VISUAL QUICKSTART GUIDE

ADOBE GOLIVE 5

FOR MACINTOSH AND WINDOWS

Shelly Brisbin

 Peachpit Press

Visual QuickStart Guide
Adobe GoLive 5 for Macintosh and Windows
Shelly Brisbin

Peachpit Press
1249 Eighth Street
Berkeley, CA 94710
(510) 524-2178
(800) 283-9444
(510) 524-2221 (fax)

Find us on the World Wide Web at:
http://www.peachpit.com

Published by Peachpit Press, a division of Addison Wesley Longman
Copyright © 2001 by Shelly Brisbin

Editor: Nancy Davis
Production coordinator: Connie Jeung-Mills
Tech editor: Steve C. Joyner
Compositor: Owen Wolfson
Indexer: Tabby Cat Communications
Cover design: The Visual Group

Notice of rights

Trademarks

Notice of liability

ISBN 0-201-70841-8

 Printed on recycled paper

9 8 7 6 5 4 3 2 1

Printed and bound in the United States of America.

Dedication

For my parents
Emma and Windel Brisbin

Acknowledgements

I would like to express my sincere thanks to:

My editor, Nancy Davis, for her encouragement, patience, eagle eyes, and juggling skills.

The Peachpit team: production coordinator Connie Jeung-Mills, compositor Owen Wolfson, indexer Cheryl Landes of Tabby Cat Communications, and cover designer The Visual Group.

Technical reviewer Steve Joyner for keeping me honest and accurate.

Richard Fenno for all his help with "the hard chapters."

My agent, Claudette Moore, who tries her best to keep me from taking on too much work at any one time.

My husband, Frank Feuerbacher, the kindest person I have ever known.

About the author

Shelly Brisbin has written about technology for fourteen years. Her specialties include the Macintosh, networking, and the Internet. She is the author of six books and hundreds of articles for magazines including *Macworld*, *MacWeek*, *NetProfessional*, *NewMedia* and *WebTechniques*. Brisbin spent four-and-a-half years as networking editor for *MacUser Magazine*. She is currently Managing Editor for Technology at Powered, Inc., in Austin, Texas. In her free time, she manages a music-related Web site and mailing list.

TABLE OF CONTENTS

INTRODUCTION

Welcome to *Adobe GoLive 5 for Macintosh and Windows: Visual QuickStart Guide*. This book is intended to help you get the most from Adobe GoLive and to acquaint you with Web page building generally.

Even if you've used Web authoring tools before, you'll probably find that GoLive is a new experience: a Web authoring tool with a comprehensive approach to page design and site management that isn't available elsewhere.

But I'm not here to sell GoLive to you. You probably own a copy or are considering making it a part of your Web publishing arsenal. Whatever the case, my goal is to give you the information you'll need to make the most of the software and to provide a convenient reference as you learn how to work with it.

Who Should Read This Book

This book is an introduction to GoLive. I cover most features of the product in enough detail to allow you to design Web pages and build Web sites quickly and easily. I've designed it so that you can easily work with GoLive, leaving the book open on your desk as you work, following the step-by-step tasks.

It is not intended as a comprehensive guide to GoLive, however. Advanced Web authors, particularly those who use animation, QuickTime authoring, and scripting will find this book a useful introduction, but may want to consult other resources for complete coverage of these features.

For some readers, this book will serve as an introduction to Web authoring, as well as a GoLive tutorial. While I do not spend a great deal of time explaining the basics of HTML or the Web, new Web authors need not fear. The step-by-step approach of this book, and the visually oriented tools in GoLive make it possible to design increasingly complex pages, even without a knowledge of HTML, the language of the Web.

If you have created Web pages before, dive right in. You won't be bored, even in the early chapters of this book. Though they are introductory, they relate specifically to GoLive, and will be useful to you as you learn the conventions of both the software and the book.

Whatever your level of Web authoring experience, use this book to jumpstart your adventure with GoLive. You'll be designing cool Web pages and complete sites before you know it.

How This Book Is Organized

Chapters 1 and 2 introduce you to GoLive's interface and basic tools. You learn how Adobe organizes tools, what they are called, and how to begin using them. Chapters 3 through 6 introduce you to basic page-building techniques, including adding and formatting text, working with page layout, and adding images and links. In Chapter 7 through 13, you'll explore more advanced topics, including the use of tables, forms, frames, Cascading Style Sheets, layers, and multimedia.

Next, Chapters 14 through 16 introduce GoLive's extensive Web site management capabilities, moving Web publishing beyond merely linking a bunch of pages. You'll see how GoLive gives you visual and logical tools to organize and maintain a killer Web site. For advanced and ambitious Web authors, Chapters 17 and 18 introduce GoLive actions—a scripting tool that uses JavaScript and Cascading Style Sheets to automate Web page activity and add special effects. You'll also learn about GoLive's animation and QuickTime authoring features.

Visual QuickStart conventions

The heart of the visual QuickStart Guide format is the step-by-step approach taken to teaching GoLive's fundamentals. You'll find instructions and tutorials on all major and most minor GoLive features and functions. Along with each step-by-step example, you'll find screen shots that depict palettes, toolbars, menus, configuration windows, and Web pages as they are created and modified throughout the book.

✔ Tips

- Each chapter contains tips that point out important tricks and suggestions for using GoLive better.

- Some tips warn you about pitfalls associated with using specific GoLive features, or issues related to specific Web browsers or HTML tags.

Mac or Windows?

GoLive is available for Macintosh, Windows 98, Windows 2000, and Windows NT computers. The tools and interface for each platform are almost identical. Since GoLive began as a Macintosh application, I've chosen to use mostly Macintosh screen shots. Windows users will find, however, that the appearance and arrangement of tools are almost identical on all platforms. In those rare cases where a tool, window, or screen differs, I've included an example from each platform.

Windows and Macintosh computers use slightly different keyboard shortcuts and other interface conventions, and GoLive typically follows the rules set down by each operating system. When there's a difference, I've noted it within the text like this:

Press Command-Option-O (Mac) or Control-Alt-O (Windows).

In the few cases where a particular feature or tool is available on one platform and not the other, the paragraph or step-by-step section is preceded by a (Mac) for Macintosh or (Win) for Windows.

What's New in GoLive 5?

GoLive 5 is the second version of the software from Adobe Systems, which acquired and renamed CyberStudio (originally developed by a company called GoLive). GoLive 5 is the first version to sport the Adobe interface that's familiar to users of Photoshop and Illustrator. The GoLive desktop features a series of palettes, each of which includes multiple functions, organized under tabs. GoLive, like other Adobe applications, packs lots of tools onto the desktop. Many of these tools, including the Objects palette, the context-sensitive Inspector, and the Document window are holdovers from earlier GoLive versions, with a slightly new look. Others are brand-new, and include tools for building tables, aligning objects, managing layers, configuring scripts, and more. If you like even more palettes onscreen, you can now "tear off" individual tabs, opening each in its own window. To do that, just click on a tab and drag it away from its current location.

Photoshop users will also recognize Adobe's handy multiple undo feature and the new History palette. Together, these options allow you to revert to a previous version of the current document. The History palette tracks changes you make to the document as you work and lets you revert to older versions with a click. For more on the History palette, see Chapter 4, "Working with Layout Tools."

Other interface improvements include more contextual menus that give you quick access to commands, and the ability to create and modify keyboard shortcuts. Learn about creating keyboard shortcuts in Chapter 1, "Learning Your Way Around."

New and improved productivity tools

GoLive 5 includes new tools that ease the process of building tables and layers (GoLive calls them floating boxes), and aligning and grouping objects. There are also enhancements to the program's Cascading Style Sheets (CSS) capabilities. With the Table palette, you can easily select all or part of a table, and sort its cells. New table-building templates can be used to quickly apply color, background, and other visual attributes to a table. The Floating Boxes palette makes it possible to manage (show/hide, lock/unlock) multiple floating boxes. You can now convert a floating box to a layout grid. With the Floating Boxes palette and the Align palette, you can align floating boxes on the page, or to a grid. See Chapter 4 and Chapter 7, "Working with Tables" for more about these features.

The Transform and Align palettes are a centralized location for aligning and grouping options. These options were available in GoLive 4, but were spread out among menus, the toolbar, and the Inspector. The Align palette is also available for aligning other elements—items on a layout grid, images, image map regions, and items within a Site Design window. Use the Transform palette to create and manage groups of objects. Once you create several elements on a page, you can select them all and group them. You can then position and size the group. Chapter 4 describes the use of both palettes.

New CSS features are detailed in Chapter 11, "Working with Style Sheets." You can now use the GoLive Site window to manage external style sheets—associating these documents with multiple HTML files that are part of your GoLive site. You can also import the contents of external style sheets into a GoLive document, making these styles available to the document as internal styles.

Code management

Several enhancements to GoLive's HTML code management tools make it easier to work with the tags that lie "under the hood" of the graphical interface.

The new 360Code feature declares a kind of hands-off policy when it comes to making unplanned modification to your source code. In previous versions, GoLive often reparsed source code, sometimes causing problems in the display of certain HTML pages. 360Code also makes it easier for several people—a designer and a developer, for example—to use different applications to edit the page without fear that saving the file in GoLive will add unwanted code to the document. Finally, 360Code ensures that non-HTML code embedded in a document won't be altered. If you want GoLive to rewrite code based on settings you customize in the Web Settings dialog box (formerly called the Web Database), you can enable this option in Web Settings.

Though GoLive has always given you the option of viewing a Web page either graphically (in the Layout Editor or Layout Preview) or as HTML (in the HTML Source Editor or HTML Outline Editor), version 5 now allows you to view the HTML code as you work in the Layout Editor, in the new Source Code palette. You can also use the new Markup Tree palette to get a look at the HTML hierarchy as you work in any of GoLive's editing views.

You have more access to the tags within your pages with the new HTML element search and replace feature. Just as you can search the contents of a document in this and previous versions of GoLive, you can now find and replace any item in a document, or a whole site—including HTML tags.

continues on next page

WHAT'S NEW IN GOLIVE 5?

HTML snippets are another new code management tool. A snippet is a block of code that can include anything on a page—code, text, links or scripts, for example—that you want to save for later use. You can use snippets to save content that you want to add to all pages on your site, such as a navigation area, header or footer, or any other bit of code that you want to keep around. Snippets are stored under the Custom tab in the Site window.

You can learn more about code management features in Chapters 10, "Working with Code," and 15, "Viewing and Managing Sites."

Graphic support and integration

If there is one area where GoLive 5 most strongly bears the Adobe stamp, it's in the area of image manipulation. Using new tools called Smart Objects, you can use GoLive together with Photoshop, Illustrator, or LiveMotion. If you have one of these applications installed on your system, you can add files created with it to a GoLive document. You can then edit the image in its native application and watch as GoLive updates the version of the file that will be part of your Web page. Smart Objects maintain a live connection between the native application and GoLive, updating the Web-format image each time you make a change to the source file, which retains its native format.

When you're finished working with an image in an Adobe graphics application, or wish to add a graphics file in almost any format, GoLive's Save for Web feature allows you to optimize the file before saving it as a Web-friendly GIF or JPEG. Save for Web uses technology from Photoshop, which was originally available in Adobe's ImageReady product.

Another GoLive-Photoshop connection is the ability to import layered Photoshop files into GoLive. Save for Web lets you optimize each layer's setting. When you import the layered file, each of the layers appears in a GoLive floating box. Alternately, you can import layers of a Photoshop file as QuickTime sprites—images that are part of a QuickTime movie. You can edit movies in GoLive's built-in QuickTime Editor.

GoLive now supports the use of tracing images. You can use a tracing image to build a pre-layout design for your page in Photoshop, then import the image into GoLive. With the Tracing Image palette, you can adjust the opacity of the image so that you can see through it more easily and fill in the page's elements over the tracing image. When you're done with the tracing image, simply delete it from the page. GoLive's new graphics integration features are covered in Chapter 5, "Working with Images."

Site management

GoLive's site management interface includes a variety of new features. Site Design, Site Reporting, and Site Templates are notable additions to the interface, while support for workgroup collaboration via WebDAV is a significant new publishing tool.

The site management interface has gotten an update in GoLive 5. In addition to an Adobe interface, the Navigation and Links views—where you get a graphical look at files and links within your site, respectively—now include additional views, called peripheral panes, that give you multiple views of your site simultaneously, if you like.

continues on next page

WHAT'S NEW IN GoLIVE 5?

With the new Site Design feature, you can build a site structure before you begin the actual site, or you can "spec out" a new section of an existing site. As you build the design, adding pages and links, you can integrate it into the actual site, or continue working on the design until you have achieved perfection. Site templates are another new site-building tool. Templates provide a quick way to set up a complete site structure in one step. You can use templates included with GoLive, or create you own, by building a site and then saving it as a site template.

Site reports give you a tool for generating reports of the contents and status of your GoLive site. You can create queries that identify problems—files that are missing or that contain broken links, for example—or you can search for site files with common elements, such as the same creation date, etc. Chapter 14, "Building Sites," and Chapter 15 will give you the whole scoop on GoLive's new site management tools.

When it's time to upload your site to a Web server, you have a new option—WebDAV. WebDAV (Web Distributed Authoring and Versioning) is a server-side technology that makes it possible for a group of designers to work collaboratively on a single Web site, all from different, even remote, locations. If your Web server supports WebDAV, you can use GoLive to upload files to it, as well as check the status of those files. When groups of people use a WebDAV server, they "check out" files to work on, make their changes, and check them back into the server so that there are no version conflicts when another user needs the file. WebDAV servers always know who has the latest version of a file. Learn about WebDAV in Chapter 16, "Publishing Your Site."

LEARNING YOUR WAY AROUND

1

When you open the Adobe GoLive application, you will see that there's a lot happening on screen. The GoLive desktop is not simply a place to create Web pages—it's an environment with professional tools and lots of different ways to look at the page or entire Web site you're working on. Like other Adobe applications, GoLive uses a number of palette windows to provide access to tools and configuration options. The Document window, where you build your pages, provides several ways to look at the same information. There's a context-sensitive toolbar showing text formatting tools as you build the page, site management options for keeping large groups of pages under control, and so on.

In this chapter, I'll give you a quick tour of GoLive, touching on the following:

◆ The GoLive desktop

◆ The Document window

◆ The toolbar

◆ The Objects and Color palettes

◆ The Inspector and View Controller

◆ Auxiliary palettes

◆ Site management tools

◆ The GoLive interface

◆ Getting help

The GoLive Desktop

The first thing you will notice when you launch GoLive is the Document window—an empty window where you will build your Web pages. The GoLive desktop also includes a number of palette windows containing tools you use to add objects, in the form of small icons, to your pages. At the top of the screen is a context-sensitive toolbar.

Figure 1.1 shows the GoLive desktop as you see it when you first launch the Mac version of the program and have not made any changes to the Preferences. We'll work our way around the desktop and its components in this chapter.

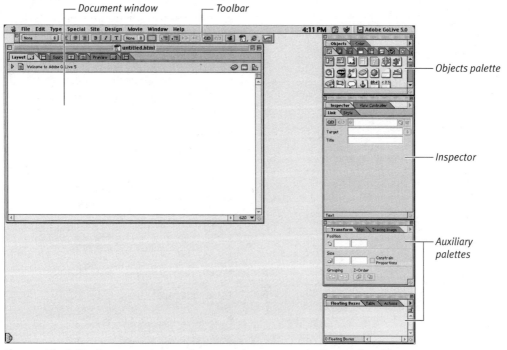

Figure 1.1 The GoLive Document window as it appears when you open the Mac version of the program. The Windows version includes the same palettes and windows that appear on the Mac.

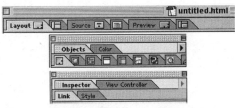

Figure 1.2 Windows in GoLive are topped by tabs that make more options available from the desktop. The Document window (top), Objects/Color palette (middle), and Inspector/View Controller (bottom) are three examples. Note that the two lower examples include not only a pair of main tabs, but palette-specific tabs below.

✔ **Tip**

■ The desktop in Figure 1.1 shows all of the items you see when you first launch GoLive. Depending upon the size or resolution of your screen, items may be placed a bit differently.

Tabbed interface

If you think there are a lot of windows on the GoLive screen, I would agree with you. On the other hand, consider the alternative. Look at the top of any window on screen. Notice the labeled tabs below the title bar (**Figure 1.2**)? Because GoLive windows are tabbed, Adobe can cram lots of tools and features into these windows, making them quickly available from the desktop.

THE GOLIVE DESKTOP

The Document Window

The Document window is where you build and view HTML pages you create in GoLive. It's visible by default when you launch GoLive. The six tabs in the Document window each provide a different view of your page, allowing you to build the page visually, using HTML code, and to see an approximation of how the page will look in a Web browser. For final page proofing, you should always use a Web browser—preferably several different ones.

Editors allow you to look at and work with the same Web page in six different ways. Use the tabs at the top of the Document window (**Figure 1.3**) to switch among the six editors for the current document.

Layout Editor (*Layout view*)

In the Layout Editor, GoLive gives you a more or less WYSIWYG (What You See Is What You Get) view of your HTML pages as you build them. You will probably spend much of your time working in the Layout Editor.

When you launch GoLive and create a new page, or open an existing one, it appears in the Layout Editor by default. To display the page in a different view, simply click the corresponding tab at the top of the main window.

Frames Editor (*Frames view*)

Use the Frames Editor to examine and work on frames-based Web pages. Frames-based pages are actually composites of two or more HTML pages. The Frames Editor shows frames and icons for each file that makes up the frameset. You will learn more about frames in Chapter 9, "Working with Frames."

Figure 1.3 Choose a page view with tabs in the Document window.

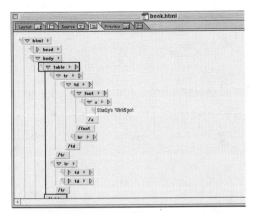

Figure 1.4 In the HTML Outline Editor, you see the page as an HTML hierarchy.

HTML Source Editor (*Source view*)

The HTML Source Editor displays the raw HTML code that makes up your page. If you know HTML, you can use the HTML Source Editor to check or edit the contents of your page. I'll have more to say about the HTML Source Editor in Chapter 10, "Working with Code."

HTML Outline Editor (*HTML Outline view*)

The HTML Outline Editor displays the HTML tags behind your Web page within a hierarchical structure. Use this view as a reminder of your page's organization and to place new elements at the correct hierarchical location (**Figure 1.4**). I cover the HTML Outline Editor in Chapter 10.

Layout Preview (*Preview view*)

In the Layout Preview, you can see an approximation of how the layout and objects you've created will look and perform when viewed from a Web browser. In many cases, the Layout Preview will look very much like the Layout Editor. You should not count on the preview for accurate representations or advanced features, like JavaScript or animation. *Always* verify your work in one or more browsers before making your pages live.

Frame Preview

The Frame Preview assembles the frames that make up a frames-based Web page and displays them as they will appear in a Web browser.

THE DOCUMENT WINDOW

The Toolbar

Just like most word processing applications, GoLive's screen is topped by a toolbar. In the Layout Editor, the toolbar is primarily used to format text (**Figure 1.5**). You can choose a style (head, body text, preformatted, and so on) and apply font size, indent, and more. You can create or break HTML links and create lists in several formats.

The toolbar is context-sensitive. Several GoLive modes, including the HTML Outline Editor and the site management interface, alter the toolbar—in other words, the toolbar changes to match what you're working on. I'll explore each set of toolbar options as we move through this book. **Figure 1.6** shows the toolbar as it appears when you work in GoLive's Navigation view, a part of the site management interface.

To use the toolbar:

1. Open GoLive. A new document appears and is displayed in the Layout Editor.

2. In the Layout Editor, type some text.

3. Select the text.

4. Choose an alignment or formatting item from the toolbar. Your text changes accordingly.

Figure 1.5 The toolbar, as it appears in the Layout Editor and the HTML Source Editor.

Figure 1.6 Here's another context-sensitive version of the toolbar—the one you see when using GoLive's Navigation view. Using the toolbar in this context, you can add or delete pages from the site, change your view of the site, or change settings associated with your site, among other things.

Internet Explorer
Netscape Communicator™

Figure 1.7 Choose a browser from the Browser menu on the toolbar. For browsers to appear there, you must set them up in the Preferences window.

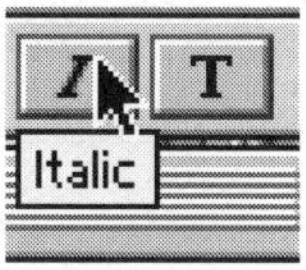

Figure 1.8 When you move the cursor over a toolbar item, a Tooltip appears. This works whether the toolbar button is active or dimmed.

✔ Tips

■ The toolbar includes a button that will open your document in a Web browser, so that you can see how your Web page will look to a visitor using that browser (**Figure 1.7**). To compare the look of your page in several browsers, use GoLive's Preferences command to add as many Web browsers as you have installed on your computer to the toolbar menu.

■ To see what a toolbar button does, move the cursor over the button. A Tooltip appears below the button (**Figure 1.8**).

The Objects Palette

Most of the tools you will use to add items to your Web pages can be found within the Objects palette (**Figure 1.9**). The Objects palette is actually composed of nine separate groups of icons, each of which is accessible from tabs at the top of the Objects palette window (**Figure 1.10**).

To use an Objects palette icon, locate the tab containing it and drag and drop the icon onto the Document window or, in most cases, you can double-click the icon. You use Objects palette icons to add text, layout grids, images, lines, Java applets, and tags that "iconically" specify most other HTML items. **Figure 1.11** shows an icon being dragged from the Objects palette to an empty Document window.

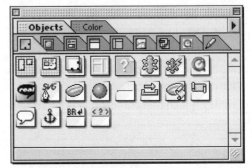

Figure 1.9 The Objects palette.

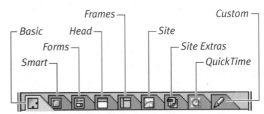

Figure 1.10 Choose from icons stored under the nine tabs of the Objects palette.

Figure 1.11 Use an Objects palette icon by dragging it from the palette into the Document window. In many cases, you can accomplish the same thing by double-clicking the icon.

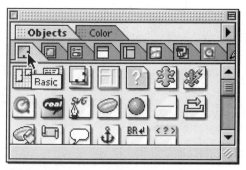

Figure 1.12 Find out what kinds of icons are stored under a tab by moving the cursor over the tab and looking at the Tooltip that appears.

Figure 1.13 To find out the name of a palette icon, move the cursor over it and note its name in the lower-left corner of the Objects palette window.

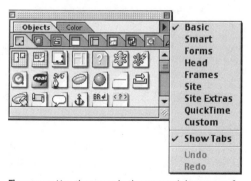

Figure 1.14 Use the menu in the upper-right corner of the Objects palette to view a specific tab or hide all of them.

✔ Tips

- If you don't see the Objects palette when you launch GoLive, choose Window > Objects (or type Command-2 on the Mac/ Control-2 in Windows) to display it.

- Objects palette tab labels appear as Tooltips when you move the cursor over the tab (**Figure 1.12**). To see labels for individual icons, move your cursor over an icon and notice that its name appears in the lower-left border of the window (**Figure 1.13**).

- Like all other windows in GoLive, the Objects palette can be resized, either to view more icons, or to get it out of your way. Just drag the Grow box in the lower-right corner of the palette to change its size. You can enlarge the palette to see all of its icons, or make it smaller and scroll to see the ones that aren't visible.

- You can move between tabs in the Objects palette by clicking them, or you can use the menu in the upper-right corner of the Objects palette. You can also use this menu to toggle the palette tabs on and off (**Figure 1.14**).

- The Objects palette shares a window with the Color palette. I'll describe the Color palette later in this chapter.

THE OBJECTS PALETTE

The Inspector

The Objects palette and the context-sensitive Inspector work together to give you control over the tools you use to build Web pages. In fact, they're the heart of the page-building interface. Once you have placed an item (text, image, multimedia file, applet, or other object) on the page, you can fine-tune its attributes in the Inspector. The Inspector window is empty until you select an object in GoLive, and its appearance and options change depending upon the object you choose.

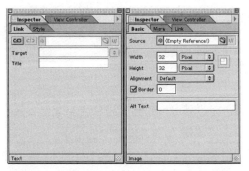

Figure 1.15 Here are the Text (left) and Image (right) Inspectors. You'll also use Inspectors to build forms, tables, multimedia files, and so on.

To use the Inspector:

1. Drag an icon from the Objects palette into the Document window, or click an object that's already there.

2. Notice that the Inspector window is no longer empty, but contains buttons and fields. (If you don't see the Inspector, choose Window > Inspector.)

3. Click another object, or type some text in the Document window, and notice that the Inspector changes again to display the options for the new object.

As you can see in **Figure 1.15**, some Inspector windows have several sets of attributes, organized under tabs. Click one of the tabs in the Image Inspector to view more options. **Figure 1.16** shows the Link tab attributes for an image.

✔ Tip

■ If you need to change an object's attributes after you've placed it on a page, just click the object, and the item's Inspector returns.

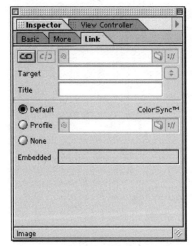

Figure 1.16 Click the Link tab in the Inspector to set more attributes for an image.

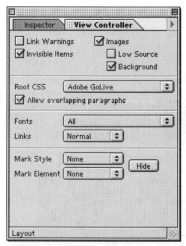

Figure 1.17 The View Controller lets you choose what items to show as you work on a GoLive document and how they should look.

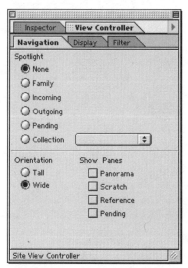

Figure 1.18 When you're working on a GoLive site in Navigation view, the View Controller provides options that control the appearance of the objects displayed in that view. You can also choose alternative ways to look at your site here.

The View Controller: An inspector for pages and sites

Notice the tab in the Inspector labeled View Controller? The View Controller is not a part of the Inspector, but another GoLive options window that just happens to share a window with the Inspector. With the View Controller, you can set options that instruct GoLive what items to show and how to display a page or a site. Like the Inspector, the View Controller is context-sensitive, changing based on what you're doing in GoLive. **Figure 1.17** shows the View Controller as it appears when you're working on a GoLive document (a page). When you work with the GoLive site management interface, the View Controller changes to give you control over what items are displayed in the text-based and graphical site views, and how they appear (**Figure 1.18**).

The Color Palette

The Color palette allows you to choose and add color to elements in your Web pages. You can color text, the background, links, table cells—almost any other element GoLive offers. Just choose a color from the palette and drag it onto an object you want to color, or use the Color field in the Inspector to add color to an object. Learn more about using color in Chapter 4, "Working with Layout Tools."

The Color palette shares a window with the Objects palette. You can either open it with a click or menu command, or activate it by using a color field in an Inspector window that supports color change.

Just like the Objects palette, the Color palette contains tabs that organize its tools and color choices (see **Figure 1.19**). Several tabs (Grayscale, RGB, CMYK) represent the color types found in image manipulation applications such as Photoshop. Other tabs (HSB, HSV, Palettes) allow you to choose colors the same way computer screens do. Still other tabs give you color options that match the Web color standard that is supported on all W3C-compliant Web browsers (Web Color and Web Name Colors). Finally, one tab (Site Color) gives you a place to store custom colors that you have associated with a site you have built in GoLive.

To open the Color palette:

◆ Choose Window > Color.

   or

   Click the Color tab in the window containing the Objects palette. The Color palette appears.

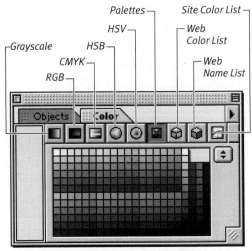

Figure 1.19 The nine tabs of the Color palette.

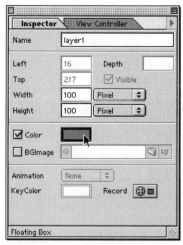

Figure 1.20 Click the Color field in the Inspector to choose a color for an object in the Document window.

To add color to text:

1. With a document open in the Document window and the Color palette visible, choose a color from one of the Color palette tabs by clicking the tab and then locating the color you want.

2. Click the Color palette's Preview pane and drag onto the text you created. The text changes color.

To color an object or background:

1. Add an object such as an HTML table, layout grid, or floating box to the Document window.

2. With the object selected, locate the Color field in the Inspector (**Figure 1.20**).

3. Click the Color field. The Color palette appears, if it isn't already onscreen.

4. Choose a color. The color appears in the Preview pane of the Color palette, and the object in the Document window changes color.

THE COLOR PALETTE

Auxiliary Palettes

The GoLive desktop contains four additional palettes. Like the Inspector, they give you access to configuration options for objects within your pages or items that are a part of your GoLive site. Each palette includes either two or three tabs, and each of these tabs performs a separate task.

The auxiliary palettes don't have names; they're simply groups containing several unrelated sets of controls, conveniently located on the GoLive desktop.

To open an auxiliary palette:

◆ Choose the palette from the Window menu.

or

With the GoLive desktop visible, click the tab of the auxiliary palette you want.

✔ Tips

■ If you don't see the auxiliary palette containing the tab you want, choose Window > Reset Palettes. All of the auxiliary palettes move to the edge of the screen (**Figure 1.21**). If they aren't currently on screen, the palettes appear.

■ When you choose a palette from the Window menu, the tab you select comes to the front. When you view all palettes by resetting them, the leftmost tab in the palette window is in front.

■ Auxiliary palettes are viewable, but not activated, unless you have selected objects, or are working in views that support them.

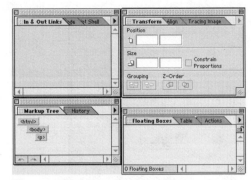

Figure 1.21 The four auxiliary palettes appear in the bottom-right corner of the GoLive desktop. The arrangement may be a bit different depending upon the size or resolution of your screen.

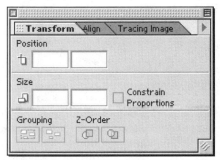

Figure 1.22 Work with groups of objects in the Transform palette.

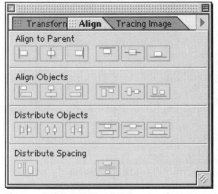

Figure 1.23 Align objects in all sorts of ways using the Align palette.

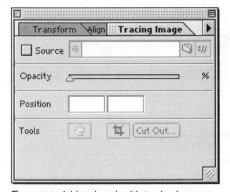

Figure 1.24 Add and work with tracing images in the Tracing Image palette.

Transform, Align, and Tracing Image palettes

The Transform and Align tabs share a palette window, and often work together. Use the Transform palette to manage groups of objects in GoLive, position and size objects, combine them into groups, etc. (**Figure 1.22**). The Align palette lets you position objects relative to one another, or to the Document window itself (**Figure 1.23**). Learn more about both palettes in Chapter 4, "Working with Layout Tools."

The Tracing Image palette, which shares a window with the Transform and Align palettes, lets you control images that can be used as frameworks for page design, or as backgrounds for HTML pages (**Figure 1.24**). A tracing image functions like a sewing pattern—you add it to a GoLive document before you place other objects, using the tracing image as a guide during layout. The Tracing Image palette gives you control of the opacity and location of the image. Chapter 5, "Working with Images," describes the use of the Tracing Image palette.

AUXILIARY PALETTES

Floating Boxes, Table, and Actions palettes

Floating boxes and tables are HTML objects that help you position text, images, and other objects on the page. (You will learn more about tables and floating boxes in Chapters 7 and 12, respectively). Actions are pre-built JavaScripts that allow you to add automated functions to your site. They are covered in detail in Chapter 17.

Floating boxes, tables, and Actions each have their own Inspectors, which become available when you create or select the item in question. Inspectors help you set up individual objects and their attributes. Auxiliary palettes do different work. In the case of floating boxes, for example, it's in the auxiliary palette where you manage multiple floating boxes, naming and positioning them relative to one another (**Figure 1.25**). The Table palette lets you manipulate the contents of table cells (by sorting the cells) and includes options for custom table formatting (**Figure 1.26**). The Table Inspector, on the other hand, assists you with building the table and its HTML attributes. What you do in the Table palette is much more specific to GoLive. Using the Actions palette, you can attach JavaScripts to objects you have already added to the page and configured. The Actions palette provides quick access to all of the actions included with GoLive (**Figure 1.27**).

✔ Tip

■ The mild-mannered palette window I've described in this section is quite small when used to display floating box names. When you click the Table or Actions tab, the palette window gets larger—a pretty unique feature among GoLive palettes. Like all windows in GoLive, you can change the size of the palette further with the grow box in the lower-right corner of the window.

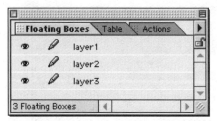

Figure 1.25 Use the Floating Boxes palette to view all of the floating boxes on a given page. You can control their visibility (whether they can be seen) and you can lock them in place.

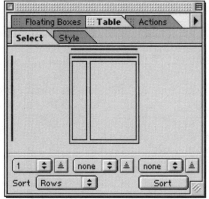

Figure 1.26 The Table palette shows the outline of the selected table. This particular one has been customized quite a bit so that it forms a framework for a complete Web page. While you do the customization in the Table Inspector, you can't really see what it looks like without the Table palette.

Figure 1.27 Set up Actions to accompany HTML elements (such as an image) in the Actions palette.

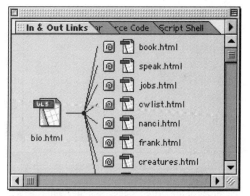

Figure 1.28 Use In & Out Links any time you want to see what the current file links to, and the condition of those links (if they are broken and what other files they are linked to).

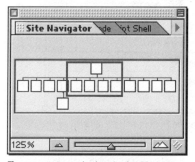

Figure 1.29 Drag the box in the Site Navigator to center the view of your Web site on the area inside the box.

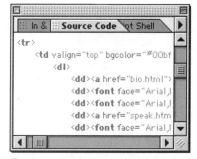

Figure 1.30 The Source Code palette gives you a view of the code for your page as you build it in the Document window.

In & Out Links, Site Navigator, Source Code and JavaScript Shell

In & Out Links is a very useful palette (**Figure 1.28**). Here you can view all of the items that link to an open Web page, as well as links within that page. The Site Navigator palette is used when you have a graphical view of a GoLive site file open, and need to move around the view (**Figure 1.29**). You'll read more about both these tabs in Chapter 15, "Viewing and Managing Sites."

The Source Code palette gives you a different view of the currently open HTML document (**Figure 1.30**). You can build your page in GoLive's Layout Editor and keep an eye on the code the program is generating in the Source Code tab. Of course, you can use the HTML Source Editor to look at and edit code, but the Source Code palette offers the advantage of two simultaneous views. There will be more about the Source Code palette in Chapter 10, "Working with Code."

The JavaScript Shell palette (**Figure 1.31**) is used in conjunction with the GoLive 5.0 SDK (Software Development Kit). While using the GoLive SDK is well beyond the scope of this book, you can read a brief overview in Appendix A, "Beyond HTML."

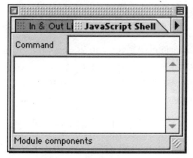

Figure 1.31 The JavaScript Shell.

Markup Tree and History palettes

The Markup Tree, like the Source Code palette, gives you an alternative view of the page you're working on (**Figure 1.32**). The Markup Tree shows the structure of your page and the individual HTML elements that make it up in terms of their relationship to the page's hierarchy. In other words, when you're working on a table, for example, you can see whether that table is nested within another table, included in a frame, or otherwise subordinate to another object on the page This is particularly useful when you're working with tables, lists, or forms, all of which have some form of tag and element hierarchy.

The History palette is like a super undo function where you can "back out" of changes you have made to your page, one at a time (**Figure 1.33**). Say, for example, you are working on a table and make several changes to its size and contents. Then, you realize that the change you made just before you added the new text to a cell should not have been made. Just locate the change you want to undo in the History palette (they are called *states*) and select it. All of your recent actions except this single change are retained. Deleting a state removes that state and those that came after it. (States are added from the top down; that is, the oldest state is at the top of the list, the most recent one at the bottom.)

The History palette gives you 20 levels of undo by default. Read more about the History palette in Chapter 4, "Working with Layout Tools."

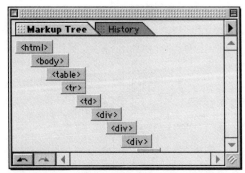

Figure 1.32 The Markup Tree palette shows the hierarchy of the current page, from the point where the cursor is at the time the palette is displayed.

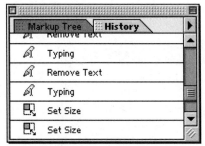

Figure 1.33 The History palette allows you to undo changes you've made as you work. Unlike the traditional Edit>Undo command, History lets you choose to undo changes in any order you like, just by selecting them.

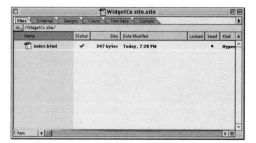

Figure 1.34 Here is a brand-new Site window, containing a home page (index.html).

Site Management Tools

GoLive includes tools for managing complete Web sites. By gathering elements of your Web site, you can make global changes to the site, organize HTML and media files, and verify that all of your links work. You can also use site management tools to view a map of your entire site, either as a collection of linked pages, or as a group of links going to and from a single page. Finally, you can upload your site to a Web server using GoLive's FTP tool.

The Site window

The Site window displays the files and other elements that make up a GoLive Web site. Like the Macintosh Finder, or Windows Explorer, the Site window displays files and folders that you can open or manipulate when making changes to the site's hierarchy. When you create a new site, GoLive creates a home page for it (called index.html). A new Site window appears as in **Figure 1.34**.

Like the Document window in GoLive, the Site window includes a number of tabs. The Site window tabs store elements of your Web site. You can drag files into the Site window to add them to your site, or you can create pages from scratch with GoLive.

In each Site window tab are the elements of your Web site. You can view each by clicking a tab at the top of the Site window. Until you add files and resources to your Web site, the Site tabs are empty.

continues on next page

The Site window tabs are Files, External, Designs, Colors, Fonts Sets, and Custom.

Each Site window tab shows different elements of your site. The Files tab displays your site's files, while the other tabs display remote URLs and email addresses, saved colors, and fonts, respectively. You can view prototype site hierarchies in the Designs tab. **Figure 1.35** shows a site with the Files tab selected and a full complement of files within it.

✔ Tip

■ The Site window also contains several secondary tabs that give you a view of specialized site objects, and allow you to set up access to your Web server. To view the secondary panes, click the button in the lower-right corner of the Site window. The resulting secondary panes appear in **Figure 1.36**. I will discuss the secondary site panes and their use in Chapter 15, "Viewing and Managing Sites."

The Navigation view

Like any Web site, a GoLive-produced site is a hierarchical grouping of HTML pages and links to other Web sites. The Navigation view is designed to make it easier for you to visualize and work with your site in these terms. You can even use the Site View to organize your site before you design its individual pages.

To view a site in the Navigation view:

1. Open a GoLive site file.

2. Choose Site > View > Navigation. The site's Navigation view appears (**Figure 1.37**).

You can work with files while using the Navigation view. Clicking once on a file displays its Reference Inspector and highlights the file's relationship to others in the site. The Reference Inspector gives you creation and location information about the file, and lets you view a thumbnail version of it.

Figure 1.35 This Site window includes files and folders that are part of the site.

Figure 1.36 The secondary pane of the Site window includes four tabs: Extras, Error, FTP, and WebDAV. The Extras tab, shown here, gives you access to objects you can use with your site, but that are not necessarily part of the site.

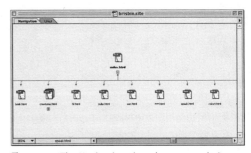

Figure 1.37 The Navigation view shows your site's contents as a hierarchy, with icons representing the files.

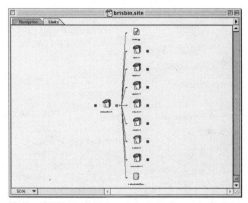

Figure 1.38 The Links view shows a page and all of the links that appear on that page. You can also view links to the page in question.

✔ Tip

■ Double-clicking a file in the Navigation view opens it. This applies to both HTML files created in GoLive and image or multimedia files that you add to your site. GoLive will hand off these "foreign" file types to the applications that created them, allowing you to edit the files.

The Links view

While the Navigation view provides an overhead view of the pages that make up your Web site, the Links view digs one step deeper by displaying links associated with individual pages.

To display pages in the Links view:

1. Open a GoLive site.

2. Choose Site > View > Links.

   or

   Open the Navigation view and click the Links tab. The Links view appears (**Figure 1.38**).

Working in the GoLive Interface

If you have used Adobe products like Photoshop or Illustrator, many of the interface elements I've described in this chapter are probably familiar to you. Because GoLive was not originally created by Adobe, some things, like the draggable palette tools, are unique, but others, like the tabbed interface, come right out of Adobe's standard playbook.

In this section, I'll show you a bit about how you can maximize your use of the interface for your needs. Things like window position and different ways of choosing the command you need make a great difference in your productivity and aren't the same for everyone who uses a piece of software.

Several ways to reach the window you want

You can open any palette or window by clicking its tab at the top of its window, but there are several other ways to reach GoLive windows.

◆ **Choose from the Window menu**: All of the windows that are open when you launch GoLive, and all of the tabs within those windows, have corresponding commands on the Window menu (**Figure 1.39**).

◆ **Use the selection menu within the host window**: If the window containing a palette you want to use is visible, choose that tab from the menu in the upper-right corner of the window, indicated by the right-pointing arrow (**Figure 1.40**). In some cases, like the Site window, commands that open additional windows are available from this menu. In the Site window, use the menu to reach the Navigation or Links view, neither of which is open onscreen otherwise.

Figure 1.39 The Window menu includes commands that open all of GoLive's palettes. The dividers between the menu items tell you which palettes share a window. The checkmarked items are visible on screen, and are the currently selected items.

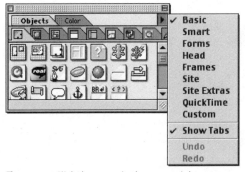

Figure 1.40 Click the arrow in the upper-right corner of a window to view a menu. In some cases, you'll see a list of tabs in the palette. In others, you'll see commands that you can use with the currently selected palette.

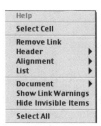

Figure 1.41 As the name implies, context-sensitive menus differ depending on where you click within GoLive. In this case, I clicked inside a table cell. I have access to both cell options and text formatting commands.

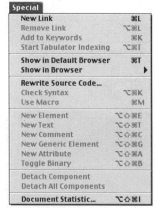

Figure 1.42 Keyboard shortcuts appear next to the commands they invoke.

◆ **Use a context-sensitive menu:**
Control-click (Mac) or right-click (Windows) almost anywhere in GoLive and you will be rewarded with a context-sensitive menu (**Figure 1.41**). In many cases, you will find access to the Inspector, or to auxiliary palettes on the menus. Since these palettes are context sensitive, what you see depends on where in GoLive (the Document window, within a table, in the Site window, etc.) you click.

◆ **The toolbar:** Like the menus I just described, the toolbar, which is always present at the top of the GoLive desktop, is context-sensitive. In some cases, the toolbar includes buttons that open GoLive windows.

✔ Tip

■ Use the Reset Palettes command from the Window menu to return palettes to their default position on the GoLive desktop.

Using keyboard shortcuts

GoLive provides a number of keyboard shortcuts for frequently used commands. You'll find shortcuts that correspond to menu items listed on all menus (**Figure 1.42**) and more shortcuts on the GoLive Quick Reference card that is included in the package.

You can also create your own keyboard shortcuts to perform commands you use often. Logically enough, the Keyboard Shortcuts command (Edit > Keyboard Shortcuts) also has a keyboard equivalent—Control-Option-Command-Shift-K (Mac) or Control-Alt-Shift-K (Windows).

continues on next page

WORKING IN THE GOLIVE INTERFACE

The Keyboard Shortcuts window gives you access to all shortcuts that are currently mapped to GoLive menu options, as well as an option to create your own set (**Figure 1.43**). That set can add shortcuts to existing ones (not all menu items have shortcuts) or you can replace the existing GoLive shortcuts with ones you choose.

To assign a new keyboard shortcut:

1. Choose Edit > Keyboard Shortcuts. The Keyboard Shortcuts window appears.

2. Choose whether your new shortcut will be an addition to your own set (highly recommended) or whether you will alter the GoLive or Adobe Common shortcuts that are already in place. The My Settings group is selected by default.

3. From the list of GoLive menus, choose the one containing the command you want to add a shortcut for and open it by clicking the triangle (Mac) or plus sign (Windows) next to the menu name. If the command you want is located on a submenu, open it.

4. Select the item to which you want to add a shortcut.

5. Click in the Shortcut field and type the shortcut. It must be a combination of a modifier key (Shift, Option or Command on the Mac; Shift, Alt or Control on Windows systems) and a letter or number. The shortcut you've chosen appears in the field (**Figure 1.44**).

6. Click Assign to confirm you choice.

7. When you have finished adding shortcuts, click OK to close the window.

✔ Tips

■ If you choose a shortcut that is already being used by GoLive, that information will appear in the Currently assigned to

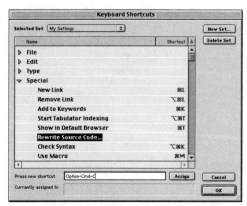

Figure 1.43 The Keyboard Shortcuts window lists GoLive's menus.

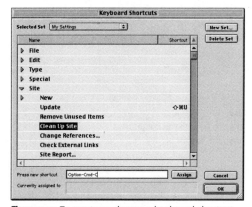

Figure 1.44 To create or change a keyboard shortcut, select a command and type the new shortcut.

WORKING IN THE GOLIVE INTERFACE

field, just below the Press new shortcut field. This is your chance to change your new shortcut, rather than replacing an existing one.

■ GoLive is picky about keyboard shortcuts. On the Mac, for example, you can't assign a function key as a keyboard shortcut, and any key combination you create must include the Command key. On Windows systems, you can't use Alt in a keyboard shortcut unless you also include the Shift key. Experiment with shortcuts until you find one that you like and will remember, once you've created it.

■ To change an existing shortcut, select a menu item, click in the shortcut field and type the new shortcut. When you click Assign, the old shortcut is replaced.

■ You can create as many sets of shortcuts as you like. The default My Settings group is the best place to make changes to existing shortcuts or to add your own small set. If you have need of several sets—perhaps several people share the machine where GoLive is installed, and each person wants his own set of short-cuts, create a set for each person in the Keyboard Shortcuts window. Doing so is as simple as clicking the New Set button, giving the set a name, and customizing the shortcuts you want to use.

To change the set of shortcuts you are using:

1. Choose Edit > Keyboard Shortcuts.

2. Choose the set you want to use from the Selected Set menu.

3. Click OK to close the window. Your new set of shortcuts becomes active.

Getting Help

There are several ways to get help when you need it in the GoLive application. The Help menu is one of these ways (**Figure 1.45**).

Electronic documentation

Adobe has included a lot of documentation with the GoLive package. You can get to it directly from GoLive, or you can read or print an Adobe Acrobat version of the user's guide.

To view GoLive help:

1. Choose Help > GoLive Help. Your Web browser opens and displays an HTML page containing links to Adobe documentation (**Figure 1.46**). The information in these documents is stored on your hard disk, so GoLive doesn't need to connect to the Internet to load these help files.

2. Click a topic on the left side of the HTML page. Subtopics appear on the right (**Figure 1.47**).

3. Click a subtopic to see the information about that topic.

✔ Tips

■ You can look for specific topics by clicking the Search button at the top of the browser window, and entering a word or phrase in the Search field.

■ GoLive Help is not a complete user's guide. If you don't find the answer to your question in the help file, don't stop looking for the answer you need. The remainder of this chapter describes your other options.

Figure 1.45 Choose a help option from GoLive's Help menu.

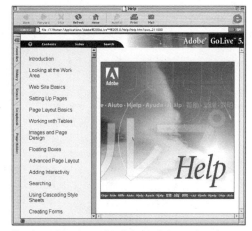

Figure 1.46 GoLive Help gives you information about lots of features.

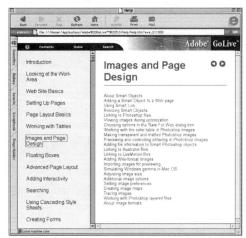

Figure 1.47 Click a topic to display available subtopics.

GETTING HELP

The PDF User Guide

The GoLive CD includes a PDF version of the printed user guide that is included with the software. The electronic version is not installed on your hard disk along with GoLive. It's located at the root level of the CD. The file is called User Guide.pdf. It's an Adobe Acrobat file. If you have Acrobat installed on your computer, you can launch the guide with a double-click. If you don't have Acrobat, you can install it from the GoLive CD. The Acrobat installer is located in the Extras folder, inside the Adobe GoLive 5.0 folder.

✔ Tip

■ At this writing, the printed and PDF versions of the user guide are not identical. The printed guide includes information about new features in GoLive 5.0, and an overview of the software. The PDF version doesn't contain these chapters. In addition, the arrangement of chapters is slightly different.

Online resources

The GoLive Help menu includes commands that will take you directly to Adobe Web resources. They include downloadable software updates, tips, user forums for GoLive users, and opportunities to buy stuff. You can also register GoLive from the Help menu. Explore the Support, Downloadables, and Adobe Online links to learn more.

GETTING HELP

YOUR FIRST GOLIVE PAGE

2

Now that you've had a walking tour of Adobe GoLive's interface and important features, it's time to dive right in and make some Web pages. In this chapter, I show the practical side of the tools introduced in Chapter 1 but keep things simple, leaving the exploration of the full power of GoLive for subsequent chapters.

In this chapter I cover:

◆ Opening and creating files

◆ Building the page

◆ Saving the page

◆ Starting a site

Opening and Creating Files

Web pages you create in GoLive can be viewed in any Web browser, or served up by any Web server. That's because, unlike files created by word processing programs, database tools or spreadsheet applications, GoLive files are plain old text files—HTML files, to be precise. You can work on a file in GoLive and immediately open it in a local browser, or upload it to a Web server for viewing over the Internet.

By the same token, you can open and edit HTML files created by other applications in GoLive. If you have an existing Web page, for example, and want to use GoLive to edit it, just open the file in GoLive.

To open a file in GoLive:

1. Launch the GoLive application by double-clicking it or by choosing it from the Start menu (Windows).

2. Choose File > Open. The Open dialog box appears (**Figure 2.1**).

3. Navigate to a file on your hard disk, and choose Open. The file opens in the GoLive Document window. The file you chose opens.

   You can now edit the file's contents, just as if you had created it in GoLive in the first place.

✔ Tip

■ By default, the Open dialog box displays all files in the current directory that GoLive can open. That includes any plain text file, whether it's a Web page, a script, a GoLive site file, or some other kind of file that's readable as text. (Site files contain information about all of the items that are part of a site you build with GoLive. You'll learn about sites in Chapter 14, "Building Sites.") You can choose to see

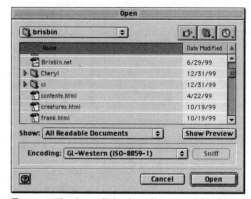

Figure 2.1 The Open dialog box shows available files and directories.

Figure 2.2 On the Mac, choose an option from the Show menu to control the type of files that appear in the Open dialog box.

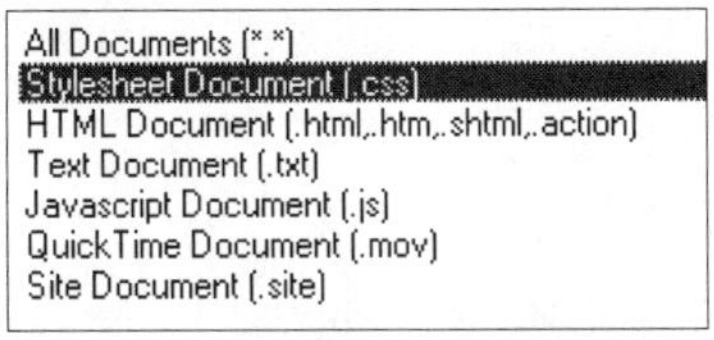

Figure 2.3 In Windows environments, the Show menu (within the Open dialog box) gives you the option of viewing several types of files that GoLive can open. Choose one of these file types, or view all file types GoLive can open by choosing All Documents.

only certain kinds of files in the dialog box by choosing an option from the Show menu (**Figure 2.2**) in the Open dialog box. (Mac). To see only HTML files created by GoLive, choose Adobe GoLive HTML page. You can also choose to see only GoLive site files, or to see all files created by GoLive by selecting All Known Documents. If you have HTML files that were created by other applications, leave All Readable Documents, the default setting, selected. The options read a bit differently in Windows environments (**Figure 2.3**), listing a variety of file types. The All Documents option allows you to view any file GoLive can open.

Creating a new file

Most of the files you create in GoLive will be HTML files—Web pages. You can also create scripts, site files, QuickTime movies, and style sheet documents. We will learn about these in later chapters. For now, we'll concentrate on HTML files—creating a new one in GoLive and building a simple Web page.

To create a new Web page in GoLive:

Choose File > New, or type Command-N (Mac) or Control-N (Windows). An empty document opens in the Document window.

It's a good idea to define a few basic parameters and settings for your Web page before you begin adding text and graphics.

OPENING AND CREATING FILES

To give your page a title:

1. In the new document you just opened, click anywhere within the title "Welcome to Adobe GoLive 5." You'll find it at the top of the Document window, to the right of the Page icon (**Figure 2.4**). When you click, notice that the entire title is selected and that there's a box around it.

2. Type a name for your page. Text you type will overwrite the original title.

   The title you type is the text that will identify your Web page when it is added to a Web browser's bookmark list. It's also the text that will appear at the top of a browser window when the page is being viewed. The title should indicate what your Web page is about in clear, concise terms.

✔ Tip

- Your page's title is not the same as the name you give it when you save the file. The name (page.html, for example) identifies this page to other sites and pages that link to it, while the title is merely an English language way to refer to the page in the browser title bar and on bookmark lists.

Size up your page

Because Web pages are viewed on a wide variety of computer monitors, some small, some large, it's usually a good idea to develop your pages so that they will appear somewhat consistently across the wide range of possible viewing conditions. In other words, pick a low common denominator that works for users with big screens and little ones. The easiest way to do this is to be sure that the window size you work with in GoLive's Layout mode is small enough to be used on a 14-inch monitor without requiring the viewer to scroll left or right.

Like most programs, GoLive lets you change a window's dimensions by dragging the grow

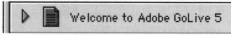

Figure 2.4 Click the default page title in the Document window to select it. Then, type a new title over the selected text.

Figure 2.5 Choose a page width (in pixels) from the Page Size popup menu.

Figure 2.6 Choose the default page size in the Window Settings dialog box.

box at the bottom-right corner of the Document window (in the Layout Editor), but that's not precise enough to ensure that every page you build has the same horizontal dimensions. The Page Size popup menu lets you choose a pixel width that's compatible with a 14- or 17-inch monitor, for example.

To choose a page size:

1. Click and hold the Page Size popup menu in the bottom-right corner of the Document window (**Figure 2.5**).

2. Choose an appropriate size for your page—the window size for which you want to design the page. GoLive includes sizes that support 14- and 17-inch monitors, and some smaller page sizes as well. The 580 (14-inch monitor) and 720 (17-inch monitor) options are probably the safest choices, since most current computer monitors are at least 14 inches. GoLive resizes the main window.

To choose a default page size for all documents:

1. Choose the window size you want to use for all pages you work with, either by choosing an option from the Page Size popup menu, or by dragging the grow box to create a window of the size you want.

2. From the Page Size popup menu, choose Window Settings. The Window Settings dialog box opens (**Figure 2.6**).

3. Be sure that HTML Windows is checked and click OK to confirm your new settings. Each new document you open will have the horizontal and vertical dimensions you've chosen.

4. To return to GoLive's default settings for this and all windows, repeat steps 1 and 2 and click the Use Default Settings button.

Setting GoLive launch preferences

When you launch GoLive, a blank document appears in the Document window, in the Layout Editor. You can change this behavior by adjusting some general preferences.

To change document preferences:

1. Choose Edit > Preferences. The Preferences window opens (**Figure 2.7**).

2. In the General Preferences section (the label is selected by default), choose an option from the At Launch menu (**Figure 2.8**). This tells GoLive whether to open a new document, to show an Open dialog box, or to open the application without displaying any document options.

3. Select an option from the Default Mode menu if you want GoLive to open documents using a mode other than the Layout Editor, which is the default.

4. If you would like GoLive to launch a specific document when you open the application, click the New Document checkbox and then click the Select button to locate a file you want to use. This is helpful if you create all of your Web pages from a single template.

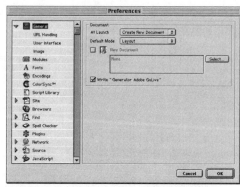

Figure 2.7 Change the way GoLive launches in the General Preferences window.

Figure 2.8 To have GoLive launch a blank document, the Open dialog box, or no document at all, choose an item from the At Launch menu.

Figure 2.9 Click the Page icon at the top of a document to view the file's Page Inspector.

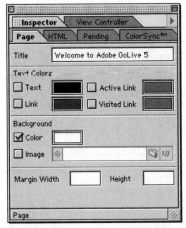

Figure 2.10 You can add a colored background or specify a custom color for text or links in the Page Inspector.

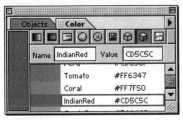

Figure 2.11 Selecting a color in the Color palette displays it in the Preview pane on the left.

Creating a Simple Page

Let's set the look of our new page. Then, we'll add some text and an image to the page.

To choose page colors:

1. Click the Page icon in the title bar of the Document window (**Figure 2.9**). Note that the Inspector now displays Page settings (**Figure 2.10**).

2. If the Inspector window isn't visible, choose Window > Inspector.

3. To select a background color for the page, click the Color field under the Background heading in the Page Inspector. The Color palette appears.

4. Select a color by clicking on it. The new color appears in the Preview pane at the left of the Color palette (**Figure 2.11**), and in the color field you clicked.

To add a background image:

1. As before, click the Page icon to open the Page Inspector.

2. In the Page Inspector, click the Image checkbox, below the Background heading.

3. Click the Browse button (it looks like a folder). A file navigation box appears.

4. Navigate to the image you want to use as a background for your Web page and click Select. You'll see the image in the main window, and visitors to your Web page will see the image behind the page's other elements.

continues on next page

✔ Tips

- If you choose a small image for your page's background, the image will repeat across and down the page, as shown in **Figure 2.12**. This arrangement would probably not be the best background for a page with text, especially if the text is fairly small in size. Choose a larger, less busy background for pages that include lots of text.

- If you choose both a background color and a background image, the image will be shown unless the user's browser does not support background images, in which case the color appears behind the page content.

To choose colors for text and links:

1. With the Page Inspector visible, click a color field for the item whose color you want to specify.

2. When the Color palette appears, choose a color. The new color appears in the color field.

✔ Tip

- If you decide to use custom colors for text, links, or background, use the Preview pane or a Web browser to check the colors you've chosen.

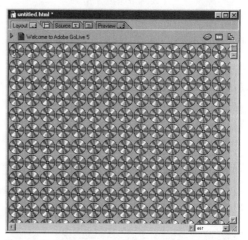

Figure 2.12 This busy page background consists of repeats of an image of a single compact disc.

Saving the Page

When you've added a few items to your new Web page, it's a good idea to save it. Saving files in GoLive is pretty much like saving them in other applications you have used.

To save a Web page:

Choose File > Save (Command-S on a Mac or Control-S on Windows) and navigate to a folder where you want to store your new page.

When you choose Save, GoLive presents the default file name, `untitled.html`. Though you should change it to something more appropriate, be sure not to remove the .html extension, or to add spaces or slashes (/) within the file name. HTML files must follow this naming convention to be recognized by servers as Web pages. Even if you're using a Mac, where file name extensions usually aren't important, keep the .html extension.

✔ Tip

■ If you are creating a Web site in GoLive, be sure to save your file to the folder that contains the rest of the HTML files that are part of your site. You will learn more about creating and storing sites in Chapter 14, "Building Sites."

Setting Up a Site

Until this point, we've been working with individual Web pages. In many cases, you'll start with a single page or two and then add new items as your needs grow. GoLive supports that way of doing things, but the real power of the software is its ability to create and maintain groups of Web pages and other elements that make up a complete Web site.

When I talk about a GoLive *site*, I mean a group of elements (HTML files, images, and other files) that form a Web site, are managed as a unit, and are saved under the umbrella of a single site file. The GoLive site file contains pointers to all of the elements of the site. It does not contain the HTML pages and other files themselves; it simply keeps them organized.

In this section, I introduce you to GoLive's site management tools by showing you how to set up a simple site. For a more in-depth look at sites, see Chapter 14, "Building Sites."

You can create GoLive Web sites from scratch, or you can import files belonging to an existing Web site into a new GoLive site file. Because we've already created a Web page, albeit an empty one, in this section we'll start a site from scratch and import your current index file into a GoLive site.

To create a new site:

1. With GoLive open, choose File > New Site > Blank. You can also choose to import an existing site from a folder on your hard drive, or download it from a Web server using FTP. I'll have more to say about using these options in Chapter 14, "Building Sites."

2. Select a location on your hard disk where you want to store your new site. You can have GoLive create a folder by leaving the Create Folder button checked in the navigation dialog box.

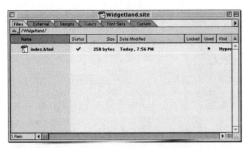

Figure 2.13 When you create a new GoLive site, you see its home page — index.html — in the Site window.

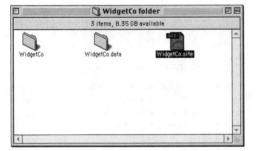

Figure 2.14 Click the site file to open your new site.

3. Name your site.

4. Click Save. The Site window appears (**Figure 2.13**). It contains a single item, a page called index.html. The page name is bold because index.html is the home page for your new site.

With a new site created, the next task is to get your home page up and running. You can either work directly with the home page GoLive has created for you (setting it up just as you did in the first section of this chapter), or you can replace the site's default home page with one you've already worked on.

To replace your site's home page:

1. Quit GoLive.

2. In the Finder (Mac) or Windows Explorer (Windows), locate and open the new site folder you just created. Notice that there are two folders and a file within the site folder.

3. Open the New Site folder (where *New Site* is the name you gave your site). Notice that the file index.html is stored here.

4. Locate the index.html file you created earlier in this chapter, and drag it into the site folder.

5. When asked if you want to replace the existing index.html file, click OK.

6. Open your site by double-clicking on the site file in the root folder of your site (**Figure 2.14**). As before, index.html appears in the Site window. If you open it by double-clicking, you'll see that the file has the title and attributes you gave it earlier.

Point & Shoot

You've learned that you can add objects like images to a Web page by locating them with the Inspector, after adding a placeholder icon to a GoLive document. GoLive provides another way to add items to a page when you work within a GoLive site. It's called *Point & Shoot*.

When you build a GoLive site, you add items including Web pages and images to it. They appear in the Site window, along with the index.html page. For this section, I'll work with an existing site. In Chapter 14, "Building Sites," you will learn how to build a site of your own.

To use Point & Shoot to add an image to a page:

1. Open a GoLive site containing GoLive documents and image files.

2. Open a GoLive document by double-clicking its icon in the Site window.

3. Arrange the document and the Site window for the current site so both are visible on screen. You only need to be able to see the icons and file names of items in the Site window (**Figure 2.15**).

4. Drag the Image icon from Basic tab of the Objects palette to the Document window. The Image Inspector appears.

5. With the image selected, click the Point & Shoot button in the Image Inspector. It is located immediately to the left of the Source field (**Figure 2.16**).

6. Drag the mouse from the Point & Shoot button to the Site window. A line appears as you drag from the Inspector (**Figure 2.17**).

Figure 2.15 Arrange the Document window and Site window so that you can see the contents of both, especially the file icons and names in the Site window.

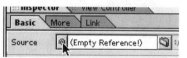

Figure 2.16 Use the Point & Shoot button to link to an image stored within a GoLive site. All Inspectors that allow you to browse to files on your hard disk also have a Point & Shoot button.

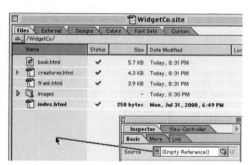

Figure 2.17 Click the Point & Shoot button and drag the mouse into the Site window. A line follows the path you draw.

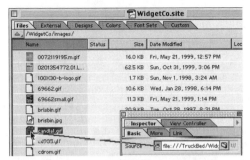

Figure 2.18 Select an item in the Site window to complete the link. When the item you want is highlighted, you can let go of the mouse button.

7. When the cursor is over an image file that you want to link to and the image file is highlighted (**Figure 2.18**), let go of the mouse button. The image appears in the Document window and the image path appears in the Source field of the Inspector, just as if you had used the Browse button to locate the file on your hard drive.

✔ Tips

■ If you want to Point & Shoot to an image or other item that is stored in a subfolder of your Web site, drag to the Site window and over the folder's icon. The folder will open to reveal the files inside. Then you can finish the link by pointing to the file and letting go of the mouse button.

■ In this example, I showed you how to Point & Shoot to an image. You can also Point & Shoot in any Inspector window that contains a Browse button with which you can create links. They all have a Point & Shoot button, too.

WORKING WITH TEXT

Adding text is just about the easiest task there is for a Web page developer. But formatting text to look the way you want it to, or getting it to appear at the precise location on the page it should, requires a bit more thought. You must add HTML tags to the text to tell browsers what typeface, size, and style you want the text to have, and you'll need more HTML tags to ensure that the text is placed properly.

Adobe GoLive's text handling features are a familiar combination of word processing and page layout tools that build the HTML you need graphically. You can create text in GoLive or copy it from elsewhere. From there, you can edit, format, position, search, spell check, and manipulate text and text blocks to polish your Web pages.

In this chapter, I cover:

- ◆ Entering text
- ◆ Formatting text
- ◆ Formatting text blocks
- ◆ Spell checking
- ◆ Finding and replacing text

Entering Text

You can add text to a GoLive document in several ways. You also have a choice of views in which to add your text. In most cases, you will use the Layout Editor, either by typing directly into the Document window or by copying or importing into a document. You can also use other views to add or edit text—more on that in Chapter 10, "Working with Code."

To type text directly into a document:

1. Open a new or existing GoLive document. Make sure that the Layout Editor appears in the Document window by clicking the Layout tab at the top of the window.

2. Type some text in the Document window.

Editing text

You can edit text in GoLive just as you can in most applications. Select text, then cut, copy, or paste it. Use your cursor (arrow) keys to move around the document, adding or deleting text as needed. Later in this chapter, you will learn how to check your spelling and use GoLive's Find & Replace tool to locate and change text when you need to.

You can also paste text into GoLive from another application, though the text will not retain formatting it may have had in the native application.

Text and Layout Grids

GoLive includes a feature called the *layout grid*. It's either a godsend for page layout, or a troublesome gimmick, depending upon your point of view. The GoLive layout grid is essentially an HTML table that you can use to position text and objects, relative to a specific position on the page, defined by the cells in the grid.

Using another GoLive tool called a Layout Text Box, you can place a block of text onto a layout grid at precisely the coordinates you want. Without the grid, text on a Web page either appears at the margin of the page, or next to an object that's on the margin. The layout grid allows you to achieve text spacing.

On the other hand, layout grids add complexity to the page. Dense tables take longer to download, and, should you need to edit the contents of the grid in GoLive's HTML Source Editor, you'll have a more difficult time than you would in either a gridless arrangement, or in a conventional table.

In this chapter, I'll show you how to add text with a Layout Text Box and layout grid. To decide for yourself whether layout grids are right for your Web pages, read Chapter 4, where I discuss grids and design in detail.

Figure 3.1 The Layout Grid icon appears on the Basic tab of the Objects palette.

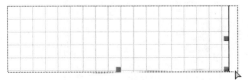

Figure 3.2 To resize a layout grid, grab the handle at the bottom-right corner of the grid and drag to change the grid's shape and size.

Figure 3.3 The Layout Text Box icon is on the Basic tab of the Objects palette.

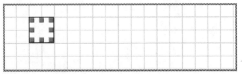

Figure 3.4 When you drag the Layout Text Box onto a layout grid, a small text frame appears on the layout grid.

Adding text using layout grids and text boxes

To add a Layout Text Box to a page, you must first add a layout grid.

To add a text frame to a page:

1. Double-click the Layout Grid icon (**Figure 3.1**) on the Basic tab of the Objects palette, or drag the Layout Grid icon into the Document window.

2. Use the mouse to grab the handle at the bottom-right corner of the grid you've created and drag the handle to the right, so that the layout grid becomes a horizontal rectangle (**Figure 3.2**).

3. Drag the Layout Text Box icon (**Figure 3.3**) from the Basic tab of the Objects palette. Like the grid, the text box has highlighted handles for resizing (**Figure 3.4**). You'll also notice that the I-beam cursor is positioned within your new frame.

   Note: You can't double-click to add the text box as you can the grid, because the text box can only be placed within the grid—you have to place it in a specific location.

4. Grab the handle at the bottom-right corner of the text box you've created and drag to the right, so that you'll be able to see what you're about to type.

5. Click within the text box and type some text.

6. Click the text box, but not on the text itself. Now you can drag the block to any position on the layout grid.

continues on next page

ENTERING TEXT

✔ Tips

- If you type or paste text into a text box without enlarging the frame first, GoLive expands the box vertically as text is entered. You can resize the frame after you enter text, but it's easier to size the box to fit the text first.

- When you click the text box, you may notice that the box is selected but that the handles aren't visible. Without pressing the mouse button, move your cursor over the text box until it displays a selector icon (when the pointer is on the border of the box). When you click, you'll see the handles and can move or resize the window. As you move, the selector icon will change to a hand icon.

- Try to use as few text boxes as possible, and align them to your layout grid.

- You can change the background color of a layout text box with the Layout Textbox Inspector (**Figure 3.5**). It appears in the Inspector window when you click a text frame's border. To change the color of the text itself, you need to select the text and use the toolbar or menus as described in the next section, "Formatting Text."

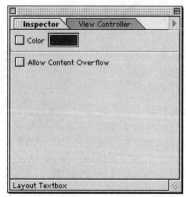

Figure 3.5 The Layout Textbox Inspector allows you to change the background color of a text box.

ENTERING TEXT

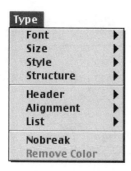

Figure 3.6 Use the Type menu's commands to format selected text.

Formatting Text

Text on a Web page, like text that appears in print, or onscreen in a word processor, can come in all styles and sizes, but it is affected by many factors, such as different browsers, browser versions, preferences, and platforms. To format text for the Web, you must apply HTML tags to it. Though GoLive insulates you from the need to know these tags, you do need to know something about the formatting features HTML supports and how to get around the limitations imposed by the Web. You apply text formatting in much the same way you would in a word processing application or page layout program. GoLive's text formatting tools are available from the Type menu (**Figure 3.6**), and many are repeated on the toolbar (**Figure 3.7**).

In this section, I'll show you a number of options for changing text size, weight (bold, italic, etc.), color, and typeface. Because we're working with HTML, rather than traditional typography tools, there are special and sometimes confusing rules for formatting text. In this section, I'll cover:

◆ Text size

◆ Text display styles

◆ Text color

◆ Fonts

◆ Font sets

In the next section, you'll learn how to format and arrange blocks of text on the page.

Figure 3.7 The toolbar includes most of the same options found on the Type menu.

Changing text size

In traditional (print) typography, the size of text on a page is expressed in *points*. There are 12 points in an inch. Most body text is 10 to 12 points, for example, and a heading might be anywhere from 14 to 36 points, or even bigger. In HTML, text size is not usually expressed in points, unless you are working with cascading style sheets (described in Chapter 11, "Working with Style Sheets"). In plain old HTML, the size of text on the page is expressed relative to the size of baseline text on the page. The actual size of the baseline is determined by the browser used to view it, and the text size settings that have been set. Though this means that your text will not appear in exactly the same way in all browsers, the size relative to the baseline will be fairly constant.

To add a bit of confusion to the mix, there's another kind of relative text sizing going on in HTML. The size of text on the Web is expressed using either the *absolute* or *relative* scale. The absolute scale provides for text sizes from 1 to 7, with 3 being the baseline. Setting text to 5 displays it at a size somewhat larger than the baseline, while 1 is smaller. **Figure 3.8** shows text sizes from 1 to 7. The relative scale works the same way, but is applied differently. Instead of an absolute number (3, 4, 5 and so on), a relative text size is expressed as −2, −1, +1, +2 and so on. The numbers on this scale are relative to the baseline. There's not much difference in appearance between absolute and relative text sizes unless browser font size preferences have been changed, in which case, the differences between font sizes on the relative scale will remain apparent, while text that was sized using the absolute scale will not grow or shrink relative to the baseline.

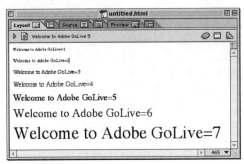

Figure 3.8 Text in this window is from 1 to 7 on the absolute scale.

Figure 3.9 You can use the toolbar's Size button to select absolute or relative font sizes.

Figure 3.10 Choose an absolute or relative text size from the Size menu.

To change the size of text:

1. Select some text in the Layout Editor.

2. Click the Size button on the toolbar (**Figure 3.9**).

   or

   Choose Type > Size. The Size submenu appears (**Figure 3.10**).

3. Select an absolute size (top portion of the menu) or a relative size (lower portion). The size of the selected text changes.

Text display styles

HTML specifies two types of text display styles: *physical* and *logical*. *Physical styles*, such as bold and italic, always look the same, regardless of the Web browser being used to view the page. *Logical styles*, such as strong and emphasis, take their visual marching orders from the user's Web browser. In general, newer browsers do a better job of displaying logical styled text than do older ones.

✔ Tip

■ Physical and logical styles should not be confused with cascading style sheets (CSS), which I'll discuss more fully in Chapter 11, "Working with Style Sheets." Style sheets allow you to specify fonts, type sizes, and other text attributes much the way you do in non-Web applications. To view them, though, a user must have a style-sheet–capable browser. Netscape and Microsoft browsers versions 4.0 and later support style sheets.

continues on next page

FORMATTING TEXT

Only three physical styles—bold, italic, and teletype—are available from the toolbar. All of the physical styles appear on the Style submenu of the Type menu (**Figure 3.11**). The rest are:

◆ Plain text

◆ Underline

◆ Strikeout

◆ Superscript

◆ Subscript

◆ Blink

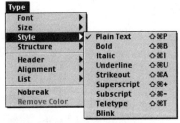

Figure 3.11 The Style menu of the Type menu contains physical styles.

✔ Tip

■ Blink is a Netscape-only tag. GoLive cannot display the blink tag in either the Layout Editor or Layout Preview. If you want to make a Web page's text flash, you'll need to preview it in a Netscape browser. But think twice before you make those pages blink. The blink tag is universally reviled among Webmasters and users alike.

Logical styles—as they're called in HTML jargon—appear on the Structure submenu of the Type menu. GoLive refers to logical HTML styles as structural styles. **Figure 3.12** shows the Structure submenu.

Because the look of text formatted with a logical style can vary depending on the viewer's browser, it's particularly important to take a look at the page using several browsers, preferably on both the Mac and Windows platforms. **Figure 3.13** compares the look of logical styles in three popular browsers—two Macintosh, and one Windows.

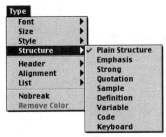

Figure 3.12 The Structure submenu of the Type menu contains logical styles.

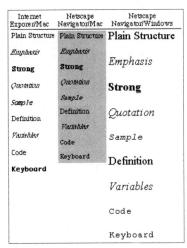

Figure 3.13 Here are logical styles, as displayed in three different browsers. Note that besides slight differences in type size and display attributes, different browsers render vertical spacing differently.

FORMATTING TEXT

Text color

As you saw in Chapter 2, "Your First GoLive Page," you can choose color for the text and links on a page in the Page Inspector. If you want to apply color to a particular block of text, you can do that by adding a color from the Color palette.

To color a block of text:

1. Select some text in the Document window.

2. Choose a color from the Color palette. For more about creating or choosing colors, see Chapter 4, "Working with Layout Tools."

3. Click in the Color palette's Preview pane and drag to the text you selected in the Document window. The text changes color.

Fonts

You can specify typefaces (commonly called fonts) in GoLive, but there are some HTML-specific barriers that limit your options somewhat and require that you observe a few special rules.

Like type sizes, described earlier in this chapter, typefaces displayed by a user's browser are subject to the behavior of that browser. If you don't specify a typeface when you build a Web page, the user's browser will provide one. If you do want to use a specific typeface, there is still no guarantee that the user's browser will display it if he or she does not have the typeface installed. HTML and GoLive allow you to specify several typefaces for a single text element: a default typeface and as many backup fonts as you like. When a user's browser displays an HTML page, it tries to use the specified default typeface and then the backup fonts in turn, looking for one that is available on the user's system. You can specify alternate font relationships in GoLive with font sets.

Font sets

Font sets are an easy way to manage groups of font choices that browsers use to locate a font with which to display your Web page. If, for example, you create a font set that includes Arial, Helvetica, and Geneva, and then use Arial to produce a page, users who don't have Arial installed can view the text in Helvetica or Geneva, depending on the fonts installed in their system.

GoLive allows you to build two types of font sets: Default (also known as global) and Page. The Default font set includes fonts that will be used with all GoLive pages you create, unless you override the default on a specific page or text selection. Page fonts are used only on the GoLive document for which you create them.

To edit a font set:

1. Choose Type > Font > Edit Font Sets. The Font Set Editor appears.

2. If it isn't already highlighted, click the Page icon in the left pane of the window. Page fonts apply only to the current document.

3. Click New in the middle pane of the Font Set Editor. A new, unnamed font set appears (**Figure 3.14**).

4. Choose a font from the pulldown menu on the right. The fonts on this menu are those currently installed in your system.

   or

   Type the name of a font you want to use, whether it is in your system or not.

5. Whether you select a font from the menu or type in the name, choose the font that you would like to specify as the first font (the one browsers try to use first) in the new set by clicking on the font that's currently in the first position on the list and choosing a font as described in the previous step.

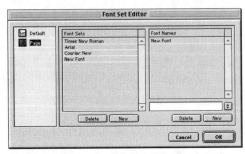

Figure 3.14 When you click New in the Font Set Editor, you can type or select the name of the first font in your new font set.

6. Press Enter to confirm your choice.

7. To add another font to the set, click New under the Font Names list and choose another font from the list, or type the name of the second font you want to add.

8. When you've finished adding fonts, click OK to close the Font Set Editor.

You can add more font sets by clicking New in the middle pane of the Font Set Editor. When you're done, the sets you've created (named for the first font in the set) appear on the Font submenu of the Type menu.

To use a font:

1. Select some text in the Document window.

2. Choose a font from the Font submenu of the Type menu. The font is applied to the text you selected.

✔ Tip

■ If you added a font to a set by typing its name into the Font Set Editor, GoLive adds that name to the source code for your page (Page fonts) or globally (Default), regardless of whether that font exists in your system, or even whether you've ever used it. If you apply that font to text in GoLive, the font will be used on a system where that font is installed. You can also see the font name by clicking on the Source tab and taking a look at the HTML code surrounding the text to which you applied the font.

FORMATTING TEXT

Setting Font Preferences

In addition to creating font sets and using them with Web pages, GoLive allows you to set the fonts that you see in the Layout Editor, when no other fonts have been specified.

To set font preferences:

1. Choose Edit > Preferences. The Preferences dialog box appears.

2. Click the Fonts label on the left side of the dialog box (**Figure 3.15**).

3. Click one of the items under the Western label to select it.

4. Choose a font and a size from the menus at the bottom of the dialog box (**Figure 3.16**).

✔ Tip

■ If you click the Font Sample triangle at the bottom of the Fonts Preferences window, you will see a sample of the font you've chosen. Change the font or size with the pulldown menu and the sample changes.

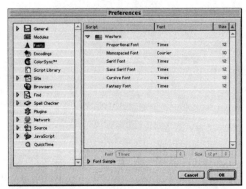

Figure 3.15 Use the Fonts Preferences window to choose display fonts in GoLive.

Figure 3.16 Choose a font and size to be used within GoLive.

Figure 3.17 Align text using the Left, Center, or Right buttons on the toolbar.

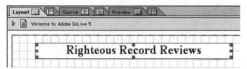

Figure 3.18 When you align text, it is aligned relative to the dimensions of the layout text box. Note: If you're not using a layout text box on a layout grid, the text is aligned relative to the width of the user's browser.

Formatting Text Blocks

Up to this point, all of the text-formatting options I've described have been intended to format text characters. Now, let's concentrate on text formatting that changes the way a block of text looks on the page, how it is indented, its relationship to other text blocks, and so on.

First, we will look at formatting options for lines of text and for paragraphs. Next, we move on to headings, lists, and alternative ways to arrange and organize text blocks.

Text alignment

You can align text to the left, center, or right margins, using buttons on the toolbar (**Figure 3.17**) or by choosing Type > Alignment and then your choice.

To align text:

1. Select some text.

2. Choose the Left, Center, or Right button from the toolbar.

   or

   Choose Type > Alignment and then Left, Center, or Right.

In **Figure 3.18**, the text is centered within the layout text box.

✔ Tip

■ If you center text in a layout text box as shown in Figure 3.18, your text will not be centered on the page, but within the box itself. You'll have to center the layout text box on the page to achieve centered text relative to the layout grid. If you want to center text over a portion of the Web page, first center the layout text box relative to the grid using GoLive's object alignment tools. You can read more about these tools in Chapter 4, "Working with Layout Tools."

Indenting text

You can indent blocks of text from the margin using an HTML element called *blockquote*. Blockquote indents text from both sides of the page. You can use it multiple times to create a deeper indent.

To indent text:

1. Click some text in the Document window. You don't need to select it.

   Choose Type > Alignment > Increase Block Indent (**Figure 3.19**). Text is indented from the left margin of the Document window or text box.

2. Repeat Step 2 to increase the indent further.

✔ Tip

- You can remove or decrease text indents with the Decrease Block Indent command.

Paragraphs and line breaks

Text blocks, like everything else on a Web page, are defined by HTML tags. Most body text is set off by paragraph tags. You can also use a line break or a heading to set off a block of text from other text blocks on the page.

You don't have to do anything special to create paragraphs in GoLive. When you type text into the Document window, GoLive generates an opening and closing paragraph tag by default. If you press Return while typing, GoLive creates a new paragraph. HTML paragraphs are separated by a blank line. If you would rather create a new text block without creating a blank line, use a line break instead. You can also use a line break to control the way text interacts with adjacent elements, such as images.

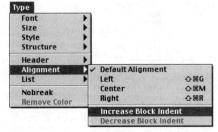

Figure 3.19 You can use the Type menu's Alignment submenu to change alignment and text indents.

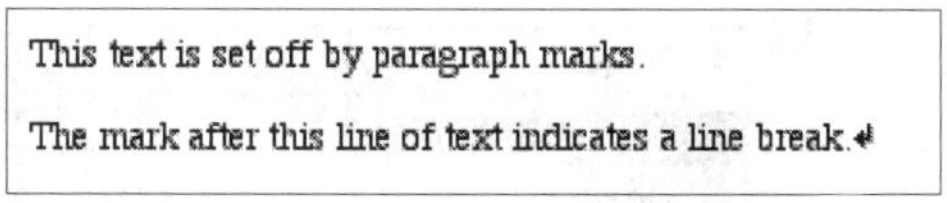

This text is set off by paragraph marks.

The mark after this line of text indicates a line break. ↵

Figure 3.20 When you create a line break, the line break character appears in the Document window.

Figure 3.21 The image is aligned to the left of a continuous block of text.

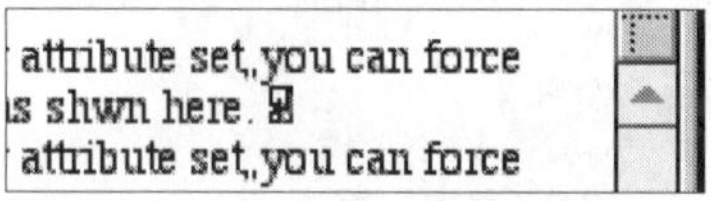

attribute set, you can force
is shwn here. ⬛
attribute set, you can force

Figure 3.22 A line break character appears when you drag the Line Break icon into the Document window or when you press Shift-Return. Select the line break character to use the Line Break Inspector.

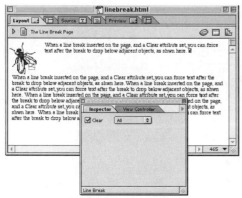

Figure 3.23 When you select the line break character and click the Clear checkbox in the Line Break Inspector, the flow of text stops until it is clear of any images that are adjacent to the text.

To create a line break:

1. Place your cursor at the location where you want the line break to appear.

2. Press Shift-Return. A line break character appears (**Figure 3.20**).

To use a line break to stop text wrap:

1. Add some text and an image to a GoLive document, either without a layout grid, or within the same layout text box, so that the position of the text affects the position of the image.

    Click the image to select it, and choose Left from the Alignment menu in the Inspector. Text wraps to the right of the image as shown in **Figure 3.21**.

2. Create a line break within the block of text by pressing Shift-Return.

    or

    Drag the Line Break icon from the Objects palette. A line break character appears.

3. Select the line break character (**Figure 3.22**) to display the Line Break Inspector.

4. Click the Clear checkbox. The adjacent menu becomes active. Notice that the All option is selected, and that the text below the line break in the Document window now falls below the image (**Figure 3.23**). The line break's Clear attribute stops text from flowing until it is clear of all images. If you choose the Left or Right attribute from the Clear popup menu in the Line Break Inspector, text will not wrap to images on the left or right of the text, respectively, following a line break.

FORMATING TEXT BLOCKS

Headings

HTML provides for six levels of headings that you can use to call attention to and organize text on the page. Like headlines and subheads in print publishing, HTML headings are larger and bolder than standard Web page text. Like paragraph tags, HTML heading tags enclose the heading text. Unlike paragraph tags, headings change the size and weight of the text they surround. Heading 1 is the largest heading choice while heading 6 is the smallest.

To create a heading:

1. Type some text in the Document window.

2. From the toolbar, choose Header 1 from the Paragraph Format pulldown menu (**Figure 3.24**).

   or

   Choose Type > Header > Header 1.
   The text is now larger and bold.

Addresses and Preformatted text

The Address and Preformatted formats are found on the toolbar's Paragraph Format menu. The Address style is usually used to identify the owner/copyright holder/author of the Web page and is traditionally located at the bottom of a Web page (**Figure 3.25**). You can't change the Address style.

Text that is preformatted does not use the HTML tags that give Web page text a typeset look. Instead, using the Preformatted format displays text in a fixed-width font. GoLive displays preformatted text using the Courier font (**Figure 3.26**). Web browsers display preformatted text in whatever fixed-width font is specified in the browser. Preformatted text is most often used to display code, or to differentiate certain passages from the rest of the text on the page.

To apply the Address or Preformatted text format, select the text and choose a format from the Paragraph Format menu on the toolbar.

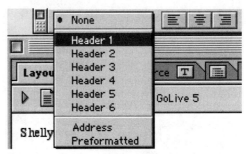

Figure 3.24 Choose Header 1 from the Paragraph Format menu in the toolbar.

Figure 3.25 An example of the Address style.

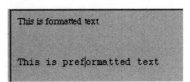

Figure 3.26 Preformatted text looks like this.

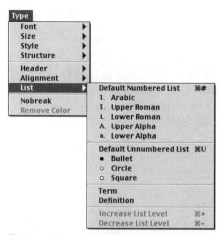

Figure 3.27 You can choose from a number of list types on the List submenu of the Type menu.

Lists

Lists are an easy way to organize content on your Web page. Whether you need to create a numbered list of instructions, an outline, or a bulleted list of links, HTML provides several formats to cover your needs.

To create a list:

1. Type the items from your list into the Document window. After typing each item, press Return.

2. Select the items in the list.

3. Choose a list format from the List submenu of the Type menu (**Figure 3.27**). The Arabic (numerals) style is shown in **Figure 3.28**.

4. With the text still selected, choose a different list format and notice how the appearance of the text changes. **Figure 3.29** shows a bulleted list.

1. General Info
2. Rides
3. Newsletters
4. Sponsors
5. Tandem Links

Figure 3.28 To format a list that looks like this, choose a numbered list from the toolbar or List submenu.

- General Info
- Rides
- Newsletters
- Sponsors
- Tandem Links

Figure 3.29 Change the list to a bulleted one to get this look.

Changing list indents

The toolbar includes two list-making options and one tool each for increasing and decreasing the indent of lists.

To change the indent of a list:

1. Select a list.

2. To add a greater indent to the list, click the Increase List Level button on the toolbar (**Figure 3.30**).

3. To move the indent back one level, click the Decrease List Level button on the toolbar.

4. To delete all list formatting, decrease the list level until the option is dimmed.

✔ Tips

■ You will find the list level options on the List submenu of the Type menu, too.

■ The toolbar buttons that allow you to indent your list further, or decrease its indent, do not work with non-list text blocks. You can only use those buttons with a list that you have already created. Besides increasing the indent of the entire list, you can also choose to indent selected items only. To do that, just select the list item whose indent you want to change and then click the Increase List Level button. Figure 3.30 shows the toolbar's list-making buttons.

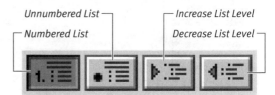

Figure 3.30 The toolbar contains four buttons for managing the display of lists.

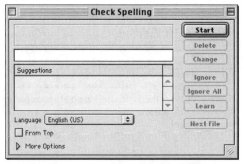

Figure 3.31 The Check Spelling dialog box.

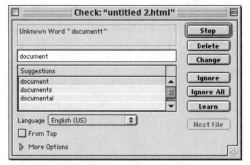

Figure 3.32 When the spelling checker questions a word, you can choose the correct spelling from the list presented in the lower pane.

Spell Checking

GoLive's built-in spelling checker can locate spelling errors in a single page or throughout your site. You can use one of several English language or non-English dictionaries, or add your own words to a Personal Dictionary. To use a non-English dictionary, select it when you install GoLive for the first time, or run the installer to add the dictionary.

To check spelling:

1. Open a GoLive document and make sure that you're working in the Layout Editor.

2. Choose Edit > Check Spelling. The Check Spelling dialog box appears (**Figure 3.31**).

3. If you would like to use a dictionary other than the default U.S. English dictionary, choose it from the Language pulldown menu. The dictionary must be installed with GoLive before you can use it.

4. Click Start.

5. The spell checker locates words that it does not recognize, whether they're misspelled or simply not included in the dictionary.

6. To correct a spelling mistake, click one of the suggestions offered (**Figure 3.32**), and then click the Change button. If you don't see a suggestion you like, type a new spelling for the word in the field provided.

   You can also tell the spell checker to simply Ignore a word that it doesn't know. Ignore All passes over all occurrences of the word.

   continues on next page

7. If the spellchecker has pointed out a word that is not misspelled, and should be added to your personal dictionary, click the Learn button.

8. To delete a flagged word, click the Delete button.

✔ Tip

■ While you have the Check Spelling dialog box open, GoLive highlights questionable words in the Document window. You may need to move the dialog box in order to see the highlighting. That's what I did in **Figure 3.33**.

If you're working in the HTML Source or HTML Outline Editor, the spell checker ignores the HTML code that surrounds your text when performing its check.

To customize the spell checker:

1. With the Check Spelling dialog box open, click the More Options triangle at the bottom of the window (**Figure 3.34**). A list of spell checking options appears.

2. Check or uncheck options to customize the way you want your spell check to work.

Figure 3.33 Move the Spell Checking dialog box out of the way to see where a misspelled word appears in your document.

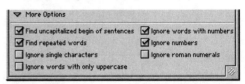

Figure 3.34 From the More Options panel of the Check Spelling dialog box, you can customize your check to ignore certain words and look for common typing errors.

Figure 3.35 Click Next File in the Check Spelling dialog box to move from the current file to the next one in your site.

To check an entire site's spelling:

1. Open a GoLive site file, so that the Site window is visible.

2. Make certain that the Site window is the front-most window by clicking on the Files tab.

3. Choose Edit > Check Spelling.

4. The Check Spelling dialog box appears and begins to check the first document in your site when you click the Start button.

5. Check spelling as you would for a local file. When the checker has finished with the first file, it opens the next (alphabetical) file in your site and begins checking.

6. To move from the current file to the next one, click the Next File button (**Figure 3.35**). The Next File button is dimmed when you do not have a GoLive site open.

✔ Tip

■ When you click Ignore All or Learn, your instructions are carried throughout the current checking session, including all of the files in your site.

Find and Replace Text

You can search one document or a whole site with GoLive's find and replace features. You can search text (including Web page content and HTML code) for characters, words, or phrases. Find and Replace works in the Layout, HTML Source, and HTML Outline Editors.

✔ Tip

■ GoLive allows you to locate and replace items within a single file (locally), a site (globally), or within a group of files you select. You can also search within site reports, which I cover in Chapter 15, "Viewing and Managing Sites." You can look for text or code, or use powerful regular expressions (commonly referred to as Grep) to utilize wildcard searching and then use the replace feature to do just that. The Element feature, which allows you to search for HTML tags and other code, is covered in Chapter 10, "Working with Code."

Finding text locally

You can search for and replace text contained in one or more files using the Find command.

To find text in a file:

1. Open a GoLive document and make sure that you are in the Layout, HTML Source, or HTML Outline Editor.

2. Choose Edit > Find, or type Command-F (Mac) or Control-F (Windows). The Find dialog box appears.

3. Type a word that can be found within the current document. **Figure 3.36** shows the Find dialog box ready to search.

4. Click Find.

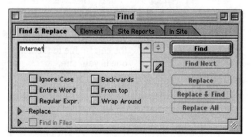

Figure 3.36 Enter text to search for in the Find dialog box.

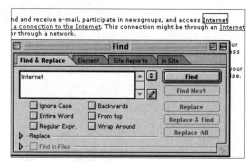

Figure 3.37 Text matching your search request is highlighted in the Document window.

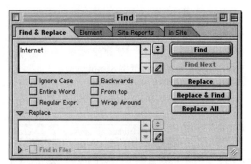

Figure 3.38 Open the Replace field by clicking on the Replace triangle in the Find dialog box.

5. When GoLive finds an instance of the word you've searched for, it highlights the word in the Document window (**Figure 3.37**). You can click Find Next to look for another instance of the word.

To find and replace text locally:

1. If the Find dialog box is not still visible, choose Edit > Find.

2. Type some text to search for.

3. If it is not already visible, open the Replace field by clicking on the triangle near the bottom of the window (**Figure 3.38**).

4. Type some text to replace the characters you're going to find.

5. Click Find. Notice in the Find window that you have the option to replace the text (Replace) or to automatically find and replace all occurrences within your document (by clicking the Replace All button). If you would rather make the decision to replace text on a case by case basis, simply click the Replace & Find button to replace, then locate another occurrence of your text, in one step.

✔ Tip

- When you use Find and Replace to change text in the HTML Source or HTML Outline Editors, you may inadvertently destroy links if they contain the text you are replacing, because the Replace command does not distinguish between text that is part of a URL and text that is part of the body of the document.

Search options

The Find dialog box includes several check-boxes that allow you to narrow your search (**Figure 3.39**).

◆ **Ignore Case** searches only for text that's capitalized just like the text you type in the Find field.

◆ **Entire Word** limits your search to results that match the spacing of the word you type. For example, if you search for "go" with Entire Word checked, you won't find occurrences of the word "GoLive".

◆ **Backwards** searches before the current insertion point.

◆ **From top** starts the search at the beginning of the document.

◆ **Wrap Around** starts a search at the current location, continues to the end of the document and begins again.

◆ **Regular Expr** tells GoLive to activate wildcard searching using regular expressions.

Searching multiple files

Searching for text in several files works very much the way it does when you're searching the currently open document.

To search multiple files:

1. Click the Find in Files triangle in the Find dialog box (**Figure 3.40**). Don't worry if the Find in Files label is dimmed (Mac). You can still open that section of the window.

2. Click Add Files. A dialog box appears, allowing you to navigate to a file you want in the upper pane.

3. Locate a file you want to search for, and select it by clicking Add. The file's name appears in the lower pane (**Figure 3.41**).

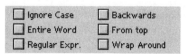

Figure 3.39 Choose one of these options to narrow or organize your search.

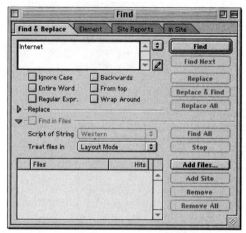

Figure 3.40 Click the Find in Files triangle to open this part of the dialog box and search for text in multiple files.

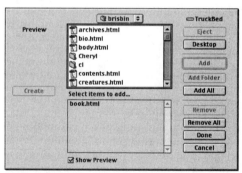

Figure 3.41 When you click Add Files in the Find dialog box, GoLive presents a file browser window where you can choose files to include in the search. Select one, click Add, and it will appear in the lower pane of the dialog box.

Figure 3.42 When you add files to a search in the Windows version of GoLive, you can choose to view all readable files, or just HTML files. Choose HTML, because GoLive can't search non-HTML files, even though it will let you add them to a search.

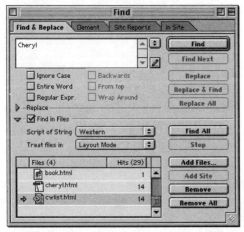

Figure 3.43 When your search is complete, GoLive shows the number of occurrences in each document in the Find dialog box.

4. Repeat Step 3 to add more files.

5. When you're finished, click Done. The files you've added appear in the Files field of the Find dialog box.

6. Use the Find and Replace commands as described above. When GoLive finds an occurrence of the text you're searching for, it opens the file, unless it's already open.

7. To open all files with a match, click Find All.

✔ Tips

■ (Mac) You can add any text file to a multi-file search list while you're browsing your hard drive. But only the HTML files you include will show up in the Files list in the Find dialog box.

■ (Windows) The Windows version of GoLive is a bit smarter about selecting files to search. In the Add Files window, you can choose to view All Files, or just the HTML files that GoLive can search (**Figure 3.42**).

■ When GoLive searches multiple files, the Find dialog box displays the number of matches found in the Files field (**Figure 3.43**). View the document with text matching your search by double-clicking on its name in the Files field.

Searching the HTML Source Editor

When HTML files with results that match your search criteria open, they do so in the Layout Editor. In a multifile search, you can choose to have GoLive look at URLs and tags, and open files with matches in the HTML Source Editor. To do so, in the Find dialog box choose Source Mode from the Treat files in pulldown menu (**Figure 3.44**).

✔ Tip

■ You can use this search option to locate HTML code in the HTML Source Editor, but you'll find much more powerful code-searching tools under the Find dialog box's Element tab, which I discuss in Chapter 10, "Working with Code."

Figure 3.44 Search the contents (including tags and URLs) of the Source view by choosing Source Mode from the Treat files in menu.

WORKING WITH LAYOUT TOOLS

In many ways, this is the most important chapter in the entire book. Here I explain how to use Adobe GoLive to construct Web pages using text, graphics, and spacing devices. I'll start by adding a layout grid to a blank page, then work my way through a design process, adding items to the page and fine-tuning each one.

In this chapter, I cover:

◆ Layout options

◆ Working with layout grids

◆ Grid objects

◆ Managing multiple objects

◆ Working with lines

◆ Media objects

◆ Browser-specific elements

◆ Managing color with the Color palette

◆ Using the History palette

The Quest for Layout

Today's Web page designers have a variety of technologies available to build pages and lay them out in a way that is not as limiting as early HTML. Three HTML layout options in particular—tables, frames, and layers—offer the Web designer more options than ever.

GoLive takes this "evolution" one step further with a very unique feature—the layout grid. Think of the layout grid as an interface to an automatic table generator. Layout grids "create" sophisticated tables that automatically include HTML code to maximize the display consistency among browsers. Of course, the value of grids is that you can use them to create sections for a page, and you can position text, graphics, and other HTML objects anywhere you choose—without having to work with HTML code.

Layers and Cascading Style Sheets

Version 4 of the HTML specification—the document that describes all elements in the language—included a major new tool for building page layouts. Layers (GoLive refers to them as floating boxes) allow you to position objects on the page without any regard for their relative location. In other words, where tables and layout grids always have some connection to the origin of the page— the upper-left corner of the page—layers are defined by the distance in pixels from the origin and thus, float on the page. You can use layers to position text, images, and media objects or even to edit animations.

A floating box, like many other tools in the Objects palette, can be placed onto a layout grid. Unlike layout grids, floating boxes can be placed anywhere on the page, and at any point in the design process.

Finally, a unique advantage of floating boxes is that you can place several of them atop each other, so they can overlap.

In summary, many of the positioning features of the layout grid can be realized using floating boxes, although page designers who need to support pre-4.0 browsers should not use them.

You'll find a complete discussion of layers in Chapter 12, "Layers and Positioning." For more on tables, read Chapter 7, "Working with Tables."

Tables vs. Grids: Which is Better?

Both traditional tables and GoLive layout grids are, in fact, HTML tables.

Layout grids are also useful tools for Web page designers, who can use them to position objects with pixel-level accuracy—making it possible to choose the exact location in the layout where an object will appear—though you should not expect that level of accuracy when a page is actually viewed in a specific browser. Objects you drag around a layout grid will snap to the grid when you complete the drag, allowing you to arrange them along the horizontal and vertical gridlines. Layout grids are also easy to build and change as you work with them.

Despite their flexibility as a way to build pages in GoLive, grids do make it even more necessary than usual for you to check your page design in several browsers as you build it to make sure that objects on a grid appear where they should, especially in relation to one another.

In some cases, a layout grid is not the right choice. Use a table instead if you are building a design containing content whose size varies by browser, such as text, which is rendered at a substantially larger size by PC browsers than by Mac browsers. This is also true of HTML for elements (see Chapter 8, "Working with Forms"). In a similar vein, stick to a table if you want to align text with an image, since you can keep the two in a single cell, and thus maintain their relationship.

If you decide to use layout grids, keep them simple. Don't load up a single grid with lots of objects (if you have 20 objects or more, chances are that the grid is too complicated) and use multiple grids if you need to build a more complex layout. Make sure that your grids are arranged vertically, not side-by-side. This keeps both grids simpler, since a grid that appears to the right of another grid must include extra code for needed columns.

The Layout Grid

With single-pixel accuracy, GoLive's unique layout grid is helpful for designers looking to control their layouts. Text, images, and other objects can be easily placed, arranged, and aligned using the grid.

Layout grids eliminate the need for using tables or frames to create multi-column pages. Grids can be customized so objects snap to their lines, painlessly aligning elements with respect to the grid and to each other. Grids can be sized to fit any page, or any portion of a page. They can also be placed on top of and adjacent to each other, though you can only place two grids side-by-side, and it's best to position them vertically, rather than side-by-side to keep the tables simpler.

Grids are not always the right solution, and you will want to read Chapter 7 ("Working with Tables"), Chapter 9 ("Working with Frames"), and Chapter 12 ("Layers and Positioning"), before you decide which layout options are best for your pages. You may choose to use more than one.

To create a layout grid:

1. Open a new GoLive document.

2. Drag the Layout Grid icon (**Figure 4.1**) from the Basic tab of the Objects palette onto the Document window, or double-click the icon. A square layout grid appears (**Figure 4.2**) in the upper-left corner of the blank page.

This grid is set to its default values, which probably will not meet your needs. You will need to use the Layout Grid Inspector to change the grid's attributes.

Figure 4.1 Choose the Layout Grid icon from the Basic tab of the Objects palette, then double-click or drag it into the Document window.

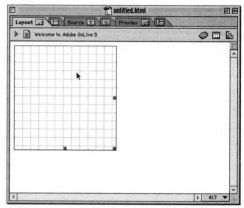

Figure 4.2 A grid appears at the first available space in the Document window. Note the three handles on the grid, used for dragging and sizing.

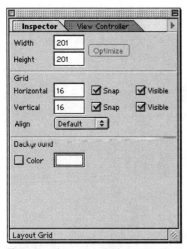

Figure 4.3 The Layout Grid Inspector controls size, position, behavior, and color of the grid.

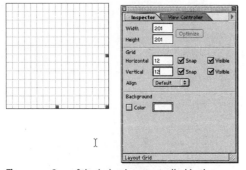

Figure 4.4 One of the behaviors controlled in the Inspector is the density of the grid. The size of the grid's cells is expressed in pixels.

To make adjustments to the layout grid:

1. Click the grid to display the Layout Grid Inspector (**Figure 4.3**). In the Layout Grid Inspector, you can resize the grid, change its horizontal and vertical gridlines, set the grid's color, and align two grids horizontally on the page.

2. With the Inspector visible, click in the Horizontal field in the Grid area. Type 12, to replace the default value of 16 pixels.

3. Press Tab. The Vertical field is now selected. Notice that the horizontal gridlines are now closer together. They are 12 pixels apart.

4. Type 12 in the Vertical field and press Tab to finish the new, denser grid (**Figure 4.4**).

   Closer grid spacing can be useful if you want to place a number of objects close together on a grid. Likewise, adding space between gridlines keeps objects further apart on the page.

✔ Tips

- By default, both the Horizontal and Vertical Snap checkboxes are selected in the Layout Grid Inspector. With Snap turned on, objects you drag onto a layout grid automatically snap to the nearest gridlines when you release the mouse.

- Turning off the Visible checkbox hides the grid from view but doesn't prevent it from snapping objects into place if the Snap option is on. Because the grid will not be visible on the finished page, hiding the grid temporarily can make previewing pages in the Layout Editor a bit easier.

continues on next page

THE LAYOUT GRID

- Grids can be resized by dragging the handles on the sides of the grid or by entering new numerical values—expressed in pixels—in the Layout Grid Inspector. They cannot, however, be repositioned, because "underneath" the grid is an HTML table; therefore, grids cannot be positioned at a *specific point* on the page.

- Grids can be optimized so that they are just large enough to contain the elements placed upon them. Clicking on the Optimize button in the Layout Grid Inspector will retain the position of the upper-left corner of the grid, but the area of the grid without objects on it will be eliminated. Optimize only works when the grid contains objects and excess space.

Positioning a layout grid

A single layout grid can be used for an entire Web page, or you can divide the page into multiple grids. A single page-wide grid forms a consistent background for the entire document and is usually a good choice if your Web page contains lots of items that are positioned or aligned relative to each another. If your page design is modular, with common sections such as a navigation bar or logo section—a grid for each section is an option, but one that should be applied carefully, making sure that each element (text boxes, for example) lines up exactly into rows and columns on the grid. (Using Snap To Grid can help with alignment.) This will minimize the number of extra cells and columns that are generated, thereby streamlining your code. In the following example, two grids accommodate a modular layout.

To size a layout grid:

1. In a new GoLive document, add a layout grid to the blank page.

THE LAYOUT GRID

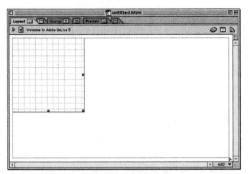

Figure 4.5 Drag the layout grid handle to the bottom-right corner of the Document window.

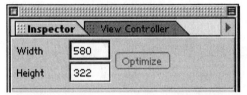

Figure 4.6 Change the grid's width in the Layout Grid Inspector.

2. Drag the handle at the bottom-right corner of the grid downward and to the right until the grid extends to the bottom and right edge of the window (**Figure 4.5**).

3. In the bottom-right corner of the Document window, click and hold the Page Size popup menu to open the menu, and select a width of 580 pixels, the common browser width for 14-inch monitors. The Document window enlarges a bit.

4. Select the layout grid and drag its bottom-right handle down to the lower-right corner of the window to once again fill the page with the grid.

   or

   Resize the grid by typing **580** in the Layout Grid Inspector's Width field (**Figure 4.6**). Now, the grid matches the pixel width of the window.

✔ Tip

■ As you drag to resize the grid, the width and height measurements in the Layout Grid Inspector change, reflecting the grid's new size in pixels. While "eyeballing" may work when dragging a layout grid, you can always enter the precise size of the grid in the Inspector's Width and Height boxes.

Using multiple layout grids

Many Web sites use a navigation bar, logo, or other standing visual elements to unify the look of the pages making up the site. Multiple layout grids make it possible to add these and other standing elements to your Web pages to use as placeholders and positioners. Even better, you can save a layout of multiple grids and their repeating objects as a Custom object snippet, and use the object to quickly and accurately add elements to new pages as you build them.

continues on next page

THE LAYOUT GRID

✔ Tip

- While grids can be placed next to one another, problems with alignment, especially when browser windows are resized, make maintaining their placement difficult. One way to use grids effectively is to confine them to a unique portion of the page, say the top or bottom. Vertical grids don't cause as many alignment problems as horizontal grids, and offer an easy way to separate recurring matter—banners, logos, or other header and footer information—from rest of the page.

To add a second layout grid:

1. Open a new page. Set the width of the page to 580 pixels and fill the Document window with a layout grid.

2. Double-click the Layout Grid icon in the Objects palette. A second grid appears in the Document window (**Figure 4.7**). In this example, secondary grid will contain your Web site's table of contents.

3. With the new grid selected, click the Layout Grid Inspector. Here you will change the settings of the grid.

4. Click the Background Color field in the Inspector (**Figure 4.8**). The Color palette (which, by default, shares palette space with the Objects palette) opens.

5. With the Color palette open, select a new background color for your layout grid, which changes the Layout Grid Inspector's Color field. The secondary grid changes to the color you've selected (**Figure 4.9**) differentiating it from the first one you created. You will find more details about choosing colors and using the Color palette later in this chapter.

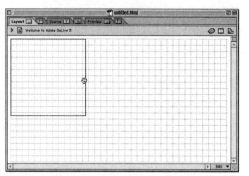

Figure 4.7 A secondary grid (to be used for a table of contents) is placed over the primary grid (which fills the entire page).

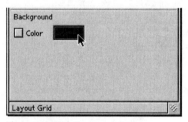

Figure 4.8 Click the Inspector's Background Color field to open the Color palette.

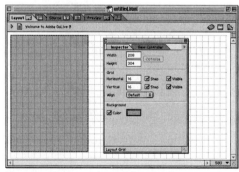

Figure 4.9 The secondary grid's color changes to the selected one.

Working with Objects on a Grid

You can add multiple objects to a layout grid, and work with them singly or as a group. Once objects are placed on the grid (unlike when they are placed in the Document window without a grid), they can be moved freely, as long as they stay on the grid. Just drag the object from one position on the grid to another. If the Snap checkboxes in the Layout Grid Inspector are activated, objects you drag will snap to the nearest gridline.

Object management tools

In this section, we will work with three GoLive tools: the Layout toolbar, the Align palette, and the Transform palette. Some of their features overlap, but each will help you align and group objects and gain more control over layout grids.

As you saw in the last section, the layout grid has its own inspector. The grid also has its own toolbar (**Figure 4.10**), which replaces the standard toolbar at the top of the screen when you work with a layout grid.

Actually, you can't use the Layout Grid toolbar's grid-related tools unless you have added an object to the grid. When you select that object, the toolbar's fields and buttons become active.

continues on next page

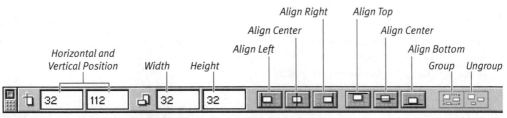

Figure 4.10 The Layout Grid toolbar appears when you select an object within a grid.

✔ Tips

- You can move an object on a grid with your keyboard's arrow keys. If Snap is selected in the Inspector, the object will move a grid square at a time, up or down, left or right. Holding down the Control and Alt keys (Windows) or the Option key (Mac) while using the arrow keys will move the object one pixel at a time. Additionally, the toolbar shows the position of the object in pixels relative to the upper-left corner —*0,0* on the *xy* axis—of the page (**Figure 4.11**).

- Objects on the grid may be resized by grabbing their control handles and dragging out (larger) or in (smaller). They may also be resized by typing numerical values in the appropriate toolbar fields.

All of the alignment tools on the Layout Grid toolbar, plus additional tools, are included in the Align palette. With it, you can align objects to the grid, as on the toolbar, but you can also align them relative to one another, or distribute them around the grid.

To align a single grid object:

1. Drag the Image icon from the Objects palette onto a new layout grid, and link to a graphic file by clicking the Browse button in the Inspector (it looks like a folder) and locating an image you want to add to the page.

2. With the object selected, click one of the six alignment buttons in the toolbar to move the picture around the grid (**Figure 4.12**).

✔ Tip

- You can also align objects within a layout grid using the Align palette (**Figure 4.13**). To open the Align palette, choose Window > Align. This palette contains the same controls as the toolbar, and then some.

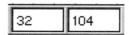

Figure 4.11 The Layout Grid toolbar shows the distance (in pixels) of a selected object from the left and top margins of the page.

Figure 4.12 Move the image around the Document window with these buttons located on the Layout Grid toolbar.

Figure 4.13 Choose an alignment option from the Align palette. You align objects relative to the grid with the Align to Parent buttons.

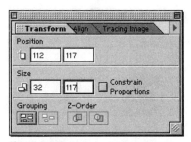

Figure 4.14 You can control an object's size and position with the Transform palette.

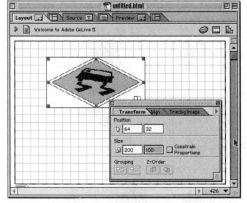

Figure 4.15 Changing the width of the graphic to 200 pixels distorts the graphic.

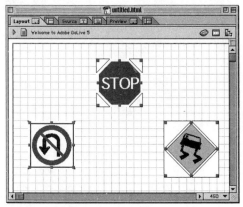

Figure 4.16 Three images are placed on the grid. All three are selected.

The Transform palette works only with objects that appear on layout grids.

To use the Transform palette to position an object:

1. Make a layout grid fill a page. Open the Transform palette from the Window menu, or click the Transform tab in the Align palette, if visible.

2. Add an Image item to the grid.

3. Use the Inspector to locate a graphic. In this case, I have linked to a 117-pixel square GIF image of a traffic sign. Note that the sign's size is visible in the Transform palette's Size boxes (**Figure 4.14**) and in the Inspector.

4. Change the numerical values in the Size boxes of the Transform palette and press Return. In **Figure 4.15**, I have changed the width of the graphic to 200, with the distorted result.

5. Return the value to its original number. Click the Constrain Proportions checkbox.

6. Enter a new numerical value in either of the Size boxes. Note that both values grow proportionately.

To align three objects with the Align palette:

1. On a new page, set the width to 580 pixels and fill the entire page with a layout grid.

2. Distribute three objects on the page more or less randomly.

3. Shift-click to select all three objects (**Figure 4.16**).

continues on next page

WORKING WITH OBJECTS ON A GRID

4. Open the Align palette. With multiple grid objects, your options for aligning and distributing are more numerous (**Figure 4.17**).

5. From the Align Objects section of the Align palette, select Top Align (which will line up all the objects with the topmost object), Center align (which will align them to the center object), or Bottom align (which will align them with the bottom of the lowest object). The objects in **Figure 4.18** are aligned to the center.

✔ Tips

■ The Align buttons on the toolbar perform the same functions as the Align palette buttons when you're aligning multiple objects, just as they do when you're aligning a single object to the grid.

■ The Align palette's four sets of buttons align the graphics with respect to the grid (Parent), to each other, or you can distribute the objects evenly around the layout, either by the average distance between the horizontal (or vertical) edges of the objects, or by the amount of white space between them.

■ To use Distribute Object or Distribute Spacing, you must select at least three objects on the grid.

■ Only the Align and Distribute buttons that can currently be used will be active in the Align palette. For example, if all selected objects are currently aligned to the bottom of the grid, you can't choose Bottom under Align to Parent.

■ Use the Distribute Objects buttons to space multiple selected objects an equal distance from each other, horizontally or vertically. Use the Distribute Spacing buttons to make the white space between the multiple selected objects equal, horizontally or vertically.

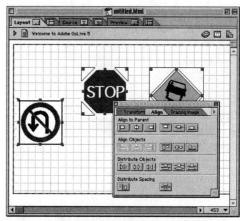

Figure 4.17 Alignment options abound for multiple selected objects. Here, the top row aligns objects to the Parent (grid) and the second row aligns them to each other. The Distribute options will equally distribute the objects or the white space between them.

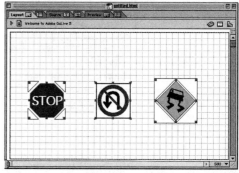

Figure 4.18 These objects are center-aligned to each other.

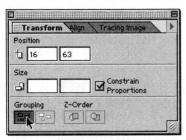

Figure 4.19 Click the Grouping button in the Transform palette to group selected objects.

Figure 4.20 Grouped objects are contained within a single border, allowing you to move them as one object when you click on the group.

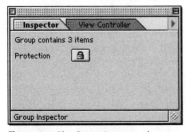

Figure 4.21 The Group Inspector lets you know how many items are in your group. You can unlock a group by clicking the padlock, which opens its hasp.

Figure 4.22 The toolbar also has Group and Ungroup buttons, which perform the same functions as the ones in the Transform palette.

Grouping objects

You can group multiple layout grid objects so that they can be moved as a single object.

To group objects:

1. Shift-click to select several objects on the layout grid and align or distribute them as you like.

2. Click the Grouping button in the Transform palette (**Figure 4.19**). The objects' individual selection handles disappear and the newly grouped object is now surrounded by a single border (**Figure 4.20**).

3. Drag the grouped object. All the elements move together.

4. When you create a group, the Inspector changes to the Group Inspector (**Figure 4.21**). Use the lock icon to lock the group so that its elements will continue to move together. Clicking the lock opens the lock's hasp, making the objects independent once again.

5. To break up a group, choose Ungroup from the Transform palette or click the lock in the Group Inspector to open the hasp and break up the group.

✔ Tip

■ The Group and Ungroup buttons in the Transform palette also appear on the Layout Grid toolbar (**Figure 4.22**).

The Rules for Lines

Lines (called *horizontal rules* in HTML) can be used to divide the Web page into visual and logical sections. They give text and graphics elements a little breathing room. Like most page elements, lines work best when you use a layout grid to position them. However, you can place lines without a grid as well.

You can vary the appearance of lines by thickness and, in Internet Explorer browsers (3.0 or later), by color. Netscape does not support the color attribute for the horizontal rule.

To add a horizontal line:

1. Double-click or drag the Line icon (**Figure 4.23**) from the Basic tab of the Objects palette to the Document window. The Line Inspector appears (**Figure 4.24**).

2. Change the settings in the Line Inspector. You can change the style to a solid rule or change the width and/or height of the line in pixels. You can also drag the line's handles onscreen to change its length (width).

3. Click one of the alignment buttons to change the line's relationship to the page or to the grid.

Figure 4.23 Select the Line icon from the Basic tab of the Objects palette.

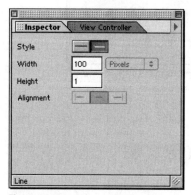

Figure 4.24 By default, the line displayed will be hollow and 100 pixels wide.

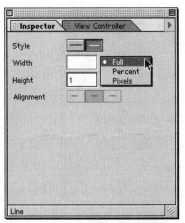

Figure 4.25 Lines existing outside of a layout grid can be assigned a width of full (the entire width of the page), as a percentage of the width of the page, or as a fixed width in pixels.

✔ Tips

- When using layout grids, you can fit a line within a grid or text frame by dragging the Line icon into the desired grid or frame. The line will snap to the width of the grid or frame.

- Lines dropped outside a layout grid can be sized in the Inspector's Width box in pixels, as a percentage of the browser window, or to the full width of the browser window (**Figure 4.25**).

- The Align tools on the toolbar and on the Align palette work when the line appears on a layout grid.

- Even if you're not using grids, you can create lines that drop easily into place. To create a line next to an image, for example, place the image first and drag the Line icon into place next to the image. The line is drawn to fill the available space.

Media Objects

Many of the icons on the Objects palette represent links between a Web page and rich media. Flash, Shockwave, RealAudio, and QuickTime are a few of the formats supported (via plug-ins) by most major browsers, and by Web authoring tools including GoLive, with links to audio, video, or animation files.

You can add placeholders in your Web pages for multimedia files, just as you would add a link to an image. The difference is that you'll need to view the media files in a Web browser or in GoLive's Layout Preview. Chapter 13, "Working with Rich Media," describes configuring plug-ins more thoroughly, and Chapter 18, "Creating Motion," gives you an overview of GoLive's QuickTime authoring tools. Here, I offer an introduction to working with media files as you build your layout.

To add a media file:

1. Choose a plug-in object (plug-in, SWF, QuickTime, RealAudio, or SVG) from the Basic tab of the Objects palette and double-click or drag it into the Document window. The Plug-in Inspector appears (**Figure 4.26**).

2. Choose the audio, video, or other media file you want to link to by clicking the Browse button (the icon that looks like a folder, adjacent to the File field), or typing a URL in the File field.

3. Continue configuring the file in the More and Attribs tabs of the Inspector.

4. Click the fourth tab, named for the plug-in type you selected. In **Figure 4.27**, it's Real, as in RealAudio.

5. Configure the plug-in-specific options here. For more on RealAudio and other plug-ins, see Chapter 13, "Working with Rich Media."

Figure 4.26 The Plug-In Inspector looks similar to the Image Inspector, and some of the options are the same.

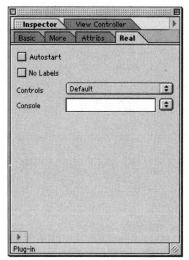

Figure 4.27 When you add a plug-in object that's directly supported by GoLive, you'll see a format-specific tab in the Inspector. This one allows you to configure RealAudio files.

Browser-Specific Elements

In their quest to dominate the marketplace, both Netscape and Microsoft have tinkered with standard HTML, adding tags that either add features to your Web page or gum up the works, depending on your point of view. GoLive supports two of these browser-specific tags, both of which have icons in the Objects palette.

✔ Tip

- Warning: Using these elements means that your Web pages either will not be compatible with both major browsers, or that you will need to create versions of the page for each.

Spacers

A spacer is a Netscape-created, Navigator-only element. It must be viewed with a Navigator 3.0 or later browser. Spacers create room between elements on the page, making it easier to combine text and objects or to create text spacing effects. Unlike alignment tags, which position items relative to other items, spacers enforce absolute boundaries. Spacers are especially useful when you work without a layout grid.

Because spacers are Netscape-only tags, consider the alternatives. If absolute positioning of text or objects is important to your layout, consider using Cascading Style Sheets (see Chapter 11, "Working with Style Sheets"). Style sheets, like spacers, don't work with all browsers; your visitors will need at least a 4.0 or later browser, but at least they work on either Navigator or Internet Explorer.

continues on next page

GoLive can create three types of spacers: horizontal, vertical, and block spacers.

- **Horizontal spacers** are most useful in formatting lines of text. Insert one at the beginning or end of a line to precisely control line breaks or the width of an area of white space.

- **Vertical spacers** can work like line breaks to divide text blocks, or they can be used to correctly position images relative to the text above or below them.

- **Block spacers** are two-dimensional, meaning that you can create a square or rectangle of white space to separate items on your page. Block spacers are used to create text indents—although perhaps not the most universal way. It's usually a better idea to use list tags as described in Chapter 3, "Working with Text," or Cascading Style Sheets, covered in Chapter 11, "Working with Style Sheets."

To insert a horizontal spacer:

1. Type some text into a document.

2. Double-click or drag the Horizontal Spacer icon (**Figure 4.28**) from the Basic tab of the Objects palette to the Document window.

3. Position the spacer either at the beginning of a line as a paragraph indent, or between words in a paragraph or headline. The text moves to accommodate the spacer (**Figure 4.29**).

4. Click the spacer to select it. The Spacer Inspector appears (**Figure 4.30**).

5. Lengthen the spacer by typing a number (in pixels) in the Width field of the Inspector, or by dragging one of the spacer's handles. There is no way to change the height of the spacer. Only block spacers have two dimensions.

Figure 4.28 Select the Horizontal Spacer icon in the Objects palette.

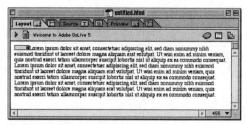

Figure 4.29 This horizontal spacer displaces the text. This indent will only be visible on Netscape browsers.

Figure 4.30 The Spacer Inspector controls the spacer's attributes.

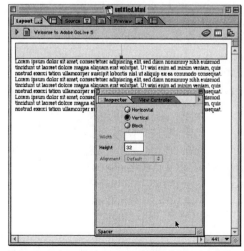

Figure 4.31 A vertical spacer's 32-pixel default height displaces several lines of this text.

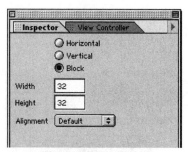

Figure 4.32 Block spacers displace objects horizontally and vertically. They can be resized in height and width, and they can be aligned.

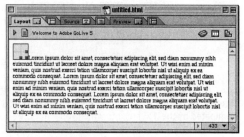

Figure 4.33 A block spacer has three handles for resizing and dragging.

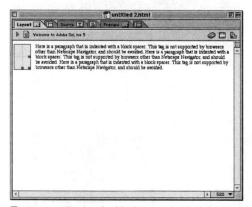

Figure 4.34 Aligning the block spacer to the left raises the paragraph so the paragraph is indented on several lines.

To insert a vertical spacer:

1. Double-click or drag the Horizontal Spacer icon from the Basic tab of the Objects palette to the Document window. Note that the icon is called Horizontal Spacer, but it makes all three types of spacers: horizontal, vertical, and block.

2. Click the Vertical radio button in the Spacer Inspector.

3. Position the spacer between two lines of text that you want to separate and click it. By default, the Vertical spacer is 32 pixels in height (**Figure 4.31**).

4. Resize the spacer by entering a numerical value (in pixels) in the Height field of the Inspector or by dragging the spacer's handle.

To insert a block spacer:

1. With the vertical spacer you've just created selected, click the Block radio button in the Spacer Inspector. The Width, Height, and Alignment fields are now active (**Figure 4.32**), and the vertical spacer has changed to a small block with three dragging handles (**Figure 4.33**).

2. Change the spacer's dimensions by using the Width and Height fields or by dragging the spacer's handles.

3. Align the block spacer to the left edge of the text by choosing Left from the Alignment menu in the Inspector. The block spacer now indents the entire paragraph (**Figure 4.34**).

✔ Tip

■ Block spacers can be aligned according to the same rules that apply to images and other two-dimensional HTML elements. For a complete explanation of the alignment options available, see Chapter 5, "Working with Images."

Scrolling marquees

Microsoft invented the scrolling marquee tag and, you guessed it, Netscape doesn't support it. Internet Explorer and WebTV do support scrolling marquees.

Unlike the other layout tools we've worked with in this chapter, marquees do not just sit there on your Web page. Scrolling marquees actually move. A scrolling marquee is a line of text that scrolls horizontally—à la the famous sign in Times Square—across your Web page.

To create a scrolling marquee:

1. Drag the Marquee icon from the Objects palette to the Document window (**Figure 4.35**). You can place it within a text box on a layout grid or directly in the window. A positioning box appears in the Document window, and the Marquee Inspector appears (**Figure 4.36**).

2. Type some text into the Text field, the large empty text box, of the Marquee Inspector. Some of the text becomes visible in the marquee (**Figure 4.37**).

3. Choose a Behavior from the pop-up menu in the Inspector (**Figure 4.38**). Scroll causes the message to scroll continuously. Slide moves the message across the screen, but keeps it on screen after scrolling once. Alternate causes the message to move into the marquee box and bounce between the box's left and right edges.

4. Select a time for the marquee to run. Selecting the Forever checkbox makes the marquee scroll continuously. Enter a number in the Loops field if you only want it to run a certain number of times.

Figure 4.35 The Marquee icon in the Objects palette resembles a scroll.

Figure 4.36 The Marquee Inspector's Basic tab is dominated by the text box into which you enter the text you want your marquee to scroll.

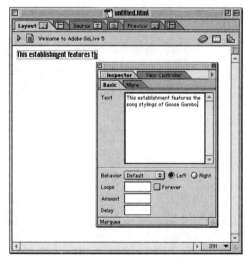

Figure 4.37 Entering text into the text box causes it to appear in the marquee as well.

Figure 4.38
The Behavior pop-up determines how the marquee moves its text.

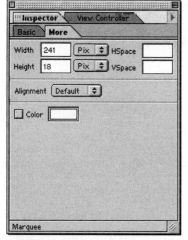

Figure 4.39 The Marquee Inspector's More tab sets the width and height measurements of the marquee, HSpace and VSpace (padding), the alignment of the marquee, and its color.

5. In the Amount field enter a value to control the scrolling speed.

6. In the Delay field, enter the scrolling delay.

7. Select the Left or Right radio button to set the marquee's running direction.

8. In the Marquee Inspector, select the More tab (**Figure 4.39**), and enter a size in either pixels or percentage for the marquee in the Height and Width fields. The marquee can also be sized by dragging its handles.

9. From the Alignment popup menu, select an alignment specification for the marquee. You can align a marquee to the top, middle, or bottom of text, if the marquee is within the flow of that text.

10. To add a color to the marquee, click the Color box in the More tab. The Color palette opens. Select a color by clicking a color. The Marquee Inspector's color box reflects the change. There's more about the Color palette later in this chapter.

continues on next page

✔ Tips

- Because text will be scrolling across the screen, it isn't necessary that the marquee be large enough to display the full line of text. Size the marquee so that it displays the number of words you'd like to be visible at any given time.

- Use the HSpace and VSpace fields, located under the More tab, to add horizontal and vertical space around the marquee.

- If you choose Alternate scrolling from the Behavior popup menu in the Marquee Inspector, make sure the marquee is wide enough to display the full line of text. Alternate bounces text from one side of the marquee to the other—it won't display text that won't fit in the visible marquee.

- Try several marquee settings to determine which one best fits your needs. As you set up the marquee, use the Layout Preview to watch the marquee's scrolling method and speed. You should also preview the marquee in an Internet Explorer browser.

- The best way to choose scrolling speed and delay options for a marquee is to experiment with different values in the Amount and Delay fields. Entering 10 in the Amount field, for example, produces a fairly slow-scrolling marquee, while 50 is dizzying. Enter some values in each field, then click the Preview tab in the Document window to see how the marquee will look in Internet Explorer. When you've approximated the look you want, open the browser and take a closer look.

- Remember that viewers using Netscape Navigator will see nothing where you've placed the marquee.

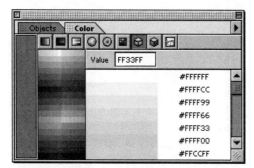

Figure 4.40 The Color palette contains nine ways to determine color. Only one, the Web Color List, contains colors that will appear predictably across all platforms.

Color Management

Placing color on a Web page is easy. Making the right choices so the colors you choose *work* presents some challenges.

Web pages are viewed on different computers, employing different color-handling conventions. To overcome this color Babel, the developers of HTML (assisted by Netscape) created a standard for Web color that makes it possible for all Web users with color-capable browsers and computers to see the same colors. Creating and adopting that standard meant adopting a chromatic lowest common denominator. Many colors available on some systems (notably the Macintosh) are not part of the "Web-safe" color set.

Whatever development platform you use, it's important that Web designers use "Web-safe" colors on their Web pages to avoid dithering, the process whereby a computer "fakes" a color by the splotchy imposition of one color over another.

There are nine ways to define and use colors in GoLive. Only one of them is specifically Web-safe.

In GoLive, all color comes from the Color palette. You'll find the Color palette in the window with the Objects palette. Just click the Color tab, or choose Window > Color. The tabs of the Color palette (**Figure 4.40**) contain the nine different ways of defining color. They are, from left to right:

♦ Grayscale (Gray Slider), which defines colors as percentages of black. The 256 levels of gray can be shown on any Web browser, but you lose the impact of color.

continues on next page

◆ RGB color (RGB Sliders), which is how
your computer monitor assembles colors
from its red, green, and blue light sources.
Values here are represented on slider bars
for each base color, which can be mixed
in near-infinite combinations.

◆ CMYK color (CMYK Sliders), the color
model most used in the printing industry.
Pigmented "process" inks of Cyan, Yellow,
Magenta, and Black are mixed for 4-color
printing. Actually, you're seeing an RGB
representation of the CMYK color model
on your computer screen. The CMYK tab
contains millions of colors that are not
Web-safe, but are useful when trying to
match a printed color.

◆ The HSB Color Wheel has a circle in which
the RGB color space is defined in hue (base
color) and saturation (color density). Pick
a color point inside the circle, then use
the Brightness slider to modify its level
of brightness.

◆ HSV Color Picker is based on the
Windows system color model. The tab's
controls are a combination of RGB percentages moderated by Hue, Saturation,
and Value controls.

◆ The Palettes tab contains the 256-color
system palette, and, from its pop-up
menu, arbitrary palettes of 16 colors and
16 levels of gray, the 34 colors reserved by
Windows for its desktop, and a Custom
palette for making up to 36 colors, so that
your site uses a consistent group of colors.

◆ The Web Color List is the most useful
group of colors because these colors can
be displayed in all browsers. Colors in
this palette appear on the left side of the
palette, with their hexadecimal code
equivalents on the right. Confusing?
Maybe so, but to the rescue comes...

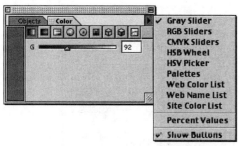

Figure 4.41 The Color palette has a handy menu for selecting the right color-naming scheme.

Figure 4.42 Click the Page icon in the Document window to open the Page Inspector.

◆ Web Name Colors, display colors with some rather odd but memorable names and hexadecimal values. Web Name Colors are not necessarily Web-safe colors, as some of these colors will dither when displayed on some systems.

◆ Site Color List, contains a visual list of all the colors used on a loaded site. This tab is very useful for maintaining color consistency in a growing site.

There are very few colors visible to the human eye that are not contained somewhere in the color ranges or gamuts of the Color palette. However, for universal and most predictable results, use the 216-color Web Color List.

✔ Tip

■ Although there are no Tooltips for identifying the tabs of the Color palette, you can click the arrow near the upper-right corner to see a selection menu for the tabs (**Figure 4.41**).

Applying color

To apply color to a page or an element in GoLive, drag the color from the Color palette to the Inspector of the item to be colored.

To apply background color to a page:

1. Open a new document.

2. With the Inspector open, click the Page icon (**Figure 4.42**) in the upper-left corner of the page, just above the Document window.

3. Under the Background heading in the Inspector, make sure Color is checked.

4. Open the Color palette (click the Color tab in the Objects palette or choose Window > Color).

continues on next page

COLOR MANAGEMENT

5. Select the Web Color List tab.

6. Choose a pleasing color from the list. You can use the eyedropper cursor and select a color by clicking one of the range of colors, or by scrolling through their names on the right side of the window. When you click to select a color, your selection will appear in the color preview pane on the left side of the Color palette, and as a selection with a hexadecimal name to the right.

7. Click and hold the mouse button in the preview pane of the Color palette. The cursor becomes a small square outline. You are now carrying a color swatch.

8. Keep holding the mouse button down as you drag the swatch onto the Color box in the Inspector (**Figure 4.43**). The selected color fills the Color box in the Inspector and fills the Document window.

✔ Tips

■ A shortcut to making a background page color is to drag a color swatch directly on to the Page icon below the toolbar.

■ Highlighted text may be colored by dragging a swatch directly on to the text.

■ To change the default color of text, drag a selected color into the Text Color box on the toolbar (**Figure 4.44**).

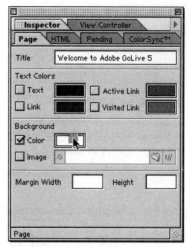

Figure 4.43 Drag the color over to the Inspector and drop it on the Color field.

Figure 4.44 Drop a selected color onto the toolbar's Text Color field to change the default text color. Selected text can also be colored using this method.

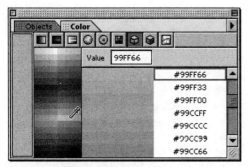

Figure 4.45 Clicking and dragging the mouse over the displayed colors changes the cursor into an eyedropper, which is used to sample colors.

Figure 4.46 Move the mouse over to the graphic that contains the color you wish to sample. The color's closest match in Web-safe colors will appear in the Web Color List as a selection.

Using the Color palette to match colors

From time to time you may want to use a color which appears in a graphic. The Color palette's eyedropper cursor will sample colors and give you an exact match in RGB, or the closest match in Web-safe colors. For example, imagine that you need to match the color of a graphic you are going to use to some other element on a page.

To match an existing color:

1. Open the page containing the graphic or other item whose color you want to match.

2. Open the Color palette. Select the Web Color List tab. Your graphic may have colors that are not Web-safe, but GoLive will locate the nearest match from the Web Color List.

3. Place your cursor over one of the 216 Web-safe colors and click and hold the mouse button. The cursor becomes an eyedropper (**Figure 4.45**).

4. Drag the eyedropper over the image (**Figure 4.46**). The eyedropper samples the color and displays the nearest Web-safe color in the Preview pane of the Color palette.

COLOR MANAGEMENT

The History Palette

The History palette (**Figure 4.47**) is watching every move you make in GoLive, and recording each one. Every change you make in the Layout or HTML Source Editor is recorded, not so much for posterity as to allow you to correct any complex bonehead mistakes that might arise, even if they straddle several steps in your page design process.

The History palette saves the 20 most recent actions you've taken—they're called *states*.

To return to a previous state:

1. After you've done some work on a page, open the History palette by choosing History from the Window menu, or by clicking the History tab in the window it shares with the Markup Tree palette. The History palette shows up to 20 actions, or "states," with the oldest on top.

2. Click an item in the History palette. The Document window is updated to reflect that page at the state you've clicked on.

3. Scroll through the History palette to view additional past actions (**Figure 4.48**). The newer states of the page dim when an older state is selected. However, as long as they are present on the History palette you can return to them. When you perform another action in GoLive, the oldest item on the History palette is removed.

✔ Tips

■ You can always use Revert to Saved from the File menu if you need to go back further than the History palette remembers, or if you haven't saved recently. Revert to Saved, as you might imagine, returns you to the last saved version of your document.

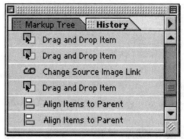

Figure 4.47 The History palette keeps a record of the last 20 steps in your development process.

Figure 4.48 This History palette shows the last 6 steps. Use the scroll bar to view more steps. To revert to one, click it and watch the Document window as it is updated.

■ Using the Edit menu's Undo command has the same result as working with the History palette does. The difference is that you can choose the items you want to undo from the palette, out of order. The Undo command forces you to go backwards in order.

■ If you switch from the Layout or HTML Source Editor to any other view (Frames Editor, HTML Outline Editor, Layout Preview, or Frame Preview), the History palette is cleared.

Working with Images

Images bring Web pages to life. They may be pictures that accompany text, buttons, or navigation elements. They may even be animated.

Unlike text that exists as part of a Web page, images are external files that are connected to a Web page via hyperlinks. HTML and Adobe GoLive allow you to specify a number of image attributes that change the appearance of pictures or alter their relationship with surrounding elements.

GoLive, which is brought to you by the same folks who built Adobe Photoshop and Adobe Illustrator, along with the new kid on the block, Adobe LiveMotion, includes a number of features that make it easier to integrate image building in other Adobe applications with GoLive.

In this chapter, I cover:

◆ Understanding images on the Web

◆ Adding images to a Web page

◆ Importing images

◆ Modifying image attributes

◆ Creating image maps

◆ Working with Save for Web

◆ Using layered Photoshop images

Using Images on the Web

Adding an image to a Web page is remarkably easy. Basically, you create a link between the page and a graphics file, and the picture appears on your Web page. But like other things on the Web, there are a few rules that make that straightforward process a bit more complicated. In other words, you need to know a bit about image formats and loading characteristics before you go dropping them onto your Web pages.

Web image formats

The two most common image types, or formats, on the Web are GIF (Graphic Interchange Format) and JPEG (Joint Photographic Experts Group). GIF and JPEG account for almost all of the still images on the Web. All browsers support both formats. You can also use the newer PNG (Portable Network Graphics) format, which is supported by current versions of Internet Explorer and some versions of Netscape Communicator. PNG, like GIF, supports 256 colors, and compresses them without the patented compression method used by GIF. Trouble is, PNG is not as universally supported as GIF, and so isn't used a great deal. Other file formats, such as QuickTime and PDF (Portable Document Format) are viewed with Web browser plug-ins. I discuss them more fully in Chapter 13, "Working with Rich Media." In this chapter, I describe how to add and use static GIF and JPEG images in your Web pages. All the rules apply to both formats.

GoLive can import images that are not HTML friendly and can then convert these graphics files for the Web when you drag them onto a GoLive document. For more about working with foreign file formats and image-editing applications, see "Smart Objects and Save for Web," later in this chapter.

Image loading characteristics

Images can make your Web page look great, but they also cause the page to load more slowly. That's usually a handicap you can deal with by planning your use of images carefully. You can control the download time of images by choosing the format that's both the most compact and appropriate for the task at hand. In this case, compact has more than one meaning. Both JPEG and GIF images are compressed, but you can shave even more download time by saving any GIFs or JPEGs at the lowest number of colors you can get away with, while still preserving the integrity of the image. You will need to make these adjustments in your image-editing software and evaluate the tradeoff between image size and quality by taking a careful look at your images.

GoLive gives you some help in creating images that are compact: you can use the Lossy slider in the Image Inspector (described more fully in "Adding Images," later in this chapter) to establish just the right balance between compression and color. You can also use the Image Inspector to *interlace* a GIF image. An interlaced image loads gradually as a Web page loads, increasing in resolution as it does so that when the page is fully loaded, the GIF is at its best quality. This option doesn't make your images any smaller, but it is a way to give your visitors a look at your graphics while a complex page loads.

continues on next page

You can also keep images compact by using smaller ones—smaller in terms of width and height, that is. There are two ways to size an image destined for the Web: size the image in a graphics program like Photoshop before you add it to a Web page, or use GoLive (or any Web page authoring tool) to adjust the size attributes of the image. I recommend you use the first method, determining approximately what size your image should be *before* you begin working in GoLive. You'll have more flexibility in dealing with images in their native applications. In this chapter, I'll show you how to use GoLive to size images, but doing so will not decrease graphic download time, because whatever measurement the image attribute shows, a Web browser still has to deliver a full-size image.

Finally, using one image, rather than several, can save on download time for your site's visitors, because each individual graphic requires a separate request to the Web server, and a separate, though usually quick, download. If you want to create a navigation element or a large graphic that looks as if it's composed of several images, try building an image map—a single image that contains several sections, often indicated by clickable hot spots. I explain how to create image maps later in this chapter (see "Creating Clickable Image Maps").

Figure 5.1 The Image icon.

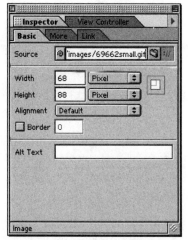

Figure 5.2 When you add an image to a page, the Image Inspector's Basic tab is displayed.

Adding Images

GoLive gives you several ways to bring images into a Web page. You can use an Objects palette icon to do it. Or, if you're working within a GoLive site, you can use Point & Shoot (dragging from the Inspector to the Site window to build a link). You can even import images in non-Web-friendly formats by dragging and dropping them from your hard drive (see "Importing Images") into a GoLive document. Finally, you can add images to your pages that were created in Adobe software products including Photoshop, Illustrator, and LiveMotion by using a GoLive Smart Object. With SmartObjects, you add a Web-friendly version of a high-quality image to a GoLive document. SmartObjects make it possible for you to edit the original image in Photoshop, Illustrator, or LiveMotion. The changes you make are then applied to the Web version.

To add an image with the Objects palette:

1. With the Layout Editor visible, drag the Image icon (**Figure 5.1**) from the Objects palette into the Document window. An image placeholder appears in the Document window, and the Inspector window displays the Image Inspector (**Figure 5.2**).

   or

   Double-click the Image icon. A placeholder appears in the Document window. If you're using a layout grid or a table to build your page, you may need to move the image placeholder to the spot where you want the image to appear.

   continues on next page

2. In the Inspector, click the Browse button (the icon that looks like a folder, next to the Source field).

3. Locate a GIF or JPEG image file that you would like to add to the Web page, and select it. The image appears in the GoLive Document window at full size (**Figure 5.3**).

To add an image with Point & Shoot:

1. If you have created a GoLive site, open it and then open the Web page where you want to add an image.

2. Double-click the Image icon on the Basic tab of the Objects palette.

3. In the Image Inspector, click the Point & Shoot button (immediately to the right of the Source label, and shown in **Figure 5.4**) and drag the resulting line to the Site window's Files tab.

4. Choose an image by dragging the line over its label or icon (**Figure 5.5**). When you release the mouse button, the image appears in the Document window.

Figure 5.3 The JPEG image I added is much larger than it needs to be.

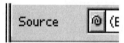

Figure 5.4 Use the Point & Shoot button to select an image within your GoLive site.

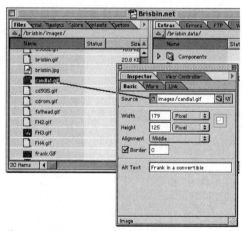

Figure 5.5 Point & Shoot from the Image Inspector to the Site window to link an image to a page.

ADDING IMAGES

Figure 5.6 Configure image import options in the Preferences window.

Importing Images

You can use GoLive either to save an imported image in a Web-friendly format for uploading with the page you're creating, or as a low-quality placeholder that you can use to preview the image on the page as you work on it.

GoLive can import Adobe Photoshop and Illustrator files as well as PICT (a Macintosh format), BMP, TIFF, PCX, and a number of other graphics formats. While you can use an application like Photoshop, or its Web image-making companion, ImageReady, to save GIFs or JPEGs for the Web, you can't fully manipulate the image once it has been saved for the Web. But GoLive allows you to both view a Web-friendly version of the image, and edit the original in its native application. When you edit the original image, the pre-view version that appears in your GoLive document is updated.

Setting Image Import preferences

To import images with drag-and-drop or as a GoLive Smart Object, you must first set Image Import preferences.

To configure image import:

1. Choose Edit > Preferences.

2. Click the triangle (Mac) or plus sign (Windows) next to the General Preferences label.

3. Click the Image item to view Image Preferences (**Figure 5.6**).

4. Click Select if you want to choose a new image import folder, or leave the default folder (within the GoLive application folder) selected.

continues on next page

IMPORTING IMAGES

5. Click the Ask User radio button to have GoLive ask how to deal with imported images. You must choose Ask User to activate GoLive's Save for Web feature, which converts images into a Web-friendly format. If you don't want to use this feature, choose the other radio button and choose a file format from the popup menu.

6. If you choose GIF or PNG, GoLive allows you to specify whether the imported image should be interlaced or not. You can choose to make JPEG images progressive or not, and how high in quality the imported image will be.

7. In the Low Source Image area, choose the color mode and where you want a low-resolution version of the imported image to be saved.

8. Click Auto-Generate by default to automatically create a low-resolution version of any image you add to a GoLive document.

9. Click OK to close the Preferences window.

With these options configured, you can drag an image (PICT, TIFF, or BMP) from the Finder (Mac) or the desktop (Windows) into a GoLive document.

✔ Tip

- When you use the Import Images feature, GoLive makes sure that all images have a three-character extension (.gif, .tif, and so on). When you add images to your pages, be sure that they include extensions in this format. Be sure that JPEG images use the .jpg suffix.

Figure 5.7 This icon represents a Photoshop file imported into GoLive. If you use the Save for Web dialog box to create a Web-friendly version, you'll see the actual image in the Document window.

Importing an image with drag-and-drop

You can add an image to a GoLive document simply by dragging its icon from the desktop of your computer into the Document window. You can then configure the image as described in the next section of this chapter, just as you would any Web page image.

When you drag a Web-format image (GIF, JPEG, or PNG) into GoLive, the image appears in the Document window. Non-Web images (TIFF, Photoshop, BMP, etc.) appear as placeholder icons (**Figure 5.7**) unless you save them in a Web-friendly format, in which case, that version of the image appears in the Document window.

Importing tracing images

Tracing images have two main uses. They can be used to bring a mock-up, created in a program such as Photoshop, into GoLive for actual page building, or they can be used as a background for the page, such as a graphic element, usually lightened in opacity, over which all the other elements of a page sit.

GoLive supports these import formats for tracing images:

- PSD (only RGB 8-bit images)
- JPEG
- GIF
- PNG
- BMP (Windows)
- TARGA
- PCX
- PICT (Mac)
- PIXAR
- TIFF
- Amiga IFF

✔ Tip

- Photoshop files are automatically changed to Web-safe colors.

To add a tracing image to a page:

1. Choose Window > Tracing Image. The Tracing Image palette opens (**Figure 5.8**).

2. Click the Source checkbox to activate the adjacent field.

3. Click the Browse button and navigate to the folder containing the file you wish to use.

4. The image is imported into your page. You may now adjust the opacity of the image with the Opacity slider in the Tracing Image palette.

✔ Tips

- You can numerically reposition the image by entering values in pixels in the Position boxes.

- Click the Move Image tool (the hand icon) to move the image and reposition it visually (while the values change in the Position boxes).

- The Cut Out tool is used to select an area of the image to be cropped. It works like an illustration or image-editing application's crop tool, removing the area of the image that falls outside the crop selection. Click the Cut Out tool when you have selected the area to be cropped.

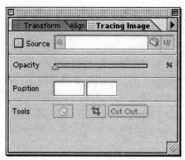

Figure 5.8 The Tracing Image palette.

Figure 5.9 Configure an image using the items under the three tabs of the Image Inspector.

Setting Image Attributes

Images on Web pages can have a variety of attributes that allow you to size, align, and arrange them. In most cases, you will configure images in the Image Inspector.

You saw the Image Inspector when you added an image to your Web page, earlier in this chapter. Take another look by clicking on an image in a GoLive document, or adding a new one. The three Image Inspector tabs (**Figure 5.9**) contain tools for setting image attributes.

Sizing an image

The Image Inspector provides three ways to size an image. You can set image width and height by typing numbers in the corresponding fields. An image can be sized by:

◆ **Pixel:** the image's size in pixels.

◆ **Percent:** the image's size as a percentage of the size of the Document window.

◆ **Image:** automatically sets the width or height measurement to that of the original image.

Pixel is the default measuring system. To use the Percent or Image option, make the appropriate choice from the Width or Height popup menu.

To resize an image:

1. Click the image you wish to resize. The Image Inspector displays parameters including the current height and width of the image.

2. To resize the image proportionally, change the unit of measure in the Height popup menu to Image.

continues on next page

SETTING IMAGE ATTRIBUTES

3. Type a number of pixels in the Width box with the Pixel option still selected (**Figure 5.10**). The image resizes proportionally in the Document window.

4. To return the image to its original size, click the Resize warning button next to the Height and Width fields in the Image Inspector.

5. If necessary, drag the image you have resized into its proper location on the page.

✔ Tips

■ To size an image proportionally (so that the width and height change by the same amount) hold down the Shift key as you drag the handle in the lower-right corner of the image in the Document window. If you change only one dimension of the image, it will appear distorted.

■ The best way to ensure that your image is the proper size is to set its width and height in the graphics program you used to create it. Besides saving you a step in GoLive, inserting a correctly sized image ensures a faster download. Images resized in GoLive (or any HTML application) maintain their original file size. That's because the image file size is not changed by the dimensions you choose for it in your HTML code. The complete file is downloaded to the user, regardless.

Aligning images

In HTML parlance, aligning an image means aligning it to adjacent text. It's not necessary to align an image to text unless you want the text and image to move together. In other words, if you want text to wrap around an image or to maintain a certain position relative to the image, you need to use the alignment tools. With a layout grid, you need to insert the image into the layout text box containing text you want the image to align to.

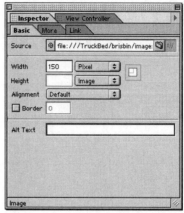

Figure 5.10 Resize an image proportionally by first choosing Image as the unit of measure for one dimension. Then, with Pixel as the measurement for the other dimension, change that measurement.

SETTING IMAGE ATTRIBUTES

Figure 5.11 Choose an image alignment option from the Image Inspector's Alignment popup menu.

Figure 5.12 Three alignment options appear in this screen shot. In each case, the image is inside a layout text box. The three images show an image aligned vertically to the text. The Top and Bottom options align the top of the image to the highest and lowest point of the text. Middle aligns the middle of the image to the baseline of the text.

Figure 5.13 The top two boxes align images horizontally to text—Left and Right. The final four boxes show images aligned to the top of the text (Text Top), middle of the text (Abs Middle), Baseline, and the bottom of the line of text (Abs Bottom). Baseline and Bottom (see Figure 5.12) are the same.

Image alignment also works (and is almost essential) if you're designing pages without a layout grid.

You can align images vertically or horizontally in one of several ways. It's simple enough to apply an alignment to an image, but it's trickier to know just which alignment to choose, because many of the choices have similar properties.

To align an image to adjacent text:

1. If you are using a layout grid, add a new layout text box to your grid. If you aren't using a grid, begin with step 2.

2. Drag the Image icon from the Basic tab of the Objects palette into the text frame.

3. With the image icon selected, locate an image with Point & Shoot or use the Browse button in the Inspector.

4. Resize the image if necessary.

5. Select the text box by clicking on the border of the box.

6. Enlarge the box a bit by dragging one of the handles to the right.

7. Type some text into the box; a sentence should do. If you're not using a layout text box, type directly into the Document window, right next to the image.

8. Click the image to select it.

9. In the Inspector window, choose an alignment from the Alignment popup menu (**Figure 5.11**). **Figures 5.12** and **5.13** show the effect of aligning images to text, using the nine available options.

SETTING IMAGE ATTRIBUTES

To add a border to an image:

1. Select the image.

2. In the Image Inspector, click the Border checkbox. The Border field becomes active.

3. Type the number (in pixels) for the border. A border appears around the image (**Figure 5.14**).

4. If you uncheck the Border checkbox, the border disappears.

Figure 5.14 This image has a three-pixel border.

Adding alternative text

Some Web browsers, such as Lynx, do not support images. In addition, visually impaired users often have difficulty navigating Web pages with images included, especially if they use screen reading software to speak the contents of Web pages. To get around this problem, you can add alternative (alt) text to an image's attributes—just a word or two. Text-only Web browsers, or browsers with graphics support turned off, display alternative text where the image would otherwise be.

To add alternative text to an image:

1. Click the image to select it.

2. In the Image Inspector, type a one- or two-word description of the image in the Alt Text field.

SETTING IMAGE ATTRIBUTES

Figure 5.15 In the Image Inspector's More tab, you can generate a low-resolution version of an image.

Creating low-resolution images

You can give your site's visitors something to look at while large image files load by adding a low-resolution version of the image to your page. This image is displayed while the higher-quality image is downloaded to the visitor's computer.

To add a low-resolution image:

1. Click the Image Inspector's More tab (**Figure 5.15**).

2. Click the Generate button. GoLive creates a low-resolution version of the image you're working with and stores it in the folder with your original image. The file name appears in the Low field. It's the same as the source image filename, with the letters *ls* inserted just before the file extension, as in mydogls.jpg.

If you would rather create your own low-resolution image, use Adobe Photoshop, GraphicConverter, DeBabelizer, or an image manipulation program of your choice to save a low-resolution version of your original image. Be sure to save the new image as a GIF or JPEG file.

To use your own low-res image:

1. Give the low-resolution image a name similar to that of the original (e.g., *imagel.gif*) and store it in the same folder as the original.

2. In GoLive, add the higher-quality version of the image to your layout.

3. Under the More tab of the Image Inspector, click the Low checkbox.

4. Click the Browse button next to the checkbox.

5. Find the low-resolution image you created earlier and click Open.

Hspace and Vspace

You can give an image some breathing room with the Hspace (horizontal space) and Vspace (vertical space) fields, also under the More tab of the Image Inspector. Enter a pixel value in these fields to create space to the left and/or top of the image. Unlike a border, which is visible, the space options simply leave an empty area around the image, and only apply it to the left and top margins.

Using an image as a link

Like hyperlinked text, images can be used to connect one Web page to another with just a click.

To link from an image:

1. Click an image you want to link.

2. Choose the Link tab in the Image Inspector.

3. Click the Link button (**Figure 5.16**). The fields become active. The Inspector now looks like **Figure 5.17**.

4. Type a URL if you want the image to link to a remote Web site. Or, if you are linking to a location within your site, use the Browse button to locate a file, or use Point & Shoot to locate an item within your GoLive site.

Figure 5.16 Click the Link button in the Image Inspector to activate the fields in the Link tab.

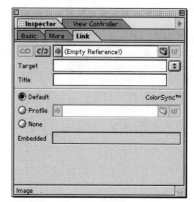

Figure 5.17 The Link tab of the Image Inspector lets you set an image as a link to another Web page.

Creating Clickable Image Maps

We've seen that you can use an image not only as decoration for your page, but also as a link to another location on the Web. Actually, you can include several links within a single image. That arrangement is called a *clickable image map,* and the locations your site's visitors will click are called *hot spots.* Some site designers use image maps to add hot spots to logos or other large Web graphics. A picture of a car, for example, might include hot spots on the tires, doors, and hood, indicating that the user can get more information about these parts of the car by clicking on the appropriate hot spot.

You can invoke image maps in two ways. The first is from the Web server, using a CGI (Common Gateway Interface) application to support the image map. The second, simpler way is to create *client-side* image maps, which are configured entirely within your Web pages. When you use a client-side image map, neither you as the page designer nor a user clicking on an image map needs to have any interaction with the Web server beyond the usual downloading of HTML files and images. Client-side maps, as you can imagine, are easier to work with. GoLive allows you to create client-side maps. Server-side image maps are outside the scope of this book.

There are two steps to creating a client-side image map: setting up the map and linking hot spots.

To set up a clickable image map:

1. Choose an image from which you will create an image map. The image you choose should be large enough to accommodate several hot spots and should include distinct sections that lend themselves to the image map treatment.

2. Add the image to a GoLive document.

3. Using the tools I've described in this chapter, make any necessary changes to the image.

4. In the Image Inspector, choose the More tab.

5. Click the Use Map checkbox. The Name field is activated, and a default map name is supplied (**Figure 5.18**). The toolbar changes to display image map tools and replaces the standard toolbar at the top of the screen. (**Figure 5.19**). You can change the map name. Use a single word or other string of characters that appeals to you.

6. Type a name for the image map in the Name field.

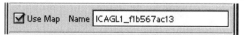

Figure 5.18 Click the Use Map checkbox to activate the Name field in the Image Inspector.

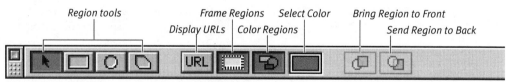

Figure 5.19 Clicking the Use Map checkbox in the Image Inspector changes the toolbar to the Image Map toolbar.

Figure 5.20 The RealAudio palette tool has a rectangular hot spot drawn on it.

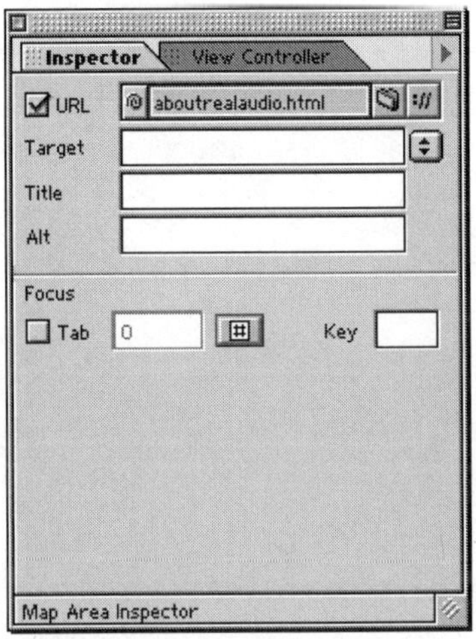

Figure 5.21 Configure the hot spot's link in the Map Area Inspector.

The Image Map toolbar contains the tools you need to create and modify image map hot spots. To create hot spots, you use the tools to draw them on the image.

To create hot spots:

1. From the toolbar, choose one of the three region tools (rectangle, circle, or polygon) that best matches the hot spot shape you want to create.

2. Draw the hot spot on your image. Handles appear at the sides and corners (**Figure 5.20**), so that you can adjust the size of the hot spot if necessary. When you add or select a hot spot, the Map Area Inspector appears.

3. With the hot spot selected, type a URL for it in the Map Area Inspector's URL field (**Figure 5.21**) or use Browse or Point & Shoot to locate a local file to link to.

4. Repeat steps 1–3 for each hot spot you want to create.

CREATING CLICKABLE IMAGE MAPS

Viewing hot spots as you work

GoLive includes tools that allow you to deal more easily with hot spots as you work with them. You can add a border or view the linked URL for the hot spot, or even choose a color for the region so that it stands out from other spots or from the image it's a part of.

Figure 5.22 Use the Frame Regions tool to add a border around the hot spot.

To enhance the display of hot spots:

1. With a hot spot selected, click the Frame Regions button on the Image Map toolbar. A border appears around the hot spot, as shown in **Figure 5.22**.

2. Click the Color Regions button on the Image Map toolbar to add color to the hot spot. This option is a convenience for the Web author. Hot spot colors do not appear within a user's browser.

3. To use a different color, click the Select Color icon. The Color palette appears, allowing you to choose a new color.

4. To display a URL on the hot spot, click the Display URLs button.

5. To remove a border, color, or URL, click the appropriate toolbar button to toggle it off. You can use any combination of border, color, and URL with your image map.

Use the Arrow button to resize or move hot spots and the Bring Region to Front or Send Region to Back items to work with hot spots that overlap one another.

✔ Tip

■ It can be tricky to select an image and its hot spots. To select a previously created hot spot, click the Arrow button on the Image Map toolbar and then, when the cursor is an arrow, not a hand, click over the hot spot. Clicking when the hand is visible (when you move the mouse over the edge of the image) selects the image, not the hot spot.

CREATING CLICKABLE IMAGE MAPS

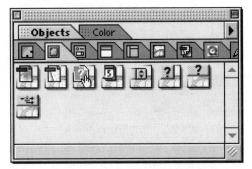

Figure 5.23 The Smart tab of the Objects palette.

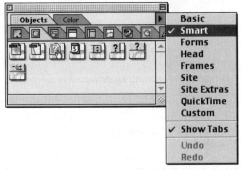

Figure 5.24 Choose Smart from the palette menu to open the Smart tab of the Objects palette.

Smart Objects and Save for Web

I've described GoLive's useful image import features and the preferences you'll need to set to make them work. But beyond importing non-GIF image formats and creating Web-friendly versions of them on the fly, GoLive provides sophisticated linking capabilities between itself and image-building applications like Photoshop, Illustrator, and LiveMotion, all from Adobe. You can add these image types to a GoLive document and optimize them for the Web while maintaining a link between the Web-friendly version of the image and the original one. When you make changes to the original, they are reflected in the Web version.

The GoLive installer is smart enough to figure out whether you have Photoshop, Illustrator, and/or LiveMotion on your hard drive when you first install GoLive, and adds a corresponding icon for each of these applications to the Smart Objects palette. When you want to import an image, just choose the appropriate smart object or drag the image from the desktop into the Document window. Either way, Save for Web opens and displays options for creating a Web image from the imported file.

To save an image using Save for Web:

1. Open the Smart tab of the Objects palette by clicking the tab (**Figure 5.23**) or choosing Smart from the palette menu (**Figure 5.24**).

continues on next page

2. If you have Photoshop installed on your computer, double-click the Smart Photoshop object (**Figure 5.25**). If you have Illustrator or LiveMotion installed, you may click one of these tools in the Smart tab. An image placeholder appears in the Document window and the Live Image Inspector appears (**Figure 5.26**).

or

Drag a Photoshop, Illustrator, or LiveMotion image from the desktop into the Document window.

3. In the Live Image Inspector, click the Browse button and navigate to an image file you want to import into GoLive. Click Open. The Save for Web dialog box, containing the image you selected opens (**Figure 5.27**).

Figure 5.25 The Smart Photoshop object.

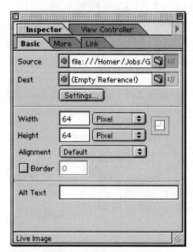

Figure 5.26 The Live Image Inspector is nearly identical to the Image Inspector. The only difference is the Dest. field that's immediately below the Source field. Dest. is filled in automatically when you import an image.

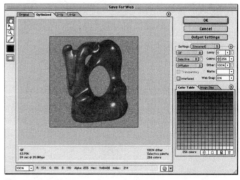

Figure 5.27 The Save for Web dialog box shows the image you have selected, and the tools you can use to optimize it for the Web. This image comes from the Adobe Photoshop tour supplied with the software.

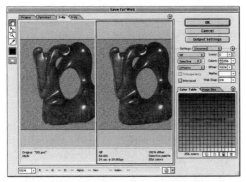

Figure 5.28 View the original and a Web-optimized version of the image.

| GIF 128 Dithered |
| GIF 128 No Dither |
| GIF 32 Dithered |
| GIF 32 No Dither |
| GIF 64 Dithered |
| GIF 64 No Dither |
| GIF Web Palette |
| JPEG High |
| JPEG Low |
| JPEG Medium |
| PNG-24 |
| PNG-8 128 Dithered |
| [Unnamed] |

Figure 5.29
Choose the format and quality for the Web-optimized image.

4. Click the Optimized tab or the 2-Up tab at the top of the window (**Figure 5.28**) so that you can see the image change as you work with it. If you click the 4-Up tab, you can work with four versions (including the original) of the image.

5. Choose one of the Web-safe image formats from the Settings menu (**Figure 5.29**). All of the formats in the menu are Web-safe. Save for Web settings allow you to use a group of settings that optimize the image for a particular format. You can change any of these settings, and save your own set if you like. The settings options available vary depending on whether you choose the GIF or JPEG format.

6. If you're satisfied with the look of the optimized image, click OK. The Save for Web dialog box closes, and GoLive saves the optimized image to your Image Import folder.

✔ Tips

■ Once you have created a smart object, you can open the image file in its native application by double-clicking it within GoLive. When you edit the file in Photoshop, LiveMotion, or Illustrator, the Web-safe version is updated.

■ When you import a Photoshop file that contains multiple layers, the Web-based version of the file becomes a "flat" file, containing no layers. You can, however, import Photoshop layers individually. See "Adding Layered Photoshop Images" in this chapter.

A tour of Save for Web

You can quickly save an image for the Web by choosing a format and clicking OK, or you can spend a little more time configuring the image and examining how it will look compared to the original.

Save for Web lets you look at the image in its original form or optimized for the Web. You can also view the two versions of the image side-by-side or add two more versions so that you can experiment with options. Choose the number of views from the tabs at the top of the window (**Figure 5.30**).

You can customize a variety of options—file format, color, dithering, and size—and save them as a custom set of settings that you can reuse with other images if you like. You can also choose one of the preconfigured group of settings that are commonly associated with the GIF or JPEG format.

Choosing Save for Web settings

The GIF and JPEG file formats each have their own set of Save for Web options that you can change to build your own setting set. **Figure 5.31** shows GIF options. JPEG options appear in **Figure 5.32**.

To set GIF optimization settings:

1. With a GIF Settings option selected in the Save for Web dialog box, enter a percentage value in the Lossy field or click the arrow next to the field to compress the image more. Using more compression is a great way to reduce file size, but can result in degradation of your image. Be sure to examine the image carefully if you use the lossy setting and strike a balance between compression and quality that you're comfortable with.

Figure 5.30 Choose the number of versions of the image you want to see.

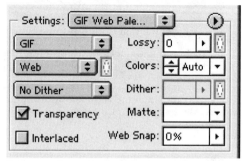

Figure 5.31 Customize the GIF image options in the Save for Web dialog box.

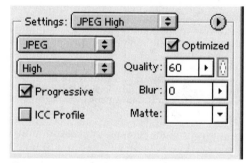

Figure 5.32 Customize the JPEG image options in the Save for Web dialog box.

2. Choose a color reduction algorithm from the pulldown menu labeled Web if you want to use a palette other than the standard Web palette for this image.

3. Choose a maximum number of colors to use in this image. Fewer colors means smaller file size.

4. Choose a dithering option from the Dithering Algorithm menu to indicate how the browser should deal with 24-bit color images that are displayed on 8-bit computer monitors.

5. Click the Transparency checkbox to maintain existing transparency within the image.

6. To avoid "halos" around your image, choose a Matte color (the color to which transparent pixels are changed) that matches the background color of your page.

7. Click the Interlaced checkbox to load a GIF image in a series of consecutive stages, with the first hint of the image displaying in the browser almost immediately.

8. Use the Web Snap field to convert colors within the image to the closest Web-safe color. GoLive will locate and use the Web-safe colors nearest to the colors in the image.

To set JPEG optimization settings:

1. With a JPEG Settings option selected in the Save for Web dialog box, click the Optimized checkbox to "streamline" the file, decreasing its file size.

2. Choose an option from the Quality menu, and/or use the Quality field to choose an option that displays the JPEG image. Higher quality settings display more color, but cause the file to be larger in size.

3. Click the Progressive checkbox to cause the image to load in stages in a browser. This option is somewhat like the Interlaced GIF option described earlier.

4. Enter a Blur value to smooth images with sharp angles or edges.

SMART OBJECTS AND SAVE FOR WEB

Adding Layered Photoshop Images

Savvy Photoshop users use layers to make complex, visually stunning layouts. Layered Photoshop documents can be directly imported into GoLive, either as described above, by "flattening" the contents of the layers into a single GIF or JPEG document, or by preserving them as individual elements. The layers are preserved as floating boxes, which can be stacked on top of one another. Using layered images will bulk up your layout because multiple image files are used to create a layered effect, but the flexibility and quality you gain are often worth the trouble and a few extra seconds of download time for your site's visitors.

To import Photoshop layers:

1. From the File menu, select Import > Photoshop as HTML.

2. Locate a Photoshop file containing layers and click Open.

3. Select a folder (or make a new one) which will contain the Photoshop components. You will usually want to store this folder within your site folder.

4. The Save for Web dialog box opens, displaying the first layer of the Photoshop document. Configure the settings and format you would like to use for the layer.

5. Click OK. The next layer appears in the Save for Web dialog box.

6. Configure it, click OK, and repeat the procedure for each layer in the document.

Once the image has been assembled, its components are contained in floating boxes, which can be manipulated and reorganized using techniques described in Chapter 12, "Layers and Positioning." The original layer numbers appear in the floating boxes.

WORKING WITH LINKS

Hyperlinks are as essential to the World Wide Web as phone numbers and e-mail are to telecommunication. Links between Web pages make it possible for people to jump instantly (surf) from place to place on the Internet.

Using links effectively is also an integral part of building a useful Web site. You use links to move visitors from page to page and to provide points of reference (in the form of navigation bars and tables of contents) for your site.

Adobe GoLive provides several ways to create links, and it supports the various kinds of links that are standard parts of HTML. In this chapter, I describe how to create text links. Chapters 5 ("Working with Images") and 13 ("Working with Rich Media") focus on linking to images and multimedia files. The process of creating these different kinds of links is quite similar, however.

In this chapter, I cover:

◆ How links work

◆ Creating links

◆ Editing links

◆ Named anchors

◆ Using targets

◆ Link warnings

How Links Work

An HTML link is a pointer from a Web page to another item on the Internet. Links can be text or images. Text links are usually designated visually on the page by underlining and by color, usually blue by default. Links have two parts: a URL (Universal Resource Locator) and a label or image that is visible in the user's browser. When a Web site visitor clicks a link's label, the Web browser uses the link's URL to locate the desired item. The browser then displays, downloads, or connects to the item.

Links can point to other pages within your site, to a remote Web site, or to non-Web resources, such as FTP servers, newsgroups, and e-mail addresses.

Anatomy of a URL

URLs contain all the information needed to turn a link into a means of transportation from one page to another. All URLs have the same structure:

`Protocol://server.domain/page.html`

(See **Table 6.1**)

Table 6.1

URL Anatomy	
ELEMENT	DESCRIPTION
Protocol	The type of link. Links to Web pages use http, while FTP links begin with ftp. E-mail addresses use mailto.
Server	Most Web URLs include "www" here, though some don't use it. A server may have another name that identifies the specific server, or there may be no server name in the URL at all. Non-Web URLs may include a server name, too, but they're not required.
Domain	The name of the site (often a version of the company's or organization's name) followed by the domain type, such as .com, org, .gov, .edu, or net.
Page	The name of the individual page to which the URL points. In most cases, entering a URL without a specified page takes you to the site's home page. When you connect to a URL with no page specified, you may see the page name index.html in the browser when you reach that page. If the link leads to a subsidiary page within a site, the page's name will appear, preceded by a slash (/) and followed by an extension (usually .htm or .html). Links to pages stored within directories include the directory name (/directory/page.html).

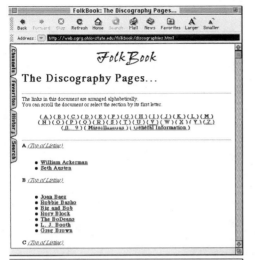

Figure 6.1 The alphabet at the top of the Folk Book Artists' Page consists of anchors that connect to lettered links further down the page.

Absolute and relative links

Links to remote sites always appear in the URL format described above. These are *absolute links*. URLs that point to files or other objects within the same Web site as the referring page may be absolute (with fully spelled out URLs), or they may be relative—using only the portion of the URL that's needed.

For example, a relative URL from your home page to a product catalog page within your site might have the URL /catalog.html, or even /products/catalog.html, if the file resides within a directory of your site. The full URL is not needed because when relative URLs are used, Web servers are smart enough to look first within their own site for requested pages. Relative URLs can point to any object within the same site, whether it's in the same directory or in a directory that is above or below the source file. You can also create links that point to locations on the same page as the link; these links are called anchors and are used to make it easier to navigate through long documents (**Figure 6.1**).

Using relative links is often simpler than typing a long, absolute URL, and it also makes things go a lot more smoothly when you need to add or change links within your site, or when you move your site from one server to another. For instance, you might move a site from an internal staging or production server to a live public server; or, from one Web hosting provider to another. By default, the links you create in GoLive will all be relative, unless you specifically choose to use absolute links. To do so, you'll need to set the "Make new links absolute" option in URL Handling Preferences in GoLive's Preferences window.

Creating Links

You can add links to your GoLive pages by using the toolbar's New Link button or one of the many Inspectors to type and configure them, or by using GoLive's various tools to create links to items stored within a GoLive site. Either way, you can link to files in your site, or to remote sites, e-mail addresses, and FTP servers.

✔ Tip

■ When you link to a remote URL, whether it's a Web site, e-mail address, FTP server, or some other resource that is not part of your site, you'll use the full URL, as described in the previous section. If you want to link to a file stored on your hard disk, and that is part of your Web site, be sure that the item you link to (HTML file, image, or multimedia file) is located within the folder that contains your GoLive site files. If you are not using GoLive's site management tools to store and maintain your site, be sure that both the file you link from and the file you link to are stored in the same relative location that they will be when you upload your files to a Web server. In other words, build your hierarchy of files and folders before you begin making links with GoLive. If you ignore this step and move files or change file or folder names after you have made links, the links will not work because the URLs you create will be incorrect.

One way to improve your chances of avoiding broken links is to build your Web site with GoLive's site management tools, as described in Chapter 14, "Building Sites."

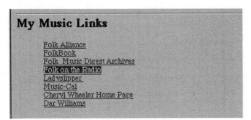

Figure 6.2 Text links should be short, but descriptive.

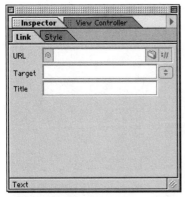

Figure 6.3 Enter your link's URL in the Link tab of the Text Inspector.

Figure 6.4 Use the toolbar's New Link button to create a link.

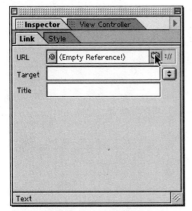

Figure 6.5 Click the Browse button to navigate to a file within your Web site.

To link text to a remote URL:

1. In the Layout Editor, select some text (a single word or short phrase) or an object that you would like to link to a remote resource (**Figure 6.2**). The Text Inspector becomes active (**Figure 6.3**).

2. Click the Link button on the toolbar (**Figure 6.4**).
   or
   Press Command-L (Mac) or Control-L (Windows). The fields in the Text Inspector become active.

3. Type a complete URL in the URL field of the Text Inspector. Be sure that the URL includes the correct protocol and syntax, i.e., http:// or ftp://.

4. Optionally, you can type a title of the item you are linking to in the Title field.

5. Choose a destination for the Link in the Target field, if you wish. For more information on using targets, see Chapter 9, "Working with Frames." Targets are primarily used to direct links within frames-based pages or sites.

To link to a local file with the toolbar:

1. In the Document window, select some text that you would like to link to another file within your GoLive site folder.

2. Choose the New Link button from the toolbar. An underline appears under the selected text, and the dimmed fields of the Text Inspector's Link tab become active.

3. In the Inspector, click the Browse button (**Figure 6.5**).

continues on next page

4. Locate the file you want to link to, and click Open. The relative URL appears in the URL field of the Text Inspector (**Figure 6.6**), and the linked text is underlined in the Document window.

Figure 6.6 When you've chosen a URL to link to, the relative URL appears in the Text Inspector's URL field.

✔ Tip

■ When you link to a file stored on your hard disk, the URL will appear in the Inspector in the format: file://drive/ folder/page.html. Don't be concerned. The actual URL that appears in the GoLive pages you will upload to a Web server do not contain this local path information, but the proper relative URL. The relative URL will work as long as you do not change the relationship between a document and an item you've linked it to. You can use this method to link to files that are part of a local Web site, whether you use GoLive to manage the site or not, as long as the directories and file locations are set up exactly as they will appear when you upload your site to a Web server.

Linking to GoLive site items

In the next few step-by-step examples, I describe how to create links between a Web page and items that are part of a GoLive Web site. GoLive site files can store pointers to HTML files, images, and even external resources—Web bookmarks and e-mail addresses, for example. Provided the files to which you are linking are within the GoLive site folder, your links will always be valid. GoLive constantly monitors changes you make and updates links automatically. You can learn about creating GoLive sites in Chapter 14, "Building Sites."

Figure 6.7
Command-click (Mac) or
Control-click (Windows)
to Point & Shoot from
a Web page to the Site
window.

To link to a site file with Point & Shoot:

1. Open a GoLive site file.

2. Open a document by double-clicking its icon in the Files tab of the Site window.

3. If the file you want to link to is not already part of your site, add it by dragging it into the Site window before proceeding to step 4.

4. In the Document window, select some text or an object that you would like to link.

5. Hold down the Command key (Mac) or the Control key (Windows) as you drag the cursor into the Site window. GoLive displays a line as you drag (**Figure 6.7**). If the Site window is hidden by other windows, it will be brought to the front as you drag over it.

6. Stop dragging when your cursor is over the file you want to link to (the line will start blinking) and release the mouse button to finish the link. You can verify that the link is complete in the Text Inspector.

Linking to site resources

GoLive sites can manage not only HTML files and images, but also bookmarks that contain URLs for remote resources. You can store the remote resources your site points to within the site file, and then Point & Shoot your way to them whenever you need to add a link.

To link to a stored URL:

1. Open a GoLive site file.

2. Open a document by double-clicking it in the Files tab of the Site window.

continues on next page

CREATING LINKS

3. In the Site window, click the External tab to display external resources that you have stored there.

4. In the Document window, select the text or object that you want to link.

5. Command-click (Mac) or Control-click (Windows) the selection and drag the resulting line to the Site window.

or

Drag and drop a URL from the Site window to the selected text (**Figure 6.8**).

6. Stop dragging when your cursor is over the item you want to link (the line will start blinking), and release the mouse button.

7. Verify that the link is complete in the Link tab of the Text Inspector.

Linking to an e-mail address

You can create a link between a Web page and an e-mail address with Point & Shoot, if the address is stored within your site file. To learn how to add e-mail addresses to a site file, see Chapter 14, "Building Sites." You can also type e-mail links directly into the URL field of the Inspector, using the format, `mailto:user@domain.com`. When an e-mail link is clicked, the user's browser opens an e-mail application, assuming that the user's system is configured to do so.

To link to an e-mail address with Point & Shoot:

1. With a GoLive site file open, open a file by double-clicking it in the Files tab of the Site window.

2. In the Site window, click the External tab to display external resources that you have stored there.

3. In the Document window, select the text or object that you want to link.

Figure 6.8 Drag a URL from the External tab of the Site window to the selected text in the Document window to create a link.

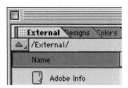

Figure 6.9 E-mail addresses are stored in the External tab of the Site window.

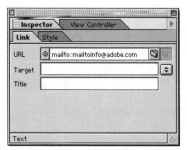

Figure 6.10 The e-mail address included in your new link appears in the Link tab of the Text Inspector.

Figure 6.11 Select text you would like to link to another GoLive document, then drag that document's Page icon over the text.

4. Command-click (Mac) or Control-click (Windows) the selection and drag the resulting line to the Site window.

   or

   Drag and drop a URL from the Site window to the selected text.

5. Stop dragging when your cursor is over the e-mail address you want to link (the line will start blinking), and let go of the mouse button. E-mail address icons look like the one in **Figure 6.9**.

6. Verify that the link is complete in the Link tab of the Text Inspector (**Figure 6.10**).

Linking open documents

You can use the GoLive Page icon to create links between open documents, whether or not they are part of a GoLive site.

To create a link with the Page icon:

1. In the Document window, select some text or an object that you would like to link.

2. Open another document.

3. Position the new document onscreen so that you can see the portion of the first document that contains the selected text or object.

4. Drag the Page icon at the top of the new document's window onto the selected text or object in your destination document (**Figure 6.11**). The link is complete.

✔ Tip

■ You can use the Page icon method whether you're working within a site or just constructing individual pages. If you're working with a site, you may prefer using Point & Shoot.

Editing Links

Once you've created links, it may be necessary to change them. A remote URL may change or you might rename a directory, or update an e-mail address. In any case, you can edit any link in the URL field of the link's Inspector or with Point & Shoot.

To edit a link in the Inspector:

1. Open the file containing the link you want to change. Make sure you're in the Layout Editor.

2. Click the link. The appropriate Inspector window appears, with the link's URL and other information displayed.

3. Type the new absolute (full) URL, or relative URL in the URL field of the Inspector (**Figure 6.12**).

✔ Tip

■ Not all Inspectors use the same terminology to refer to the field where you find a link. In the Text Inspector, for example, the field has no name, just icons of the Link and Unlink buttons. If you are working in the Image Inspector, the field is called Source. Plug-in Inspectors use the term File (**Figure 6.13**). Whichever Inspector you're working with, the field you want to edit is the one that links the object in the Document window to a URL.

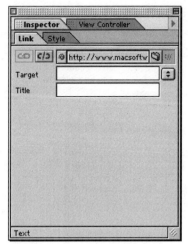

Figure 6.12 Select a URL in the Inspector and type the new URL over it.

Figure 6.13 To link to a plug-in file, you use the File field in the Plug-in Inspector.

To edit a link within a site:

1. Open your GoLive site, if it isn't already open.

2. Open the file containing the link you want to change.

3. If you are linking to an external URL or an e-mail address, click the External tab in the Site window. Otherwise, proceed to step 4.

4. In the Document window, Command-click (Mac) or Control-click (Windows) on the link.

5. Drag the resulting line into the Site window.

6. Let go of the mouse button when the line connects with the new object (file or URL) you want to link to. The new link is complete.

✔ Tip

- You can use GoLive's site management tools to update all occurrences of a link within your site at the same time. See Chapter 15, "Viewing and Managing Sites," for more details about updating sites. The Site window's error icons also let you know which pages contain broken links.

To delete a link:

1. In the Document window, select the linked text.

2. From the toolbar, click the Unlink icon. The link is deleted.

EDITING LINKS

Named Anchors

Named anchors are a special kind of link. Rather than linking one page to another, named anchors are used to navigate within a single page—linking a list of headings at the top of a page to subsequent sections of the document, for example—or linking to a location in the middle of a different page. Clicking on a named anchor link scrolls the browser to the appropriate point on the page, or opens another page in the middle, displaying the specified anchor point.

You can begin by creating links, then making named anchors to go with them, or you can set up the anchors first. The first method works best if you're creating a single link that connects to a single anchor. Creating the anchor (or anchors) first works best if you plan to create several links that point to a single anchor point, or if you are designing a navigation scheme or table of contents that goes with an existing document.

To create a named anchor on the current page:

1. With a document open in the Layout Editor, select the text or object you want to link from.

2. Command-click the text or object and drag the resulting line through the document until you reach the point where you would like the anchor to appear (**Figure 6.14**).

3. Release the mouse button, the line will blink, and an anchor icon appears in the Document window (**Figure 6.15**). The Link Inspector is now active and displays a unique anchor name.

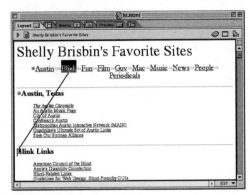

Figure 6.14 Command-click the item you want to link, and drag to the location where you want the anchor to appear.

⚓ Blink Links

Figure 6.15 The anchor icon appears next to the text to which it's anchored in the Document window when the anchor is complete.

Figure 6.16 The Anchor icon is available on the Basic tab of the Objects palette.

Figure 6.17 The Anchor Inspector becomes active when you add an anchor by dragging the Anchor icon to the Document window.

✔ Tips

■ Not all browsers place anchors properly. For best results in GoLive, position the anchor point in a text frame or within a table, rather than on a bare layout grid.

■ Anchors work best when they appear at the left margin of a window.

■ As always, it's a good idea to check your work by previewing it. Open your document in a Web browser rather than GoLive's Layout Preview, then click the link you've created to see whether it properly moves to the anchor.

To create anchors before linking them:

1. With a document open, drag the Anchor (**Figure 6.16**) icon from the Basic tab of the Objects palette to the Document window. An anchor icon appears where you release the mouse button, and the Anchor Inspector becomes active (**Figure 6.17**).

2. In the Name field, type a unique, one-word name for the anchor.

3. Create more anchors within your document.

4. Locate some text or an object (in the current document or in any other document that is part of your GoLive site) that you would like to link to one of the anchors you just created.

5. Select the text or object and Command-click (Mac) or Control-click (Windows) the selection.

continues on next page

NAMED ANCHORS

6. Drag the resulting line to the anchor you created earlier and release the mouse button (the line will blink). The link is now complete.

7. Repeat steps 3 and 4 to add more links to the anchor you've created.

When a Web page visitor clicks on the new link, the anchor point comes into view. If the anchor appears in a different document, that document opens and displays the page at the point of the anchor location.

✔ Tip

■ You can create as many links to a single anchor as you like, from any number of documents. Just Point & Shoot from each link to the anchor.

To move an anchor:

◆ In the Document window, click the Anchor icon and drag it to its new location on the page. Any links you've created will now point to the new location.

To delete an anchor:

1. Click an Anchor icon to select it.

2. Press the Delete key to remove the anchor. Now, you need to remove links to the anchor you've just deleted.

3. Locate the link that leads to the anchor and select it.

4. Click the Remove Link button in the toolbar. The link is removed.

✔ Tip

■ It's important that you delete the anchor before you break the link. Even if you select a link and click the Unlink button in the Inspector, the link stays intact if there's an anchor in place.

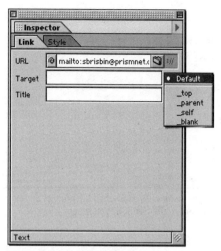

Figure 6.18 To target a link, choose from the Target menu in the Text Inspector.

Links and Targets

When a site visitor clicks a link, the resulting Web page usually opens in the same browser window, replacing the previous page. In some cases, you might want to open a link in a new window or in a frame. Opening a new window for a link preserves access to the previous page, and opening a link in a frame allows you to link to a remote site without the user leaving your site. The link attribute that allows you to choose where a link should open is called a *target*.

There are four kinds of target attributes:

◆ _top

◆ _blank

◆ _parent

◆ _self

Specifying a _top target replaces the current contents of the browser window with the linked page. A _blank target opens the link in a new window. The _parent and _self links are used in frames-based Web pages. I'll describe their use in Chapter 9, "Working with Frames."

To apply a target to a link:

1. Create a link using any of the methods described in this chapter.

2. In the Text Inspector, choose a target type from the Target pulldown menu (**Figure 6.18**).

Link Warnings

GoLive can alert you to broken links using a variety of link warnings. You can turn link warnings on and off to determine the status of your links. By default, problem links are highlighted in red. You can change the color in the Preferences window's General: User Interface Preferences, if you like.

To change the color of link warnings:

1. Choose Edit > Preferences.

2. Click the triangle (Mac) or plus sign (Windows) next to the General label in the left side of the Preferences window to view more options.

3. Click the User Interface item. The resulting screen (**Figure 6.19**) includes a color box for changing the color of link warnings.

4. Click the color box. A color picker appears. **Figure 6.20** shows the Apple (Mac) color picker. **Figure 6.21** shows the choices available under Windows.

5. Choose a color from one of the panels. If you need help with the color picker, see your system's Help feature.

6. Click OK. The new color appears in the Link Warnings color box.

7. Click OK again, to close the Preferences window.

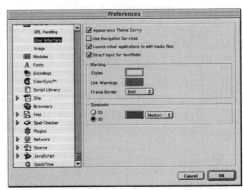

Figure 6.19 Change the color of Link Warnings under User Interface in the General Preferences window.

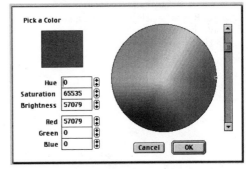

Figure 6.20 Pick a link warning color from the Mac OS Color Picker.

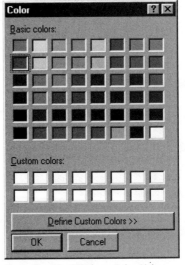

Figure 6.21 The Windows Color Picker.

LINK WARNINGS

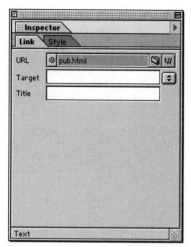

Figure 6.22 Broken links appear in the link warning color in the Inspector.

To locate errors with link warnings:

1. With a document open, choose Edit > Show Link Warnings (or press Command-Shift-L on the Mac, or Control-Shift-L in Windows). If the Edit menu command says "Hide Link Warnings" instead, link warnings are already available. Proceed to the next step.

2. Scroll through your document to locate links that are highlighted (in the color you chose when you set Link Warnings preferences).

3. When you locate a broken link, click it to place your cursor within the link. The Text Inspector becomes active, displaying the broken link. The link text field is in the color of your link warnings (**Figure 6.22**).

4. Repair the link.

✔ Tip

■ GoLive will display link warnings for images and multimedia files, too. The procedure for finding and fixing broken links is exactly the same. When an image or media file link is broken, you'll see a red (or whatever color you want to use for link warnings) border around the image box. Of course, you'll also notice that the image itself is missing, since its link is no longer in place. To locate the source of the break, you may need to examine all tabs of the appropriate Inspector.

WORKING WITH TABLES

7

HTML tables are among the most useful Web page design tools available. You can use them to display information in rows and columns or build multi-column layouts, where the table's grid pattern isn't even visible.

Table building is among the best reasons to use a WYSIWYG Web authoring tool like Adobe GoLive. It's a whole lot easier to build and edit tables using a graphical interface than it is to write the HTML code in a text editor.

In this chapter I cover:

◆ Table basics

◆ Inserting tables

◆ Editing tables

◆ Adding table content

◆ Nesting tables

◆ Using table styles

◆ Converting tables to grids

About Tables

Tables are a versatile HTML feature that you can use to create grid-like page elements such as spreadsheets, calendars, or other items that use columns and rows. Tables are also an important design tool because they allow you to "fake" multi-column layouts in HTML. GoLive employs this fakery to create layout grids (covered in Chapter 4, "Working with Layout Tools").

You can use grids to create columns, or simulate frames, but conventional HTML tables allow you to create and manage a large number of columns and rows simultaneously.

Inserting Tables

Adding a table to a GoLive document is very much like adding any other object.

To create a table:

1. With a document open, double-click or drag the Table icon (**Figure 7.1**) from the Basic tab of the Objects palette to the Document window. By default, a three-by-three cell table appears in the Document window (**Figure 7.2**).

2. Select the table. If you deselected the table after you created it, place your cursor on the top, left, or right border of the table. The cursor will change into a two-sided arrow on the right border (**Figure 7.3**), or into an arrow with a box below it (**Figure 7.4**) on the top or left border. Click the border to view the Table Inspector (**Figure 7.5**).

Figure 7.1 The Table icon.

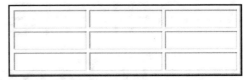
Figure 7.2 Dragging the Table icon into the Document window creates a three-by-three table.

Figure 7.3 Select the table by clicking on the right border. The cursor changes to a two-sided arrow.

Figure 7.4 When you move the cursor to the left or top border of a table, an arrow cursor with a box appears, allowing you to select the table.

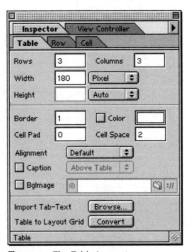
Figure 7.5 The Table Inspector.

Figure 7.6 Here's the table after being expanded to contain five columns.

3. Type 4 in the Rows field of the Inspector.

4. Press Tab. The table expands downward to add a new row.

5. Type 5 in the Columns field.

6. Press Tab. The table expands to the right, adding two columns (**Figure 7.6**).

✔ Tips

■ If adding rows and columns has changed the table's position relative to other items on the page, you can move the table by moving your cursor to the left or top border of the table. When the cursor changes to an arrow with a box, click and drag the border to move the table to the desired location.

■ Clicking on the top or left border is also the quickest way to delete an entire table. Click and then press the Delete key.

Editing Tables

You can change any aspect of a table with
the Table Inspector or the Table palette. We'll
talk more about the Table palette a little later
in this chapter. You can also change many
table attributes by clicking and dragging
internal and external table borders.

Resizing tables

You can resize table cells, rows, and columns,
and even the table itself by dragging table
gridlines or by typing values into the appropriate fields in the Table Inspector.

✔ Tip

- If you plan to add rows and columns to
  a table, it's a good idea to do so *before*
  resizing the table, because placing new
  cells will expand the table on the page,
  possibly shifting other elements of your
  layout out of their proper positions. You
  can fix that, of course, but it's better to
  plan your tables and their dimensions
  from the start.

To resize a table horizontally:

1. Move the cursor to the right edge of the
   table. The cursor changes to a blue, two-
   sided arrow.

2. Drag the border to the left to shrink the
   table horizontally. All of the cells decrease
   in size proportionally.

✔ Tip

- Dragging the right border of a table to the
  right expands the table and all of its cells.

Figure 7.7 With the Option key (Mac) or Alt key (Windows) held down, the cursor changes to a light blue, two-sided arrow. You can now drag cell borders right or left to change the width of columns.

To resize a table vertically:

1. Hold down the Option key (Mac) or the Alt key (Windows) and move the cursor to the lower border of the table. The cursor changes to a dark blue, two-sided arrow (**Figure 7.6**).

2. With the Option or Alt key held down, click the border and drag the border downward to expand the table vertically. The cells increase in size proportionally.

✔ Tips

- To shrink a table vertically, drag the border upward.

- You can also resize the table using the Inspector. With the table selected, be sure that the Table tab is visible and type values (in pixels) in the Width and Height fields.

- By default, the Inspector displays the width of a table in pixels, but the height is set to Auto. The first time you drag the table's border to resize the table vertically, the Inspector's Height measurement changes from Auto to Pixel and allows you to edit the table height from the Inspector.

To resize a column:

1. Place your cursor on the right border of an interior cell of the table. Hold down the Option (Mac) or Alt (Windows) key. The cursor changes to a light blue, two-sided arrow (**Figure 7.7**).

2. Drag the border to the left to shrink the table cell and its column, or to the right to expand the column. Unlike resizing the table, resizing columns does not affect adjacent columns, although it does narrow the table as a whole.

To resize a row:

1. Place the cursor on the lower border of a cell within the table. Hold down the Option (Mac) or Alt (Windows) key. The cursor changes to a light blue, two-sided arrow (**Figure 7.8**).

2. Drag the border downward to expand the row, or up to shrink it. Unlike resizing the table, resizing a row does not affect adjacent rows.

Customizing table items

You can change the appearance of individual table cells, rows, or columns.

To customize a cell:

1. Click within a table cell. Type a few words of text. Having text within the cell will make it easier for you to see the impact of the changes you make in these steps.

2. Click the bottom or right border of the cell and Control-click (Mac) or right-click (Windows) and choose Select cell from the context-sensitive menu. A marquee appears within the cell (**Figure 7.9**) and the Table Inspector displays the Cell tab (**Figure 7.10**).

3. To align text within the cell vertically, choose Top, Bottom, or Middle from the Vertical Alignment menu.

4. To align text within the cell horizontally, choose Left, Right, or Center from the Horizontal Alignment menu. By default, text in table cells is aligned to the middle and left of the cell.

5. To cause the selected cell to span three rows within the table, type 3 in the Row Span field. The result appears in **Figure 7.11**.

Figure 7.8 Placing the cursor on a cell's border and holding down the Option key (Mac) or Alt key (Windows) displays the light blue, two-sided resizing cursor.

Figure 7.9 When you click the border of a table cell, a marquee appears, indicating that the cell is selected.

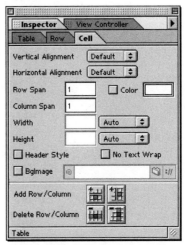

Figure 7.10 The Table Inspector's Cell tab appears when you select an individual cell.

1994				December
	January	February	March	April
1995	May	June	July	August
	September	October	November	December

Figure 7.11 The leftmost column in this table has a row span of 3.

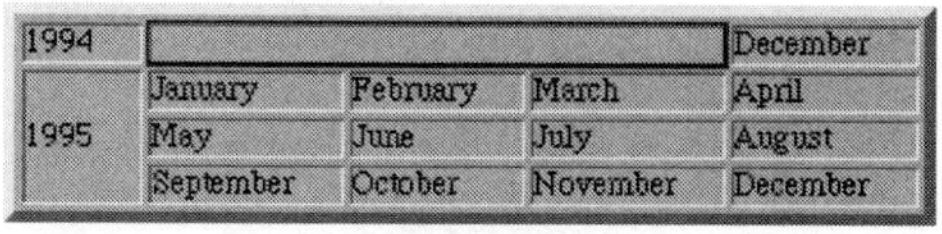

Figure 7.12 A column span of 3 looks like this.

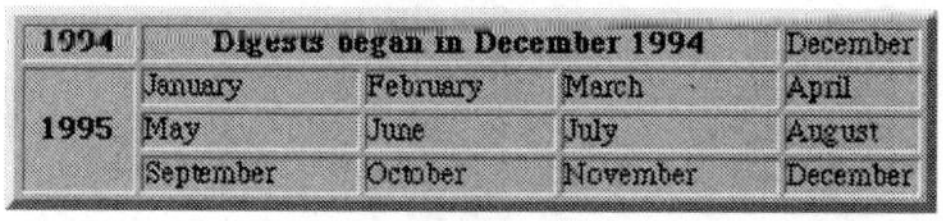

Figure 7.13 Table headers are centered, and appear in bold type.

6. To cause a cell to span three columns, type 3 in the Column Span field. The result appears in **Figure 7.12**.

7. To color the cell, click the Color field in the Cell tab of the Table Inspector and make a choice from the Color palette. The cell's color changes.

8. Click the Header Style checkbox to center cell text and make it bold (**Figure 7.13**).

9. Click the No Text Wrap checkbox if you want to prevent text from wrapping at the end of a line.

10. Click the BgImage checkbox to choose an image that will appear in the current cell. (Note that background images are only supported by Internet Explorer browsers.)

✔ Tips

- It is usually easiest to resize cells by dragging their borders, as described in the previous section. But if you want a precise measurement, use the Width and Height fields to resize them. First choose Pixels from the appropriate popup menu, and then enter a value.

- If you are creating a table that will be empty—not filled with text or another object—insert a non-breaking space in the cell. If you don't do this, any background color or borders of the cells will not appear, giving the table a strange look. To add a non-breaking space, select a table cell and Control-click (Mac) or right-click (Windows) and choose Insert . You can also use Option-Spacebar (Mac) or Alt-Spacebar (Windows) to achieve the same result.

- You can format multiple table cells at once by selecting them together. First, select a cell. With the Shift key held down, select another cell. Now you can format the cells together, using options in the Table Inspector's Cell tab.

To customize a row:

1. Shift-click the left border of a row to select the row.

2. In the Table Inspector, choose the Row tab (**Figure 7.14**).

3. Choose an alignment for the row from the Vertical Alignment popup menu. You can align text within the selected row to the top, middle, or bottom of the cells.

4. Choose an alignment from the Horizontal Alignment popup menu. You can align text within the selected row to the left, right, or center of the cells.

5. Choose a custom height for the selected row by selecting Pixels from the Height popup menu and then typing the height measurement you want.

6. Click the Color field to view the Color palette. Choose a color. The row is updated with the new color.

7. Click the Cell tab of the Table Inspector.

8. Click the Header Style checkbox if you want text in this row to be centered and bold.

9. Click the No Text Wrap checkbox to prevent text from dropping to a second line within the row.

10. Click the BgImage checkbox and choose an image if you want the row to include a background image. (Background images are only supported by Internet Explorer browsers.)

✔ Tip

■ To select all items in a row or column except the currently selected item, Shift-click the left border (row) or top border (column). The previous selection is deselected.

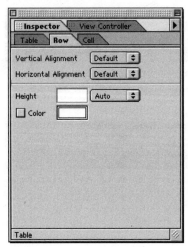

Figure 7.14 The Row tab of the Table Inspector.

To customize a column:

1. Select a column by Shift-clicking on the top border.

2. In the Cell tab of the Inspector, choose an alignment for the column from the Vertical Alignment popup menu. You can align text within the selected column to the left, center, or right edge of the cells.

3. Choose an alignment from the Horizontal Alignment popup menu. You can align text within the selected column to the left, right or center of the cells.

4. Click the Color field to view the Color palette. Choose a color for the column.

5. Click the Cell tab of the Table Inspector.

6. Click the Header Style checkbox if you want the column's text to be bold.

7. Click the No Text Wrap checkbox if you want to keep column text on a single line. This option increases the width of the column as text is added.

✔ Tip

■ It's a good idea to click outside a table you've been working on before you select an entire row or column. Because Shift-clicking a cell or group of cells inverts any previous selections, it's possible that Shift-clicking will cause cells outside your target row or column to be affected by changes you make in the Table Inspector. Clicking outside the table before you Shift-click will prevent this possible effect.

EDITING TABLES

To change the appearance of a table:

1. Select the table by clicking on the top or left border.

2. In the Table tab of the Inspector, type a value (measured in pixels) in the Border field. **Figure 7.15** shows a table with a six-pixel border.

3. Click the Color field and choose a color for the table from the Color palette.

4. Type 2 in the Cell Pad field to create extra vertical space within each cell. **Figure 7.16** shows the table we've been working on, with a two-pixel pad in each cell.

5. Enter a different value to change cell spacing. The Cell Space field controls the amount of space between cells. By default, cells are spaced two pixels apart.

6. If you are not using a layout grid, choose an option from the Alignment menu to place the table, relative to the page you're working on. You can align the table to the left or right or leave it unaligned.

Adding and removing cells

Once you have created a table, you can add new cells in the form of captions, rows, or columns.

Captions

A caption is a table cell that spans the entire width of the table, and appears at the bottom or top of the table. By default, captions are centered over the table, but you can format text in any way you like. A caption can also appear at the bottom of a table, and can consist of as many lines of text as you like. Aside from the requirement that there be only one caption per table, and that the caption must either appear above or below the table, a caption is just like any other table row.

Figure 7.15 This table has a six-pixel border.

Figure 7.16 Adding cell padding increases the space between cells in a table.

Click on a month link to see a list of daily digest files				
1994				December
	January	February	March	April
1995	May	June	July	August
	September	October	November	December
	January	February	March	April
1996	May	June	July	August
	September	October	November	December
	January	February	March	April
1997	May	June	July	August
	September	October	November	December
	January	February	March	April
1998	May	June	July	August
	September	October	November	December

Figure 7.17 This table has a caption above the other cells.

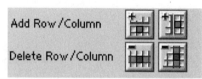

Figure 7.18 Add a row or column with these buttons in the Cell tab of the Table Inspector. The buttons below delete rows and columns.

Help
Insert Column
Insert Column Right
Insert Row
Insert Row Below
Delete Column
Delete Row
Split Cell
**Insert **
Convert To Grid
Import TabText...
Document ▶
Show Link Warnings
Hide Invisible Items
Cut
Copy
Clear
Select All
Grammarian ▶

Figure 7.19 Select a table cell and Control-click (Mac) or right-click (Windows) to see a context-sensitive menu where you can add or remove rows and columns.

To add a caption:

1. Select a table.

2. In the Table tab of the Table Inspector, click the Caption checkbox.

3. Use the adjacent popup menu to place the caption above or below the table.

4. Type a caption in the cell created above or below the table. The table shown in **Figure 7.17** has a caption above it.

To remove a caption from a table, uncheck the Caption checkbox in the Table Inspector.

✔ Tip

- In effect, a caption is like a table cell that spans the full width of a table, with centered text. You can achieve the same effect by selecting a cell in the bottom or top row of a table and choosing a Column span (in the Cell tab of the Table Inspector) that equals the total number of columns in the table.

To add a row:

1. Select a table cell that lies below the position your new row will occupy.

2. In the Cell tab of the Table Inspector, click the Add Row button (on the left) (**Figure 7.18**).

   or

   Control-click (Mac) or right-click (Windows) and select Insert Row from the popup menu (**Figure 7.19**). A new row appears above the selected cell.

3. To add a row below the current one, choose Insert Row Below from the context-sensitive menu.

To add a column:

1. Select a table cell that lies to the right of the position the new column will occupy.

2. In the Cell tab, click the Add Column button (on the right). A new column appears to the left of the selected cell.

   or

   Control-click (Mac) or right-click (Windows) and select Insert Column from the menu. A new column appears to the left of the current cell.

3. To insert a column to the right of the current cell, choose Insert Column Right from the context-sensitive menu.

Adding cells to the bottom or right edge of a table

When you use the Add Row/Column buttons to add cells to a table, the new cells appear above or to the left of existing cells. You can add cells to the bottom or right edge of the table by adding rows or columns in the Table tab of the Table Inspector. First select the table, or a cell, and switch to the Table tab of the Inspector. Add the number of rows or columns you want to add to the current number and type the result in the Rows or Columns field. You can also add single rows or columns with the context-sensitive menus, as described in the previous section.

Removing cells

The process of removing table rows and columns mirrors the process for adding them. You can use the Delete Row/Column buttons in the Cell tab of the Table Inspector.

With a cell selected, from the context-sensitive menus (Control-click on the Mac or right-click in Windows), choose Delete Row or Delete Column.

Adding Table Content

HTML tables can include any element you can put on a Web page, including text, images, and multimedia objects. You can type directly into the table, use the Objects palette to add objects, or drag and drop items into a table from the desktop.

To add text:

1. Click in one of the table's cells—not on the border.

2. Type the text.

3. Press Tab. The insertion point moves to the next horizontal cell. Tabbing from the last cell in a row moves the insertion point to the first cell in the next row.

✔ Tips

■ When you type text into a table cell and the text exceeds the visible boundaries of the cell, the cell grows downward to accommodate the text. So, if you're typing the contents of your table from scratch, you should complete the typing before you finish sizing the table cells.

■ When you add an image to a table (either by drag-and-drop or using the Image Inspector to place the image) the table cell grows to accommodate the image. If you resize the image, the cell's size changes too, though not in direct proportion to the image.

■ If a table cell is blank, its gridlines won't display properly. You can avoid this problem by adding a non-breaking space to any empty table cell. To add a non-breaking space, select the empty cell and Control-click (Mac) or right-click (Windows) and choose Insert   from the menu.

ADDING TABLE CONTENT

Importing table content

You can add content to a table by typing or by importing the contents of a tab-delimited text file into your GoLive document. The fields (which will become table cells) in your file must be separated by tabs, and each record (row) must include a carriage return at the end.

To import table content:

1. Create a new table or place your cursor in a cell within an existing table. This will be the first cell to accept imported text.

2. In the Table Inspector, click the Import Tab-Text button.

3. Locate a tab-delimited file in the dialog box that appears. When you click Open, the file's contents appear in the table (**Figure 7.20**).

4. Resize the table, and its rows and columns, so that the data fits correctly on the page.

✔ Tip

■ There's no need to add empty table cells before importing text. GoLive will add the needed cells when you add the text with the Import Tab-Text button.

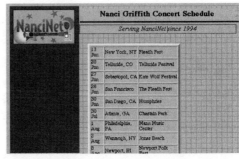

Figure 7.20 When you import a tab-delimited file into a GoLive table, you may need to adjust the table's appearance to display the data correctly.

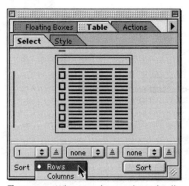

Figure 7.21 When you have selected cells to sort, choose whether to sort by Rows or Columns in the Table palette.

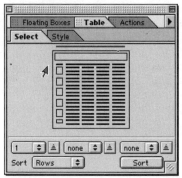

Figure 7.22 To select a table row, click to the left of the row in the Table palette.

Sorting table content

You can sort the contents of table rows and columns, in much the same way you can in a spreadsheet program. This is useful if you want to change the order of table data without retyping it. You can sort a table by row or column, in ascending or descending order, using multiple criteria.

To sort the contents of a table:

1. Create or select a table containing cells you want to sort.

2. Open the Table palette, either by choosing Window > Table, or clicking on the Table tab in the palette, if it's visible onscreen. Note: The Table *palette* and the Table *Inspector* are two distinct interface objects.

3. In the Select tab, select the table or the portion of the table you want to sort by clicking on the table cells that appear there. If you want to sort rows in the table, you must select the column containing the row cells you want to sort. If you are sorting table columns, select all of the rows affected.

4. Choose Rows or Columns from the Sort popup menu (**Figure 7.21**).

5. Click the Sort button.

✔ Tips

- You can select the table or its cells in the Document window, or in the Select tab of the Table palette. It's usually easier to use the Table palette.

- The techniques you use to select table cells in the Document window apply to cells in the Select tab as well. To select multiple cells, click one cell, then Shift-click each additional cell you want to select. To select a complete row in the Table palette, click to the left of the row as shown in **Figure 7.22**.

To sort by multiple criteria:

1. Select the whole table or specific cells you want to sort in the Table palette or in the Document window.

2. In the Table palette, choose whether you will sort by rows or columns.

3. From the first (leftmost) popup menu above the Sort menu, choose whether the first row or column will be the first criteria by which you sort. If it isn't, choose a number other than 1 from the menu.

4. If you want to sort in descending order rather than ascending order, click the arrow next to the first menu, as shown in **Figure 7.23.**

5. From the next popup menu, choose the sort order for the second selected row or column.

6. Repeat steps 3–5 if you have more rows or columns to sort.

7. Click the Sort button.

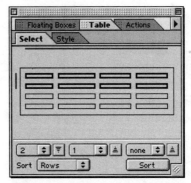

Figure 7.23 The second selected row in this table will be sorted first in descending order. Then, the first row will be sorted in ascending order. It's a strange way to sort a table, but it illustrates the point.

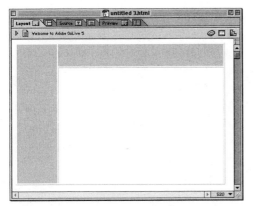

Figure 7.24 This three-cell table creates a structure for the page. The cell on the left has a row span of 2. The new table will be added to the lower-right cell—the body cell of the page.

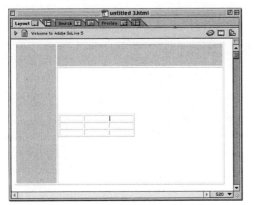

Figure 7.25 When you add a second table, it is aligned, by default, to the left and to the vertical center of its parent cell.

Nesting Tables

It's often useful to use multiple tables on a page: one serving as a container for all or part of the page, with a second table, *within* the first, providing a modular-like structure for a smaller section of the page, perhaps a site navigation scheme. Such an embedded table is also an effective way to structure tabular information, like a calendar or spreadsheet. Placing a table within another table is called *nesting* tables. You can nest as many tables as you like, but it's best to use as few as you can to keep your page simple. Nested tables can add to page download time, and make it a bit of a challenge to manage and edit a group of tables. First, I'll show you how to nest tables, and then I'll describe some ways of working with them.

To nest a table:

1. Add a table to a document. Format the table to provide a structure for your page, or a part of it. **Figure 7.24** shows a large table that divides the page into three sections.

2. Choose a cell within the first table that will contain a second table and drag the Table icon from the Objects palette into the cell. The new table appears, centered vertically in the table cell (**Figure 7.25**).

3. Select the parent cell—the one containing the new table.

continues on next page

4. In the Cell tab of the Table Inspector, choose Top from the Vertical Alignment popup menu. The second table now appears in the upper-left corner of the cell (**Figure 7.26**).

5. Select the second table (the one you just added) and configure it, using the Table Inspector. Add rows and columns as needed, and then add the table's content.

✔ Tips

■ Selecting a cell within a nested table can be a challenge, because it requires a steady hand to get the cursor just where you want it. To select a cell in a nested table, click it, and then press Control-Return. Press Control-Return again to select the entire nested table. One more press of these keys selects the cell in which the nested table lies. One more? You've selected the parent table.

■ Using the HTML Outline Editor view is another way to get your bearings when using nested tables. Click the Outline tab in the Document window and look for the <table> tags that indicate the tables that are part of your page. You can select the table you want by clicking on one of these tags. From there, you can configure or edit it in the HTML Outline Editor, or you can switch back to the Layout Editor and work in the Table Inspector or Table palette.

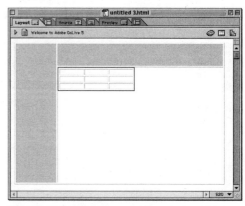

Figure 7.26 To align the new table to the top of the parent cell, choose the appropriate option in the Cell tab of the Table Inspector, and then select and configure the new table.

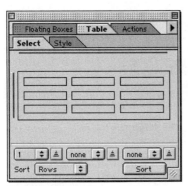

Figure 7.27 The Table palette displays the currently active table.

Figure 7.28 Choose a table style from the Style popup menu in the Table palette.

Using Table Styles

Just as many applications include templates that allow you to quickly add a unique look to a word processing document or spreadsheet, GoLive provides a selection of pre-defined table styles that come complete with color, borders, and other attributes.

To use a table style:

1. Add a new table to a document.

2. Choose Window > Table to open the Table palette. You can also reach it by clicking the Table tab in the palette in the group that also includes the Floating Boxes and Actions tabs (**Figure 7.27**).

3. Click the Style tab.

4. From the Style popup menu (**Figure 7.28**), choose a table style. I chose Seventies.

5. Click the Apply button. The table changes to reflect the new style (**Figure 7.29**).

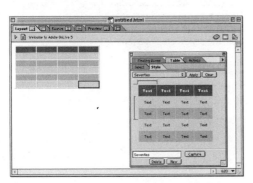

Figure 7.29 When you apply a style to a table, it is reflected in the Table palette and on the table.

To change table styles:

1. Be sure that the table is selected.

2. Choose a new style from the Style popup menu in the Table palette.

3. Click the Apply button.

4. To remove a style, click the triangle in the upper-right corner of the Table palette and choose Undo Select TableStyle from the menu (**Figure 7.30**).

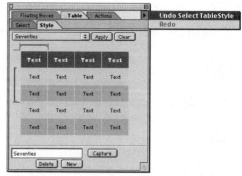

Figure 7.30 To remove a table style, choose Undo Select TableStyle.

To change rows or columns that use a table style:

1. Select a table and set a style for it, as described in the previous section.

2. In the Style tab of the Table palette, drag the end of the bracket that appears above or to the left of the table to add or remove columns or rows from the styled area (**Figure 7.31**).

✔ Tip

■ Because some predefined styles alternate the colors used in a table style, it's not always possible to add or remove affected table cells by dragging the bracket as described above.

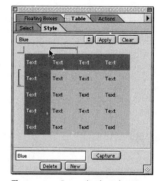

Figure 7.31 Drag the bracket to add or remove columns or rows from the styled area of a table.

To create your own table style:

1. Set up a table. Customize it any way you like, as described in earlier sections of this chapter.

2. Save your work.

3. In the Table palette, click the Style tab, then click New.

4. Give your custom table style a name.

5. Click the Capture button. Your style is added to the Style popup menu, and is now available for use with any table.

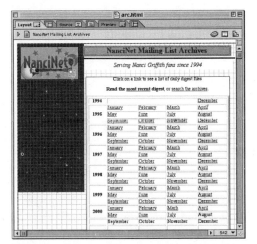

Figure 7.32 Select a table to convert to a layout grid.

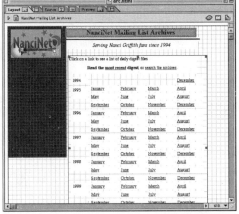

Figure 7.33 When you convert the table, the cell grid disappears and is replaced by text boxes. Notice that the text boxes take up more room than do the table cells.

Converting Tables to Layout Grids

GoLive allows you to break tables out into text frames, within a layout grid. This feature allows you to redesign a page by moving its tabular content around freely.

To convert a table to a layout grid:

1. Select a table (**Figure 7.32**).

2. In the Table tab of the Inspector, click the Convert button next to Table to Layout grid.

   or

   Control-click (Mac) or right-click (Windows) and choose Convert To Grid from the popup menu. The table is replaced onscreen by a layout grid. Each former cell is now a text box (**Figure 7.33**).

WORKING WITH FORMS

Forms add interactivity to your Web pages. Guest books, search engines, and product ordering systems are just a few of the applications that use forms. Basically, a form is a Web page component that allows a user to send information to the owner of the page, by sending data to a Web server. A form can contain one or more elements that allow user input. Web servers accept the input and return information or confirmation to the Web site visitor, based on the way server software is programmed to respond.

To use forms with your Web site, your Web server (run by your company or an ISP) must have a CGI (Common Gateway Interface) application—or the functional equivalent—installed that supports the forms you create. Before you design any forms, be sure that you will be able to use them with your server. Find out whether you have CGI access to your server, either through an ISP or your corporate IS manager. If your server does not support interactive forms, you can skip this chapter. In this chapter, I cover:

- How forms work

- Creating and configuring forms

- Basic and special form elements

- HTML 4.0 form elements and features

How Forms Work

To a Web site visitor and, perhaps, to a Web page designer, forms look and behave just like any other Web page element. Most forms are integrated with text and graphics, and their appearance is usually designed to complement the overall look of the page.

What differentiates forms is how they work behind the scenes. When a user enters text in a form, clicks a checkbox, and hits the Submit button, the form's work is done. From that point on, the Web server takes over.

A Web server must be running a script or CGI application designed to process the information Web site visitors submit. CGI applications are often written in Perl, C, or other computer languages. The CGI application transfers data entered into a Web page form into a database on the Web server. If, for example, the site visitor is using a form to reach a search engine, the database sends the search result to the server, which sends it back to the user via the CGI application. The result is an HTML page containing search engine hits.

When you create a form page, you have two tasks: designing the form so that it looks the way you want it to, and creating the hooks that allow your form to work with a Web server and CGI application. Those hooks are loosely analogous to Web URLs that link one page to another. With the hooks in place, a CGI can accept data from, and return data to, a site visitor's Web browser.

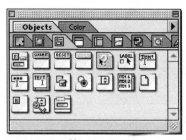

Figure 8.1 The Objects palette's Forms tab.

Figure 8.2 The Form icon.

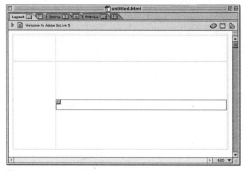

Figure 8.3 The Form element encloses all objects that are part of your form.

Creating Forms

Like other HTML elements, Adobe GoLive supports forms through a set of palette icons. They are stored under the Forms tab of the Objects palette (**Figure 8.1**).

Each icon activates the context-sensitive Inspector, where you configure the form to work with your Web page and the script or CGI that processes your form's input. (The input comes from the users.)

Before you begin dragging Form icons onto your page, take some time to design the form you want to build, preferably on paper. Choose the fields and labels you want to use and draw the page as you would like it to appear on the Web, positioning and aligning form objects so that they are easy for your site visitors to locate and use.

When you're ready to begin building the page, you will probably discover that positioning form elements, even with a design for the page in hand, is a tricky proposition. The easiest way to build form-based pages is to use either tables or floating boxes (covered in Chapters 7 and 12, respectively) to hold form elements. You can use table cells to align form objects with other objects and with their labels. Keeping a form within a table also makes it easy to move the entire form from one part of the page to another, if necessary.

To create a form element:

1. Add a table, floating box, or any other constraining structure in which you want to position form objects.

2. Click the Objects palette's Forms tab to display the form-creation icons.

3. Drag the Form icon (**Figure 8.2**) onto the table. GoLive creates a form box, indicated by a frame and a small F (**Figure 8.3**).

continues on next page

4. Place the form element in the upper-left corner of the area where your form will be. If the form is located in a table cell, select the cell and align the contents of the cell to the top of the cell, using the alignment options in the Table Inspector's Cell tab. That will move the form element to the upper-left corner of the cell.

The Form Inspector allows you to configure your new form. In order for the form to work, you must connect it to a CGI application on your Web server and provide the server with other information about how to work with the data that will be transferred from the form.

To configure the form:

1. Click the Form element to make the Form Inspector visible (**Figure 8.4**).

2. Type a unique name for the form in the Name field.

3. In the Action field, type the directory or URL of the CGI application that will process data entered into the form. You will need to get this information from the Webmaster of your site, or from your Internet service provider.

4. To specify the target window for your form's output, choose a target in the Target field. By default, the form's results will appear in the current browser window. You usually won't need to specify a target unless you're using frames on your page.

5. Choose an option from the Encode popup menu if your site uses encryption. Your Webmaster or ISP will be able to tell you which option to select.

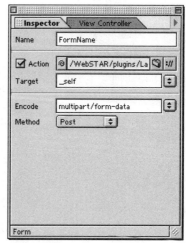

Figure 8.4 Set up the interaction between the form and the CGI in the Form Inspector.

6. From the Method popup menu, choose Post or Get to specify the way the form's output will be returned to the user. Post is usually the better choice.

The Post method returns form responses (such as search results) separately from the rest of the Web page, pasting the data into the page that's generated for the user. Get, on the other hand, appends the form response to the URL of the results page, making the URL long and cumbersome.

✔ Tip

■ The quickest way to specify actions for your forms is to set each action you use as an external item within your site. You can then Point & Shoot from the Form tag Inspector to the External tab to reach the CGI you need.

You've just linked your form to the Web server, making it possible for the form to send and receive information. You've also set up a container for all the elements that will become part of your form. In order for your form to be useful, you now need to add fields, buttons, and other elements with which your Web page visitors can interact.

✔ Tip

■ Many Web designers will never write a CGI application, though they should understand how CGIs work and, specifically, the demands of the CGI that will be used to process form data. To learn more about CGI programming, check out *Perl and CGI for the World Wide Web: Visual QuickStart Guide*, by Elizabeth Castro.

CREATING FORMS

Adding Form Elements

Think of the Form tag you just created as a container; it encloses the rest of the items that make up your Web page form and includes instructions (the Method and Action elements) that indicate how the form's input and output should be handled. Every element of the form must fall between the <FORM> and </FORM> HTML tags. You'll see these tags only if you examine your page with GoLive's HTML Outline Editor or HTML Source Editor. When you add form elements in the Layout Editor, they should be added to the area bounded by the Form tag you added in the previous section. All items included within a form tag are controlled by that tag.

Figure 8.5 The Text Field and Password Field icons, and a text field as it appears in the Layout Editor.

✔ Tip

- The Form element Inspectors shown in the next few sections include a section labeled Focus. I'll describe how to use Focus later in this chapter. For now, I will concentrate on options related to the specific form elements.

Text and password fields

Text fields allow users to enter a single line of text into a form. Text fields can contain names, addresses, search engine queries, or just about anything else that can be expressed in a single line of text. If you need to accommodate multiple lines of text, use the Text Area field, described in the next section. The Password field element is identical to the Text field except that it supports password entry, which conceals text as it is entered.

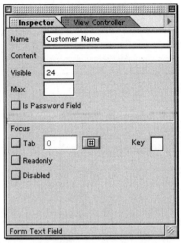

Figure 8.6 The Form Text Field Inspector.

To create a Text or Password field:

1. With a Form container in place and configured as discussed earlier in this chapter, drag the Text Field icon (**Figure 8.5**) from the Forms tab of the Objects palette to the form area. The field is displayed in the Document window, and the Form Text Field Inspector appears (**Figure 8.6**).

2. Type a name in the Name field.

3. If you want the field to contain default text (such as "Type Your Search Request Here"), enter it in the Content field. If not, leave the Content field blank.

4. In the Visible field, enter the number of characters you want to be visible to the user. The field may actually contain more characters. The field's visible contents will scroll horizontally as a user types beyond the number you've chosen to make visible.

5. Enter a larger number in the Max field if you want to give the user more room to type but don't want the entire field to be visible.

6. Leave the "Is Password Field" checkbox unchecked unless you're creating a password field.

✔ Tips

■ When you choose a name for your field and other form elements, keep in mind that the field names are used by your Web server's CGI application to connect the form to an underlying database or to a text file that accepts the form data. Your field names should exactly match the field names of your database or text file, and be intuitively linked to the form you're working with.

continues on next page

ADDING FORM ELEMENTS

- You create a Password field using exactly the same procedure you used to make the Text field. When you add the Password Field icon into the Document window, the Inspector selects "Is Password Field." Simply adding a Password field to a form does not password-protect the page. Password fields require a connection to a CGI script that passes passwords to the Web server.

When you're designing forms, you can choose to label or not label the fields. To give each form element (such as a text field) a label, you'll need to create a location for it (text frame, table cell, or floating box) and leave room in your page for the label. Alternatively, you can use the Content and Value fields found in most form elements to label the fields internally.

You can resize a text field by dragging one of the field's two handles. As you drag, the value in the Inspector's Visible field changes.

Text area fields

A text field contains a single line of text, but text *areas* allow you to provide multiple lines in which a user can enter information. You can use text areas to provide visitors a place to submit comments about your site, for example.

To create a text area:

1. Drag the Text Area icon from the Forms tab of the Objects palette to the area containing the form, within the Document window (**Figure 8.7**). The Form Text Area Inspector appears (**Figure 8.8**).

2. Name the text area.

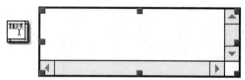

Figure 8.7 The Text Area icon and a text area.

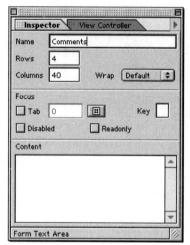

Figure 8.8 The Form Text Area Inspector.

Figure 8.9 The Check Box icon and a checkbox.

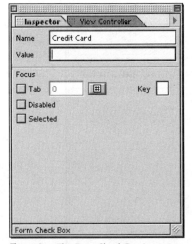

Figure 8.10 The Form Check Box Inspector.

3. If you want to change the default size of the text area, do so by increasing or decreasing the values in the Columns and Rows boxes or dragging the text area's handles to alter the field's size.

4. Use the Wrap popup menu to tell the form whether or not to wrap the text at the end of each line—usually a good idea. Unless you choose a wrap option, text in the field will continue past the field's boundary.

Checkboxes and radio buttons

Adding a set of checkboxes or radio buttons to your form provides a way for site visitors to choose from a number of options. Radio buttons allow users to choose a single option from a group of several options. Checkboxes allow the user to pick one or more items from a group.

To create a checkbox:

1. Drag the Check Box icon from the Forms tab of the Objects palette to the form area in the Document window. A checkbox appears (**Figure 8.9**).

2. In the Form Check Box Inspector (**Figure 8.10**), type a name for the checkbox.

3. In the Value field, enter the information that should be passed to the Web server when a user submits a form in which the checkbox is selected.

4. If you want the box checked by default, click the Selected checkbox.

5. Create additional checkboxes by repeating the steps above.

ADDING FORM ELEMENTS

To create a set of radio buttons:

1. Using the Radio Button icon, drag several radio buttons from the Forms tab of the Objects palette to the form area (**Figure 8.11**).

2. Instead of a name for a single checkbox or field, the Form Radio Button Inspector (**Figure 8.12**) asks for a group name, which represents all the radio buttons you will use as part of this series. Type a group name in the Group field.

3. Type a value for this particular radio button in the Value field. The value is transmitted to the Web server if the user selects the corresponding radio button.

4. Repeat steps 2 and 3 for each button you created, entering the group name that applies to all of them in the Group field as you go. Once you've created a group, you can choose that group's name from the popup menu associated with the Group field.

Submit and Reset buttons

The Submit and Reset buttons are an important final step to make your forms truly interactive. After filling out a form, the user clicks the Submit button, sending the information off to the server. A Reset button clears the form, which is useful if the site visitor decides to erase the data he or she has entered.

To create a Submit or Reset button:

1. Drag the Submit Button icon (**Figure 8.13**) from the Forms tab to the form area in the Document window.

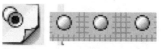

Figure 8.11 The Radio Button icon and three radio buttons.

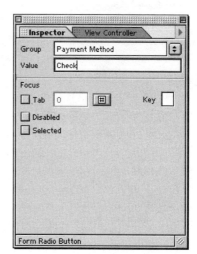

Figure 8.12 The Form Radio Button Inspector.

Figure 8.13 The Submit and Reset Button icons, and the buttons they create.

Figure 8.14 The Form Button Inspector.

2. In the Form Button Inspector (**Figure 8.14**), choose a name for the button.

3. If you want the button text to say something other than "Submit Query," click the Label checkbox and type your new label. It will appear within the button.

Because you used the Submit Button icon, GoLive has chosen Submit as your button's type (at the top of the Button Inspector). Leave it unchanged.

✔ Tip

- You create a Reset button using exactly the same procedure you did to make the Submit button. When you drag the Reset Button icon onto the main window, the Inspector selects Reset, rather than Submit, as the button type.

Popups and list boxes

You can display a list of choices within your form using a popup menu or a list box. They perform the same basic function but look a bit different from each other.

✔ Tips

- Popups and list boxes can be used like radio buttons and checkboxes, but they're much easier to configure as a group. They also take up less space on the page—a design bonus or drawback, depending on the look you're trying to achieve.

- A popup menu looks just like a Macintosh popup menu. (Windows users call them drop-down menus.) Only a rectangle is visible until you click it to pull down the menu. List boxes, on the other hand, display more of their contents on the Web page. Simply clicking on an item from the list box selects it.

- Configuring these two form elements is similar.

ADDING FORM ELEMENTS

To create a popup menu:

1. Drag the Popup icon (**Figure 8.15**) from the Forms tab of the Objects palette to the form area.

2. Name the popup in the Name field of the Form Popup Inspector (**Figure 8.16**).

3. If you want site visitors to see more than one popup item, enter that number in the Rows box.

   Note that making multiple rows visible makes your popup identical to a list box and defeats the purpose because your Popup is turned into a list box. The same goes for the Multiple Selection checkbox, which lets users select more than one item from the popup.

4. By default, the Inspector shows three items that you can edit and include in a popup menu. You can include as many items as you like in the popup. You can modify them, add items, or delete items here. To modify an item, first select it.

5. Rename the labels and values with names you want to appear in the popup menu.

6. To select the item by default, click the checkbox to the left of the Label name at the bottom of the Inspector.

7. To add new items to the popup, click New and type the new item's name and value in the appropriate fields.

✔ Tip

■ With a popup menu item selected in the Inspector, you can create another by clicking the Duplicate button. This is handy if you have several popup items with similar names and values. Just select the duplicate you create and edit its information.

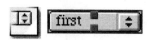

Figure 8.15
The Popup icon and a popup menu.

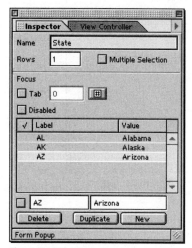

Figure 8.16 The Form Popup Inspector.

ADDING FORM ELEMENTS

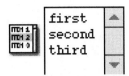

Figure 8.17 The List Box icon and a list box.

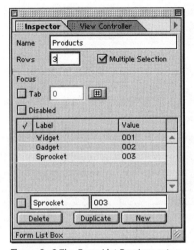

Figure 8.18 The Form List Box Inspector.

To create a list box:

1. Drag the List Box icon (**Figure 8.17**) from the Forms tab of the Objects palette to the form area.

2. In the Form List Box Inspector, give the list box a name (**Figure 8.18**).

3. Because the whole idea of a list box is to view several options, use the Rows box to enter the number of items you want to be visible on the list. You can display as many list box items as you like, but more than five or six may occupy more vertical space on the page than you want.

4. Click "Multiple Selection" if you want to permit the user to select several options from the list.

5. Follow steps 4–7 of the "Popup menu" section, above, to finish your list box.

✔ Tips

- List boxes have scroll bars, allowing you to display some rows and make others available by scrolling. Choose the number of rows you think will both look best on the page and also display the items you think will be most popular, saving site visitors the extra mouse movement to scroll down the entire list.

- You can change the number of visible rows using either the Inspector or by dragging the handle on the list box downward.

Input Image

The Input Image element allows you to substitute an image for the Submit or Reset button. Configuring it is similar to configuring an image you add to a page.

To create an input image:

1. Drag the Input Image icon (**Figure 8.19**) into the form area. An image placeholder appears.

2. Browse or Point & Shoot to locate the image you want to use.

3. Configure the image's attributes, as described in Chapter 5, "Working with Images."

4. In the More tab of the Input Image Inspector, type a name of the input image in the Name field, next to the Is Form checkbox, which should be checked (**Figure 8.20**).

✔ Tip

■ You can turn a previously placed image into a button by clicking the Is Form checkbox in the More tab of the Image Inspector. Optionally, you can name the image, as a part of the form, in the Name field to the right of the Is Form checkbox.

Figure 8.19 The Input Image icon.

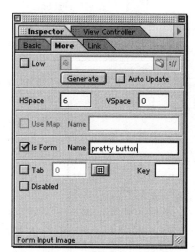

Figure 8.20 The More tab of the Input Image Inspector is where you enter the name of the image. This tab, and the rest of the Inspector, is identical to the standard Image Inspector.

Elements that interact with the server

Several HTML elements are very useful in maintaining communication with the Web server, enhancing security, and allowing users to upload files to your site. Configuring these elements requires very specific information about your CGI application and Web server, so while I will describe them here, I will leave the details to you and your Webmaster, who can tell you the values that should be entered in the Inspectors for each of these items.

Hidden field

Hidden elements are not a visible part of a form. Instead of holding information entered by a form user, hidden elements store information that has already been collected. For example, if your Web site includes one form that asks for a user's name and address, and a second form where the user can place an order, a hidden field can link the information on the two forms by providing the user's name and address to the second form.

Key generators

Key generators insert an encryption key into the transaction between Web site visitor and Web site owner. Keys are often used when forms contain financial transactions or personal information. When a site visitor submits a form, the Web server sends a dialog box to the visitor, asking the visitor to accept or decline the key so that the transaction can be completed.

File browser

The File Browser element lets you open a window to the FTP directory on your Web site. Using a File Browser, site visitors can access and download files, provided they have been granted private access (with a username and password), or public access, known as *anonymous FTP.*

ADDING FORM ELEMENTS

HTML 4.0 Form Elements

The latest version of the HTML specification includes several new form tags and a couple of features that can help users navigate your forms. The catch is that your Web site's visitors must use a 4.0 (or later) browser to view and use the new tags and features. In addition, some of these tags are only supported by *one* of the major browsers (Netscape Navigator or Internet Explorer).

Button

An HTML 4.0 button is similar to the Submit and Reset buttons I described earlier in this chapter, except that you can customize its appearance and function with the Text Inspector.

To create a button:

1. Add a button (**Figure 8.21**) to the form by dragging the Button icon from the Forms tab of the Objects palette.

2. Move your cursor over the button until it changes from a hand to an I-beam. You can now type text in the button and customize that text just as you would any other text in your document. Just select existing text, or type some, and apply formatting from the toolbar or from the Type menu. If you click the text, notice that the Inspector window changes to the Text Inspector, allowing you to add a link or other attribute of your choice. (This is an example of how the *context-sensitive* Inspector works.) The button in **Figure 8.22** includes text formatted as a heading and italicized.

3. Click the border of the button to select the entire button. The Form Button Inspector becomes active.

4. In the Inspector (**Figure 8.23**), choose a name and value for the button.

Figure 8.21 The Button icon.

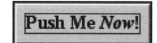
Figure 8.22 The text in this button has been styled using HTML text formatting.

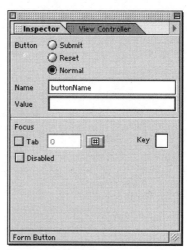
Figure 8.23 The Button element uses the same Inspector you used to configure Submit and Reset buttons.

Figure 8.24 The Label icon.

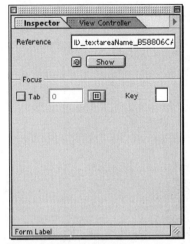

Figure 8.25 The Form Label Inspector as it appears when the label has been associated with a form field.

Label

It seems like a pretty simple matter to create a text label for a form element such as a radio button or checkbox. HTML 4.0's Label form element is a nifty way of linking a label with a button or a box because clicking on the label activates the button or box, much as clicking on a label in the Inspector activates the button or box associated with it. In other words, an HTML 4.0 label belongs to and is part of the form element it describes.

To create a label element:

1. Create or locate a checkbox, radio button, or any other form element you would like to label. Make sure that you have configured your form elements before trying to create a label.

2. Drag the Label icon (**Figure 8.24**) from the Forms tab of the Objects palette to your form.

3. Double-click the label to select the text, and type the label name.

4. Select the label by clicking on its border.

5. Position the label icon near the item you want to connect it to.

6. Command-click (Mac) or Alt-click (Windows) the label (not the text inside it) and Point & Shoot the resulting line to the box, button, or other element you want to link to. Note that the Form Label Inspector becomes active (**Figure 8.25**), and that it now displays an ID number in the Reference field that connects your label to the form element.

✔ Tip

■ Just like an HTML 4.0 button tag, you can format label text when the text (not the label) is selected. Formatting the text ensures that your labels are consistent with the look and feel of your page.

HTML 4.0 FORM ELEMENTS

Fieldset and legend

The Fieldset element provides a physical grouping for other form elements. You can work with and move a group of buttons, checkboxes, or radio buttons around as one once they've been added to a Fieldset. The legend option allows you to label the group.

To create a fieldset and legend:

1. Drag the Fieldset icon (**Figure 8.26**) from the Forms tab of the Objects palette to the form. A fieldset appears in the Document window, with the word Legend at the top.

2. In the Fieldset Inspector (**Figure 8.27**), choose an alignment for the Fieldset legend or uncheck the Use Legend box to disable this feature altogether.

3. If you plan to use a legend, click the word *Legend* in the Document window and change the word *Legend* to a title of your choice.

4. Drag a table (either one you've worked on already or a new one) into the Fieldset box you just created. The Fieldset box expands to hold the table.

5. Drag some radio buttons or other form elements into the Fieldset box and table. Add labels to the table to complete the fieldset.

✔ Tips

- You can vary the alignment of a fieldset's legend with the Alignment popup in the Fieldset Inspector. By default the legend is aligned to the top of the fieldset.

- Fieldsets are only supported by Internet Explorer 4.0 (and above).

Figure 8.26 The Fieldset icon.

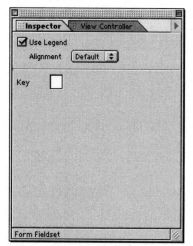

Figure 8.27 The Fieldset Inspector.

HTML 4.0 Form Features

You may have noticed several items under the Focus label of many form element Inspector windows. These items specify the HTML 4.0-specific features I'll cover in this section.

HTML 4.0 form features supported in GoLive are:

◆ Tabbing chains

◆ Access keys

◆ Read-only elements

◆ Disabled elements

Tabbing chains

Filling out a long online form is much easier if you can move from one field to the next using the Tab key. GoLive and HTML 4.0 give you a way to create and control the order in which users move from field to field. It's called a *tabbing chain*.

Form elements that support tabbing chains are:

◆ Text and password fields

◆ Text areas

◆ Submit and Reset buttons

◆ Checkboxes and radio buttons

◆ Popup menus and list boxes

◆ Labels

To create a tabbing chain:

1. Open a document that contains form fields that require the user to make text entries, such as a text field or text area.

2. Choose Special > Start Tabulator Indexing. Small yellow boxes with question marks appear next to the indexable fields in your form (**Figure 8.28**).

3. Click the boxes in the order you want the tabs to appear. The question marks change to reflect your clicks (**Figure 8.29**).

4. Choose Stop Tabulator Indexing from the Special menu. When visitors type into your form's fields and press Tab, their cursors will move into subsequent fields in the order you've specified here.

✔ Tip

■ You may have noticed a checkbox and a field labeled Tab in the Inspector of form elements that support tabbing chains (**Figure 8.30**). You can activate or change the tab order of fields within your forms in this Inspector field.

Access keys

Defining an access key within a form element allows the user to activate the element or field by typing a specific keyboard shortcut.

Form elements that support access keys are:

◆ Text and password fields

◆ Text areas

◆ Submit and Reset buttons

◆ Checkboxes and radio buttons

◆ Labels

◆ Legends

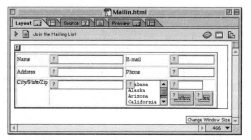

Figure 8.28 When you start tabulator indexing, yellow boxes containing question marks appear within each form field.

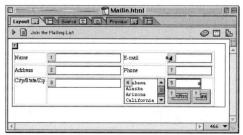

Figure 8.29 To set the tab order, click each box in turn to give the field a number. Here, I've already set the tabbing order for several fields. The user will type name and street address information and then be moved into the E-mail field.

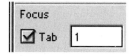

Figure 8.30 To add a form element to a tabbing chain, click the Tab checkbox and enter a number to establish the position this field will occupy in the tabbing chain.

To create an access key:

1. Select a supported form element in the Document window.

2. In the Inspector, type an alphanumeric character in the Key field.

3. Test your new key in a browser that supports access keys, such as Internet Explorer for Windows. To activate a key, type Command-accesskey (Mac) or Alt-accesskey (Windows).

✔ Tips

■ It's a good idea to include some sort of label or other visual cue on the page, so that your visitors will know that the form field includes an access key.

■ Many possible access keys are already used by browsers. A browser key will override access keys you create if they are identical.

Read-only elements

You can use read-only elements to prevent visitors from editing the contents of a form field. If, for example, you want to limit the visitor to submitting a pre-defined text string, you could create a field that includes it.

Form elements that support read-only elements are:

◆ Text and password fields

◆ Text areas

◆ Submit and Reset buttons

◆ Checkboxes and radio buttons

◆ Popup menus and list boxes

To create a read-only element:

1. Select the element you want to make read-only in your document.

2. In the Inspector, add text that you would like to appear in the field.

3. Click the Readonly checkbox.

HTML 4.0 FORM FEATURES

Disabled elements

You can disable any form element. While it may seem silly to create an element only to disable it, you can use a JavaScript to bring disabled elements to life conditionally—the item will be disabled unless it is activated. You could, for example, create two versions of the same form page for use in a sales transaction. If a customer makes a purchase from your site and checks a "Gift Wrap" checkbox on the order form, a second form could include paper style and color options. If on the other hand, the customer doesn't click "Gift Wrap" when placing the order, a second version of the order confirmation form appears, identical to the first, but without gift wrap options displayed. Those elements are disabled form elements, rendered unavailable by a JavaScript when the customer chooses whether or not to have the package gift wrapped.

To disable a form element:

1. Choose the form element you wish to disable.

2. Write a JavaScript (or choose a GoLive Action) to enable the element conditionally. For more information about GoLive Actions, see Chapter 17, "Using Actions."

3. Select the element in the Document window.

4. In the Inspector, click the Disabled checkbox.

WORKING WITH FRAMES

Think of frames as multi-paned windows to your Web site. Instead of a single, scrollable page full of text and images, framed pages display two or more pages within the same browser window. Usually, framed pages (*framesets*, in HTML-speak) contain a main pane and one or more smaller panes. Panes may include scroll bars that permit you to move through the frame independent of the other elements on the page. Some frames, used for navigation menus or logos, remain stationary in the browser as you click through other pages within the frameset.

Many Web designers use frames as navigation tools. For instance, a frame can display a site-wide table of contents alongside each individual page. Other sites use frames to force visitors to view advertisements or other banner images.

In this chapter, I cover:

- ◆ How frames work
- ◆ Creating frames
- ◆ Adding content to frames
- ◆ Adding frames and framesets
- ◆ Adding NoFrames content
- ◆ Adding inline frames

How Frames Work

Most Web pages consist of a single HTML file. Frame-based Web pages, on the other hand, actually display several HTML documents at once, each in its own pane of the browser window. **Figures 9.1a** and **9.1b** show a couple of design options available using frames.

To use frames, you'll need to create and link several files into a frameset. Although the files you need will vary based on the arrangement of your frames, these are the most basic ones:

◆   A frameset document

◆   A navigation document

◆   A body document

The frameset document contains instructions on how the browser window and its panes should look when filled with frame content, and how they are positioned on the page. The frameset document doesn't include text or images, just the HTML code needed to describe how the frames that are a part of the frameset should be displayed in the browser window.

The file I'm calling the navigation document contains a table of contents (including links) of pages that can make up your Web site, and it will appear in the main pane when you click.

The body document is a placeholder for content (and the HTML code used to describe it) that will appear in the main pane of the browser window.

You can add advertising banners, text, images, or other items using additional frame documents. Like basic navigation and content frames, you specify the frame size and appearance within the frameset document.

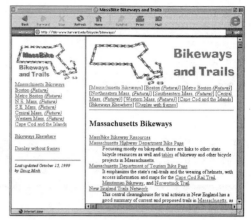

Figure 9.1a The MassBike links page uses two frames: a table of contents on the left and a body frame containing individual links.

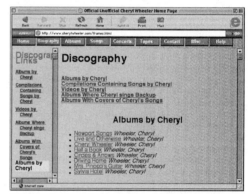

Figure 9.1b The Web site for singer/songwriter Cheryl Wheeler uses navigation frames on the left and top of the page, with a third frame containing the body of the page.

HOW FRAMES WORK

Frame caveats

Frames are not really a full-fledged part of the HTML standard. Netscape Communications introduced frame tags as an extension to HTML. At this writing, only Netscape browsers (Navigator and Communicator) and Microsoft Internet Explorer support frames. Although browser software from Netscape and Microsoft dominates the marketplace, Webmasters who use frames run the risk of creating pages that users of other browsers cannot view. The solution for some is to create both frame-filled and no-frames versions of their Web sites.

Even when site visitors use browsers that support them, frames can be problematic for Web site visitors. Although frames make it possible to look at more of your site at once, they also limit the user's ability to use the mouse and cursor to move freely. For example, if you're used to using the Page Down key to scroll through a Web page, you'll find that impossible to do in some framed pages unless you first click in the frame you want to navigate.

Frames also decrease the amount of visible screen space available to display Web site content. Contents areas and navigation frames leave less room for the main pane. However, the same is true of other highly structured site design methods that use tables to create navigation elements fixed to the side or top of the browser window. The challenge is to leave as much space as possible in the main frame while retaining readability within smaller frames.

Creating Frames

Once you've decided which portions of your Web site belong in frames, you can create a page with a *frameset*. Framesets specify the way a group of frames on the page will look and interact.

All the tools you need to create and customize frame-based pages can be found under the Frames tab of the Objects palette (**Figure 9.2**).

To create a frame document:

1. Open a new Adobe GoLive document.

2. Switch from the Layout Editor to the Frames Editor by clicking the Frames Editor tab in the Document window. The result looks like **Figure 9.3**.

3. Choose the Frames tab from the Objects palette.

4. Drag a frameset icon (all but the upper, leftmost icon are framesets) from the palette onto the Document window.

   The configuration I chose as an example is displayed in **Figure 9.4**, along with the corresponding frameset icon from the Objects palette.

Figure 9.2 The Object palette's Frames tab contains tools you can use to create a variety of framesets.

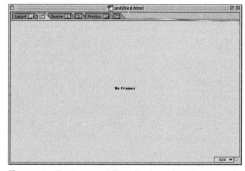

Figure 9.3 The Frames Editor displays the structure of a frameset page. It's blank when no frames are present.

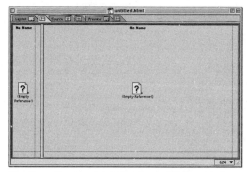

Figure 9.4 Here's a simple frameset, displayed in the Frames Editor.

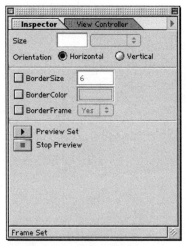

Figure 9.5 The Frame Set Inspector sets all preferences for frames within a frameset. To set options for individual frames, click within them and use the Frame Inspector.

Figure 9.6 When you attempt to resize a frame, be sure that your cursor is positioned on the border between frames, rather than within one of them.

5. Click the border between the two frames to bring up the Frame Set Inspector (**Figure 9.5**). If you don't see the Inspector, choose Windows > Inspector.

Options you choose here apply to all frames within the frameset. You can change the set's orientation, specify the thickness of the border, the border color, and whether there should be a border frame. You can also tell GoLive whether or not to preview frames within the Frames Editor. When you work with individual frames within the set, you'll have other configuration options.

To arrange frames:

1. Click and hold the mouse button inside the leftmost frame on your page, and drag to the right, across the Document window. When the frame you've selected reaches the other frame onscreen, the two change places.

2. Drag the frame to the left to return it to its original position.

To resize frames:

◆ By default, the smaller frame, sometimes called a sidebar, is very narrow. To widen it, click and drag the border of the frame to the right. I'll need the extra space, because I'm going to use the frame as a table of contents for a Web site, as you'll see in the next set of steps.

✔ Tip

■ Be careful to position your cursor on the border of the frame, as shown in **Figure 9.6**, rather than the outline of the scroll bar (to the left of the cursor). As we've seen, dragging from inside a frame moves the entire frame. All you want to do at this point is resize it.

To configure frames:

1. Click within a frame. The Frame Inspector becomes active (**Figure 9.7**).

2. If you wish, choose Pixels or Percent from the Size popup menu and enter a number in the adjacent field. To have the frame sized automatically when a visitor views the page (based on the contents of the frame and the browser and operating system being used) choose Scale instead. Scale tells the browser to use all available space—space not assigned to other elements—to the frame.

3. If you wish, type a name for the frame in the Name field. The name describes the frame, and is also used with the target attribute, described later in this section. The name should consist of alpha-numeric characters only, and should not include any spaces.

4. In the Scrolling popup menu, choose Yes or No to determine whether your contents frame will have scroll bars, or leave Auto selected to allow the browser to add bars only when the content is long enough to warrant them. In this example, I'll turn off scrolling because the table of contents won't be long enough to require scrolling. Leaving off the scroll bars also conserves valuable screen real estate.

5. Click the Resize Frame checkbox if you want to prevent the frame from being resized by the browser or by a user who changes the size of the window. This is useful if you want to maintain the exact size of a frame in order to properly display a logo, image, or other object.

6. Click the Preview Frame button to see the contents of the frame document that you constructed in the Frames Editor.

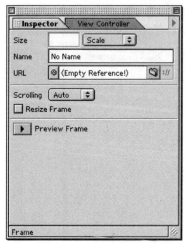

Figure 9.7 Name and configure individual frames in the Frame Inspector.

7. Save your frame document. Because this example Web site uses only one frameset, I'll save and name the file `frameset.html`. Remember that this document won't contain any content, just instructions for the display of framed pages.

I named the page `frameset.html` so that it would be obvious which document we were working with. Chances are, though, that you'll want to use a different name (`index.html` or `home.html`, for example) if your new, framed look will be the home page of your site.

✔ Tips

- If you want to use a frames-based page as your home page, name it `index.html`, `default.html`, or some other name that your Web server recognizes as your home page.

- Even if your server doesn't have set rules about how your page should be named, Webmasters redesigning existing sites to include frames will want to preserve their previous home page URLs by giving the frame page the same name as the previous home page.

- Some Webmasters avoid this naming headache (as well as problems caused for people whose Web browsers don't support frames) by offering framed and non-framed versions of home pages and sites. In that case, create a page that offers that choice, and name it `index.html` and let site visitors click the version of their choice. In that case, you can name your framed document anything you like and can link to it from your index page.

CREATING FRAMES

Adding Content to Frames

With your framework in place (pun intended), it's time to dress up those window panes with some content. Although frames can simply provide windows to individual Web pages, they are much more powerful when used as a navigation aid for your entire site. The example frame structure I'm using in this chapter does that. The contents frame offers a list of available pages within the site, and the larger frame (I'll call it the body frame) displays the page your site visitors clicked from the table of contents.

Like the frame document itself, the body frame is a container for information. The contents of the body frame change depend on the hyperlink a user selects.

To add a body page to your frameset:

1. Open a new document.

2. Click the title bar (labeled "Welcome to Adobe GoLive 5" by default) and change the title to body.

3. Save your document as body.html.

4. Open the frameset.html document you created in the preceding section. Switch to the Frames Editor.

5. Click in the larger of the two frames (on the right) to select it.

6. Browse or Point & Shoot from the Frame Inspector and locate and select the file you want to appear in the body frame by default. This is probably your home page.

   or

   Drag a file from the Site window or from the Finder (Mac) or from Windows Explorer or the desktop (Windows) into the body frame.

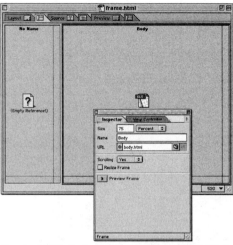

Figure 9.8 With the body Frame Inspector fields filled in, the question mark in the body frame changes to a page icon, and the frame's name appears at the top of the page.

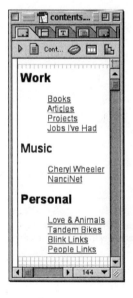

Figure 9.9
The contents.html page will appear as a navigation frame on each page of my Web site. I narrowed the window so that it would be easier to work with.

7. In the Frame Inspector, name the frame Body. If you want to add scroll bars to the frame, select an option (Yes or No). **Figure 9.8** shows the completed body Frame Inspector and the frame itself.

8. If you check Resize Frame, those who view your page will be able to shrink or enlarge the frame in their browser windows. Otherwise, the frame is always the same size you created it.

The contents frame contains a fixed, non-resizable HTML page, usually including links that activate the body frame. You can also add text, graphics, or any other element you'd like to appear in the navigation frame. The contents of the body frame change based upon the link a site visitor activates. Web page designers often set the body frame to load a site's home page, as described in the next section.

When you're designing your contents frame, remember that it will probably be quite narrow. Limit your text elements to headings and listings, and keep logos and graphics small. Of course, you *can* make your contents frame as wide as you like, but you'll be sacrificing valuable body frame screen space with every expansion of the contents frame.

To add a contents frame:

1. Open a new GoLive document.

2. Title your document contents and save it as contents.html.

3. Type the text for your table of contents. **Figure 9.9** shows my table of contents page.

continues on next page

I included several elements: headings and listings (including links to individual pages). Your next task is to create hyperlinks that connect the listed items to the body frame. Although connecting frames is similar to creating links or anchors for a normal page, it comes with one added wrinkle: the target.

Targets tell the Web browser where a link should be displayed: in a new window, at the top of a page, or, in this case, in a frame that is part of the current frameset.

To create targeted links:

1. Open contents.html. Be sure that frameset.html is also open.

2. In contents.html, select an item from your table of contents list.

3. Click the Link icon on the toolbar and complete the link by typing, browsing, or using Point & Shoot to locate a file within the Files tab of your Site window.

4. Connect the new link to the main frame (Body) of your frameset (frameset.html) by filling in the Target field of the Inspector. Because this is the first frame link you've created, you need to type the word Body (the name you gave to your main frame) in the Target field. The completed Inspector looks like **Figure 9.10**.

5. Save the contents.html document.

6. Bring frameset.html to the front.

7. In the Document window, choose the Frame Preview tab. You should see the contents document in the left frame and an empty pane on the right (**Figure 9.11**).

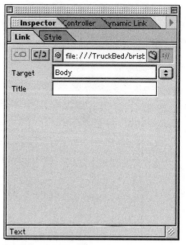

Figure 9.10 In the Inspector, you can target links that appear in the navigation frame to the body frame, so that the links will appear there when clicked by site visitors.

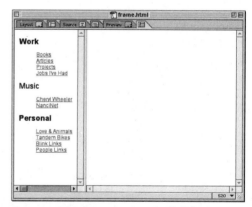

Figure 9.11 With the contents.html file linked to frameset.html, you can preview the navigation bar in the Frame Preview mode.

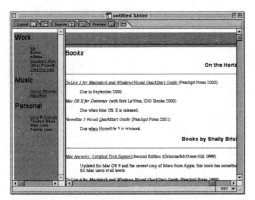

Figure 9.12 In the Frame Preview mode, clicking the properly configured link in the contents frame displays the requested page in the body frame.

8. Click the link you just created in the contents frame. The page you've linked appears in the body frame (**Figure 9.12**).

9. Repeat steps 2–5 for each table of contents element you'd like to connect to a document that will appear in the main frame.

✔ Tip

■ When you choose targets in the Link Inspector, use the popup menu. Once you create the first link you'll notice that the target menu now includes the word *Body*. Naming the frame "Body" in an earlier step added this item to the menu. This shortcut does not work, however, unless the frameset document (`frameset.html`) is open.

Does the contents frame look right to you in Frame Preview mode, and/or in your Web browser? Do the line breaks occur where you want them to? If not, you can adjust the contents frame's width in the Frames Editor. Here's how.

To tweak the contents frame:

1. Open `frameset.html` and choose the Frames Editor.

2. Click the contents frame.

3. In the Frame Inspector window, click the Preview Frame button so that `contents.html` will appear in the contents frame.

4. To adjust the width of the frame, drag the border to the left or right (depending upon whether you think the contents frame is too wide or too narrow), and note the impact the movement has on line breaks and available space within the body frame.

5. For that extra measure of accuracy, click the Frame Preview tab in the Document window and verify the look of your frames.

Adding Frames and Framesets

GoLive allows you to create framesets in a wide variety of configurations. The Frames tab of the Objects palette suggests a number of options, including the simple two-frame arrangement I've been using in this chapter. You can also modify existing framesets by adding new frames, one at a time. You can even use multiple framesets on the same page, creating nested framesets, though this is not usually a good idea. Because more framesets create denser code and because they add even more variability than usual to the way different browsers display frames, be extremely careful with nested framesets, avoiding them when possible.

To add a single frame:

1. Open the frameset.html document you've been working with and switch to the Frames Editor.

2. Drag the Frame icon (**Figure 9.13**) from the Objects palette to the main window, dropping it into the body frame. A new frame appears.

3. Click the new frame and drag it upward so that it switches places with the body frame, as shown in **Figure 9.14**. I'm going to use this frame as a banner.

4. Click the new frame. Now you can use the Frame Inspector to resize it.

5. In the Size popup of the Frame Inspector, note that the default setting is Scale. Choose Percent from the menu. You can now enter a number (try 25) that states the frame's size as a percentage of the available vertical space. The upper frame shrinks. Now you're ready to add content to your new frame by dragging an HTML file into it.

Figure 9.13 Add a single frame to your frameset with the Object palette's Frame icon.

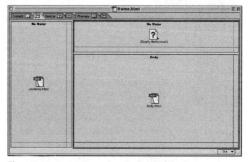

Figure 9.14 Dragging a frame upward and over another frame causes the frames to switch places.

✔ Tip

■ If you'd rather use the mouse than the keyboard, you can resize the frame by dragging its border, so long as either Pixel or Percent is chosen in the Frame Inspector's Size popup menu.

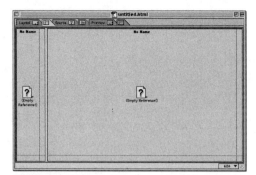

Figure 9.15 Add a two-frame set to the document.

 Figure 9.16 Choose a horizontal, two-frame set from the Frames tab of the Objects palette.

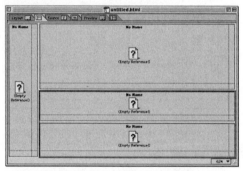

Figure 9.17 This page includes a vertical frameset, whose right frame is bisected by a horizontal frameset.

If you want to add a group of frames to an existing frames-based page, simply drag a frameset from the Objects palette to the main window. Each frameset on a page operates as a separate entity, meaning that the attributes you set for one frameset do not apply to other sets on the same page. On the other hand, placing additional framesets on a page can and does affect the position of other framesets.

To add nested frames:

1. Open a new GoLive document and add a frameset containing two vertical frames (**Figure 9.15**).

2. Drag a frameset icon that creates two horizontal frames (**Figure 9.16**) from the Frames tab of the Objects palette into the right-hand frame in the Document window. The result looks like **Figure 9.17**. Notice that the two new frames take half the available space in the existing frame—the same amount of space a single frame (as described in the previous section) would have taken.

continues on next page

ADDING FRAMES AND FRAMESETS

✔ Tip

■ The easiest way to configure a frameset when there are multiple framesets on the page is to click a part of the frame border that is not shared with the other frameset. In the example in this section, click the vertical border, above the secondary frameset (**Figure 9.18**) to choose options for the primary frameset. To set up the secondary set, click the border between its two frames (**Figure 9.19**). The Inspector changes to show the attributes of the second frameset.

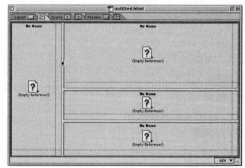

Figure 9.18 To select the first frameset, click above the second frameset.

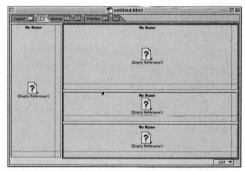

Figure 9.19 Click the border between the two frames of the second frameset to select that frameset. When you do, the Inspector changes to show the second frameset's attributes.

Adding Noframes Content

Not all Web browsers support frames: 2.0 versions of Netscape Navigator and Microsoft Internet Explorer don't, and neither do text-only browsers like Lynx. Using the <noframes> tag, you can design your pages so that browsers that don't support frames will display a frame-less version of your page. The <noframes> tag encloses HTML that is displayed when a non-frames browser accesses the page. You can create a complete, frameless version of the page, or a simple message directing the user to a non-frames version of your site, or to a frames-capable browser.

Adding a <noframes> element to a frameset in GoLive requires you to work with HTML source code; you can't do it in the Frames Editor.

To add a noframes element:

1. Create a page for visitors whose browsers do not support frames. You may create one from scratch, or copy and paste the contents of your framed pages into the new page.

2. Save the page.

3. Open a GoLive document containing a frameset.

4. Switch to the HTML Source Editor by clicking the Source tab at the top of the Document window.

5. Locate the opening <frameset> tag, and type <noframes> after the frameset tag.

6. Return to the page you created in Step 1, and switch to the HTML Source Editor.

continues on next page

ADDING NOFRAMES CONTENT

7. Locate the opening <body> tag and copy everything below (or after) it and above (or before) the closing </body> tag to the clipboard.

8. In the frameset document, paste your noframes content into the HTML Source Editor, following the <noframes> tag.

9. Type </noframes> to finish the tag.

10. Save and preview the page in both a frames-capable browser and a browser that does not support frames.

✔ Tips

- If you include a full copy of a Web page within <noframes> tags, you'll have to update two copies of the page whenever a change is made. And because the <noframes> items are invisible in GoLive's Layout Editor, you must perform these updates in the HTML Source Editor. If you update your pages frequently, consider creating a simple message in the <noframes> section that asks users to upgrade to a frames-capable browser.

- It's very important to remove <head> and <HTML> tags from documents you copy into <noframes> tags. A Web page must only have one set of these tags. GoLive creates the tags at the beginning and end of all HTML documents, including the frameset document that contains the <noframes> element.

Adding Inline Frames

Standard frames always have at least one edge along the browser window's margin. *Inline frames*, also called floating frames, are not constrained in this way, but can "float" in the middle of a page. Inline frames are a Microsoft addition to the HTML standard, and are compatible only with Internet Explorer browsers (version 3.0 and above). You can create inline frames in GoLive, but you must use Internet Explorer to preview them.

Unlike standard frames, inline frames can appear within any HTML page. You don't need to create a frameset, or use other frames with an inline frame. Inline frames have many of the same attributes as image tags. Like images, inline frames take a position on a Web page relative to other items on the page.

To add an inline frame:

1. Open a GoLive document to which you would like to add an inline frame.

2. Switch to the HTML Source Editor.

3. At the location on your page where the inline frame should appear, type `<iframe SRC="filename.html">` where *filename.html* is the name of the document that will appear in the frame.

4. Set any additional attributes, such as size or background color, just as you would when setting up an image.

5. Type `</iframe>` to close the inline frame element.

6. Save the document.

7. View the document with Internet Explorer by choosing Internet Explorer from the toolbar's browser menu (if you've configured this option in GoLive Preferences), or by opening Internet Explorer and then the document that includes the inline frame.

Working
with Code

Adobe GoLive is a visual tool for Web site development that allows you to design sites without getting your hands dirty or having to learn or edit HTML code. But as appealing as visual page design is, there are times when it is necessary to work with HTML directly.

GoLive includes two HTML editing views: the HTML Outline Editor and the HTML Source Editor. The HTML Outline Editor presents HTML pages in a hierarchical, organized fashion. The HTML Source Editor breaks down all barriers between the Web page author and the HTML underlying the page.

Once you've had your first taste of Web page coding, you'll learn about some specialized HTML tags that add information about your document, such as Head tags. You can work with and add your own HTML tags in Web Settings, a tool that helps you and GoLive keep up with the ever-changing HTML standard. In this chapter, I cover:

◆ Using the HTML Outline Editor

◆ The Markup tree

◆ Working with the HTML Source Editor

◆ Using the Source Code window and Layout Editor together

◆ Head tags

◆ Using Web Settings

◆ Dynamic components

Using the HTML Outline Editor

Think of the HTML Outline Editor as a bridge between WYSIWYG Web page development and the dark recesses of the HTML language. Like the layout environment, the HTML Outline Editor can display images and text.

The HTML Outline Editor displays a hierarchical version of your Web page with HTML tags around the text and graphic elements. **Figure 10.1** shows a Web page in the Layout Editor and a portion of the same page in the HTML Outline Editor.

To view a document in the HTML Outline Editor:

1. Open a GoLive document.

2. In the Document window, click the HTML Outline tab (**Figure 10.2**) to switch to the HTML Outline Editor. The page's outline appears.

To view the outline of a new page:

1. Open a new document.

2. Click the HTML Outline tab to view the outline. Even without text or images, the empty page already has an outline, containing the required structure for the page (**Figure 10.3**).

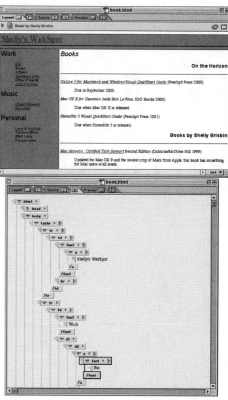

Figure 10.1 Here is a Web page in the Layout Editor (top) and the same page in the HTML Outline Editor (bottom).

Figure 10.2 Click the HTML Outline tab to view a page in HTML Outline Editor.

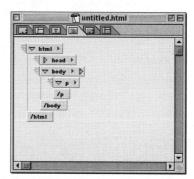

Figure 10.3 A new page as it appears in the HTML Outline Editor.

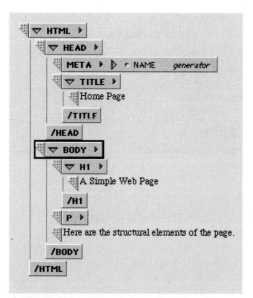

Figure 10.4 This basic outline shows structural attributes and tools you use to control the outline.

Anatomy of an outline

The outline that appears when you view a new GoLive document contains all the essential elements of an HTML page. In the HTML Outline Editor, these elements are displayed the way the HTML language expects them to be when a page is translated for viewing on the Web. The HTML tags are arranged hierarchically. Several required elements (HTML, HEAD, and BODY) lead the hierarchy and, like many tags, must also be *closed* at the end of the outline, or they will not work properly.

Boxes within the outline represent HTML tags and Web page content. Tag contents appear in subordinate (child) lines within the outline. Tag lines also contain the structural, and display attributes of HTML tags. These appear when you expand the outline. In addition to Web page text, you can view images and other objects, just as you can in the Layout Editor. **Figure 10.4** shows a basic Web page with labels indicating the components described in the next section.

Structural attributes

The HTML Outline Editor uses three structural components:

◆ **Boxes** indicate HTML tags. These outline elements' "children"—lower-level items in the hierarchy—contain both content (images and text) and attributes used to display the content properly.

◆ **Indents** indicate an item's position within the HTML hierarchy. <P> (paragraph) tags appear under and to the right of the <BODY> tag, because paragraphs are contained within the BODY element. The same goes for BODY tags themselves, which are contained within the HTML tag.

◆ **Vertical lines** between tags indicate that the tags are paired open and close tags, as in <I> and </I>.

USING THE HTML OUTLINE EDITOR

Outline Editor tools

HTML tag entries contain tools that let you manipulate the tag within the outline.

◆ **The drag-and-drop handle** moves a tag when you click and drag the handle through the outline.

◆ **The collapse/expand triangle**, when clicked, shows or hides content and settings for an HTML tag.

◆ **The show/hide attributes triangle**, to the right of an HTML tag, shows or hides attributes associated with the tag. In some cases, clicking the triangle displays a popup menu from which you can choose attributes.

◆ **The HTML tag name** is itself a tool. Command-clicking it displays a popup menu of other HTML tags that you can replace it with if you choose.

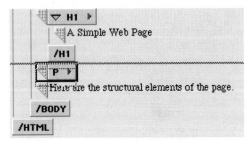

Figure 10.5 Move HTML tags with the drag and drop handle.

Editing in the HTML Outline Editor

The tools you use to add or rearrange items in the Layout Editor (the Objects palette, drag-and-drop, and the toolbar) are all available in the HTML Outline Editor.

To drag and drop within an outline:

1. In HTML Outline Editor, click and drag the drag-and-drop handle (to the left of an HTML tag) up or down. As you drag, a box outline representing the item you're moving, along with its content and attributes, moves across the screen (**Figure 10.5**). A horizontal line appears as you drag over other tags to indicate where the item will be displayed when you complete the drag.

USING THE HTML OUTLINE EDITOR

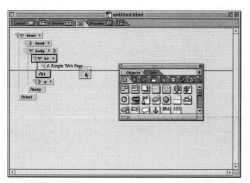

Figure 10.6 Drag an icon from the Objects palette into the HTML Outline Editor to add a new tag.

2. Release the button when you reach the location where the tag is to be placed.

3. Click the Layout Editor or Layout Preview tab to examine the change you've made.

To add tags with Objects palette tools:

1. With the HTML Outline Editor visible in the Document window, select an icon from the Basic tab or the Forms tab of the Objects palette and drag it into the Document window. A horizontal line indicates where the tag is as you move the tool through the window (**Figure 10.6**).

2. Release the mouse button when you reach the desired location for your tag. Empty tag attributes appear.

✔ Tips

■ Unlike in the Layout Editor, dragging a palette icon to the HTML Outline Editor does not display an Inspector. If you want to use the Inspector to configure a new tag, return to the Layout Editor after you add the tag and click the object. Otherwise, use the HTML tag attributes described in this chapter to configure it.

■ You can add any icon from the Basic or Forms tab to the HTML Outline Editor, with one exception: you cannot add a layout text box. The layout text box is not actually an HTML tag but a GoLive layout convention.

To add tags with the outline toolbar:

1. Click at the location in the outline where you want a new HTML tag to appear.

2. From the toolbar, choose New Element (Mac) or New Tag Item (Windows) (**Figure 10.7**). The tag appears in the HTML Outline Editor (**Figure 10.8**).

3. Command-click (Mac) or Control-click (Windows) the mouse button on the new tag to view the Tag Type popup menu (**Figure 10.9**).

4. Choose the type of tag you want from the menu. The tag appears onscreen.

5. Click and hold the mouse button on the new tag's show/hide attributes triangle to view a list of attributes that match the tag you've created (**Figure 10.10**).

6. Choose an attribute. In many cases, choosing an attribute brings up another show/hide triangle, allowing you to choose more attributes by clicking and selecting them from a menu. **Figure 10.11** shows an attribute that adds a specific image to the IMG tag.

✔ Tips

■ The outline toolbar options described in this section are also available from a context-sensitive menu. When you Control-click (Mac) or right-click (Windows) on an element in the HTML Outline Editor, you'll see a menu that allows you to add new tags, attributes, text, and comments.

■ If you are creating a tag that has lots of available attributes, such as an IMG tag, it may be easier to add the tag in the Layout Editor and use the Inspector to configure it.

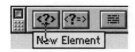

Figure 10.7 In the HTML Outline Editor on the Mac, choose New Element from the toolbar.

Figure 10.8 This is an undefined HTML tag in the HTML Outline Editor.

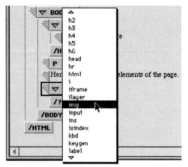

Figure 10.9 Command-click (Mac) or Control-click (Windows) to view the menu of available tag types.

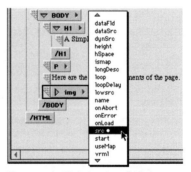

Figure 10.10 Click the show/hide attributes triangle to view tag attributes.

Figure 10.11 This IMG tag includes a SRC attribute, and a pointer that allows you to set a path to a specific image.

USING THE HTML OUTLINE EDITOR

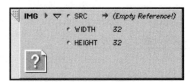

Figure 10.12 An image tag with some basic attributes configured.

Figure 10.13 Chose New Text (Mac) or New Text Item (Windows) from the toolbar.

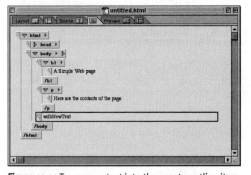

Figure 10.14 Type some text into the empty outline item.

- Using a palette icon to add a tag is also simpler than creating each attribute from scratch because the tool brings basic attributes along when you add it to an outline. **Figure 10.12** shows the result of dragging an IMG (image) icon from the Objects palette.

- On the other hand, some tags support browser-specific attributes. These are not available through the Inspector windows, but you will find them in the tag's attributes menu in the HTML Outline Editor.

To add text to an outline:

1. In the HTML Outline Editor, place the cursor where you want new text to appear.

2. From the toolbar, choose New Text (Mac) or New Text Item (Windows) (**Figure 10.13**). A text box appears (**Figure 10.14**).

3. Type the text over the highlighted place-holder text. When you preview your page, the text you typed will conform to the HTML tag surrounding it.

To add HTML comments:

1. In the HTML Outline Editor, place your cursor at a location where you would like to insert an HTML comment. A comment is a note to you or to someone else working on the Web page. It will not be visible to those who visit your Web site.

2. From the toolbar, choose New Comment (**Figure 10.15**). A blank text box appears in the outline.

3. Type your comment. HTML comments do not appear on the page when you preview it or upload it to the Web. In the Layout Editor, a comment is represented by a small icon. Within the HTML Outline and HTML Source Editors, they appear in a different color from HTML text (**Figure 10.16**).

✔ Tip

■ You can also add comments by dragging the Comment icon from the Objects palette to the HTML Outline Editor.

To add attributes to an HTML tag:

1. In the HTML Outline Editor, click an HTML tag to select it.

2. Click and hold the show/hide attributes triangle to view the popup menu containing all attributes supported by this tag (**Figure 10.17**).

3. Choose an attribute.

4. Type a number, choose a color, or make any other selections appropriate for the attribute you've chosen.

5. Repeat steps 2–4 to add more attributes.

Figure 10.15 Choose New Comment from the toolbar.

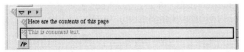

Figure 10.16 You can view HTML comments in the HTML Outline or HTML Source Editor.

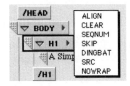

Figure 10.17 Click the show/hide attribute triangle to pick an attribute.

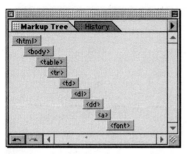

Figure 10.18 Clicking in the Document window shows the hierarchical display of the tag you select in the Markup Tree palette.

The Markup Tree

The HTML Outline Editor is an extremely useful way to look at HTML structure and hierarchy on a Web page. But what if you want to figure out where one particular tag or item fits within the hierarchy: is it within a <p> or <div> tag, or outside of it, for example? You could use the HTML Outline Editor, but one of the quickest way to check out an individual tag is with the Markup Tree palette.

The Markup Tree, which by default shares a window with the History palette, displays the hierarchy of the current page, relative to the location you've clicked within the document. If your cursor is inside a table cell, you'll see a view of the hierarchy in the Markup Tree that places the cell within the table and within whatever structure that table might be a part of, all the way up to the opening <html> tag of the page. You won't see the full hierarchy, including paragraphs or other tables, just what's relevant to the current tag.

To use the Markup Tree palette:

1. Open a GoLive document with content already in it.

2. Choose Window > Markup Tree or click the Markup Tree tab in the palette that also contains the History palette.

3. Click somewhere in the middle of the Document window.

4. Note the affect on the Markup Tree palette (**Figure 10.18**).

5. Click again, elsewhere in the document and note the change in the Markup Tree.

Using the HTML Source Editor

Although most Web page design may occur in the Layout Editor, and the HTML Outline Editor offers a convenient way to examine HTML structure, the HTML Source Editor provides an unvarnished view of the code and content that makes up a Web page. In the HTML Source Editor, there is nothing between you and the code that instructs a browser how to display your Web page.

The HTML Source Editor is a text editor, where you can see and edit all of the tags, attributes, paths, and text that form the HTML page. **Figure 10.19** shows a Web page in the HTML Source Editor. You can type directly into the HTML Source Editor, move around with the cursor, cut and paste, and drag-and-drop text. Like other GoLive Editors, the HTML Source Editor supports drag-and-drop editing and allows you to use palette icons to add tags.

To view a document in the HTML Source Editor:

1. Open a GoLive document.

2. Click the Source tab (**Figure 10.20**) to switch to the HTML Source Editor. The view changes to show the HTML code underlying the page.

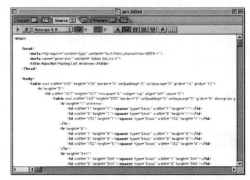

Figure 10.19 A document in the HTML Source Editor.

Figure 10.20 Switch to the HTML Source Editor by clicking the Source tab in the Document window.

```
<html>
   <head>
      <meta name="generator" content="GoLive CyberStudio (
      <title>Home Page</title>
   </head>

   <body>
      <h1>A Simple Web Page</h1>
      <p>Here are the structural elements of the page.
   </body>

</html>
```

Figure 10.21 A basic Web page in the HTML Source Editor.

Examining the HTML Source Editor

When you look at an HTML page in the HTML Source Editor, you see the same HTML tags that appear in the HTML Outline Editor. **Figure 10.21** shows a basic Web page with only two lines of text. The rest of the tags here represent the HTML hierarchy.

All text within <> brackets (and colored differently than the page's content) represent HTML tags. Most lines are indented according to the tags' placement within the HTML hierarchy. Those indents are not displayed on your Web page—they are created merely to remind you where you are on the page. You can change the way the HTML Source Editor displays HTML with Source Preferences, discussed later in this chapter.

You can type new text or tags into the HTML Source Editor, and you can format text in the HTML Source Editor using either menus or the toolbar. In addition to the standard text formatting toolbar, the HTML Source Editor includes an inline toolbar for setting Source view-specific options.

✔ Tip

■ When you type more than a line's worth of text in the HTML Source Editor, GoLive wraps to the next line, just as many word-processing applications do. But the wrap you see in the HTML Source Editor is not identical to what you see in a Web browser. If you want to control exactly where lines of text break, you should either create a
 (line break) tag at the end of each line or use the <p></p> tag pair to create a paragraph, which breaks the line at the end.

To format text using the toolbar:

1. Select some text in the HTML Source Editor (**Figure 10.22**).

2. Click the Bold button on the toolbar. Bold tags appear around the selected text (**Figure 10.23**).

✔ Tips

■ You can use all menu and toolbar formatting tools to add HTML tags to text. You can see the results when you look at a page in the Layout Editor or Layout Preview.

■ Format an entire paragraph by triple-clicking to select it. Then choose a formatting tool to add tags.

To set HTML Source Editor preferences:

1. Choose Edit > Preferences. The Preferences dialog box appears.

2. Click the Source label on the left side of the window (**Figure 10.24**).

3. In the General Source Preferences window, choose options that control the way you work with text and tabs in the HTML Source Editor, and the way they look. Choose whether tags will appear in bold, lines are indented, etc. The changes you make are reflected in the sample pane at the bottom of the Preferences window.

Figure 10.22 Select some text in the HTML Source Editor.

Figure 10.23 Choose Bold from the toolbar to add the <B> tags around the text.

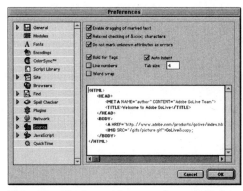

Figure 10.24 The General Source preferences window.

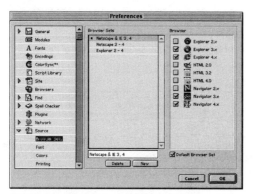

Figure 10.25 Choose a new browser set if you want to ensure that your pages conform to a particular browser's supported tags.

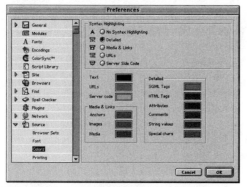

Figure 10.26 Syntax Highlighting preferences let you color text and tags in the HTML Source Editor.

Browser sets specify how the HTML Source Editor deals with tags associated with a particular browser, when checking tag syntax.

To choose browser sets:

1. Click the triangle (Mac) or plus sign (Windows) next to the Source icon, to view more Source preferences.

2. Click the Browser Sets label (**Figure 10.25**).

3. Choose a new browser if you want GoLive's syntax checker to match your tags with additional browsers.

4. When you click a browser name on the left, GoLive checks the appropriate boxes on the right.

5. You can add a browser by clicking New, naming the new browser set, and checking off HTML standards to apply.

To set font preferences for the HTML Source Editor:

1. Click the Font label under Source preferences.

2. Select a typeface, size, and style for text within the HTML Source Editor. This typeface appears within the HTML Source Editor only, not on the pages you publish on the Web. You can see how your changes will look below the font options.

To set color and printing preferences:

1. Choose the Colors item under Source preferences (**Figure 10.26**).

2. Use the "Detailed," "Media & Links," or "URLs" button to support different levels of text coloring within the HTML Source Editor. Leave "No Syntax Highlighting" selected if you don't want to see colored links, tags, or text.

continues on next page

USING THE HTML SOURCE EDITOR

3. To highlight code in your page that runs on the Web server, click "Server Side Code."

4. If you want to change the displayed colors of tags or text, use the Color palette to apply a new color to each type of text, tag, or attribute.

5. If you intend to print your HTML Source Editor pages, click Printing under the Source label on the left side of the Preferences window.

6. Click Printer Specific Settings to activate options in this window.

7. Choose syntax highlighting and/or fonts for printing if you would like to use fonts different from those you use to display the page onscreen.

The HTML Source Editor toolbar

In addition to the inline formatting toolbar that occupies its own window above your GoLive documents, the HTML Source Editor includes a context-sensitive toolbar, designed to help you find and fix problems. The toolbar (**Figure 10.27**) works with the preferences you set in the previous section to give you quick access to syntax highlighting and error-checking options.

To check HTML syntax:

1. With a document open in the HTML Source Editor, click the Check Syntax button (**Figure 10.28**) on the HTML Source Editor toolbar. GoLive opens a pane above the HTML code, displaying any syntax errors (**Figure 10.29**). The pane won't open if there are no errors on the page.

2. Click an error message to see the problem highlighted in the document.

3. Fix or delete the tag in question, and the error message disappears.

Figure 10.27 The HTML Source Editor toolbar provides access to syntax highlighting options.

Figure 10.28 Click the Check Syntax button on the HTML Source Editor toolbar to check for tagging errors in your document.

Figure 10.29 Syntax errors found in the HTML Source Editor look like this and appear in a pane above your HTML document.

Figure 10.30 Choose the level of syntax highlighting you wish to see in the HTML Source Editor by toggling these toolbar buttons.

Figure 10.31 Choose browser sets from the popup menu on the HTML Source Editor toolbar.

✔ Tips

- You've already seen that you can set syntax highlighting levels in the Preferences window. You can also change them from the HTML Source Editor toolbar. The buttons shown in **Figure 10.30** allow you to turn highlighting off and specify whether you'd like to see detailed highlights, media and links, or just URLs.

- When you instruct GoLive to check HTML syntax, it does so according to the current browser set. As I explained earlier, you can use a browser set to ensure that the tags you use comply with the specs for one or more browsers. To select a new browser set, simply choose it from the popup menu on the HTML Source Editor toolbar (**Figure 10.31**).

Using the Source Code Window and Layout Editor Together

If you don't relish the idea of having to switch between the Layout Editor's graphical representation of your page and the HTML Source Editor, there is a way to have your code and graphics, too.

The Source Code window, which can be open while you're in the Layout Editor, presents a live look at the underlying HTML code as you create it. Each time you complete a Layout Editor action, like dragging a palette tool or adding some text, the Source Code window's contents update to reflect your action, and the window scrolls to the code you're adding or editing in the Layout Editor.

To use the Source Code window:

1. With a document open in the Layout Editor, choose Window > Source Code. The Source Code window appears, containing the page you're working on (**Figure 10.32**).

2. Resize and arrange the window so that you can see both it and the Document window.

3. Make changes in the Document window and watch the corresponding changes in the Source Code window.

✔ Tip

■ You can edit HTML or content in the Source Code window. To see your changes in the Document window, click the window.

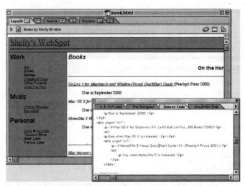

Figure 10.32 Position the Source Code view so that you can see it and the Document window on your screen.

Head Elements

HTML pages have two main parts: the body (signified by enclosing <BODY> and </BODY> tags), and the head (signified by <HEAD> and </HEAD> tags). All the text and graphics that make up the page appear between body tags and can be edited in GoLive's Layout Editor. Head tags, although they usually don't contain visible page elements, can store lots of information about the page that visitors to your site can use when searching for your site. More importantly, head tags offer a means of controlling the display and other properties of Web pages. Head tags can vary the behavior of a page based on the user's browser, for example. Many head tags also contain scripts that execute when the page is loaded.

The most basic head tag is the <TITLE> tag, which specifies the name of your page (for use in a Web browser's bookmarks list). You fill in the title tag when you replace the words "Welcome to GoLive" at the top of the Document window with your title.

Other head tags are optional and must be entered in the Layout, HTML Source, or HTML Outline Editor. In this section, I describe head tags available from the GoLive Objects palette, and explain how to add and configure them.

Adding head tags

Like other HTML elements, head tags can be added to a Web page from the Objects palette. There's a tab just full of them, called the Head tab (**Figure 10.33**). To add head tags this way, you must drag a palette icon to the Head section in the Layout Editor. You can easily configure each tag's attributes and content within an Inspector window specific to that tag. If you prefer, and if you are familiar with HTML, you can use the HTML Outline or HTML Source Editor for editing, but—unless you prefer to type raw HTML—you'll want to create the head tags in the Layout Editor and use the Inspector to set them up.

✔ Tip

■ Don't confuse *head* (which appear within the <HEAD> and </HEAD> tags, above the Web page's body) with *headings,* which use <H1>, <H2>, and so forth. Headings format text within the page, and appear between the <BODY> and </BODY> tags. GoLive makes this HTML distinction a bit of a challenge by referring in the tool- bar to headings as headers—but they really are headings.

To add a head tag to a Web page:

1. Open a new or existing GoLive document in the Layout Editor.

2. Click the small triangle in the title bar of the Document window (**Figure 10.34**). The Head section opens (**Figure 10.35**).

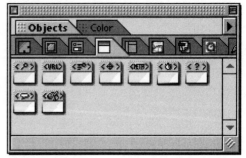

Figure 10.33 The Objects palette's Head tab contains a tool for each kind of head tag.

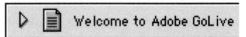

Figure 10.34 Click the triangle next to the page title to open the Head section.

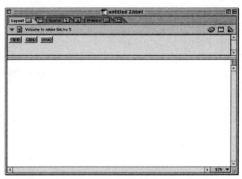

Figure 10.35 The Head section appears at the top of the Document window.

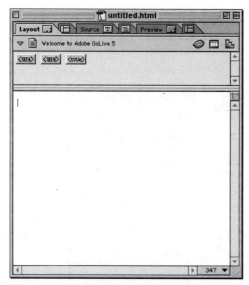

Figure 10.36 When you open the Head section of a new GoLive document, you will find three head tags there. The two meta tag icons look alike. When you click on one, you can see the difference between them in the Inspector.

3. Drag an icon from the Head tab of the Objects palette into the Head section of the Document window.

4. Click the new tag to display its Inspector.

✔ **Tip**

■ You can add a head element by double-clicking the palette icon if the Head section of the page is open.

Default head tags

When you open a new GoLive document, it contains three head tags. These icons are visible when you open the Head section in the Document window (**Figure 10.36**).

◆ **meta http equiv** indicates the character set used on the page. By default, the character set is text/html;charset=ISO-8859-1.

◆ **meta name** identifies the application that created the Web page. In this case, that's GoLive.

◆ **title** indicates the title of the page. The title is the name that appears at the top of a browser window, on a list of bookmarks, and in the bar just above the Head section in GoLive.

You can change the values in any of these head tags by selecting the tag in the Head section and configuring the tag in the Inspector.

Base

The Base head item allows you to specify a base URL for Web pages within your site, making it possible for you to use relative URLs within the site. You can use a Base head tag to specify the root—the base—URL from which all other navigation flows. However, you don't have to use a Base head to do this. Most Web servers will correctly resolve relative URLs when the linked files are stored within the same site.

To set up a Base tag:

1. Using the Base palette icon, add a Base tag to the Head section (**Figure 10.37**).

2. Click the Base item to display the Base Inspector (**Figure 10.38**).

3. Click Browse or use Point & Shoot to locate a base document.

4. Choose "Write Base always absolute" to use an absolute, rather than a relative path, to locate the base document.

Keywords

The Keywords element allows you to insert keywords into your document that Web crawlers and search engines can use to categorize and add your page to their databases.

To set up a Keywords tag:

1. With the Keywords palette icon, add a Keywords item (**Figure 10.39**) to the Head section of a document.

2. Click to display the Keywords Inspector (**Figure 10.40**).

3. Click in the keyword field near the bottom of the Keywords Inspector.

4. Type a keyword and press Add. The keyword appears in the upper field.

5. Repeat for each keyword you want to add.

Figure 10.37 The Base palette icon and head tag.

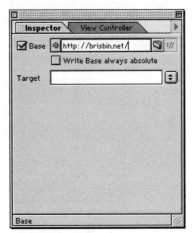

Figure 10.38 The Base Inspector.

Figure 10.39 The Keywords palette icon and tag.

Figure 10.40 The Keywords Inspector.

Figure 10.41 Select a keyword and click an arrow to move the keyword up or down the list.

Figure 10.42 The Link palette icon and tag.

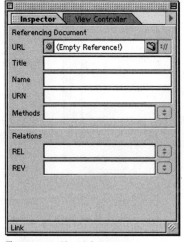

Figure 10.43 The Link Inspector.

✔ Tips

- Here's another way to add a keyword. Within a GoLive document, select a word or phrase you would like to use as a keyword and choose Special >Add to Keywords. GoLive creates a keyword element (if one doesn't already exist) and adds your keyword. You can verify that the new keyword has been added by selecting the element in the Head section area and having a look at the Inspector.

- To change the order in which keywords appear in the list, select a keyword and click the up or down arrow near the bottom of the Inspector (**Figure 10.41**) to move it.

- To delete a keyword, activate the Inspector, click the keyword you want to remove, and click Delete.

Link

The Link head tag adds a link between one page and others within your site.

To set up a Link tag:

1. Using the Link palette icon, add a Link element (**Figure 10.42**) to the Head section.

2. Click to display the Link Inspector (**Figure 10.43**).

3. Type, browse, or Point & Shoot to a URL you want to link to this page.

4. Enter the related page's title in the Title field if you like.

5. If you're linking to an anchor, type it in the Name field.

6. Leave the URN and Methods fields blank unless you use these attributes. Most Web authors don't.

continues on next page

HEAD ELEMENTS

7. In the REL field, type the relationship of your page to the linked page that follows, e.g., if the page you're working on is a subsidiary of the page to which you're linking.

8. Type the reverse relationship in the REV field.

Meta

Meta tags provide a variety of ways to supply information about the document to Web page visitors. By default, GoLive includes the meta information for file format, character set, and file creator in documents you create. You can also add other meta heads, or even alter those created by default.

To set up a Meta tag:

1. Using the Meta icon, add a Meta tag (**Figure 10.44**) to the Head section of a GoLive document.

2. Click to display the Meta Inspector (**Figure 10.45**).

3. Choose HTTP Equivalent or Name from the popup menu. HTTP Equivalent attributes are used to simulate the page's head information when it is sent by the server to the browser. A Name attribute specifies the name of the meta information.

4. Type a name for the HTTP Equivalent or for the Name attribute you want to enter.

5. In the Content field, type the meta tag content that you want sent from the server to the browser.

 Figure 10.44 The Meta tag icon and its associated tag.

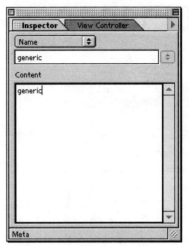

Figure 10.45 The Meta Inspector.

Figure 10.46 The Refresh icon and element.

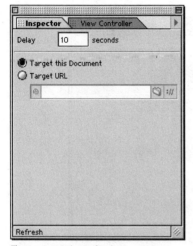

Figure 10.47 The Refresh Inspector.

Refresh

The Refresh element updates a Web page at intervals you set. This head tag is useful when you're creating pages with elements that change frequently (news items that are removed or updated regularly, for example), and want them to reload without user intervention.

To set up a Refresh tag:

1. Using the Refresh icon, add a Refresh element (**Figure 10.46**) to the Head section of a GoLive document.

2. Click the element in the Head section to display the Refresh Inspector (**Figure 10.47**).

3. Choose the Delay interval in seconds.

4. Click the Target this Document button to apply the refresh rate to the page you're working with. Otherwise, you can choose Target URL if you want the browser to replace your page with a new page. This is useful if you want to redirect users to a new URL when they type an outdated one into their browser. If you choose Target URL, use the Browse button or Point & Shoot to locate a URL.

IsIndex

The IsIndex element adds a search field to the Web page, allowing visitors to search a site by entering a text query. In most cases, it's more desirable to use a form (see Chapter 8, "Working with Forms") as an interface for site searching. Whether you use a form or IsIndex element, you will need to connect the page to a CGI application, which actually performs the search. The IsIndex element is obsolete ("deprecated") in the HTML 4 and XHTML standards—you can achieve the same results much more easily with a form—but in the interest of completeness, here's how to configure it.

Figure 10.48 The IsIndex icon and tag.

To set up an IsIndex tag:

1. Using the IsIndex icon, add an IsIndex element (**Figure 10.48**) to the Head section.

2. Click to display the Isindex Inspector (**Figure 10.49**).

3. In the Prompt field, type the text you want to appear adjacent to the search field.

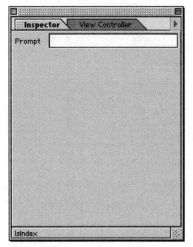

Figure 10.49 The IsIndex Inspector.

✔ Tip

■ When you are ready to upload this Web page to your server, you need to connect the IsIndex tag to a CGI application. To do this, switch to the HTML Outline Editor and locate the IsIndex tag. Click the collapse/expand triangle. In the ACTION attribute, click the arrow (**Figure 10.50**) and choose a CGI file or type the URL in the dialog box.

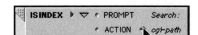

Figure 10.50 In the HTML Outline Editor, configure the IsIndex tag's ACTION attribute to connect to a server CGI.

Figure 10.51 The Tag icon and tag.

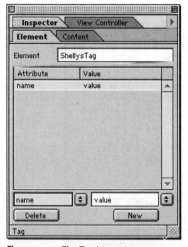

Figure 10.52 The Tag Inspector.

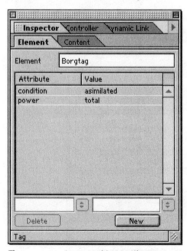

Figure 10.53 A tag and its attributes appear in the Tab Inspector.

Adding unknown tags to the Head section

As the HTML standard develops, new tags become available to Web developers. You can add a head tag that is currently unknown to GoLive (whether it's one you've made up, or a new one from the W3C) with the Tag icon found in the Head tab of the palette.

To set up an unknown tag:

1. Using the Tag icon, add the Tag element (**Figure 10.51**) to the Head section.

2. Click to display the Tag Inspector.

3. Type a name for your new tag in the Element field.

4. Click New to add an attribute to the new tag. The new attribute box is selected when you click (**Figure 10.52**).

5. Type a name for the attribute.

6. Type a value for the attribute.

7. Repeat steps 4–6 to add additional attributes. **Figure 10.53** shows a new tag with several attributes.

✔ Tip

■ Along with the Comment icon, discussed in the next section, the Tag icon is the only one you can add to both the Head and Body sections of a document. When you double-click either one, it appears in the Head section.

HEAD ELEMENTS

Comment

Comment tags add a non-displaying comment to your Web page head.

To set up a Comment tag:

1. Using the Comment icon, add the Comment element to the Head section (**Figure 10.54**).

2. Click to display the Comment Inspector (**Figure 10.55**).

3. Type the comment in the Inspector.

Script

The Script element adds JavaScript to the head, allowing the script to execute when a visitor opens a Web page.

To set up a Script tag:

1. Using the Script icon, add the Script element (**Figure 10.56**) to the Head section.

2. Click to display the Head Script Inspector (**Figure 10.57**).

3. Type a name for the script.

4. Choose a browser version from the Language popup menu. The JavaScript dialect appears in the lower portion of the Inspector window.

5. Click the checkbox next to the Source field to activate the field, then locate a script with the Browse button or Point & Shoot.

6. To edit or create a script, click Edit. The JavaScript interface appears. (For details on creating and editing JavaScript, see Chapter 17, "Using Actions.")

Figure 10.54 The Comment icon and head tag.

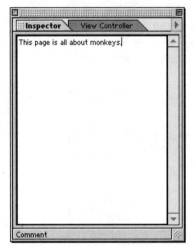

Figure 10.55 The Comment Inspector.

Figure 10.56 The Script icon and head tag.

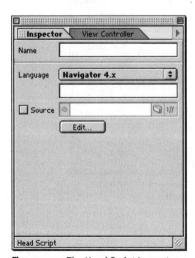

Figure 10.57 The Head Script Inspector.

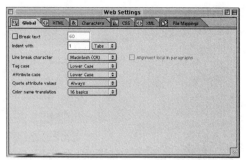

Figure 10.58 The Global tab lets you customize the look of HTML in the HTML Source Editor, among other things.

Web Settings

All of the tags, characters, and styles GoLive provides for constructing your Web pages are stored in a database called Web Settings. When you work with tags, GoLive uses Web Settings to specify these tags and their attributes. The software's syntax- and error-checking tools depend on the database to check the validity of tags entered or edited by hand in the HTML Source Editor. You can use Web Settings to look up tags and attributes and to add new ones. As HTML evolves, new tags and attributes are likely to come into common use. With Web Settings, you can keep GoLive up-to-date.

Like many other GoLive tools, Web Settings appears as a tabbed window. The Web Settings window contents are available under six tabs. They are Global, HTML, Characters, CSS, XML, and File Mappings.

To open Web Settings:

◆ Choose Edit > Web Settings. The Web Settings dialog box appears (**Figure 10.58**).

Global settings

The Web Settings Global tab (**Figure 10.58**) is really an extension of the HTML Source Editor preferences you set earlier in this chapter. Like those options, the global items in Web Settings allow you to customize the look and behavior of your HTML code. Here, you can choose text wrap, indent, and line break options, as well as case and color naming preferences.

The HTML tab

The HTML tab (**Figure 10.59**) is the heart of the Web Settings window, because it contains all of the tags that GoLive (and those of the current HTML standard) recognizes and uses. By default, tags are grouped together under logical headings. Each tag listing includes a short description that explains the tag further. Clicking on a tag displays a related Inspector.

To locate a tag:

1. In the Web Settings window, click the HTML tab (**Figure 10.59**).

2. Locate a tag category, such as Table. Scroll through the tag categories if necessary. Categories contain individual tags, which in turn contain attributes.

3. Click the triangle to open the tag category, revealing individual tags, attributes, and/or values.

4. Click the desired tag. A Web Settings Element Inspector, complete with information specific to the tag you selected, appears (**Figure 10.60**).

5. Note the Inspector settings for the tag you're working with. The settings tell you what the tag is (Tag Name, Comment) how the tag appears (Structure), the amount of space used to format a tag (Content), and whether or not it needs an End tag to complete it.

6. Click the Output tab in the Inspector to set how much space will appear before and after the tag in the source code (**Figure 10.61**).

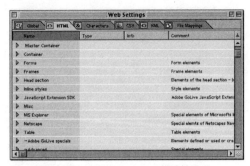

Figure 10.59 The HTML tab of the Web Settings window displays categories that contain individual HTML tags and their attributes.

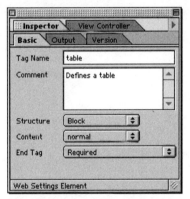

Figure 10.60 Selecting a tag in the Web Settings window brings up a corresponding Inspector window.

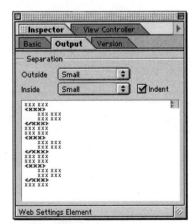

Figure 10.61 Look at the structure of a tag in the Output tab of the Web Settings Element Inspector.

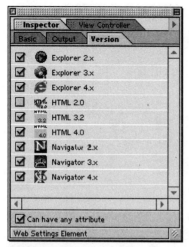

Figure 10.62 Click the Inspector's Version tab to see which HTML version and browsers support it.

7. Click the Version tab. GoLive displays a list of browsers that support the tag (checked) (**Figure 10.62**).

8. If you chose a tag with a triangle next to its name in the Web Settings window (the table caption tag is a good example), expand the tag to display the tag's attributes and/or values. These are the same attributes you can edit in the Inspector when you add a tag to your Web page.

9. Keep clicking to expand the tag and its attributes fully.

✔ Tip

■ Take a look at the various options in the Inspector. Though the Structure, Content, and End Tag popups can be edited, for example, it's almost always a bad idea to change the default options of existing tags. Web Settings stores tags and their configurations according to HTML standards, and altering a tag could cause serious problems if you're not sure you know what you're doing.

To add a new tag to the database:

1. With the HTML tab showing, click once on a category label (one of the headings in the window) into which your new tag would logically fit, based on its relationship to existing HTML elements.

2. Control-click (Mac) or right-click (Windows). From the context-sensitive menu that appears, choose Add Element. A new tag label appears in the Web Settings window, and the Web Settings Element Inspector opens.

3. Name the tag in the Inspector. Use the actual text of the tag as it will appear in your HTML code.

continues on next page

WEB SETTINGS

4. Describe your new tag in the Comment field.

5. Configure the tag by choosing Structure and Content parameters from the popup menus in the Basic tab.

6. In the Output tab, make choices about the amount of space surrounding the tag.

7. Finally, in the Version tab, assign the tag to browsers that support it.

✔ Tip

■ Adding a browser or HTML standard in the Version tab doesn't mean that your new tag will be supported by that version of HTML. It's just a reference. Before you use Web Settings to add new tags to your pages, check an HTML reference book or Web site for detailed information about new tags, their attributes, and which browsers support them.

Tag attributes

You can add attributes to existing tags or to those you've created. Attributes allow a Web author to configure features of a tag, such as its alignment, value, font, and so on.

To add an attribute:

1. With the HTML tab active in the Web Settings window, select a tag.

2. Control-click (Mac) or right-click (Windows) and choose New Attribute from the menu. The Web Settings Attribute Inspector appears. Like the Web Settings Element Inspector, the Web Settings Attribute Inspector provides fields for naming and describing the attribute (**Figure 10.63**).

You can also choose a default condition for the attributes tag when the attribute is not specified. For instance, if you add an alignment attribute, you might choose to make the default alignment left.

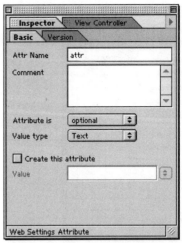

Figure 10.63 Create or edit new tag attributes in the Web Settings Attribute Inspector. You don't type attribute values here, but instead name and set options for a tag attribute.

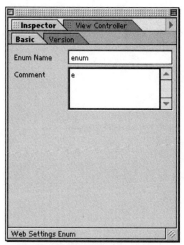

Figure 10.64 Configure a new enumeration in the Web Settings Enum Inspector.

3. Use the Attribute is popup menu to tell the database whether or not the attribute is optional or required.

4. Choose a value from the Value type popup menu.

5. Click the Version tab to identify browsers and HTML versions that support the attribute.

Enumerations

Some tag attributes include a fixed set of options. An alignment attribute, for example, includes options to align the attribute to the left, right, or center. This group of options is called an *enumeration*.

To add an enumeration:

1. In the HTML tab of the Web Settings window, click an attribute belonging to an HTML tag. The attribute you choose must have an Enum. Value type. You'll see a value in the Enum column in the Web Settings window.

2. Control-click (Mac) or right-click (Windows) on the attribute and choose Add Enum from the menu. The Web Settings Enum Inspector appears (**Figure 10.64**).

3. Type a name for the enumeration in the Enum Name field.

4. In the Version tab, choose an HTML version supported by the tag of which the enumeration is an element.

The Characters tab

While the HTML language displays alphanumeric characters just as they are typed, a number of non-alphanumeric characters require that you surround them with HTML tags. To display a special character, you must surround it with an ampersand (&) and a semicolon (;) like this:

`<H1>M&ouml;ntag</H1>`

uml indicates that the accented o in *Montag* should have an umlaut over it.

The Characters tab of the Web Settings window stores the HTML name of the character, a description of the character, and the code needed to generate it on a Web page.

Special characters are displayed under the Characters tab in three sections:

- **Basics** includes punctuation marks, such as quotation marks, colons, etc.

- **Characters** includes accented letters and other characters that are not part of the ASCII character set.

- **General Punctuation** includes dashes and spaces.

Basics characters include the ampersand, the greater than sign, and the quotation mark. Most alphanumeric characters (many of them with accent marks used in languages other than English) are stored under the Characters section, while the General Punctuation section includes several: en dashes, em dashes, and a non-breaking space character.

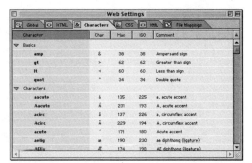

Figure 10.65 You can add or modify codes associated with alphanumeric characters in the Characters tab of the Web Settings window.

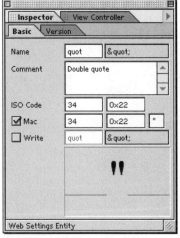

Figure 10.66 Configure a character in the Web Settings Entity Inspector.

To view a character:

1. In the Web Settings window, click the Characters tab (**Figure 10.65**).

2. Locate the quot entity under the Basics section and click it. The Inspector now displays the Web Settings Entity Inspector (**Figure 10.66**).

The Inspector displays the name, code, and description of the character. In addition, you'll find the ISO and byte codes (the byte code is to the right of the labeled ISO code) that identify the character within the HTML standard, and the Mac code that identifies the character to the Mac OS, if it is specific to the Mac. (The Mac code option is available in both Macintosh and Windows versions of GoLive). The Write option (unchecked in this example) can write the contents of the adjacent text box to the HTML code, instead of adding the name of the special character being defined. Finally, the lower pane of the Inspector shows how the character looks when displayed in a browser.

To add a new character:

1. Decide within which section of the Web Settings window your new character best fits and click the section heading.

2. Control-click (Mac) or right-click (Windows) on the heading you've chosen and choose New Entity from the menu.

3. Give the character a name; the HTML code will be filled in automatically.

4. Type a descriptive name for the character.

continues on next page

WEB SETTINGS

5. Determine the correct ISO code, byte code, and (if applicable) Mac code for the character. Be sure you have this information before creating a new character. Without it, your character will not appear correctly in Web browsers.

6. Click the Version tab to specify HTML versions and browsers that support the character.

✔ Tips

■ Like HTML tags, characters you add in the Web Settings window will not necessarily be supported. The character must have an ISO code and byte code, and browsers must support it.

■ You can edit special characters, but changing an existing character's codes will make it inoperable, and may cause errors in your Web page.

The CSS tab

The CSS tab of the Web Settings window aids you in displaying Cascading Style Sheet content in GoLive. It isn't intended to provide an editable style sheet. With the CSS tab, you can select style sheet display methods that correspond to several popular Web browsers. GoLive uses the default style sheet you select to preview style sheet content in the View Controller. When you use the View Controller to preview style sheet content, GoLive will approximate the fonts, text properties, and positioning of your pages. Changing the default style sheet in the CSS tab allows you to see how styled content will look in various browsers.

The CSS tab also includes a few options that control how style sheets are created.

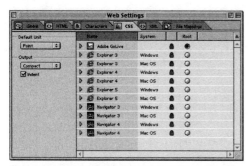

Figure 10.67 The CSS tab of the Web Settings window is where you can choose the default style sheet set you want to use.

To set style sheet options:

1. Click the CSS tab (**Figure 10.67**).

2. Choose a default unit of measure from the popup menu. This unit will apply to all style sheets applied in GoLive, unless you choose to override the default in a specific case.

3. Choose an Output option to control how the style sheet code appears in the HTML Source Editor. By default, the code display is compact; the successive menu options display the CSS code in the HTML Source Editor with more white space between words and lines.

4. Leave the Indent checkbox alone if you want the style sheet code to be indented from the left margin.

To choose a default style sheet:

1. In the CSS tab, choose a browser from the list in the right side of the Style Sheet tab, and click its heading. The CSS Style Sheet Inspector displays details about the browser, its platform, and the screen resolution it uses.

2. Click the Source tab to see the style sheets supported by the browser. You can view the style sheets individually in the Web Settings window by expanding the heading.

3. In the CSS tab, click the Root button to select the current browser as the default style sheet.

The XML tab

GoLive recognizes and reads XML (Extensible Markup Language), the simplified dialect of the SGML language, which is also the parent of the HTML language. XML can be used to structure information on the Web. The XML tab of the Web Settings window (**Figure 10.68**) displays the XML structures supported by GoLive.

In the current version of GoLive, you can view XML tags and their attributes, but you can't add your own XML tags.

The File Mappings tab

GoLive uses information stored in the File Mappings tab to open files that were created by applications other than GoLive. When you double-click an image or media file in the Document or Site window, GoLive opens it in the application that created it. The File Mappings tab (**Figure 10.69**) includes a large number of file types, but you can add new ones or change the configuration of existing ones.

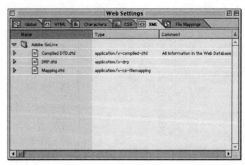

Figure 10.68 The XML tab in the Web Settings window.

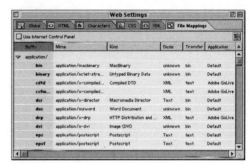

Figure 10.69 The File Mappings tab.

WORKING WITH STYLE SHEETS

You can do a variety of things with basic HTML tags; you can arrange objects and format text, but you can't position text precisely, and you can't always format it exactly as you need to. If you're used to using style sheets in word processing and desktop publishing tools, HTML's limitations can be frustrating.

Adobe GoLive includes support for Cascading Style Sheets Level 1 (CSS1), a method of separating formatting instructions from structure and content. You can use GoLive's familiar tools and Inspectors to avoid most of the coding normally associated with creating style sheets.

In this chapter, I cover:

- How style sheets work

- Types of style sheets

- Creating style sheets

- Selectors

- Adding properties

- Cascading and inheritance

- Applying style sheets

How Style Sheets Work

Cascading style sheets consist of instructions, known as *rules*, on how to format text in a document. Style sheets contain individual styles that specify formatting that can redefine an HTML tag throughout a page, or they can alter a passage or block of text. There are lots of variations, which I describe throughout this chapter.

Like other HTML pages and tags, style sheets require certain syntax to work, and that syntax varies depending on the way the style sheet is intended to work with your document. Similarly, individual styles use syntax to tell a Web browser how to interpret it, and what changes to make in text display and position.

What style sheets are good for

Style sheets allow you to create and save sets of formatting instructions for blocks of text within your Web pages. You can use these rules to globally apply consistent formatting to pages and blocks of text, without having to recreate complex tags or run the risk that you might apply them inconsistently throughout your site. Once rules have been established, you can quickly apply styles with simplified tags that represent the formatting you have built. This makes it easier to establish a consistent design for your pages and to apply it quickly throughout your site without having to remember the parameters you need.

Most importantly, style sheets provide some capabilities that have, up to now, been unavailable to Web authors. You can use them to specify the precise position of text on the page and to set measurements for margins and vertical and horizontal spacing, though not all browsers support style sheet-based positioning fully.

Style sheet syntax

It's easiest to think of style sheets and their components as a hierarchy. Style sheets can either be contained in a style sheet document to which pages refer, or contained in code that is embedded in the head section and/or body of a Web page. Each style sheet contains styles, also known as style rules, that specify formatting. Each style is defined by its *selectors, properties,* and *values.*

A selector describes how the style interacts with the documents to which you apply it. Properties identify the type, display, or positioning elements that you want to format with the style. Finally, each property supports *values* that specify the way the element will appear, including relevant measurements.

Style syntax looks like this:

```
Selector {property:value;}
```

As you'll see later in this chapter, there are several types of style sheet selectors. In the following example, the selector is an HTML tag, <H1>, which creates a large heading.

```
H1 {font-family:palatino;}
```

A single style may have multiple attributes, as follows:

```
H1 {font-family:palatino;
    font-size:36pt;}
```

Of course, GoLive doesn't require you to type style sheet information. You generate it using the tools I describe in the "Creating Style Sheets" section of this chapter.

Using CSS1 correctly

Cascading Style Sheets is part of the HTML
4.0 specification, approved by the World
Wide Web Consortium (W3C), the organization that attempts to create and enforce
Web standards. In order for a Web browser
to recognize and interpret style sheets properly, it must support the CSS1 language.
Even within CSS1, there are a few style elements that version 4.0 browsers either don't
support at all, or only support incompletely.
This is because both Netscape and Microsoft
have incomplete implementations of CSS1.
As I proceed through this chapter, I'll note
these inconsistencies, so that you can plan for
them when constructing your own style sheets.
You can learn more about the W3C's official
CSS1 guidelines at http://www.w3.org/
TR/REC-CSS1.

Types of Style Sheets

All types of style sheets support the same content-formatting options (properties) and most of the same style rules (selectors), but they differ in the way they connect to Web pages. *Internal* style sheets format the content of a single HTML document, whereas *external* style sheets can be used to change the appearance of a group of documents. Within each category are two methods for applying style sheets and styles to text.

Internal style sheets

There are two types of internal style sheets: *embedded* and *inline*. Each is actually within the HTML page it supports. An embedded style sheet is included in the document's Head section. Embedded style sheets apply formatting or positioning properties to all occurrences of an HTML tag within the document. They are contained within the <STYLE></STYLE> tag and use the syntax described above to specify individual styles.

Inline style sheets are included in the body of an HTML document, and apply styles to specific tags only. In other words, if you create an inline style to change the color of an <H2> tag to blue, the style rule would appear next to the heading you want to change (in GoLive's HTML Source Editor or HTML Outline Editor), and would apply only to that instance of the heading. To make all <H2> headings in a document blue, you would need to add an embedded style rule to the Head section of the document.

Inline style sheets use class attributes to apply formatting to the location of the HTML tag whose appearance you want to change.

External style sheets

You can use external style sheets to apply styles to one or more documents—your whole Web site, for example. External style sheets can be *linked* and *imported*.

Linked style sheets (using the <LINK> tag in a document in which you want the style to appear) are the easiest to understand. All styles for a site can be stored in a single style sheet document that you link to each HTML document to which the styles should be applied.

Imported style sheets, like linked ones, are contained in style sheet documents that you link to an HTML document in which you want to use the styles in the import document. Within the HTML document, you add import instructions to the <STYLE> tag, with a link to the document containing styles. An advantage of imported styles is that, unlike linked styles, you can import a style or styles that can, in turn, import more styles. Imported styles are only supported by Internet Explorer at this writing.

✔ Tip

- GoLive supports imported style sheets, in that it can display them in the style sheet window and preview their results correctly, but you can't use GoLive tools to edit an imported style sheet. To change an imported style sheet, you need to edit it in a text editor before importing it.

TYPES OF STYLE SHEETS

Figure 11.1 Click the Style Sheet button to open the Style Sheet window.

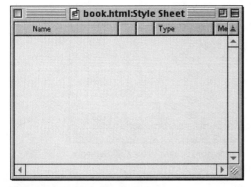

Figure 11.2 The Style Sheet window.

Figure 11.3 Choose New Class Selector from the toolbar to add a class selector to a style sheet.

Creating Style Sheets

In GoLive 5, there are two ways to create a style sheet, and two ways each to apply internal and external ones. In this section, I'll describe how to generate both style sheets and rules. In the "Using Style Sheets" section, I'll explain how to connect internal and external style sheets to HTML documents. Also, later in this chapter, I'll show you how to configure each style sheet property that specifies the appearance or position of items controlled by the style sheet.

To create an internal style sheet:

1. With a document open, click the Style Sheet button located above the Document window, at the right edge of the title bar (**Figure 11.1**). A new Style Sheet window appears (**Figure 11.2**).

2. After setting up styles, choose File > Save. Leave the style sheet's name as GoLive created it. The name refers to the document the style sheet supports.

To add a style to a style sheet:

1. With the style sheet file open (the Style Sheet window should be visible), choose New Class Selector from the toolbar (**Figure 11.3**).

   or

   Control-click (Mac) or right-click (Windows) within the Style Sheet window. Choose Add Class Selector from the menu. A new folder called Internal appears in the Style Sheet window, with a style called *.class* within the folder, under the appropriate heading. You could also have chosen New Tag, or New ID, to create these kinds of style selectors. You'll learn more about selectors in the next section.

   continues on next page

CREATING STYLE SHEETS

2. To begin configuring the style, click the *.class* item to activate the CSS Selector Inspector (**Figure 11.4**).

3. Name the style. Do not use spaces or underscores in the style name.

4. Click the other tabs in the CSS Selector Inspector to configure the style's properties. I'll walk you through configuring each property in the "Adding Properties" section of this chapter.

5. Once you've configured one or two properties, click the Basics (Pencil) tab (where you named the style) in the Inspector. Notice that your properties appear in the pane below the name of your style (**Figure 11.5**).

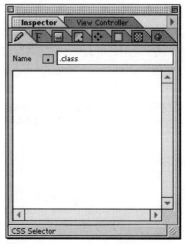

Figure 11.4 The tabs in the CSS Selector Inspector allow you to configure styles.

To create an external style sheet:

1. Choose File > New Special > Stylesheet Document. An untitled style sheet window opens.

2. Add styles to the style sheet as described in the previous section, and configure style properties.

3. Save the style sheet to the folder containing your site's Web pages. Notice that the sheet's default name contains the suffix .css. When you rename the sheet, be careful to retain the .css suffix so that the style sheet can be recognized by your visitors' Web browsers.

Figure 11.5 Once you have configured a style, its properties appear in the Inspector.

Figure 11.6 Choose New Element Selector from the toolbar to add a tag selector.

Selectors

Style sheet selectors tell the style sheet how an individual style relates to the style sheet and the documents it supports. GoLive recognizes three types of style sheet selectors.

◆ Tags

◆ Classes

◆ IDs

Tag selectors

Tag selectors allow you to apply style rules to any HTML tag within a document. Applying a tag selector tells GoLive (and the browser a visitor uses to view your page) to "style" all occurrences of the tag according to style properties you specify. You can use tag selectors with all four types of internal and external CSS1 style sheets.

To apply a style to a tag selector:

1. Open a new or existing style sheet document, along with a document to which you want to define a tag selector. Type some text in the document and format the text as a level one heading.

2. With the style sheet document at the front, choose New Element Selector from the toolbar (**Figure 11.6**).

   or

   Control-click (Mac) or right-click (Windows) and choose Add Element Selector from the menu. The new tag appears in the Style Sheet window.

3. In the CSS Selector Inspector, type H1. Do not include the usual < and > brackets.

4. Configure the new style's properties under the property tabs of the Inspector. Notice that the text in your document changes as you specify style options.

✔ **Tip**

■ Previous versions of GoLive and the user's guide for the current version refer to tag selectors as just that. In GoLive 5, tag selectors are chosen with commands that refer to "element selectors." We're not sure if the problem is language (GoLive is developed in Germany) or typographical, but elements and tags are the same when it comes to style sheets using GoLive.

Class selectors

Unlike tags, class selectors apply style formatting to specific text blocks, rather than to all occurrences of a particular HTML tag.

To create a class selector:

1. With a style sheet window open, choose Add Class Selector from the toolbar or from the context-sensitive menu (**Figure 11.7**).

2. In the CSS Selector Inspector, name the class. You can use any name you like, because classes don't depend on or expect to see an HTML tag as the identifier within the style sheet code.

3. Configure the class style with the property tabs of the Inspector.

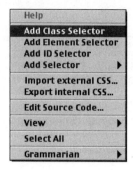

Figure 11.7 Add a class by choosing Add Class Selector from the context-sensitive menu. You reach the menu by Control-clicking (Mac) or right-clicking (Windows) within a style sheet window.

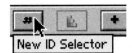

Figure 11.8 Choose New ID Selector from the toolbar to add an ID selector.

ID selectors

ID selectors apply a chosen style to a single text block or element. ID selectors can be used only once within an HTML document.

To create an ID selector:

1. With a style sheet window open, choose New ID Selector from the toolbar (**Figure 11.8**).

   or

   Choose Add ID Selector from the context-sensitive menu.

2. In the CSS Selector Inspector, name the ID. You can use any name you like, but it must be preceded by a pound sign (#).

3. Configure the ID style with the property tabs of the Inspector.

SELECTORS

Adding Properties

Throughout this chapter, I've referred to style sheet *properties*. Properties are the specific formatting elements you use to change the appearance or position of text with style sheets. All style sheet types and selectors use the same set of properties.

Properties are truly the nuts and bolts of style sheets, because they add formatting capabilities that are otherwise unavailable to Web authors who use standard HTML. For example, using a style sheet property, you can specify that all level 2 (H2) headings should be 18 point Helvetica, with 36 points of leading—referred to as line height in CSS parlance—above the heading. Try doing that with basic HTML!

The seven categories of style sheet properties supported by GoLive are:

◆ Font

◆ Text

◆ Margin

◆ Positioning

◆ Border

◆ Background

◆ List

In this section, I'll describe how to configure style sheet properties. But first I need to explain a couple of unique configuration elements: measurements and color handling.

✔ Tips

■ Just because you can create a property doesn't mean that it will work with all HTML 4.0 browsers. Unfortunately, browser vendors are inconsistent about the way they support properties. It's important that you test style sheet–enhanced pages with all major browsers before making your pages live.

■ If you don't choose an option in one of the property tabs of the CSS Selector Inspector, the style you create will not have a property associated with that option. In other words, the default for all style properties is not to change the styled area in any way.

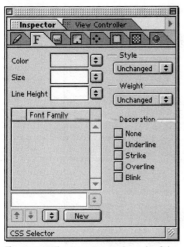

Figure 11.9 The Font Properties tab of the CSS Selector Inspector.

Measurements

Style sheet properties support a measurement scheme that is different from standard HTML. Although they do support the familiar pixel and percentage measurements, for example, you'll also find that style sheets accept measurements in picas, centimeters, inches, and more. Units of measure supported by style sheets are:

◆ **Absolute measurements:** point, pica, millimeter (mm), centimeter (cm), and inch.

◆ **Relative units:** em, ex, and pixel. Em measures the item relative to the height (in points) of the current font. Ex measures text relative to the letter X, also in the current font. Pixels are relative to the resolution of the screen.

◆ **Percent unit:** expresses styled text as a percentage of the default.

◆ **Keyword units:** ranging from XXSmall to XXLarge measure text, like standard HTML size tags, relative to the default size.

Color

Colors are also handled differently within style sheets than they are in basic HTML document. Style sheets support only 16 colors from the W3C RGB color palette. They are named on popup menus within the property tabs of the CSS Selector Inspector, or you can drag them from the Color palette.

To set font properties:

1. Open a style sheet document and create a style.

2. In the CSS Selector Inspector, click the Font Properties tab (**Figure 11.9**).

continues on next page

ADDING PROPERTIES

3. Choose a font color (if you want to change it) from the popup menu, or drag a color from the Color palette. GoLive will interpret the color you choose from the Color palette to conform to the 16-color palette.

4. Type a number in the Size field and choose a unit of measure from the popup menu.

5. Type a Line Height and choose an option from the popup menu, using one of the same measurement units. Line Height is referred to as *leading* in the print publishing world.

6. To apply a new typeface, choose a font family from the popup menu at the bottom of the Inspector (**Figure 11.10**), or click New to add a new family which you can define.

7. Choose font style, and/or decoration options in the Inspector.

8. To change the font's weight, choose a number from 100 to 900 from the popup. Choosing Normal applies a weight of 400, while Bold equals a weight of 700. Font weights are absolute, but the Bolder and Lighter options are relative to the default, or to any existing style from which this new style inherits properties.

To set text properties:

1. Click the Text Properties tab in the CSS Selector Inspector (**Figure 11.11**).

2. Edit Text Indent, Word Spacing, and Letter Spacing values the same way you chose sizes when you chose font properties, as described above.

3. Choose an option from the Vertical Align popup menu to relate the styled text relative to its baseline.

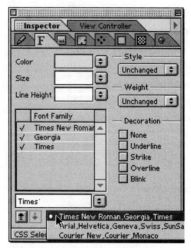

Figure 11.10 Choose a font family from the popup menu.

Figure 11.11 The Text Properties tab of the CSS Selector Inspector.

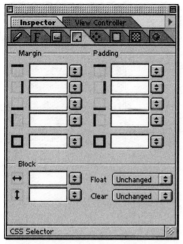

Figure 11.12 The Margin Properties tab of the CSS Selector Inspector.

4. Use the Font Variant to specify capitalization (small caps) if you like. Leaving the popup menu unchanged has no effect on the capitalization of style text.

5. Choose an option from the Transformation popup menu if you want styled text to always be capitalized, uppercase, or lowercase. Leaving the menu unchanged has no affect of capitalization.

6. Use the Alignment popup menu to align lines of text with respect to one another.

To set margin properties:

1. Click the Margin Properties tab in the CSS Selector Inspector (**Figure 11.12**). The "box" defines the area of the document controlled by the style you are creating— its margins.

2. If you don't change margin properties, the boundary is the text itself. If you do, there will be space between styled text and other elements of the page.

3. Choose margins for the box to create it. You only need to choose margins for those boundaries you want to extend.

4. Choose padding to create space between the styled text and the margin you've created.

5. You can use the Block option (horizontal and/or vertical) to define width and height of the box. This property is most useful when you need to include an image within the styled box.

ADDING PROPERTIES

To set border properties:

1. Click the Border Properties tab in the CSS Selector Inspector (**Figure 11.13**). Unlike the margin properties we created earlier, which create an invisible boundary around the element you are styling, border properties specify a visible border for the styled element.

2. Choose left, right, top, and/or bottom border thickness by typing values and using the popup menus to choose a measuring unit.

3. Choose colors for borders from the popup or with the Color palette.

4. Choose the type of border (solid, dotted, etc.) from the popup menus.

5. If you want a uniform border on all sides, use the box field and popup menu (**Figure 11.14**).

To set background properties:

1. Click the Background Properties tab in the CSS Selector Inspector (**Figure 11.15**). Use these options to add a background color or image to the box that surrounds your styled text.

2. Click the Image checkbox, then the Browse button to locate a file you would like to use as a background image.

3. Choose a Repeat option to tile the background image within the box. Repeat X tiles the image horizontally; Repeat Y tiles it vertically. Setting the option to Once means the background won't repeat.

4. Choose an Attach option to specify whether or not a background image should scroll as a visitor scrolls within the browser window.

5. Choose Top and Left measurements to position a background image relative to the box in which it is located.

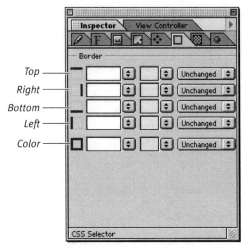

Figure 11.13 The Border Properties tab of the CSS Selector Inspector.

Figure 11.14 Make the border uniform on all sides with the box options in the Border Properties tab of the Inspector.

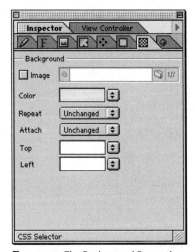

Figure 11.15 The Background Properties tab of the CSS Selector Inspector.

ADDING PROPERTIES

Figure 11.16 The List Properties tab of the CSS Selector Inspector.

Figure 11.17 Click the List Properties tab in the CSS Selector Inspector to create a new property.

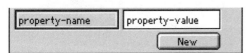

Figure 11.18 Click New and type a name and value for the property.

6. To create a colored background, choose a color from the Color palette or the popup menu.

To set list properties:

1. Click the List Properties tab in the CSS Selector Inspector (**Figure 11.16**). List properties allow you to customize bullets or other list item markers that appear within HTML lists.

2. Click the Image checkbox and locate an image to use as an alternative list item marker.

3. From the Style popup, choose an HTML list style to use.

4. From the Position popup, choose Inside (to set the list item marker inside the first line of text) or Outside (to set the list item marker apart from the remaining lines of text, as it does with a regular HTML list).

Unsupported properties

You can add properties to style sheets that are not directly supported in the CSS Selector Inspector, if you want to use a style property that is supported by a new browser, for example.

To add an unsupported property:

1. Create a new class, ID, or tag selector and select it.

2. In the CSS Selector Inspector, click the List Properties tab (**Figure 11.17**).

3. Click the New button (**Figure 11.18**) to add a property.

4. Type the property's name and value in the fields provided and press Enter to confirm.

5. Click the Basics tab of the Inspector to see the new property, along with any others you have applied to this style.

ADDING PROPERTIES

Cascading and Inheritance

CASCADING AND INHERITANCE

As you have seen in this chapter, style sheets can be implemented in a number of ways, and can even work together to define the appearance or position of individual HTML elements, or all the elements on a page or pages. Before I describe applying style sheets in GoLive, you need to understand some of the rules that govern how style sheets work together and how they interact with HTML elements. A full discussion is beyond the scope of this book, but you can use these principles to plan your style sheets, especially if you plan to apply several style sheets to a single document or HTML element.

Since multiple style sheets and rules are applied to a single HTML element, and since styled elements are displayed in browsers with a variety of visual characteristics—text size, and typeface, for example—it's important for a Web designer to understand how CSS sorts out all the competing hierarchies. That's where the *cascading* in Cascading Style Sheets comes in. Cascading sets the relative precedence of one type of style sheet over another when several style sheets apply to the same HTML element. Cascading also tells the browser how to display styled content, based on the appearance precedence.

Selector hierarchy

The more specific a style sheet selector is— the more directly it impacts the HTML element in question, the more likely it will actually be applied, either along with or instead of a rule that is more general. That means that a style rule that is applied to a particular tag will override a style that is applied to all tags that are like (and including) the tag in question. ID selectors, which apply only to a single HTML element, override class selectors, which override tag selectors.

Precedence

As I've mentioned earlier, browsers display styled content (and HTML content in general, for that matter) in different ways, depending on the platform (Mac, PC, or UNIX) and the maker of the browser (Microsoft, Netscape, or another developer). If a user changes his browser's display settings, those settings take precedence over the settings defined by the browser maker. By the same token, style sheet properties defined by a Web page designer take precedence over the user's settings and the browser's default settings. The concept of precedence gives the Web page developer a measure of control over the look of content that uses style sheets.

Another element of precedence is the distinction between kinds of style sheets. Those that are embedded in an HTML document have higher precedence than external style sheets do, and external style sheets that are linked to an HTML document have a greater precedence the farther down the document their links appear. In other words, an external style sheet that is referenced at the top of the document has a lower precedence than one that appears after it. Finally, imported style sheets have a higher precedence than do linked external style sheets.

Inheritance

HTML is hierarchical. A <P> tag occurs within a <BODY> tag, which occurs within <HTML> tags, for example, and text-formatting tags also appear within other tags. If you add a <B> tag inside an <H2> tag that already includes a font attribute, all of the text within the <B> tag will also use the font that is applied to the <H2> tag. This is called *inheritance*, and it applies to style sheet selectors as well as HTML tags and attributes.

Using Style Sheets

When I defined the two general types of style sheets (internal and external) and the four ways of applying them, I noted that *attaching* styles to one or more HTML documents differentiates the process of building style sheets in GoLive much more than *creating* them does. As promised, here's the scoop on adding the styles you've created to HTML pages.

First I'll explain how to apply internal style sheets, in the form of classes and IDs, and then move on to linking and importing external styles.

Applying classes

Unlike tag styles, which apply automatically to all matching HTML tags in a document, classes—which apply to conditional instances of text—must be specifically connected to relevant text.

To apply class styles to text:

1. Create and configure a class-based style in a document to which you want to add the style.

2. Click some text to display the Text Inspector.

3. Click the Style tab to display classes available to this document.

4. Choose the way you want to apply the style by clicking in the appropriate column, next to the style you're working with (**Figure 11.19**). A checkbox appears beside the option you choose. (See **Table 11.1** for style type definitions).

5. Click the Preview tab in the Document window to see how the styles you applied have changed the appearance of the text. For added verification, open the page you're working on in one or more Web browsers.

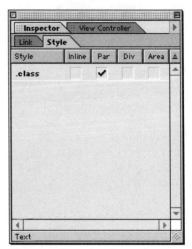

Figure 11.19 To apply a class style to text, choose the Style tab in the Text Inspector and click in the column that indicates the kind of style you want. A checkmark appears.

Table 11.1

Style Type Definitions	
STYLE TYPE	DOES THIS
Inline	Styles the selected text with a class that applies only to that span of text.
Par	Styles a full paragraph.
Div	Styles selected text and separates it from other elements on the page, allowing you to align it independently.
Area	Applies a class to the entire body section of the current HTML page.

Applying IDs

Unlike most operations in GoLive, applying an ID style requires you to edit HTML code. You'll need to locate the text you want to style, modify the existing formatting slightly, and add the ID tag. Here we go!

To apply an ID selector:

1. With an ID created and configured, click the Source tab in the Document window to display the HTML Source Editor.

2. Locate the text you want to format with an ID.

3. To apply an ID to all text enclosed within HTML tags, insert the ID selector within the start tag of your text block, by adding ID=idname. Here are two examples:

   Original code:

   ```
   <H2>One Day Sale!</H2>
   <P>All bicycles 50 percent off,
   today only.</p>
   ```

   With IDs added:

   ```
   <H2 ID="salebanner">One Day
   Sale!</H2>
   <P ID="redandlarge">All bicycles 50
   percent off, today only.</P>
   ```

4. To apply an ID only to a portion of text that falls within tags, use this syntax:

   ```
   <P>All bicycles <SPAN
   ID="salebanner">50
   percent</SPAN>off, today only.</P>
   ```

5. Verify your work by returning to the Layout Editor, or, better yet, checking out your new ID styles in a CSS-capable browser.

Referring to external style sheets

Like ordinary hyperlinks, external style sheets are referenced in an HTML page with links between two documents.

To refer to an external style sheet:

1. Open a GoLive document to which you want to add external style sheet references.

2. Open the style sheet (for this page) by clicking the Style Sheet button.

3. In the Style Sheet window, Control-click (Mac) or right-click (Windows) and choose Add Link to external CSS from the contextual menu (**Figure 11.20**). A new item appears in the window and the External Style Sheet Inspector appears.

4. In the Inspector, click the Browse button (or use Point & Shoot) to locate a document containing styles you want to use in the current document.

   or

   With the Site window visible, locate the .css document within the Site window and drag it onto the page icon at the top-left edge (near the page title) of the Document window.

   The Style Sheet window now includes the name of the document, a checkmark indicating that the link is valid, and the URL (**Figure 11.21**). The document is updated automatically to reflect the newly linked style or styles.

5. If the current document refers to multiple style sheets, use the up and down arrows to move the current style sheet up or down in the cascading order.

6. To take a look at the external style sheet, click Open in the External Style Sheet Inspector.

Figure 11.20 Link to an external style sheet with the contextual menu. You can reach it within the Style Sheet window.

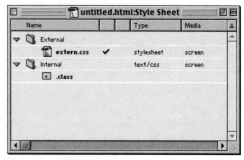

Figure 11.21 When an external style sheet is successfully linked to the current HTML document, a checkmark appears next to its label in the Style Sheet window.

USING STYLE SHEETS

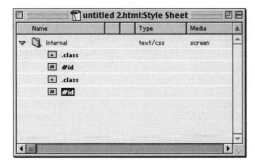

Figure 11.22 When you import styles from an external style sheet to an internal one, the styles are added to those that already appear in the Style Sheet window.

Importing and exporting styles

You can add styles that are part of other documents or that are included in external style sheets by importing them.

To import an external style sheet into a document:

1. With an internal style sheet open (click the Style Sheet button in the upper-right corner of the Document window), Control-click (Mac) or right-click (Windows) and choose Import external CSS from the menu.

2. In the dialog box that appears, locate the external style sheet (with a .css extension) you want to import and click Open. The styles from the external style sheet are added to the current document's internal sheet (**Figure 11.22**).

3. Change the properties of the imported style sheet in the CSS Selector Inspector, if you wish.

To export an internal style sheet:

1. With an internal style sheet window open, Control-click (Mac) or right-click (Windows) and choose Export internal CSS from the menu. A Save dialog box appears.

2. Choose where you want to save the exported style sheet and name it (don't delete the .css extensions that GoLive has added to the default title).

3. Save the new .css file. It is now available for use as an external style sheet.

Duplicating and deleting styles

You can easily add new styles based on those you've already created, or remove styles from a style sheet.

To duplicate a style:

1. With an internal or external style sheet open, click a style you want to duplicate.

2. Choose Duplicate from the toolbar (**Figure 11.23**).

   or

   Control-click (Mac) or right-click (Windows) and choose Duplicate from the menu. A duplicate style appears in the Style Sheet window.

To delete a style:

1. Click any style in an internal or external Style Sheet window.

2. Control-click (Mac) or right-click (Windows) and choose Clear from the menu.

   or

   Press Delete. The selected style is deleted.

Figure 11.23 Choose Duplicate from the toolbar to add a copy of the selected style to the current style sheet.

USING STYLE SHEETS

LAYERS
AND POSITIONING

Absolute, predictable precision—never the strong suit of HTML—is nonetheless what designers crave from the Web.

Floating boxes—Adobe GoLive's mixture of JavaScript, Cascading Style Sheets (CSS), and HTML—have several advantages over layout grids. (This combination of tools is often called Dynamic HTML, or DHTML, though the term is controversial among Web developers, and somewhat imprecise.) Floating boxes act like miniature HTML pages nested within a page. Floating boxes can contain any sort of object, including text, images, or multimedia, and can themselves be animated. Floating boxes can be stacked on top of each other in definable layers, opening up a whole new dimension for designers.

Unlike layout grids or tables, floating boxes can be positioned anywhere on the page.

In this chapter, I cover:

- ♦ How layers work
- ♦ Adding and using floating boxes
- ♦ Style-sheet positioning

How Layers Work

Dynamic HTML (DHTML) is a collection of techniques using JavaScript, layers, and Cascading Style Sheets to control movement on a page in space and time.

DHTML layers, are implemented as floating boxes in GoLive. They add two important capabilities to GoLive's toolbox—precise positioning relative to each other and stacking.

Layers, in the form of floating boxes, can effectively divide a page into sections, much like a table or layout grid. Layers can be positioned precisely—at least in theory—on the page, without regard to the location of other elements.

You can stack and overlap layers, either to achieve a layout goal, or to simulate movement on the page. You will learn more about using layers to animate pages in Chapter 18, "Animation and QuickTime." With layers, a section of your page can have its own unique look. Attributes can be defined in a layer rather than for the entire page. Style sheets can be used to define layers, while the underlying page can be left to the default display preferences of the receiving browser.

Figure 12.1 The Floating Box icon is on the Basic tab of the Objects palette.

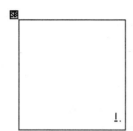

Figure 12.2 The floating box placeholder has a number, identifying it for layer ordering.

Figure 12.3 Click the edge of a floating box (when the cursor is a hand) to select a floating box or move it around the Document window.

Figure 12.4 Each floating box is represented by the SB icon in the upper-left corner of the Document window. This page has two floating boxes.

What does the SB stand for?

You may notice the tiny initials SB in the upper-left corner of the Document window when you add a floating box (**Figure 12.4**). GoLive's roots are in Hamburg, Germany, where Schewbende Büchse is how they say floating box. The SB indicator appears for each floating box you add, and you can click it to select individual boxes.

Floating Boxes

Floating boxes are based on the HTML tag `<div>`. This encloses objects and text in moveable boxes, visible in the Layout Editor but invisible to receiving browsers. Pre-4.0 browsers support `<div>`, but you can't view stacked or overlapping floating boxes in these older browsers. Everything within the `<div>` tag and displayed in the floating box in the Layout Editor is bounded by the box. Everything inside the box is positioned, aligned, or otherwise related to the box, rather than to a table, or to the page as a whole. When you move a floating box, its contents come along.

To create a floating box:

1. Choose the Floating Box icon (**Figure 12.1**) from the Objects palette and either drag it into the Document window, or double-click it.

   An empty floating box appears. Note that the box is numbered in the lower-right corner (**Figure 12.2**). This identifies it for ordering the layers of the Document window. A tiny placeholder box bearing the initials SB (see sidebar) appears at the upper left of the Document window, indicating the presence of a floating box in the layout.

2. Without clicking the mouse, move the cursor over the new box.

3. When the cursor changes from an I-beam to a hand (**Figure 12.3**), drag the box to another position in the Document window. Unlike most other elements, you can drag a floating box around the Layout Editor, even if the page does not contain a layout grid or table.

4. With the box selected, change the size of the box by dragging one of the handles on the sides or corners of the box.

FLOATING BOXES

To change a floating box's attributes:

1. Select the floating box. The Floating Box Inspector appears.

2. To better identify the floating box, type a descriptive name in the Name field of the Inspector (**Figure 12.5**). The name will become more useful to you if you use multiple floating boxes.

3. The distance from the top-left corner of the Document window to the floating box is expressed in pixels. Change the values in the Top and Left fields in the Inspector to move the box on the page.

4. Leave the Visible box checked so that the box will appear on the page.

5. Enter a value in the Depth field to set the order in which multiple floating boxes are stacked. You need not enter anything in the Depth field if you have one floating box, or if the boxes don't overlap.

6. Adjust the Width and Height of the box (measured in pixels, percent, or Auto). Pixels is the default.

7. Click the Inspector's Color box to add a color to the box. Clicking the Color box opens the Color palette, allowing you to select a color.

8. To add a background image to the floating box, click the BGImage button. Then Point & Shoot or browse to the file you wish to use.

We'll explore the Animation area of the Floating Box Inspector in Chapter 18.

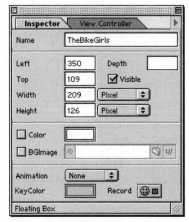

Figure 12.5 The Floating Box Inspector controls the attributes of the selected floating box.

Figure 12.6 These three floating boxes contain three types of content and are spaced around the page.

Adding content to a floating box

If you know how to add content to the Document window, you already know how to add content to a floating box.

Think of a floating box as a miniature Web page. You can type text directly into the box or add images and other elements that constrain the text. You can even place tables within the box. The boundaries of the box constrain everything within it, regardless of what's on the outside. To add content, use palette icons or any other method that can be used in the Layout Editor.

In **Figure 12.6**, I have typed some text into one of the boxes, named it Headline 2, added a GIF image to another floating box, and put a photograph in a third floating box. Note the SBs in the upper-left corner of the Document window. You can use them to select each floating box.

✔ Tips

■ There's little reason to do so, but you can even place tables or a layout grid within the boundaries of a floating box. Just because you *can*, though, doesn't mean you *should!* Floating boxes eliminate the need for most display structures like tables.

■ If you do need to add a table to a floating box, you can minimize table-related problems within a floating box by setting the box's depth to a value greater than zero (the default is empty), and setting the table's width to Auto.

FLOATING BOXES

A word about positioning types

As I mentioned earlier, floating boxes do not interact with the content on the base page. Objects and text outside a floating box flow down the page, regardless of floating boxes that are there. For example, in **Figure 12.7**, I have flooded the example from Figure 12.6 with text. The text does not wrap around the three floating boxes. In the case of floating boxes that are completely filled with opaque content (like the two images in the figure), text outside the floating box is hidden by the box. On the other hand, the page text interferes with the transparent text box. To correct this situation, you could set a color for the floating box containing the headline. However, the text in the base page still does not wrap (**Figure 12.8**).

You can create boxes (layers) that form a boundary around their content but which are themselves part of the flow of the page. Text wraps around such a layer and you can align the box to text, just as you can align an image or media object to adjacent text. For more on positioning, see "Positioning Text with Style Sheets" in this chapter.

Figure 12.7 Text floods the page, ignoring the three floating boxes. Two of the three floating boxes are opaque and do not displace or wrap any of the underlying text. The headline's floating box is not opaque, but still has no effect on the text beneath it.

Figure 12.8 Setting the top floating box's color to white makes the box solid and the type easier to read, but still has no effect on what's beneath it.

Floating Boxes as Layers

Floating boxes can be effectively used to deploy overlapping content on a Web page. The visual effect of overlapping graphic images can free up your designs from the humdrum, where everything is in its own separate box.

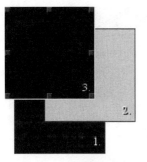

Figure 12.9
Three overlapping floating boxes each have a Z-Index at the bottom-right corner of the box.

The CSS code for keeping track of which layer sits atop which other layer is a numerical scale called the *Z-Index*. Each new layer brought onto the page is assigned a value and a layer hierarchy is built as additional objects are added. The higher the object's z-index, the closer it is to the top of the stack.

A floating box's Z-Index number is displayed in the lower-right corner of the box (**Figure 12.9**). You can change the Z-Index in the Depth field of the Floating Box Inspector.

Managing multiple floating boxes

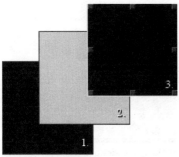

Figure 12.10 Three overlapping floating boxes are stacked atop each other.

If you use floating boxes merely as a way to organize a Web page and do not overlap them, manipulating each floating box is fairly easy. Simply select and configure the box or move it as needed. If, on the other hand, you group and stack floating boxes to form layers, you will need to use the Floating Boxes palette, a window that allows you to manage and manipulate the order of floating boxes.

To reorder layers with the Floating Boxes palette:

1. Add three floating boxes to a GoLive document. In **Figure 12.10** I have built a page with three floating boxes. Then, using the Inspector, I colored and named them.

continues on next page

FLOATING BOXES AS LAYERS

2. Using the Floating Box Inspector, change the order of the boxes. The lowest box in the stack will have the lowest number, and vice versa. I have reversed the order of my boxes in **Figure 12.11**.

3. Choose Window > Floating Boxes. The Floating Boxes palette (**Figure 12.12**) opens. This palette will look familiar to Photoshop users used to working with the Layers palette.

4. Select a layer and click its pencil icon, graying it out. That layer will now be locked in place until you click the pencil icon again.

✔ Tip

- You can use the Floating Boxes palette to control the visibility of the box. Click the eye icon next to the name of the box. When the eye is grayed out, the box is invisible. You can also make the box invisible by unchecking the Visible box in the Floating Box Inspector, when the box is selected.

Using a grid with floating boxes

You can use a grid to position floating boxes on the page. Unlike the standard layout grid element, the grid you use to position floating boxes is not a page element, but a helper tool that's only visible while you are dragging a floating box in the Layout view. You can set the gridlines as close together or far apart as you like, and force floating boxes to snap to the grid as you drag.

To set floating box grid options:

1. Click the arrow in the upper-right corner of the Floating Boxes palette and select Floating Box Grid Settings from the menu (**Figure 12.13**). The Floating Box Grid Settings dialog box (**Figure 12.14**) appears.

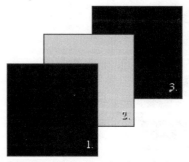

Figure 12.11 After changing the order in the Floating Box Inspector, the stacking order of the boxes is now reversed.

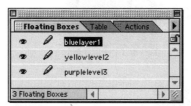

Figure 12.12 The Floating Boxes palette shows each floating box on the page, and allows you to lock or hide each box.

Figure 12.13 Click the right-pointing arrow in the Floating Boxes palette to see a menu containing the Floating Box Grid Settings menu item.

Figure 12.14 Create a grid for your floating boxes in the Floating Box Grid Settings dialog box.

Figure 12.15 Floating boxes allow you to overlap design elements as part of the design process.

2. In the Vertical spacing and Horizontal spacing boxes, choose the number of vertical and horizontal pixels between gridlines.

3. Click the Snap checkboxes to cause a floating box to snap to the nearest gridlines.

4. Click the Visible while dragging checkboxes if you want to see the grid as you move a floating box.

5. Click the Prevent Overlapping checkbox to keep floating boxes from being stacked.

6. Click OK to close the dialog box. The results appear in the Document window.

✔ Tips

■ The eye icon on the Floating Boxes palette does the same thing as the Visible checkbox in the Floating Box Inspector: it controls the display of the box and its contents.

■ All of the transform and alignment techniques you learned in Chapter 4, "Working with Layout Tools," can be used to align and distribute floating boxes. The toolbar's buttons perform the same functions.

■ Experiment! You can add dramatic effects to your pages. Just by tightening up the layers in **Figure 12.15**, the three elements change the layout while opening up the page with more white space.

FLOATING BOXES AS LAYERS

Positioning Text with Style Sheets

Yet another approach to precise placement is the use of Cascading Style Sheets to position text. Blocks of text act like floating boxes, controlled by the Position tab in GoLive's CSS Selector Inspector. Though a full discussion of positioning properties of CSS is beyond the scope of this book, here is a look at GoLive options for positioning elements with CSS.

The options in the Position tab of GoLive's CSS Selector Inspector define a block of text formatted with a style (see Chapter 11, "Working with Style Sheets") to control its position, clipping behavior, position in the order of the stack, what to do if it overflows, and visibility.

Style sheets make it possible to format and display text somewhat more precisely than does standard HTML. Most style sheets allow you to choose fonts, borders, colors, and other text properties. I have more to say about style sheets in Chapter 11. In this section, I cover style sheet positioning properties that allow you to do with text what you can do with a layer—put it exactly where you want it.

✔ Tips

- You may get more from the following section if you first read about creating style sheets in Chapter 11.

- You can also learn a lot about style sheets and positioning properties from online sources. Check out Builder.com's (`http://www.builder.com/Authoring/CSS/?tag=st.bl.3880.pro_h.bl_CSS`) style sheet article, with lots of information about positioning properties. You'll find a very helpful positioning lesson within WebMonkey's style sheet tutorial at `http://hotwired.lycos.com/webmonkey/98/15/index4a.html`.

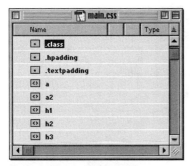

Figure 12.16 Open the Style Sheet window and select a style.

Figure 12.17 Click the Position Properties tab of the CSS Selector Inspector.

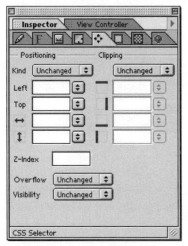

Figure 12.18 Set style sheet-related options in the Position Properties tab of the CSS Selector Inspector.

To create a style's positioning properties:

1. Open a document with an internal style sheet. Open the Style Sheet window (**Figure 12.16**) by clicking the Style Sheet button in the upper-right corner of the Document window.

2. Select a style in the Style Sheet window. The CSS Selector Inspector opens.

3. Click the Position Properties tab, which looks like a 4-pointed hollow star (**Figure 12.17**). The available positioning options appear when you click the tab (**Figure 12.18**).

4. From the Kind menu in the Position Properties tab, select one of the three methods of positioning:

   ◆ **Absolute** sets the position from the top-left corner of the document. Use pixels unless you have a very compelling reason not to. The element will behave like a floating box.

   ◆ **Static** allows the element to flow with the text.

   ◆ **Relative** sets up a parent relationship with whatever container is holding the element and controls its position within that parent as x and y coordinates from its upper-left corner.

5. Enter the size of the element in the Width and Height fields.

6. Set the stacking order of the element with respect to other elements on the page in the Z-Index box. The higher the number, the higher the element will appear in the stack.

continues on next page

POSITIONING TEXT WITH STYLE SHEETS

7. Under Clipping, select a method to deal with text when the element overlaps adjacent elements (**Figure 12.19**):

Figure 12.19 The Clipping menu's choices determine how the style's elements interact with adjacent elements.

   ◆ **Auto** sets the area of the element within the clipping rectangle in relation to the outer edge of the element.

   ◆ **Inherit** adopts the clipping method employed by the parent element.

   ◆ **Rect** allows you to set the cropping dimensions (left, right, top, bottom, and/or auto) of the element contained within the clip rectangle.

   ◆ **Unchanged** has no effect on what happens when content won't fit into boundaries you set. It is the default.

8. Select a setting from the Overflow popup menu to set how the browser will display content that does not fit into the boundaries you have defined for the element.

   ◆ **Visible** forces the content to display, even if it's outside the element box.

   ◆ **Scroll** adds a horizontal or vertical scrollbar to the element. The element's content is clipped (cannot be seen) and scroll bars are added to make the extra (hidden) content visible by scrolling left to right, and/or up and down.

   ◆ **Hidden** hides overflowing content.

   ◆ **Auto** lets the browser sort things out. It may (or may not) add scroll bars.

9. From the Visibility popup menu, select a setting to determine whether the element is to be visible or not on the page.

   ◆ **Inherited** adopts the display settings of the parent element. By default, it is not inherited.

   ◆ **Visible** allows the element to be seen on the browser when the page is loaded.

   ◆ **Hidden** causes the element not to be visible when the page loads on a browser.

POSITIONING TEXT WITH STYLE SHEETS

WORKING WITH RICH MEDIA

You can add multimedia to your Web pages in much the same way you add GIF or JPEG images. Like images, some multimedia files are displayed *inline*—as part of the Web page. Others are displayed in their own windows.

Multimedia formats supported on the Web include QuickTime video, Flash, Shockwave, RealAudio, and a number of other sound, video, animation, and publishing formats. Adobe GoLive can also display and execute Java applets, JavaScripts, and (on Windows machines) ActiveX controls, though not as reliably as browsers do. In order for the user to view multimedia files, Web browsers must either directly support the appropriate format or support and have *plug-ins installed.* A plug-in is software that is automatically activated when a multimedia file is called for and which can play or display the files.

In this chapter, I cover:

◆ Setting up plug-ins

◆ Setting plug-in preferences

◆ Configuring existing JavaScripts

◆ Java applets

◆ ActiveX controls

Setting Up Plug-ins

You add multimedia content by dragging palette icons into GoLive documents and then configuring attributes that control the way the plug-in content appears on a Web page. Like a Web browser, GoLive can display media files once you have installed plug-in software in the GoLive Plug-In folder. Just drop the plug-in into the Plug-Ins folder, inside the Adobe GoLive 5 folder. You'll also need to install plug-ins before trying to configure media files with GoLive, since the plug-in gives GoLive information it needs about the file type you're using.

Adding media content

The GoLive Objects palette includes a generic plug-in icon and four icons for specific media types. You configure all plug-ins using the Plug-in Inspector. To set up items related to a specific plug-in, you work in the Inspector's fourth tab, which is named for the plug-in you're configuring. Otherwise, the Inspector for all plug-ins is the same, though there are a few tweaks associated with different formats. I'll show you how to add and configure a generic plug-in, then move into options for specific file formats.

To add plug-in content to a document:

1. Drag (or double-click) the Plug-in icon (**Figure 13.1**) from the Objects palette to the Document window. A plug-in icon appears, and the Plug-in Inspector appears (**Figure 13.2**).

2. In the Inspector, browse or Point & Shoot to a media file you want to add to the page. The plug-in placeholder in the Document window now shows the name of the media file you've chosen (**Figure 13.3**).

Figure 13.1 The Plug-in icon.

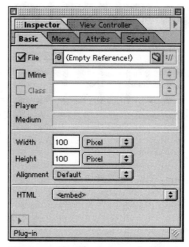

Figure 13.2 The Plug-in Inspector's Basic tab is where you choose a media file and a MIME type.

Figure 13.3 The plug-in placeholder shows the name of the media file you've just linked.

SETTING UP PLUG-INS

Figure 13.4 Choose a MIME type from the list. There are two ways to add MIME types: add a plug-in to the GoLive Plug-Ins folder, or add the MIME type in the Preferences window, in the Plugins section.

Figure 13.5 When you associate a MIME type with a plug-in placeholder, the image within the placeholder changes to reflect the MIME type and the name and contents of the fourth tab of the Plug-in Inspector become specific to the type you're working with.

Figure 13.6 Click the Play button to view a media file, once you have chosen a MIME type.

To configure a plug-in file:

1. If it isn't selected, click a plug-in place-holder that is linked to a media file (as described in the previous section) to select it and activate the Plug-in Inspector.

2. Click the Mime checkbox (**Figure 13.2**) to activate the popup menu containing a list of media file types. The MIME type identifies the media file to Web browsers and plug-ins, letting them know which application to use when opening the file. If you don't see a MIME type you want, check to be sure that the proper plug-in was installed in the Plug-Ins folder inside the Adobe GoLive 5.0 folder. If it's not there, quit GoLive and install it, then return to the Plug-in Inspector and choose the correct MIME type, which should now appear on the menu.

3. Choose a MIME type from the menu (**Figure 13.4**) that matches the media file you're linking to. When you do, the Player and Medium fields are filled in with the names of the application that will play your media file, and a description of the type of file it is. Also, the fourth tab of the Plug-in Inspector is renamed for that media type, and the picture on the plug-in placeholder in the Document window changes (**Figure 13.5**).

4. Click the Play button in the bottom-left corner of the Plug-in Inspector (**Figure 13.6**) to get a quick peak (or listen) to your media file. This will also verify that you've selected the correct MIME type.

continues on next page

5. Resize the plug-in placeholder if you like by dragging one of its handles or by typing new height and width values in the corresponding Inspector fields. If you are working with a video file, you may have noticed when you played it that the image didn't fit in the placeholder box. That's a pretty good indication that you need to resize the box (**Figure 13.7**).

6. Align the plug-in placeholder to Web page text with the Alignment popup menu. The same rules that govern the alignment of images to text apply when using plug-ins. For a full description of alignment options, see Chapter 5, "Working with Images."

7. From the HTML popup menu, choose the HTML tag that determines how the browser chooses which plug-in or application will play a media file. The safest setting is <object> & <embed> which supports most browsers and computer platforms.

8. Click the More tab in the Plug-in Inspector (**Figure 13.8**).

9. Give the file a name in the Name field, if you wish. It's not essential.

10. To link the media file to a page or site containing instructions on how to install the plug-in needed to view the media file, click the Page checkbox and type a URL for the instructions page. (You can also browse or Point & Shoot to the page you want). The installation instructions will only be presented if the user's browser detects that the needed plug-in is not installed on the system.

Figure 13.7 When you play this QuickTime movie, you can see that it doesn't fit in the default placeholder. Resize the box by dragging its handles, or by choosing new dimensions for it in the Plug-in Inspector.

Figure 13.8 The More tab of the Plug-in Inspector includes more media file configuration options.

11. Choose an option from the Palette popup menu to determine whether the plug-in will appear in the foreground or background. Leaving the Default option selected places the plug-in in the Background. The Palette option only changes the behavior of the plug-in in Windows browsers.

12. Use the HSpace and VSpace fields to set a distance (in pixels) between the plug-in and other content on the page.

13. Click the Is Hidden checkbox to cause the media file to play when the page it is on is loaded. This option is often used to play a sound when a visitor opens a page.

✔ Tips

■ To learn more about MIME, including media types associated with particular multimedia files, check out `http://www.oac.uci.edu/indiv/ehood/MIME/MIME.html`. You'll find information about media types in RFC 2046.

■ The third tab in the Plug-In Inspector, Attribs (attributes), allows you to add additional attributes to plug-ins. These are attributes for which GoLive has not created Inspector options. If you need to add additional attributes, click the Attribs tab, then click New to activate the name and value of the attribute. When you enter this information, the attribute is added to the HTML.

SETTING UP PLUG-INS

Configuring specific plug-in types

The four media types that GoLive supports with palette icons and custom Inspector tabs are:

◆ QuickTime

◆ RealAudio

◆ Flash

◆ SVG

You add these plug-in types to a document with palette icons included for each. The Plug-in Inspector is the same for these media types as it is for generic plug-ins we worked with in the previous section. Unless otherwise noted in this section, use the instructions in the previous section to configure the first three Inspector tabs. The fourth tab is specific to the plug-in you're working with.

QuickTime

QuickTime is a video format invented by Apple, but compatible with Macs and Windows machines. QuickTime files can be movies or links to video streams. They can include sound, too. You can add existing QuickTime movies to your Web pages, or you can build them with GoLive's QuickTime Editor. See Chapter 18, "QuickTime and Animation," for details on how to use the QuickTime Editor.

To configure a QuickTime file:

1. Drag (or double-click) the QuickTime icon (**Figure 13.9**) from the Basic tab of the Objects palette. The Plug-in Inspector appears, with the File and Mime checkboxes already checked. The Mime field is filled out; it says video/quicktime (**Figure 13.10**).

2. Browse or Point & Shoot to link to a QuickTime file, and resize or align the plug-in placeholder if you want to.

Figure 13.9 The QuickTime plug-in icon from the Objects palette.

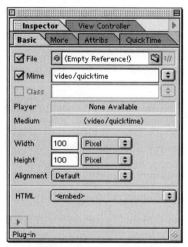

Figure 13.10 When you use the QuickTime icon to add a movie placeholder, GoLive fills out the appropriate MIME and player information in the Plug-in Inspector.

Figure 13.11 The QuickTime tab of the Plug-in Inspector includes QuickTime-specific options.

Figure 13.12 The Plug-in placeholder includes a small bar at the bottom to represent the size of audio controls, which appear in a browser or in GoLive's Layout Preview.

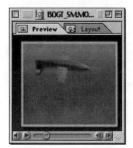

Figure 13.13 Here is a movie in Layout Preview, with audio controls included.

3. Choose <object> & <embed> from the HTML popup menu to support the widest array of browsers, as described in the previous section on general plug-in configuration. Leave other options in the Basic tab unchanged.

4. Click the More tab and then the Code checkbox. This activates the adjacent field. Browse or Point & Shoot to locate the code base—a file containing supporting code needed to play QuickTime files. (Optional)

5. Click the QuickTime tab of the Plug-in Inspector to configure items specific to QuickTime (**Figure 13.11**).

6. Click the Show Controller checkbox if you want QuickTime controls to appear below the movie when it plays. In the Layout Editor, the controls are represented by a bar at the bottom of the Plug-in placeholder (**Figure 13.12**). In the Layout Preview, you'll see the movie and the audio controls (**Figure 13.13**).

7. Click the BGcolor checkbox, and choose a color if you want the movie to play over a colored background. (For details on using the Color palette, see Chapter 4, "Working with Layout Tools.")

8. Choose the Cache checkbox to instruct the browser to cache the movie in RAM as the file is downloaded.

9. Type a number between 0 (lowest) and 100 (highest) to set the volume of the movie's sound.

10. Leave the Autoplay checkbox selected if you want the movie to play automatically when the page is opened. Otherwise, uncheck the box.

continues on next page

11. Type a value (as a percentage of the movie file's current size) in the Scale field to shrink or enlarge the movie's play area. Leaving the field blank displays the movie at its original size.

12. Click the Loop checkbox to play the video continuously. If you choose a loop, checking the Palindrome option (which becomes available when you click the Loop checkbox) will play the movie forward, then backwards. Then the process starts again.

13. Click Play every frame to prevent the browser plug-in from dropping frames. Frames are dropped to improve playback speed, and forcing the browser to display every frame can slow down playback.

14. Click the Link checkbox, then type a URL, browse, or Point & Shoot to locate a file that will be a destination link of the QuickTime file.

15. If you created a link in the previous step, you can choose a target page or frame from the Target popup menu.

✔ Tips

■ If the Code checkbox in the More tab, or the Link checkbox in the QuickTime tab is grayed out, be sure that you have chosen the <object> & <embed> option from the HTML popup menu in the Basic tab. This will activate the checkboxes, as well as the Open Movie button in the QuickTime tab.

■ GoLive includes QuickTime movie authoring tools, which allow you to modify and add effects to movies within GoLive. I have more to say about editing movies in Chapter 18.

Figure 13.14 The RealAudio plug-in icon.

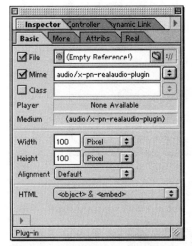

Figure 13.15 The Basic tab of the Plug-in Inspector looks like this when you add a RealAudio plug-in.

Flattening QuickTime movies

In order for a QuickTime movie to play smoothly on the Web, it must be *flattened*—saved in a format that Web browsers can accept and that can play without dropping frames or appearing "jerky." You can flatten movies before or after you've configured them within GoLive, by using the QuickTime Editor.

To flatten a QuickTime movie:

1. Open a QuickTime movie in GoLive's QuickTime Editor by choosing File > Open and locating the movie file.

   or

   Select a movie that is already included on a GoLive Web page, click the QuickTime tab in the Plug-in Inspector, and click the Open Movie button.

2. Choose Movie > Flatten Movie.

3. Save and close the movie file.

RealAudio

RealAudio, the audio format from RealNetworks, can, like QuickTime, present pre-recorded content and/or streaming audio. It's often used to add sound clips to music sites and to provide streaming radio broadcasts.

To configure a RealAudio file:

1. Drag (or double-click) the Real icon (**Figure 13.14**) from the Basic tab of the Objects palette. The Plug-in Inspector appears, with the File and Mime checkboxes already checked. The Mime field is filled out; it says audio/x-pn-realaudio-plugin (**Figure 13.15**).

2. Choose <object> & <embed> from the HTML popup menu.

continues on next page

3. Click the More tab and then the Code checkbox. This activates the adjacent field. Browse or Point & Shoot to locate the code base—a file containing supporting code needed to play RealAudio files.

4. Click the Real tab in the Plug-in Inspector (**Figure 13.16**).

5. Click the Autostart checkbox to begin audio playback when the page containing the plug-in is loaded.

6. Leave No Labels unchecked if you want visitors to see the name and other information about the audio file when it is played.

7. From the Controls menu, choose which controls you want to appear in the Web page. You can make one selection. To add more controls, you must add another instance of the Real icon and choose the control you want in the Real tab. Fortunately, the default option provides most of the controls you might want to include (**Figure 13.17**). To view other options, choose one from the Controls menu and then click the Play button in the Plug-in Inspector to view the controls and hear the file in the Document window.

✔ Tips

- The default controls for RealAudio plug-ins include Rewind, Play, Fast Forward, and Stop.

- Don't like the scrunched up controls in **Figure 13.17**? Just drag the handle in the plug-in placeholder to make it wider and not as tall.

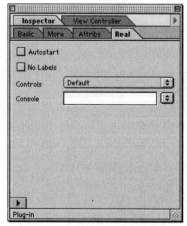

Figure 13.16 The Real tab of the Plug-in Inspector.

Figure 13.17 When you choose the Default controls from the Controls submenu, and play the clip, a preview of the controls appears in the Document window.

Figure 13.18 When you select an audio MIME type, the placeholder icon in the Document window, and the fourth tab of the Plug-in Inspector are updated.

Figure 13.19 Add audio attributes in the Plug-in Inspector's Audio tab.

Other audio formats

Though they don't have their own plug-in, the GoLive Plug-in icon supports audio formats in addition to RealNetwork's audio format.

To set up other audio formats:

1. Add a Plug-in icon to a GoLive document.

2. Select an audio MIME type from the Mime menu (you'll have to click the Mime checkbox to activate the popup menu). The fourth tab of the Inspector changes to read Audio and the place-holder icon is updated (**Figure 13.18**).

3. Configure options in the Basic and More tabs of the Plug-in Inspector as described in the section on configuring generic plug-ins, earlier in this chapter.

4. Click the Audio tab of the Plug-in Inspector (**Figure 13.19**).

5. If you plan to call the audio file with a script (a JavaScript or GoLive Action)— supported by Netscape browsers and the LiveAudio plug-in—click the Is Mastersound checkbox and give the audio file a name in the More tab.

6. Click Autostart to have the audio file play when the page is loaded.

7. To cause the sound to repeat automatically, click Loop, and enter the number of repeats in the adjacent field.

8. To specify start and stop times for the audio file, enter them in minutes and seconds in the Starttime and Stoptime fields.

9. Choose a volume level (from 1 to 100) for playback.

10. Choose how and whether to display a controller for the sound from the Controls menu. A controller, if you choose to display one, can include start, stop, and pause buttons, as well as a volume control.

SETTING UP PLUG-INS

Flash (SWF)

Macromedia Flash is a versatile animation, video, and audio format that's often used to build interactive presentations, animations, and other nifty custom Web page components. Flash files use the extension, .swf.

To configure a Flash file:

1. Drag (or double-click) the SWF icon (**Figure 13.20**) from the Basic tab of the Objects palette. The Plug-in Inspector appears, with the File and Mime checkboxes already checked. The Mime field is filled out; it says application/ x-shockwave-flash (**Figure 13.21**).

2. Configure any items in the Basic or More tabs of the Plug-in Inspector that you want to.

3. Click the SWF tab of the Plug-in Inspector (**Figure 13.22**).

4. Click Autoplay to begin playing the Flash file when the page opens.

5. Click the Loop checkbox to play the movie continuously.

6. From the Quality popup menu, choose a setting from Low to Best. The higher the quality setting, the better the movie will look, though it will play more slowly at higher settings.

7. Choose an option from the Scale menu to tell the browser how to deal with a differential between the size you've specified for the plug-in, and the actual Flash movie. Default forces the movie to appear in the space you've provided for it and may add borders to maintain a proper aspect ration. The No Border option retains the aspect ratio by cropping the movie if necessary. Choose Exact Fit to keep the movie in the space available, and make no correction for aspect problems.

Figure 13.20 The SWF plug-in icon.

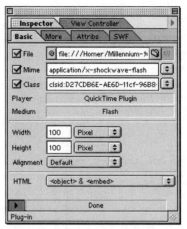

Figure 13.21 The Basic tab of the Plug-in Inspector looks like this when you add an SWF plug-in.

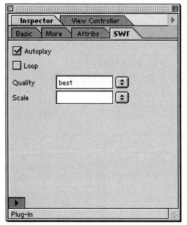

Figure 13.22 The SWF tab of the Plug-in Inspector.

Figure 13.23 The SVG plug-in icon.

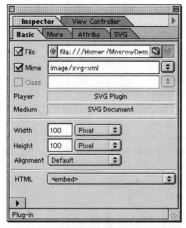

Figure 13.24 The Basic tab of the Plug-in Inspector looks like this when you add an SVG plug-in.

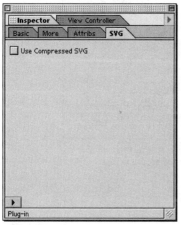

Figure 13.25 The SVG tab of the Plug-in Inspector.

SVG

SVG stands for Scalable Vector Graphics. It is a language that describes vector graphics within XML. (XML is a language that allows Web developers to build custom tags.) SVG allows you to build scripted animation and add editable text labels to images, among other things. At this writing, SVG is under review by the W3 Consortium, the arbiters of Web standards, but chances are good that it will become a part of the Web specification.

SVG is a big deal in GoLive because Adobe has made a big commitment to it, including tools in its Illustrator drawing program that allow you to export Illustrator images in SVG format.

To configure an SVG file:

1. Drag (or double-click) the SVG icon (**Figure 13.23**) from the Objects palette to the Document window. The Plug-in Inspector appears, with SVG settings configured in the Basic tab (**Figure 13.24**).

2. Choose other attributes in the Basic and More tabs of the Plug-in Inspector.

3. Click the SVG tab (**Figure 13.25**).

4. If you intend to use compressed SVG files, click the Use Compressed SVG checkbox. You must store both the compressed and noncompressed versions of the file in the same folder and upload them to your Web server.

Adding plug-in attributes manually

Many plug-in formats have attributes similar to those specified in the plug-in–specific definitions I've described. You can add these attributes manually, using the Plug-in Inspector's Attribs tab. The plug-in has its own set of attributes, which you will need to know before you can configure it. Attribute information is usually available from the Web site of the company whose plug-in file you want to add. In the following example, I will add some of the same attributes we used to configure an audio file.

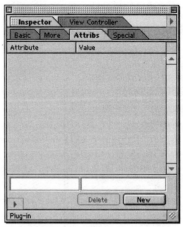

Figure 13.26 The empty Attribs tab of the Plug-in Inspector.

To add attributes manually:

1. Select a plug-in placeholder pointing to a media file that you have already placed.

2. In the Plug-in Inspector window, click the Attribs tab (**Figure 13.26**).

3. Click the New button to set up a new attribute. A pair of fields appears in the Attribs window. The Attribute field is selected.

4. Type autostart in the Attribute field and press Tab.

5. Type true in the Value field and press Enter. The attribute is complete and it appears in the upper portion of the window (**Figure 13.27**). The new autostart attribute tells a Web browser to play the content associated with this plug-in when the page is loaded.

6. Click the New button again.

7. Type loop in the Attributes field and type three in the Value field. Adding a loop attribute means that the sound plays continuously. I chose to play it only three times, so as not to annoy the site's visitors. If you had typed *true* instead of *three*, the sound would play continuously.

Figure 13.27 The Attribs tab with a new attribute configured.

✔ Tip

- Microsoft's Internet Explorer browser supports a few IE-specific plug-in attributes. To learn about these, check out Microsoft's Developer Center at http://msdn.microsoft.com/ie/

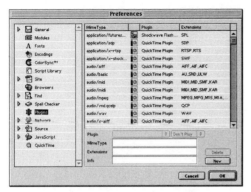

Figure 13.28 The Plugins Preferences window.

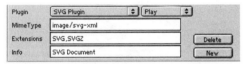

Figure 13.29 View or edit a media type by selecting it in the Plugins Preferences window.

Setting plug-in preferences

Most Web browsers that support plug-in playback allow you not only to use plug-ins but also to choose which file formats are read by each plug-in. Some of these choices are automatic. Besides movies, the QuickTime 4.0 plug-in (the current version at this writing, and the one included with GoLive, though QuickTime version 5 is currently in beta testing) supports a variety of sound files that are listed in GoLive's Plugins Preferences window. GoLive automatically associates a plug-in with each file format it knows about, and vice versa.

You can change these relationships if you would rather use different plug-ins to play files of a given format. You can also tell GoLive not to play the media files at all, if you choose.

To change plug-in/ media relationships:

1. Choose Edit > Preferences.

2. Click the Plugins Preferences icon. Scroll through the window to find it, if necessary. The Plugins Preferences panel (**Figure 13.28**) shows media formats, the plug-in used to play them, and the file extension associated with each format.

3. Select a MIME type from the list. Editable fields become available in the lower portion of the window (**Figure 13.29**). You can edit the MIME type, plug-in, and extension; delete the selected item; or create a new one. If the media type you chose can be read by multiple installed plug-ins, the plug-in menu will include several options.

4. Leave the Play/Don't Play menu alone so that files can play when you open a Web page that contains them.

continues on next page

SETTING UP PLUG-INS

✔ Tips

- All the formats listed in the Plugins Preferences window were entered there automatically by the plug-ins stored in the Plug-Ins folder. To use a plug-in with GoLive, you need to store a plug-in in the Plug-Ins folder. Note that you can't use an alias of a plug-in file. You must make a *copy* of it and drop it into GoLive's Plug-Ins folder.

- You can use the Plugins Preferences window to create entries for new media formats, but that is usually not necessary. When you add a new plug-in to the Plug-Ins folder and launch GoLive, the plug-in software registers the media formats it supports and displays them under Plugins Preferences.

- The Plugin popup menu in the Preferences window is a good way to remember which plug-ins support which formats. When you select a format and click the menu, only those plug-ins that support the format you've selected are available.

- The QuickTime plug-in supports a large number of audio and video formats. You may be able to reduce the number of different plug-ins you use by selecting QuickTime whenever it is available.

JavaScript

Netscape originally created JavaScript as a scripting language to enhance Web pages. JavaScript can be used to give life to a Web page with moving banners, animation, and other decorative touches. JavaScript can also be used to give instructions to Java applets or link multiple applets together.

The most common and powerful use of JavaScript these days is the manipulation of HTML pages and elements with scripted *actions*. Actions can create effects or invoke Dynamic HTML (DHTML) functions. For more on using actions built with JavaScript, see Chapter 17, "Using Actions."

Unlike Java, JavaScripts are composed of code that is part of your Web page or used by it. Java applets are actually programs that are downloaded to and run in a Web browser. GoLive's Script Editor allows you to write your own scripts and embed them within a document. You can also add pre-built scripts to a document using the JavaScript palette icon. Finally, GoLive includes an SDK (Software Development Kit) that allows you to extend GoLive's functionality using JavaScript. You can use the SDK to build your own palettes and tools and other add-ons to the basic GoLive application. You can learn some basics of the SDK in Chapter 17.

In this chapter, I concentrate on adding existing JavaScripts to Web pages. To learn to build your own scripts in GoLive or any other JavaScript-capable editor, check out one of the many good JavaScript resources available, both in print and online. Start with *JavaScript for the World Wide Web: Visual QuickStart Guide*, by Tom Negrino and Dori Smith. On the Web, there's Netscape's JavaScript documentation at `http://developer.netscape.com/docs/manuals/javascript.html`.

JAVASCRIPT

To add an existing JavaScript to a Web page:

1. With a GoLive document open in the Layout Editor, double-click or drag the JavaScript icon (**Figure 13.30**) from the Objects palette to the Document window. A JavaScript placeholder and the Body Script Inspector appear (**Figure 13.31**).

2. Name the script.

3. Choose a language (the name and version of the target browser you want to support) from the Language popup menu. GoLive enters a JavaScript dialect to match your choice in the dialect field, which is the unlabeled field immediately below the Language popup menu.

4. Click the Source checkbox to activate the Reference field and Browse button.

5. Browse or Point & Shoot to link to a JavaScript file. Once you've linked the JavaScript file to the current page, the Edit button becomes active, allowing you to open the Script Editor and modify the script, if you choose.

✔ Tips

■ To ensure the highest possible browser compatibility for your JavaScript, choose an older browser version from the Language popup menu. The tradeoff, of course, is that older browsers and script dialects don't include all of the features of newer offerings. At this writing, I recommend choosing Navigator 3.x (JavaScript 1.1) if you want to be conservative. Use Internet Explorer 5.x (Jscript 5.0) to ensure support for all the latest JavaScript features.

Figure 13.30 The JavaScript icon.

Figure 13.31 The Body Script Inspector.

■ If you want to use a later version of JavaScript, consider creating a page that supports older browsers or doesn't use JavaScript at all as an alternative for older browsers. You can implement this solution either by detecting the user's browser (with a browser switch action, as described in Chapter 17) or simply by asking the user to click a link to reach a non-JavaScript page.

JavaScript

Figure 13.32 The Java Applet icon.

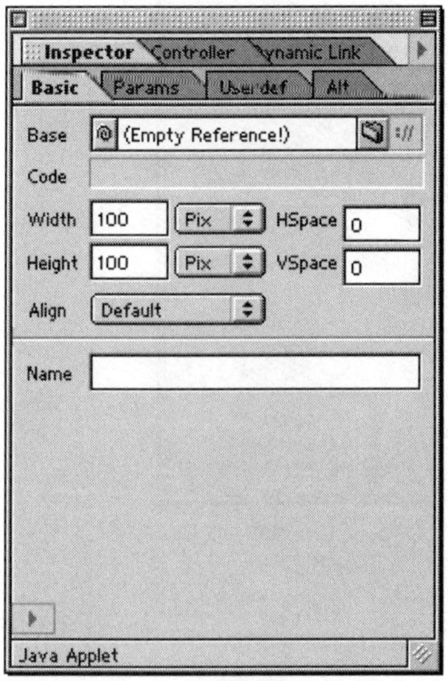

Inspector Controller ynamic Link
Basic Params User def Alt

Base @ (Empty Reference!)
Code
Width 100 Pix HSpace 0
Height 100 Pix VSpace 0
Align Default

Name

Java Applet

Figure 13.33 The Java Applet Inspector.

Java Applets

Despite the similarity of their names, JavaScripts and Java applets are not the same thing at all. As I pointed out earlier, JavaScripts are usually (but not always) fairly small pieces of code that are embedded in a Web page's HTML code. Java applets, on the other hand, are complete programs, written in the Java language, that are called by and may even appear within a Web page but are not part of that page. Java applets can be database interfaces, games, or any number of other applications.

You don't write Java applets in GoLive. For that, you'll need Java development tools and enough knowledge of the Java language to create applets. You connect existing applets to GoLive pages, specifying the appearance of the applet primarily within the applet itself. HTML (and GoLive) allows you to specify basic size, spacing, and alignment options, but the rest is up to the applet developer. You can preview applets in GoLive because, like newer Web browsers, GoLive supports Java.

To add a Java applet to a document:

1. Open a GoLive document.

2. Double-click or drag the Java Applet icon (**Figure 13.32**) from the Basic tab of the Objects palette to the Document window. The Java Applet Inspector appears (**Figure 13.33**).

3. Browse or Point & Shoot to locate a Java applet. The applet's location (Base) and Code appear in the Inspector.

4. Resize the applet if you like, either by dragging the placeholder's handles in the Document window or by typing new dimensions in the Inspector's Width and Height fields (in pixels).

continues on next page

5. If the applet is not on a layout grid or if it is within a layout text box, you can add horizontal and vertical space between the applet and adjacent text with the HSpace and VSpace fields. You can also use the Align popup menu to align the applet to adjacent text.

6. Name the applet by typing a unique name (one that's not being used by any other applet on the page) in the Name field.

7. To add alternative text or HTML that will be displayed by browsers that support Java but whose Java option is disabled, click the Alt tab of the Java Applet Inspector (**Figure 13.34**).

8. Type the alternative text in the Alt Text field.

9. If you want to display an HTML object when Java support is turned off in a browser, click the "Show alternative HTML" checkbox.

10. Add HTML objects directly to the Java applet placeholder with palette icons, or type HTML directly into the placeholder.

✔ Tip

■ You can view the contents and action of a Java applet in two ways: click the Play button in the Java Applet Inspector or view your document with Layout Preview.

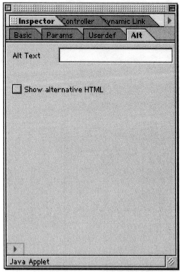

Figure 13.34 Make accommodations for browser users who have their Java support turned off.

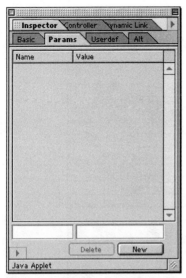

Figure 13.35 The Params tab of the Java Applet Inspector.

To add Java parameters:

1. Select a Java applet in the Document window.

2. In the Java Applet Inspector, click the Params tab (**Figure 13.35**). Parameters are applet-specific attributes.

3. Click New to set up a new parameter.

4. Type the name of the parameter in the Param field when it appears. Press Tab.

5. Type a value for the parameter in the Value field. Press Return to confirm your entry. The new parameter appears in the window above.

ActiveX

Microsoft's ActiveX is often thought of as an alternative to Sun's Java language, an improvement on current plug-in technology, and a way to add interactivity to Web sites. Unlike Java, ActiveX is not platform-independent. It's a proprietary technology that is supported primarily by Windows versions of the Internet Explorer browser.

You can add ActiveX controls—the equivalent of plug-ins, or applets—to a Web page in all versions of GoLive, but you won't be able to view them in the Mac version. GoLive's Windows version includes more ActiveX configuration options than the Mac offering. On the Mac, you can link to a control, but that's about all.

✔ Tip

■ Unlike most GoLive palette icons and Inspectors, those related to ActiveX aren't named intuitively. To set up an ActiveX control in GoLive, you use the Object icon and Object Inspector. To make things even more confusing, the GoLive documentation refers to these items as W3Cobjects. W3C stands for World Wide Web Consortium. It's the standards body that says what is and isn't part of the Web specification.

To add an ActiveX control to a Web page:

1. With a document open in the Layout Editor, double-click or drag the Object icon from the Basic tab of the Objects palette (**Figure 13.36**). The Object Inspector appears (**Figure 13.37**).

2. (Windows) Click the Select button. A list of ActiveX controls currently installed on your system appears (**Figure 13.38**).

Figure 13.36 Begin an ActiveX control with the Object icon from the Basic tab of the Objects palette.

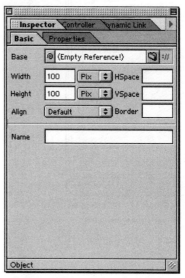

Figure 13.37 Use the Object Inspector to configure ActiveX controls.

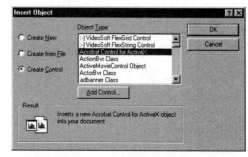

Figure 13.38 Choose an ActiveX control from the list in the Insert Object dialog box.

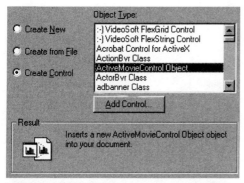

Figure 13.39 When you select an ActiveX control from the list of controls installed on your computer, a brief description of the control appears in the Insert Object dialog box.

Figure 13.40 Configure the ActiveX control in the Properties tab of Object Inspector.

3. (Windows) Click a control in the list. Notice that a brief description of the control appears in the dialog box (**Figure 13.39**). Click OK to choose the ActiveX control.

4. Locate an ActiveX control on your hard disk with the Browse button or Point & Shoot. The control's location (Base) appears in the Inspector.

5. Resize the control if you want, either by dragging the placeholder's handles in the Document window or by typing new dimensions in the Inspector's Width and Height fields.

6. If the control is not on a layout grid, or if it is within a layout text box, you can add horizontal and vertical space between the control and adjacent text with the HSpace and VSpace fields. You can also use the Align popup menu to align the control to adjacent text.

7. Name the control by typing a unique name (one that isn't being used by any other control on that page) in the Name field.

To add ActiveX Properties:

1. With an ActiveX control selected, click the Properties tab in the Object Inspector to display the Properties window (**Figure 13.40**).

2. To create a new property, click New.

3. Type the property's name in the Name field and press Tab.

4. Type a default value for the property in the Value field. Press Return to confirm the attribute.

5. Repeat steps 2–4 to add additional properties.

ACTIVEX

BUILDING SITES

A Web site is the sum of its parts: HTML pages, images, scripts, and multimedia files. Juggling a large number of site elements and organizing Web content so that it is easy for users to navigate make site management a necessity for most modern Webmasters.

Adobe GoLive includes a full-fledged site building and site management interface that allows you to organize, visualize, and manage your Web pages and other components of your site. You can also design a site before you build it, or plan for and modify an existing site's elements and structure.

The first step is to design and build your site. Next, you can add items as you create or acquire them.

In this chapter, I cover:

◆ Using site tools

◆ Creating sites

◆ Designing sites

◆ Adding resources to your site

◆ Fine-tuning preferences

Using Site Tools

You build GoLive sites with several tools, commands, and preferences. I cover each one as I work through the process of creating a site, but here's an overview. You will use many of these tools to create sites in this chapter, and others to manage and publish them in Chapter 15, "Viewing and Managing Sites," and 16, "Publishing Your Site."

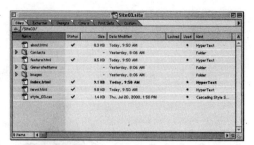

Figure 14.1 The Site window displays files and folders that make up a GoLive site.

The Site window

The Site window is where the action is. You add, rearrange, and link files from here. Under its six tabs, you store files, external URLs, site designs, colors, font sets, and custom items (**Figure 14.1**).

The Site window looks and works much like the Mac Finder or Windows Explorer/Browser. You can view and sort files and folders and move items between folders within the site. You can even drag items into and out of the Site window from the Finder or Windows Explorer.

Figure 14.2 The Site tab of the Objects palette.

The Site tab of the Objects palette

The Site tab contains icons that you can use to add elements to the site by dragging them into the Site window (**Figure 14.2**). They support the addition of new pages, colors, URLs, fonts, and other items to a GoLive site.

The toolbar

With a GoLive site open, the context-sensitive toolbar adds several site management items (**Figure 14.3**). You can create new folders, update a site's links, check and change preferences, and locate files.

Figure 14.3 The toolbar contains site management tools when a GoLive site is open.

Figure 14.4 The Site Settings window contains settings for uploading and mapping your site.

Figure 14.5 Site Preferences give you control over the behavior and appearance of elements within the Site window.

Site Settings and Preferences

You can edit site-specific parameters within the Site Settings dialog box. Most of the options relate to publishing your site on a remote Web server (**Figure 14.4**). Site Preferences, which are contained within the Preferences dialog box (**Figure 14.5**), have more to do with the way you work with sites as you build and manage them.

Inspector/View Controller

Each site file has its own Inspector that allows you to configure and view options specific to that file (**Figure 14.6**). These properties are specific to the file's relationship with the site—for example, you don't use the File Inspector to align or resize image files, but you can use it to choose files for uploading to the Web, and to look at a thumbnail view of the file, among other things. Other site objects—folders, colors, fonts, URLs—have associated Inspectors, too. The View Controller lets you show or hide labels and tabs within the Site window (**Figure 14.7**).

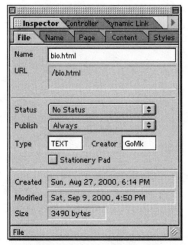

Figure 14.6 Configure the characteristics of individual site files in the File Inspector.

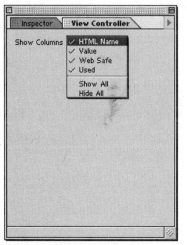

Figure 14.7 In the View Controller, you can show or hide labels and tabs.

The Site menu

Most of the commands on the Site menu allow you to add site elements or make global changes and verifications. You can also reach the Navigation view and Links view, which I discuss in Chapter 15, "Viewing and Managing Sites."

Navigation and Links views

The Navigation and Links views provide a graphical look at the contents of your site. Where the Site window offers a view of the files and resources themselves, the Navigation view shows the relationships between HTML files. Those relationships are defined by links. The Links view takes the display one step further, showing all links coming to and from a page. I'll cover the Navigation view and Links view in Chapter 15 when I discuss organizing and managing sites and their contents.

Design window

You can use the Design window (**Figure 14.8**) to "sketch" your ideas for site designs before putting them into effect. Like the Navigation and Links views, the Design window provides a graphical representation of the site, but it's not a view of the pages or hyperlinks you're currently using: it's a place to build prototypes that may (or may not) eventually become elements of your site.

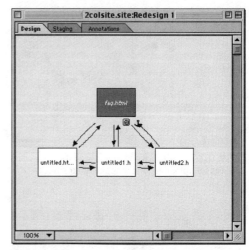

Figure 14.8 You can create a sketch of a new group of pages you would like to add to your site in the Design window.

Creating Sites

To begin a GoLive site, you first create the site structure and then add HTML and media files to it.

Site structure in GoLive

A GoLive site is a collection of files, but it's also a GoLive structure that gives you access to tools and views that make building a site easier. When you create or import a site, GoLive creates a site file and two folders: the *site* folder and the *site data* folder. The site file is your site's master control: it knows where every site object is and whether the links between them actually work or not. Inside the site folders are the files that make up the site; HTML, images, multimedia, scripts, and so on. The site data folder contains items that support the site—site designs, stationery files, and other items that you use in GoLive—but that you don't upload to a Web server.

✔ Tip

■ GoLive saves the site file, site folder, and site data folder into a single folder when you create a site. It's a good idea to save these site components to a new folder, making it easier to keep track of your site's pieces.

Start the site

There are four ways to start your site:

◆ **Create a blank site** Build a brand-new site, completely from scratch.

◆ **Create a new site based on a site template** GoLive includes several templates—sample sites with HTML pages, images, and a site structure that you can use as the basis for your own site.

◆ **Import an existing site that is stored on a local hard disk** If you have built pages in GoLive without building a site, or if you have built HTML pages in another Web development application, you can add them to a new GoLive site.

◆ **Import a site that is stored on a server, using FTP** You can download your existing site from a server and add its contents to a new GoLive site.

To create a blank site:

1. Choose File > New Site > Blank.

2. Choose a location for your site. Leave the Create Folder checkbox selected to have GoLive create a folder that contains the Site file and the other components of the site. You don't need to use the New Folder button.

3. Name your site and click Choose. The Site window appears (**Figure 14.9**).

A new blank site includes one HTML file: `index.html`. This blank file is the home page for the new site.

To copy a site from a template:

1. Chose File > New Site > Copy from Template.

2. In the Copy Site from Template window, choose a template. To see a thumbnail of each one's site structure, click a template label (**Figure 14.10**).

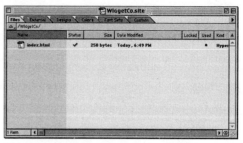

Figure 14.9 When you create a new site, the Site window displays the home page (index.html).

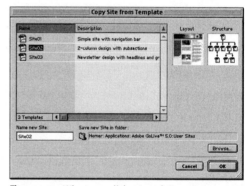

Figure 14.10 When you click a template, you see a thumbnail version of a sample page, and of the site hierarchy.

Figure 14.11 Choose the folder containing site files you want to import, and the HTML file you want to use as your site's home page.

3. Give your site a name in the Name new Site field.

4. To choose a location for your site, click the Browse button and navigate to the location you want. By default, GoLive will store template sites within its own folder hierarchy, so you will probably want to save the site elsewhere.

5. Click OK to begin copying the template files to your new site folder. When the process is complete, the Site window opens. It contains the HTML files and other items associated with the template.

To import a local site:

1. Choose File > New Site > Import from Folder. In the dialog box that appears, locate the folder containing your site files and its home page (e.g., index.html).

2. Under the "Please select an existing site folder" label, click Browse and locate the folder containing your site files.

3. Back in the Import Site Folder dialog box, click Browse under the "Please select the home page" label, and choose the site's home page. When you're ready to import the site, the window should look like **Figure 14.11**.

4. Click Import to begin building your GoLive site. When the site has been imported, its contents appear in the Site window.

✔ Tip

■ You can also import a site by dragging and dropping a site folder and/or home page into the Import Site Folder dialog box.

CREATING SITES

307

To import a site using FTP:

1. Choose File > New Site > Import Site from FTP.

2. In the Import Site from FTP Server dialog box (**Figure 14.12**), type the server URL and directory path in the appropriate fields. If you're not sure of the directory path, leave it blank and click the Browse button and navigate to your directory, if you're connected to the Internet. GoLive will fill in the correct path for you—which may be blank (i.e., empty, null).

3. Enter a username and password in the appropriate fields.

4. Click the Advanced button if you want to change the port number associated with this server. That's not usually necessary. Find out from your ISP or the administrator of the server whether you need to specify a port number.

5. Locate the home page of the site to be imported by clicking Browse under the appropriate label.

6. Click Import to begin importing the site. When the import is complete, the Site window appears, containing the newly imported site.

7. Choose a folder on your hard disk to accept the imported files.

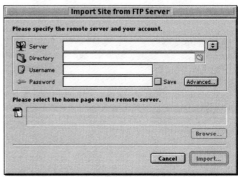

Figure 14.12 Enter information about the FTP server and choose a home page.

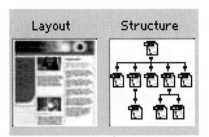

Figure 14.13 When you select a GoLive template, you see the layout of the home page and the page structure of the site.

Designing Before You Build

GoLive gives you two ways to plan your site before you build it. The advantage of planning is that you can think through all sorts of issues, including the number of pages you want, what will be on them, and how they will link to one another. By planning ahead, you can also build prototypes that you can show to others before building a complete site. Once you receive the approval or support you need for your design, you can begin building the site. It's also a whole lot easier to make modifications to your site plan before you begin filling pages with content.

Using templates

I described GoLive templates briefly in "Start the site," earlier in this chapter. Now let's take a look at the templates included with GoLive, what they are composed of, and how to build your own.

The GoLive package includes three sample templates. They are:

◆ A simple site with a navigation bar

◆ A 2-column design with subsections

◆ A newsletter design with headlines and graphics

When you create a new site with a template, GoLive shows you the layout of the site and its structure (**Figure 14.13**). The templates Adobe provides include a hierarchy of HTML pages (GoLive documents), along with images, and Cascading Style Sheet documents. The template sites also include font sets and color sets. I'll describe font and color sets in the "Adding Files and Objects" section of this chapter.

The GoLive files that are part of the templates include layout and navigation aids that you can customize for your needs. If you view the site template in Navigation or Links view, you will see the site's structure in graphical terms.

Make your own template

You can use an existing site as a template for other sites. When you do turn a site into a template you can use it as the basis for a new site—just as you can with those included by Adobe.

To create your own template:

1. Quit GoLive and locate a site you would like to turn into a template.

2. Copy the folder containing the complete site (the folder that contains the site file, site folder, and site data folder) into the Site Templates folder within the Adobe GoLive folder.

3. Launch GoLive and open the site you've copied.

4. Hold down the Shift key and click the Site Settings button on the toolbar (**Figure 14.14**). The Site Settings dialog box opens, with the Template Info label selected (**Figure 14.15**).

5. Type a description for the new template.

6. Click the Set button under the Layout label and choose an image to represent the layout of the site.

7. Click the Set button under the Structure label to add an image representing the site's structure.

8. Click OK to close the Site Settings dialog box.

✔ Tip

■ Wondering where to get images for the layout and structure thumbnails? Try taking a screen shot of the site's home page and another of the Navigation view, with the site fully expanded. Save the screen shots along with the site and use the Set buttons in the Site Settings window to add the thumbnails.

Figure 14.14 Hold down the Shift key while clicking the Site Settings button on the toolbar to view the Template Info section of the Site Settings window.

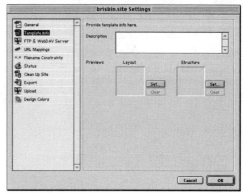

Figure 14.15 Set up a site template in the Template section of the Site Settings dialog box.

Figure 14.16 To work with designs, or to create a new one, first click the Designs tab in the Site window.

Figure 14.17 The Design window has three tabs. You create and draw the design in the Design tab, and use the other two tabs to prepare the design to "go live" and to annotate it, respectively.

Building a site design

Using a site design, you can create a mockup of a site—or a portion of a site—before you build it, or even plan for additions to the site after you've begun working with it. You can create as many designs for a single site as you like. Site designs are merely prototypes—their contents are not part of your live site—until you anchor the design to the site or to a page within it. Once anchored, you can submit the design and make it part of the live site, which in turn adds its files for uploading to your Web server.

Like the Navigation view, a site design is a graphical representation of connected pages within a site. You work with each design you create in its own Design window, accessible from the Site window or from the Design menu. Each design includes a navigation view, where you draw and arrange design elements, a staging view where you prepare the design to become part of your site, and an annotation view, in which you can make notes about the design.

You can anchor a site design to a page within the existing site before you begin, or after you've worked on the design, but you must do so before the design can become part of the live site. In the following series of steps, I'll describe a design that is anchored to an existing site page.

To create a site design:

1. Open a site and click the Designs tab in the Site window (**Figure 14.16**).

2. Choose Design > New Site Design. An untitled design label appears in the Design tab.

3. Rename Untitled Design if you wish.

4. Open the design by double-clicking it. The Design window opens (**Figure 14.17**).

To anchor a design to a page within a site:

1. Open a site and choose a page to which you want to anchor a new design. For example, say you want to add a weekly newsletter to your existing site. You could anchor a design for the newsletter hierarchy to the current What's New page.

2. Open an existing site design by clicking the Design tab and then double-clicking the design you want to work with.

3. Move the Design window so that the Site window (and the page you want to link to the design) and the Design window are both visible on screen.

4. Drag the page's icon from the Site window into the Design window (**Figure 14.18**). A new design section appears in the Design window (**Figure 14.19**).

✔ Tips

- You can anchor a design to a site, rather than a single page, by creating a new site and anchoring the design to the home page (index.html, by default).

- The easiest way to anchor a new design to a page is to first move the Design window to the right, click in the Site window, choose the Files tab and finally, select the page you want to add. Go back to the Design window and drag the still-selected page from the Files tab into the Design window.

- If you've been working on a site for some time and already have a complex site structure, you might want to anchor a page to a design from within the Navigation or Links view. The procedure is the same: drag the page to which you want to anchor the design into the Design window.

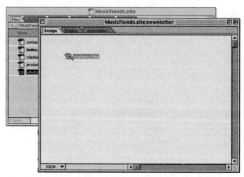

Figure 14.18 To anchor a design to a page, drag the page's icon from the Site window to the Design window for a new design.

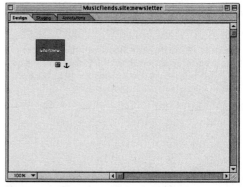

Figure 14.19 When you anchor a page to a design, a new design section box is created in the Design window.

Figure 14.20 Choose the Design Section icon from the Site tab of the Objects palette to add a new section to a site design.

Parts of a design

You can add the following elements to a site design:

◆ **Section:** A group of pages within a design usually defined as a new branch of the site hierarchy. Adding a section creates a new page, the section page.

◆ **Page:** Individual HTML pages can be added to sections or subsections as children.

◆ **Link:** A link defines a relationship between pages in the design.

◆ **Group:** Organize sections or pages into a group in order to move all items in the group at once.

The GoLive documentation also refers to an item called a subsection. Subsections are merely sections that are part of other sections.

Adding design elements

When you create and anchor a design to a site, you create a section that serves as the top level of the design's hierarchy. You can add pages and links to that section, and other sections at an equal (sibling) level or a lower (child) level. A section is actually an HTML page with links to other pages—its children. When you select a section, you can configure its section properties—how it relates (links) to child pages and its page properties.

To add a section to the design:

1. Open a site containing a design and click the Design tab to view the design.

2. Double-click the design to open it.

3. Drag the Design Section icon (**Figure 14.20**) from the Site tab of the Objects palette into the Design window. A new section appears.

✔ **Tip**

■ You can't double-click the design-related palette icons to add them to a design. You have to drag them over.

DESIGNING BEFORE YOU BUILD

To configure a design section:

1. With a section selected, click the Object tab of the Section Inspector (**Figure 14.21**). You will now configure the section's page properties.

2. Give the section a name. The name will become the label for the section if you choose that option in the View Controller. (I describe configuring the View Controller later in this chapter.)

3. Enter a directory name for the section in the Target Dir. field. Doing this will set up a new directory (folder) to hold the files that are part of this design section.

4. Change the Filename from `index.html` if you like. It might be confusing to have multiple files with the same name, though section files appear in their own directories.

5. Change the Page Title. The title will appear on the title bar in a user's browser when the page is loaded.

6. Click the Section tab of the Section Inspector (**Figure 14.22**).

7. In the New Filename field, enter a base name (everything before the ".html") for all pages within the section. When you create a new (child) page within this section, its name will begin with the characters you enter in this field.

8. If you want child pages of this section to appear in their own folder, enter a name for the folder in the Folder field.

9. If you want the child pages to be based on an existing stationery file, choose it from the Use Stationery menu.

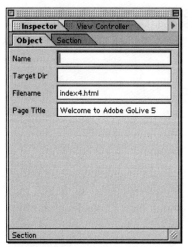

Figure 14.21 When you add a new section to a design, the Section Inspector displays the Object tab.

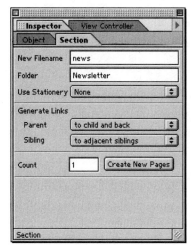

Figure 14.22 The Section tab of the Section Inspector gives you control of section-wide properties.

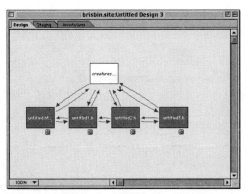

Figure 14.23 This design includes a section page and four child pages. The arrows going in both directions from each box indicate links in each direction.

10. If you want to add links between the current section and other sections, choose options from the Parent and Sibling menus.

11. To add child pages to the section, enter a number in the Count field and click the Create New Pages button. **Figure 14.23** shows a design containing a section and four child pages. The pages all link in both directions.

✔ Tip

■ The Parent and Sibling menus in the New Pages dialog box allow you to add links to pages above (parent) or on the same level (sibling) as the currently selected item. You can specify links that join the selected item either to *and* from child and sibling pages, or only to those pages from the currently selected page. You can also link to only a single adjacent page, or choose not to generate any links at all.

Design pages

You can add new pages to your design in a number of ways, making them children or siblings of existing pages. I described one way in the previous section—you can add pages as you configure a section. You can even create pages that are (or will become) sections with child pages of their own.

To add a child page to an existing section:

1. Click the section to which you want to add a child page.

continues on next page

DESIGNING BEFORE YOU BUILD

2. Control-click (Mac) or right-click (Windows) and choose New > Page from the menu (**Figure 14.24**).

or

Choose New Child Page from the toolbar.

or

Choose Design > New Page. A child page appears below the section page, with arrows connecting the two and indicating links (**Figure 14.25**).

3. If you have configured the parent of this page, some fields in the Object tab of the Page Inspector are already filled out.

4. Add a name and page title in the Object tab.

To add multiple children to a page:

1. Click the section to which you want to add children.

2. Control-click (Mac) or right-click (Windows) and choose New Pages from the menu.

or

Choose Design > New Pages.

3. The New Pages dialog box appears (**Figure 14.26**). Here you can configure all the same options available in the Object tab of the Page Inspector for the pages you are creating.

4. Enter the number of pages you want to add.

5. Leave the Filenames field unchanged if you have already configured it for this section. If you want all of the child pages you are currently creating to have a different base filename, type it now.

6. Choose a stationery file for the new pages from the Stationery menu if you want to base your new pages on an existing template.

7. Choose options from the Parent and Sibling menus to create links between the new pages themselves and/or to their parents.

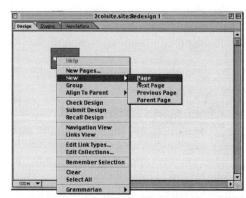

Figure 14.24 Select a page in the Design window and add a new child page with the contextual menu.

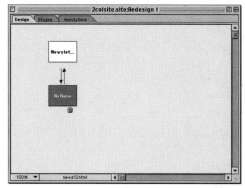

Figure 14.25 When you create a new child page, links between parent and child appear.

Figure 14.26 Add multiple pages and configure them in the New Pages dialog box.

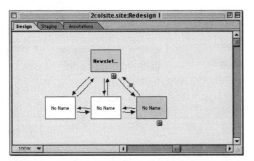

Figure 14.27 Click on a link between two pages in the Design window to select the link. Notice when you do that Point & Shoot icons appear below the page icons that the link connects.

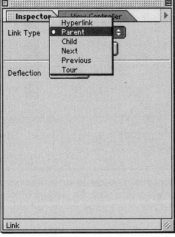

Figure 14.28 Change the Link Type in the Link Inspector to establish a family relationship between the selected object and its neighbors.

Adding other page relationships

You can add parents or siblings to any page you create: when you add a sibling, you can choose to add a Previous Page (which appears to the left of the selected page) or Next Page (which appears to the right). Commands to add parents and siblings appear in the contextual menu, on the toolbar, and on the Design menu.

Links

When you add new pages to a site design by selecting a parent or sibling, GoLive adds links between the selected page and the new one(s) you create. The links generated depend on the options you choose in the Generate Links section of the Section tab of the Inspector, or in the New Pages dialog box. You can change these links, or add links to pages that don't have them, with the Link Inspector, or by drawing links between unlinked pages in the Design window.

To change existing pending links:

1. In the Design window, click on a line that connects two pages (**Figure 14.27**). The link is selected and the Link Inspector appears.

2. In the Link Inspector (**Figure 14.28**), choose a link from the Link Type menu.

To add a pending link:

1. Add an unlinked page by dragging the Design Section icon from the Site tab of the Objects palette into the Design window.

2. Click the new section page to select it. Notice the Point & Shoot icon that appears below the page.

continues on next page

3. Click and drag from the Point & Shoot icon to another page in the Design window (**Figure 14.29**). When the two pages are linked, the Link Inspector appears.

4. Choose the link type from the Link Type menu to establish a family relationship between the two objects.

✔ Tips

■ Just because you drag a new design section page alongside an existing one does not create a sibling relationship. Using the preceding steps to link two visually parallel sections will make them siblings in reality by linking them, rather than simply siblings in appearance. Choose Next or Previous to link the two pages as siblings. If you want the pages to link in both directions—with links to and from each page to the other—make a second link. To do that, Point & Shoot from the page you just linked to back to the first page.

■ When you create links between pages, you can alter their appearance with the Deflection menu in the Link Inspector. You might choose to do that in a large design where you want to rearrange the link lines between pages. To change the angle of the link line, click on a line and choose an option from the Deflection menu. The options are expressed in percentages.

■ You can change the appearance of your design and its contents in the Design Colors section of the Site Settings dialog box. To change colors, choose Site > Settings and click the Site specific settings checkbox. The color choices are now activated (**Figure 14.30**). Click one you want to change, and select a color in the dialog box that appears.

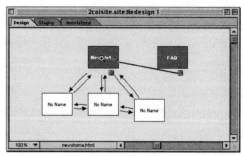

Figure 14.29 Create a new link between pages by dragging from the Point & Shoot icon of one page to the second page.

Figure 14.30 Choose colors to use with your site designs in the Design Colors section of the Site Settings window.

DESIGNING BEFORE YOU BUILD

Adding Files and Objects

Once you have created or imported a site, you can add files and objects to it. These objects include new files (HTML, images, multimedia, and external scripts), URLs, addresses and site objects. Site objects include font sets and color sets. Font sets and color sets are GoLive-specific features that allow you to quickly add a color or font that has been previously defined within your site.

Adding files

There are several ways to add files to a GoLive site: you can create new files as you build the site, drag and drop files from your hard disk, or import files, as you saw in the "Start the site" section of this chapter.

When you add files, GoLive checks to see whether they contain hyperlinks and tries to reconcile them with other files in the site. If you have instructed GoLive to check external URLs, it will connect to the Internet and attempt to verify that the links in your new files are good.

To create new files within your site:

1. Open a site.

2. Choose File > New to create a new document.

3. Add text, images, or other content to the page.

4. Save the document to your site folder—the folder on your hard disk that contains other files that are part of your site. The new file appears in the Site window.

✔ **Tip**

■ Be extremely careful to save new files to the correct folder. A GoLive site includes two root-level folders, one named for the site—MySite, for example—and another called <sitename>.data—MySite.data. HTML files, images, and multimedia files should be saved to the MySite folder, not the MySite.data folder, which contains site design files and other files used by GoLive to build your site's infrastructure.

To add files from the Site menu:

1. Open a new or existing site.

2. Choose Site > New > Page. A new page appears in the Site window, with the filename selected (**Figure 14.31**).

3. Type a filename for the new page.

To add files from your hard drive:

1. In the Site window, Control-click (Mac) or right-click (Windows) and choose Add Files from the menu. A dual-pane file dialog box appears.

2. Browse to the first file or folder you want to add to the site.

3. Select the item and click Add (file) or Add Folder (folder). You can also click Add All to add everything in the current folder. Items you add appear in the lower pane of the dialog box (**Figure 14.32**).

4. When you've added all the files you want to, click Done.

5. GoLive may ask you to update the files you've added in a dialog box (**Figure 14.33**) where each file to be updated is listed and indicated with a checkmark. Update all the files you added by clicking OK. GoLive copies your files and folders to the site folder and updates the Site window.

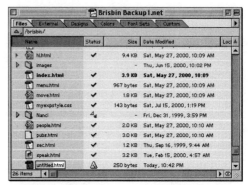

Figure 14.31 When you add a new page from the Site menu, an untitled page appears in the Site window.

Figure 14.32 Add files or folders to your site in this window. Double-clicking a selected item in the upper pane adds the item to the list of files and folders to be imported (in the lower pane).

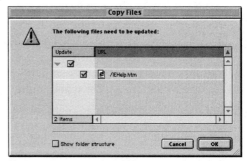

Figure 14.33 When you add files to your site, GoLive presents a dialog box listing the files and giving you the chance to check their links or to leave broken links unmarked.

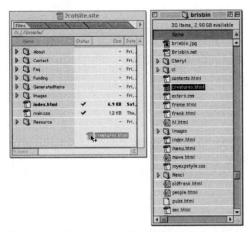

Figure 14.34 You can add a file or folder to a GoLive site by dragging it from the Finder (Mac) or Windows Explorer (Windows) to the Site window.

To add files to a site with drag-and-drop:

1. Open a site.

2. In the Site window, be sure that the Files tab is visible.

3. In the Finder (Mac) or in Windows Explorer (Windows), locate the folder containing the files you want to add to the site and open it.

4. Drag the files you want to add (or the whole folder, if you like) into the Site window (**Figure 14.34**) and release the mouse button. GoLive examines the files you've added and copies them to the site's folder.

✔ Tip

■ If you begin dragging a folder or file to the Site window and realize that the Files tab is not visible, you can drag the file or folder over the Files tab to bring it to the front. With that done, drag over the window and let go of the mouse to complete the addition to your site.

Adding non-file resources to a site

In addition to locally stored HTML files and graphics, GoLive sites can store pointers to external resources, and references to custom colors and font sets. Once included in a site, these resources can be added to pages with Point & Shoot.

You can import groups of external resources or add them one at a time. There are three ways to import multiple URLs: add files to a site that contain external links (those URLs are automatically added to the External tab of the Site window), or import resources from bookmark or address book files. You can also add single external resources much the way you would a new file.

Importing external resources

If you are creating a site from scratch using GoLive (rather than updating an existing site), you may not have external URLs or e-mail addresses stored in your site. However, you may have bookmark files or address books that include this kind of information, with no way to add them to a new Web site other than cutting and pasting. GoLive allows you to import bookmark files and address or nickname files. When you are ready, you can use Point & Shoot linking to add URLs and addresses to a page within your site.

To import bookmarks or addresses:

1. In the Site window, click the External tab.

2. Choose File > Import > Favorites as Site Externals.

3. In the dialog box that appears, locate a favorites (Internet Explorer) or bookmarks (Netscape Navigator) file and click Open. The URLs stored in the favorites or bookmarks file are imported into the site and stored in a folder called Favorites or Bookmarks, respectively.

4. Click the triangle (Mac) or plus sign (Windows) to the left of the new folder to display its contents. If your bookmark or favorites file contains folders, GoLive preserves them when you import the file into a site (**Figure 14.35**).

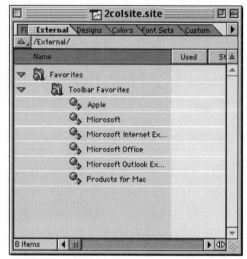

Figure 14.35 When you import a favorites file from Internet Explorer, its URLs appear in the External tab of the Site window.

Figure 14.36 Use the URL icon from the Site tab of the Objects palette to add a new URL to the Site window.

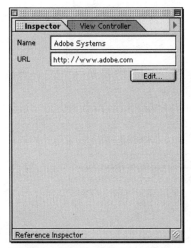

Figure 14.37 Create a new URL in the Reference Inspector.

Figure 14.38 Add an address to a site with the Address icon, found in the Site tab of the Objects palette.

To add a single URL:

1. Click the External tab of the Site window if it isn't already visible.

2. In the Site tab in the Objects palette, double-click or drag the URL icon (**Figure 14.36**) into the Site window.

   or

   Control-click (Mac) or right-click (Windows) in the External tab of the Site window and choose New URL.

   or

   Choose Site > New > URL. An untitled URL appears under the External tab in the Site window, and the Reference Inspector appears (**Figure 14.37**).

3. In the Reference Inspector, type a name for the URL in the Name field.

4. Type the full URL in the URL field.

✔ Tip

- Another way to add a new URL to a GoLive site is to drag it from a Web browser. In the browser, select the link that represents the URL and drag it into the External tab of the Site window.

To add a new address:

1. Double-click the Address icon (**Figure 14.38**) or drag it from the Site tab of the Objects palette into the External tab of the Site window.

   or

   Control-click (Mac) or right-click (Windows) in the External tab of the Site window, and choose New Address from the menu.

   or

   Choose Site > New > Address. The Reference Inspector appears.

continues on next page

ADDING FILES AND OBJECTS

2. Type a name for the address in the Name field.

3. Type the e-mail address into the URL field. The finished address appears in **Figure 14.39**.

✔ Tip

■ GoLive helps you enter addresses by filling out the portion of the URL for you (when addresses are used as links, these links are URLs). When you add a new address with the Address icon, or via a menu, the URL field of the Reference Inspector includes the `mailto:` required to begin e-mail address links. If you delete the mailto accidentally and type `info@adobe.com`, GoLive adds the leading `mailto:` to complete the URL.

Adding site colors

You can store colors within a site, much as you do files and external resources. You'll find this option useful if you have created a custom color in the Color palette, and to uphold a sitewide color scheme. Like other site objects, colors can be added to a Web page with drag-and-drop or Point & Shoot.

To add colors to a site:

1. In the Site window, click the Colors tab (**Figure 14.40**).

2. Double-click the Color icon (**Figure 14.41**) or drag it from the Site tab of the Objects palette to the Site window.

or

Control-click (Mac) or right-click (Windows) in the Colors tab of the Site window, and choose New Color from the menu.

or

Choose Site > New > Color. An untitled color appears in the Site window, with its name selected.

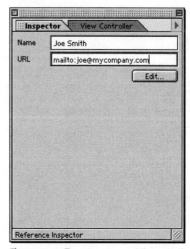

Figure 14.39 Type a name and the e-mail address you want to add in the Reference Inspector.

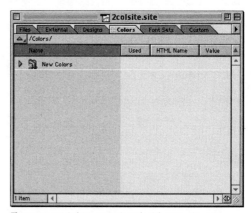

Figure 14.40 Colors associated with your site are stored under the Colors tab.

Figure 14.41 Add a new color to a site with the Color icon, found under the Site tab of the Objects palette.

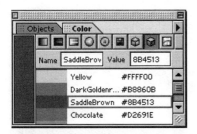

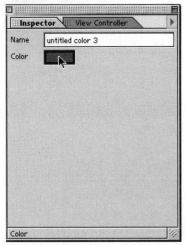

Figure 14.42 Drag a color into the Color Inspector's Color field to save the color in the site.

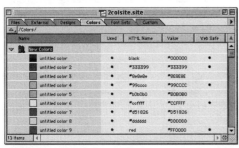

Figure 14.43 Colors that are Web-safe are indicated by a bullet in the Web-safe column of the Site window's Colors tab.

3. Give the color a descriptive name and press Return to confirm the name.

4. Double-click the new color. Both the Color palette and the Color Inspector appear.

5. Choose a color from one of the Color palette tabs. (For more information about creating and customizing colors, see Chapter 4, "Working with Layout Tools.") The color appears in the Preview pane.

6. Click and drag from the Preview pane into the Color field in the Color Inspector (**Figure 14.42**).

   or

   Drag the new color onto the Color box in the Site window to apply the color to the Site Color item you have created.

✔ Tips

- You can also add site colors by first selecting a color in the Color palette and then dragging it from the Preview pane to the Colors tab of the Site window.

- When you add a new color, GoLive examines it to determine if it is Web safe—one of the 216 colors supported by all Web browsers and computer platforms. If it is Web safe, a bullet appears in the Web Safe column of the Colors tab (**Figure 14.43**). It's a good idea to choose a Web Safe color.

ADDING FILES AND OBJECTS

To make an existing site color Web safe:

1. In the Site window's Colors tab, click the color you want to change.

2. In the Color Inspector, click the Color field. The Color palette opens.

3. Choose a new color in the Web Safe tab of the Color palette.

4. Drag the new color from the Preview pane to a color icon in the Site window. The color changes along with its HTML Name and Value. Look for the bullet in the Colors tab of the Site window to confirm that the new color is Web safe.

Adding font sets

Font sets allow you to save and use fonts with your Web site. You can store font sets as part of a site, just as you do custom colors.

To add a font set to a site:

1. In the Site window, click the Font Sets tab (**Figure 14.44**).

2. Drag or double-click the Font Set icon from the Site tab of the Objects palette to the Site window (**Figure 14.45**). An empty font set item appears in the Site window.

3. In the Font Set Inspector (**Figure 14.46**), name the font set.

4. Click New. The field near the bottom of the Inspector becomes active, along with a menu to its right. Click and hold the menu to view a list of available fonts.

5. Choose a font from the list.

6. If you want to add more fonts to the set, repeat steps 4 and 5.

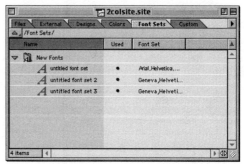

Figure 14.44 You can store font sets in the Font Sets tab of the Site window.

Figure 14.45 Add a font set to the site using the Font Set icon from the Site tab of the Objects palette.

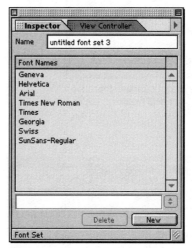

Figure 14.46 The Font Set Inspector shows the fonts included in the selected font set.

To use a font from an existing document:

1. Open a GoLive document that contains custom fonts. The document need not be part of a site.

2. If a GoLive site is not already open, open it.

3. In the Site window, click the Font Sets tab.

4. In the Document window, select some text that uses the font you wish to add to the site.

5. Drag the text into the Site window. A set appears in the Site window, and the Inspector changes to display the Font Set Inspector.

6. Type a name for the font set in the Font Set Inspector and press Return to confirm the name of your font set. The font used in this set appears in the Font Set Inspector.

✔ Tips

■ You can copy font sets or colors between sites. With two sites open, click a font set or color in the Site window and choose Edit > Copy. In the destination site, paste the font set or color into the Site window's Font Sets or Colors tab, respectively.

■ For details about how to safely add font sets that will be recognized by most browsers, see Chapter 3, "Working with Text."

■ Any time you add an item to a site via the Site window, GoLive determines whether or not the item is currently in use within the site. For example, if you copy a font set used within the site in the way I described above, a bullet will appear in the Used column of the Font Sets window.

Fine-tuning Preferences

The Preferences and Site Settings windows include options that change the way you interact with your site. I've covered some of these options in the course of adding files and resources, and I'll cover more when I discuss publishing Web sites in Chapter 16. For now, though, there are a few settings you may find useful as you work on your site.

To set site preferences:

1. Choose Edit > Preferences.

2. Click the Site icon to display site-related options (**Figure 14.47**).

   ▲ To control how GoLive scans a site to verify that links are working, check Reparse only modified files and/or Reparse files only on harddisk rescan.

   ▲ Allow the use of aliases to files outside the site hierarchy by checking Create URL mapping for alias to folder.

   ▲ Spring-loaded folders in a site file behave just like folders on your desktop. If you drag an item onto a folder and hold down the mouse, the folder opens.

   ▲ Display full path shows the path from the root level to the selected item, in the Site window.

   ▲ Leave Ask before deleting objects checked to receive a warning when you remove a file from a site.

   ▲ Automatic backup of site file creates a backup within the site folder. It's not a backup of the components of your site, but of the GoLive site file that keeps track of them.

   ▲ Use the fields under the Names for new items label to specify default file and folder names used within sites.

   ▲ Choose options for deleting files under the When removing files label.

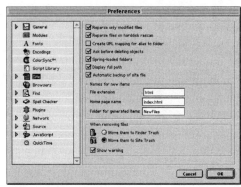

Figure 14.47 Set file management and naming options in the Site Preferences window.

VIEWING AND MANAGING SITES

The real value of site building tools lies not only in creating a well-organized site, but also in maintaining it. Large sites often become unmanageable because of the vast number of links and confusing hierarchical relationships. Adding, deleting, and moving files tends to introduce errors. And things change on the Web; over time, links get broken.

Adobe GoLive's site management tools allow you to take a visual and logical look at your site and find and correct errors efficiently. You can also use these tools to diagram and report on the contents and condition of your site.

In this chapter, I cover:

- ◆ Working with site objects
- ◆ The Site window
- ◆ Custom site objects
- ◆ The Navigation view
- ◆ The Links view
- ◆ Peripheral panes
- ◆ Collections
- ◆ Troubleshooting sites
- ◆ Site reports

Working with Site Objects

Files, URLs, e-mail addresses, colors, and font sets are all objects within a GoLive site. Each type of object can be configured, renamed, and moved, just as items within a document can be. Also, like layout objects, site objects can be configured within the Inspector.

Managing site files

Unlike layout objects—text boxes, images, and multimedia, for example—files that are part of a site are all configured using the same Inspector.

Because the Site window provides a view to the actual files that make up a site, you can perform some site management tasks in the Finder (Mac) or Windows Explorer (Windows), if you prefer. Like these operating system–based file managers, the Site window is organized into files and folders (GoLive calls them groups, but they look and act just like folders or directories). You can also use the Site window's Files tab to view file attributes (file type and its location on the disk) and to sort files by their status. Finally, you can open and rename files, just as you do in the Finder or in Windows Explorer.

To rename a file in the Site window:

1. Click a file name in the Files tab of the Site window to select the file.

2. Type a new name, overwriting the old one. Don't forget to preserve the file's extension (.html, .gif, etc.).

3. Press Return to confirm the name. If the file is linked to others in your site, GoLive will search for URLs that need to be changed and present you with a window containing files that should be updated (**Figure 15.1**).

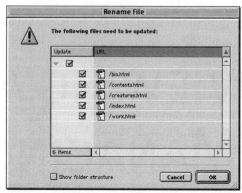

Figure 15.1 When you change a file's name or location within a site, an update dialog box appears, allowing you to choose whether to update references to that file that occur within other site files.

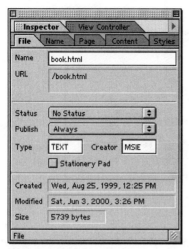

Figure 15.2 The File Inspector allows you to rename a site object and see information about that object.

4. To change all URLs that refer to the file whose name you're changing, click OK. If you don't want to change a specific file reference, uncheck the checkbox next to its name and then click OK to change the others.

To rename a file with the Inspector:

1. Click a file in the Site window. The File Inspector appears (**Figure 15.2**).

2. Type a new name in the Name field. Don't forget to keep the file extension.

3. Update the links to the file as described in the previous set of steps.

To move a file within a site:

1. Locate a file you want to move. Drag it into the folder you want to move it to. GoLive displays the Update window and asks if you would like to update the file's URL and its connection to other files in your site.

2. Click OK to update the site.

✔ Tips

■ You can change URLs and e-mail addresses, too. Using the same options you find in the familiar Finder (Mac) or Windows Explorer (Windows) interface, you can change the name, but not the address, or the URL itself. Changing the name within the site will not update your Web page.

■ To edit a URL or address, select the item in the External tab of the Site window and edit the URL in the Inspector. When you're done, GoLive will present the update dialog box and give you the chance to correct references to the URL within your pages.

■ If the External tab contains no URLs or addresses, choose Site > Get References Used. GoLive will update the External tab with URLs and addresses it finds in the files that make up your site.

To preview a file's contents:

With a file selected in the Site window, click the Content tab of the Inspector. A thumbnail representation of your HTML file or image appears (**Figure 15.3**).

✔ Tips

■ In order to see the thumbnail in the Content tab of the File Inspector, you may need to update the thumbnail information. To do that, choose Site > View > Navigation, then choose Design > Update Thumbnails. When the update is complete, each file in the site should have a thumbnail.

■ You can add an image to a document from the File Inspector by clicking on the thumbnail in the Inspector's Content tab and dragging it into the Document window (**Figure 15.4**).

■ You can play a multimedia file in the Content tab, just as you can in the Document window. GoLive provides built-in support for QuickTime and QuickTime VR files. Other multimedia formats will play if the appropriate plug-ins are present. For a complete discussion of plug-ins, see Chapter 13, "Working with Rich Media."

■ You can drag-and-drop images or multimedia files to the Document window. You can't drag-and-drop HTML thumbnails within a document.

■ (Mac) Another useful capability of the File Inspector, at least on the Macintosh, is the ability to change the file's creator code. This is useful if you have added an HTML file to your site that was not created with GoLive. If you try to open the file by double-clicking it in the Site window, it will open with the application that created it, rather than with GoLive. To learn how to change the file's creator, see the next step-by-step section.

Figure 15.3 The Content tab of the File Inspector shows a thumbnail of GoLive-created HTML files, and any image files that are in a Web-compatible format.

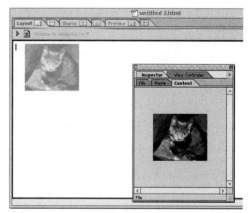

Figure 15.4 Drag an image thumbnail from the Content tab of the File Inspector into the Document window to add the image to a document.

Figure 15.5 One way to add a new folder to a site is to drag the Folder icon from the Site tab to the Site window.

To change a file's creator code to GoLive (Mac only):

1. In the Site window, select an HTML file that was created with an application other than GoLive.

2. Under the File tab of the File Inspector, change the entry in the Creator field to GoMk.

3. If the Type field contains an entry other than TEXT, change it to TEXT.

4. Return to the Site window. The file's icon has changed to that of GoLive and the page preview appears in the Content tab of the File Inspector.

Using site folders

If you have a large Web site, managing lots of site files can be a challenge. GoLive recognizes and uses your site's imported folder hierarchy. You can also add new folders to organize files logically. You can create groups that store pages, media files, URLs, and e-mail addresses.

To create a site folder within a site:

1. With a site open and the Files tab visible, Control-click (Mac) or right-click (Windows) and choose New Folder from the contextual menu.

   or

   Choose Site > New > New Folder.

   or

   Drag the Folder icon (**Figure 15.5**) from the Site tab of the Objects palette to the Site window. A selected folder appears in the Site window.

continues on next page

2. Type a new name for the selected folder, and click outside the folder to confirm the name.

or

Type a name for the folder in the Folder Inspector (**Figure 15.6**).

3. In the Site window, add HTML files to your new folder by dragging them onto the folder's icon.

4. View the contents of the folder by clicking on the triangle (Mac) or plus sign (Windows) to the left of the Folder icon, in the Site window.

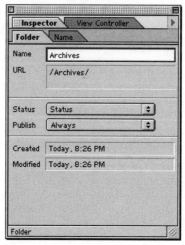

Figure 15.6 You can name and view information about site folders in the Folder Inspector.

WORKING WITH SITE OBJECTS

Figure 15.7 Click the button in the lower-right corner of the Site window (the two-headed arrow) to view the secondary site window as a pane of the primary Site window. Clicking the button again closes the pane.

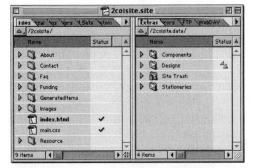

Figure 15.8 When you open the secondary site window, you see four tabs. The active tab contains folders for several kinds of site objects.

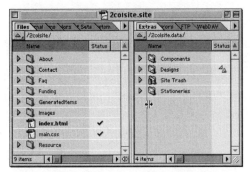

Figure 15.9 Drag the border between the primary and secondary site windows to change their sizes. To give more room to both windows, drag the grow box in the lower-right corner of the Site window.

A Closer Look at the Site Window

In the previous chapter, I showed you how to view and add items to a GoLive site in the Site window. In this section, I will introduce you to Site window features you can use to manage your site. I'll also show you how to find and organize the items in the Site window so that they're easier to work with.

Expanding the Site window

When you open a new GoLive site, it appears in the Site window, which contains six tabs. You can expand the window to view four more tabs in the *secondary site window*. You use the tabs in this window to work with several specialized types of GoLive site objects, and they provide access to windows you will use to view errors and to upload your site to a Web server.

To view the secondary site window:

1. Click the button in the lower-right corner of the primary Site window (**Figure 15.7**). The button looks like a two-headed arrow. The secondary site window opens as a pane to the right of the primary pane of the Site window (**Figure 15.8**).

2. Enlarge the Site window to see more of both the primary and secondary panes.

3. To view more of one pane or the other, click and drag the border between the two panes (**Figure 15.9**).

I'll have more to say about the secondary pane in "Custom Site Objects," later in this chapter, and in Chapter 16, "Publishing Your Site."

Changing your view

When you open the second pane of the
Site window, your view of the primary pane
shrinks. As I described above, you can easily
change the size of the window and of each
pane within it. You can also control which
Site window columns you see and how wide
they are.

To add or remove columns from the Site window:

1. With a site open, choose Window >
   View Controller.

   or

   Click the View Controller tab in the
   window containing the Inspector.

2. Click the Show Columns popup menu
   in the View Controller to view the list of
   columns you can display in the Site window. The currently displayed columns
   are indicated with a checkmark
   (**Figure 15.10**).

3. Select a column from the menu. The
   column you chose is no longer visible in
   the Site window.

✔ Tips

- Choose Show All or Hide All from the
  View Controller popup menu to view all
  available columns, or to hide all of them.
  If you hide all columns, only the filename
  and its icon appear in the primary pane
  of the Site window.

- Like the Site window, the View Controller
  is context-sensitive, and shows different
  columns depending upon which Site
  window tab is visible. When you click
  the Colors tab, for example, the View
  Controller shows columns for the HTML
  Name of the color, value, Web safe status,
  and whether or not the color is currently
  in use.

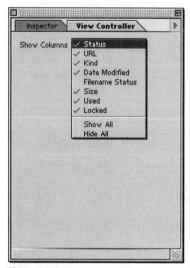

Figure 15.10 Choose a column or columns
to view in the View Controller's Show
Columns popup menu.

Figure 15.11 Click the arrow to change the sort order for Site window columns.

Sorting items in the Site window

Each of the columns in the Site window can be used to sort the objects in the site. By default, these items are sorted alphabetically by object name.

To sort items in the Site window by any column value, click the column heading. To change the sort order from ascending to descending, click the arrow to the right of the column labels (**Figure 15.11**).

Custom Site Objects

You can store more than files and URLs within a GoLive site. There are several special categories of site objects that give you access to frequently used information and templates or code fragments you can use to build pages.

Snippets

Snippets are sections of code, text, objects, or even layout grids that you save and use when you need to reuse the item on several pages within the site. An obvious use for snippets is the creation of boilerplate text, logos, or navigation elements. GoLive lets you store snippets with individual Web pages or with a site. In either case, snippets are stored in the associated Custom tab.

The sixth tab in the GoLive Site window is the Custom tab (**Figure 15.12**). It's empty until you add the first snippet to it. Like other tabs in the Site window, you can store individual items or create folders to store a group of items. Once you've stored a snippet with a site, you can add it to any page in the site by dragging it from the Custom tab to the Document window.

Creating snippets

You can create a snippet by copying text or objects from a GoLive document or from other applications. Snippets you copy from within GoLive appear as HTML code when you view them in the Snippet Inspector, while text you copy from a word processor, for example, appears as text when you view the snippet and when you copy it into a GoLive document.

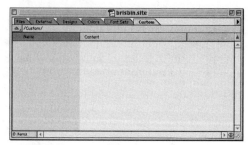

Figure 15.12 The Custom tab of the Site window is empty until you add snippets.

Figure 15.13 Select the text and/or object you want to turn into a snippet.

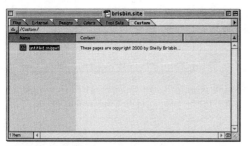

Figure 15.14 Snippets appear in the Custom tab as untitled. The Content column shows a portion of the text or HTML code that makes up the snippet.

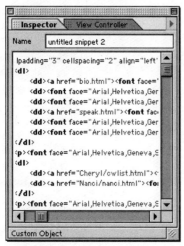

Figure 15.15 The Custom Object Inspector shows the text and code within the snippet, as well as the snippet's name. You can edit the snippet's contents in the Custom Object Inspector.

To create a snippet based on a GoLive object:

1. Open a GoLive document containing an item you would like to turn into a snippet—a navigation bar or boilerplate copyright notice is a good example.

2. Select the object. If it is contained within a table, floating box, or layout grid, be sure to select the enclosing structural object if you want to include it as part of the snippet (**Figure 15.13**). All of its content will come along when you copy the container to the Clipboard.

3. Choose Edit > Copy to copy the object.

4. Open a GoLive site if one is not already open.

5. Click the Custom tab.

6. Choose Edit > Paste to paste the snippet into the tab. An untitled snippet item appears (**Figure 15.14**), along with the Custom Object Inspector (**Figure 15.15**).

7. Name the selected snippet in the Custom tab or in the Name field of the Inspector.

To add a snippet from outside GoLive:

1. In the document containing the item you want to turn into a snippet, select the item.

2. Copy the item to the Clipboard.

3. Open a GoLive site and select the Custom tab in the Site window.

4. Paste the snippet content.

5. Name the selected snippet.

CUSTOM SITE OBJECTS

To edit a snippet:

1. Select the Custom tab in the Site window.

2. Click a snippet to display the Custom Object Inspector.

3. Within the Inspector, edit the HTML code and/or text that forms the snippet. Any changes you make will be reflected when you add the snippet to a GoLive document.

To use a snippet in a document:

1. Select the Custom tab of a site.

2. Open the document where you would like to add the snippet. Move the Document window so that you can see the snippet you want to copy to the document.

3. Drag the snippet from the Custom tab to the Document window (**Figure 15.16**).

✔ Tip

■ You can copy snippets from one site to another. Just select a snippet in the Custom tab, and choose Edit > Copy. Open the site file to which you want to add the snippet, select the Custom tab in the Site window, and choose Edit > Paste to add the snippet.

Stationeries

Like snippets, Stationeries let you keep track of items you want to reuse as you build your site. While snippets save chunks of HTML code, stationeries are GoLive documents that you can use as the basis for new documents. For example, if every page on your site includes the same navigation bar and logo, you can build a stationery that includes these elements and then build new pages by adding content to the stationery file, which acts as a template.

Stationeries are stored in the Stationeries folder under the Extras tab of the Site window.

Figure 15.16 To use a snippet, drag it from the Custom tab of the Site window into a GoLive document.

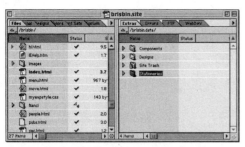

Figure 15.17 Expand the Site window to view the Stationeries folder in the secondary pane.

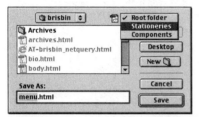

Figure 15.18 Choose Stationeries from the popup menu to save your template to the Stationeries folder within your GoLive site.

Figure 15.19 When you save a new stationery document, the secondary pane of the Site window displays the contents of the Stationeries folder, including your new file.

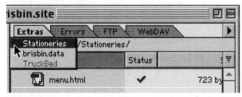

Figure 15.20 To view all the folders in the Extras tab of the secondary pane of the Site window, click and hold the triangle next to the Stationeries folder label and choose Site.data, where *Site* is the name of the site you're working on.

To locate the Stationeries folder:

1. Open the Site window and expand it if the secondary pane isn't visible. The Extras tab is selected.

2. Click the triangle next to the Stationeries folder in the secondary pane (**Figure 15.17**).

To create and save a stationery document:

1. With a site open, create a GoLive document and add the items you want to appear on your stationery document.

2. Choose File > Save As.

3. In the dialog box, click the popup menu (**Figure 15.18**) and choose Stationeries. You should now see the Stationeries folder label at the top of the dialog box.

4. Click Save. The new stationery appears in the Stationeries folder of the Site window (**Figure 15.19**).

✔ Tips

- You can also create a stationery document by dragging from the Files tab of the Site window into the Stationeries folder of the Extras tab. When you do, the original file is moved, not copied. To copy the original, hold down the Option key (Mac) or Alt key (Windows) as you drag from the Files tab.

- When you save a new stationery document to the Stationeries folder, GoLive opens the folder in the secondary pane of the Site window. To view all of the folders in the pane, click the triangle next to the folder's label (**Figure 15.20**).

CUSTOM SITE OBJECTS

341

To open a stationery document using the Objects palette:

1. Choose the Site Extras tab from the Objects palette, then click the popup menu at the bottom of the Objects palette and choose Stationery Pads (**Figure 15.21**).

2. Drag a stationery icon into the Site window's Files tab.

3. Rename the new document.

4. Open the file. It contains all the text and objects of the stationery document.

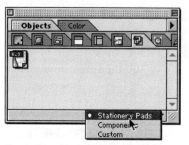

Figure 15.21 Choose Stationery Pads from the popup menu in the Site Extras tab of the Objects palette to view any items you have saved to the Stationeries folder within your site hierarchy.

To open a stationery document from the Site window:

1. Open the secondary pane of the Site window and make sure the Extras tab is visible.

2. Double-click the stationery document you want to work with. You'll see a dialog box asking if you would like to modify the file, or create a new one. If you create a new file, GoLive opens an untitled document containing all of the items in the stationery document.

3. Choose Create to open an untitled file. You can now add anything you like to the file, leaving the original stationery document unchanged.

4. Choose File > Save As and then click Root folder from the popup menu in the Save dialog box. You should now see the root folder of your site in the dialog box.

5. If you wish, navigate to the folder within your site where you want to save the new file.

6. Name the file (including the .html extension) and click Save.

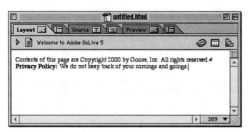

Figure 15.22 This new document contains text for a copyright notice and privacy policy that will appear at the bottom of the site's pages.

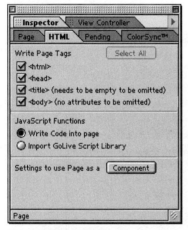

Figure 15.23 The Page Inspector's HTML tab is where you declare a page to be a component.

Using components

Say you have a site with hundreds of pages. At the bottom of each page is a footer containing a copyright notice and the site's privacy policy. Wouldn't it be nice if you could change the footer information once and have all your pages automatically change?

That's just how GoLive's components work. Unlike stationeries, which also allow you to save files for reuse, component-based content can be changed dynamically—editing the component file updates any document that includes that component. GoLive saves a component as an HTML file, linked to as many pages as you choose. This makes components a useful way to deploy buttons and other navigational schemes, logos, headers, and mastheads.

Components can include any text or object that can be described with HTML. To create and use a component, you first build the source file, which contains the content you want to use on pages throughout your site. Then, you add a reference to the source file to each page where you want component content to appear.

To create a component source file:

1. Open a GoLive site.

2. Create a document containing the content you want to include in the component. In **Figure 15.22**, I have created a copyright notice and privacy policy for a site.

3. Open the Page Inspector by clicking the Page icon below the toolbar and then click the HTML tab (**Figure 15.23**).

4. Click the Component button. The Component button dims. You can now save the file as a component.

5. Choose File > Save As and choose Components from the popup menu in the Save dialog box.

To apply a component:

1. Open a document to which you want to add a component.

2. Open the Smart tab from the Objects palette.

3. Drag the Component icon (**Figure 15.24**) from the Smart tab into the Document window (**Figure 15.25**). The placeholder for a component is a heavy box with a rounded upper-left corner. The Component Inspector appears (**Figure 15.26**).

4. In the Inspector, click the Browse icon.

5. Navigate to the Components folder within your site's Site.Data folder and select the component you want to use. The component's content appears in the document with a box surrounding it.

✔ Tips

- You can also use Point & Shoot to link a component placeholder with the component source file. In the Component Inspector, click the Point & Shoot icon and drag to the component you want to use in the Site window.

- Components stored in the site's Components folder appear in the Site Extras tab. You can add an existing component by dragging its icon from the Site Extras tab to the document.

- Although components may be any shape or size, they need to be the only object displayed on the horizontal line they occupy. They cannot share a horizontal space with another object, like an image or text block. Components are ideal for headers, footers, copyright notices, and other elements that occupy an entire horizontal unit of the page.

Figure 15.24 The Component icon appears in the Smart tab of the Objects palette.

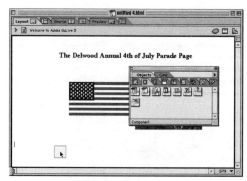
Figure 15.25 Drag the Component icon from the Smart tab of the Objects palette into the Document window.

Figure 15.26 The Component Inspector appears when you add a component placeholder on the page.

Figure 15.27 When you edit a component source file and save it, GoLive verifies that you want to update all files using this component. Uncheck any files you don't want to update.

To edit a component you have already placed:

1. In a document containing a component, double-click inside the component. The component source file opens.

2. Make any changes to the component, and save the source file.

3. In the Updating Component window (**Figure 15.27**), confirm that you want to update all of the files containing this component. When you click OK, the component is updated.

The Navigation View

To this point in the chapter, we've been working in the Site window, a file-hierarchy–oriented view of your GoLive site. You can also look at your site graphically, as a hierarchy of pages (Navigation view) or as a collection of links (Links view). In this section, I'll show you the Navigation view, and how you can use it to approach your site as a hierarchy of dependent pages.

Think of the Navigation view as a bird's eye view of your Web site. Starting with your home page, the Navigation view displays miniature representations of each page in the site and the relationships that connect them to one another. The home page is the *parent* page for the entire site. Each linked page is a *child* of the home page and a *sibling* to other pages on that level. The Navigation view shows these relationships in graphical terms, just as the Design view does (see Chapter 14, "Building Sites").

To examine a site with the Navigation view:

1. Open a site.

2. Click the Navigation View button from the toolbar.

   or

   Choose Site > View > Navigation. The Navigation view (**Figure 15.28**) appears. It shows an icon for the site's home page: in this case, index.html.

3. Click the plus sign below the page icon (**Figure 15.29**). The HTML pages at the root level of your site's folder hierarchy appear (**Figure 15.30**). Note that these pages are not necessarily linked to the home page. To expand the hierarchy further, click the plus sign below any page icon in the Navigation view.

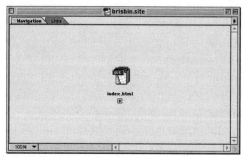

Figure 15.28 When you open the Navigation view for the first time, your home page appears alone in the window.

Figure 15.29 Click the plus sign below an icon in the Navigation view to see children of that page.

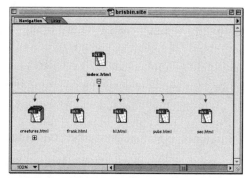

Figure 15.30 This site includes a home page and several child pages.

Figure 15.31 Click the Unfold All button to expand the view of the site in the Navigation view. Click it again to collapse the site.

✔ Tip

■ You can completely expand the Navigation view by clicking the Unfold All button (**Figure 15.31**) on the toolbar. To collapse the site, click the button again.

THE NAVIGATION VIEW

Figure 15.32 Click the Toggle Orientation button on the toolbar to change the Navigation view's orientation on screen.

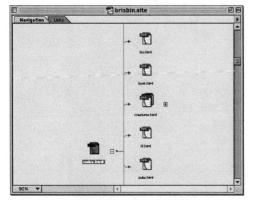

Figure 15.33 When you use the Toggle Orientation button, the Navigation view changes from horizontal to vertical.

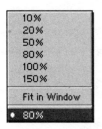

Figure 15.34 Reduce or enlarge the Navigation view with the magnification popup menu in the lower-left corner.

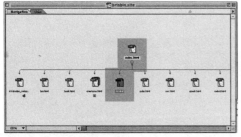

Figure 15.35 When Navigation view items are spotlighted, they appear in a colored box or circle.

Navigation view display options

You can adjust your view of the site in Navigation view in several ways. Changing the site's orientation is one of the most useful ways, especially if your site includes a large number of files. By default, the site appears in a horizontal (wide) orientation. Clicking the Toggle Orientation button on the toolbar (**Figure 15.32**) rotates the view (**Figure 15.33**).

You can also take a different look at your site by reducing or enlarging the Navigation view. To do that, choose a magnification percentage from the popup menu in the lower-left corner of the Navigation view (**Figure 15.34**).

Spotlighting items in Navigation view

You can focus on a particular portion of your site—a single page or related elements in the page hierarchy—using GoLive's spotlight feature. When items in the Navigation view are spotlighted, they are distinguished from other items in the view by a colored box or circle (**Figure 15.35**).

There are several spotlight options available.

◆ **Family** spotlights a page's children, the page itself, and its parent.

◆ **Incoming** spotlights all pages with links to the selected page.

◆ **Outgoing** spotlights pages to which the selected page is linked.

◆ **Pending** indicates pages with pending links to the selected page.

◆ **Collection** points to pages that are part of a collection containing the selected page.

To spotlight pages within a site:

1. With the Navigation view visible, choose Window > View Controller to bring the View Controller tab to the front. If the Inspector is visible, you can simply click the View Controller tab (**Figure 15.36**).

2. Make sure the file you want to include as part of the spotlight is visible. Expand the Navigation view if necessary. Then, select the file.

3. Choose a Spotlight option in the View Controller.

    or

    Choose a Spotlight option from the Navigation Pane menu (**Figure 15.37**) in the upper-right corner of the Navigation view window. The spotlighted page is highlighted in the Navigation view (**Figure 15.38**).

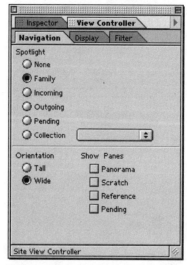

Figure 15.36 Choose a Spotlight option from the View Controller.

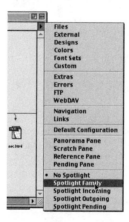

Figure 15.37 You can choose a Spotlight option from the Pane menu in the upper-right corner of the Navigation view window.

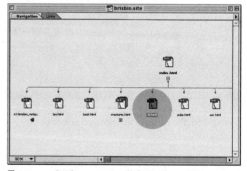

Figure 15.38 When you spotlight an incoming page, the spotlight is a circle.

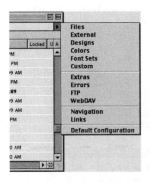

Figure 15.39
You can open the Links view by choosing that option from the Pane menu in the Site window.

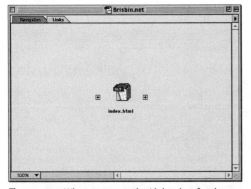

Figure 15.40 When you open the Links view for the first time, your home page and plus signs indicating links to (left) and from (right) appear.

The Links View

When you're ready to move from a high-level, file-centric view of your site to a link-centric one, you'll also move from the Navigation view to the Links view to do your work. The Links view presents your site in terms of the actual hyperlinks that exist between pages. This may or may not correspond to the file hierarchy you have built. In fact, the Links view is a great way to verify, for example, that all of the pages in your site's root directory have links back to the home page. If a page in the directory isn't linked to another page, you won't see it in the Links view when you expand it out from the home page.

To view a page in the Links view:

1. Open a GoLive site.

2. Choose Site > View > Links.

   or

   Click the right-pointing arrow in the upper-right corner of the Site window (called the Pane menu) and choose Links (**Figure 15.39**). The Links view window appears (**Figure 15.40**). Notice that the window also contains a tab for the Navigation view.

✔ Tip

- If you are working in the Navigation view, you can reach the Links view by clicking the Links tab.

Viewing links

When you first open the Links view, an icon representing your home page appears. Just as in the Navigation view, plus signs let you expand the Links view to see more of your site. But instead of displaying files that appear below the home page in the folder hierarchy, as the Navigation view does, the Links view displays links to (on the left) and from (on the right) your home page.

To view links to or from the current page:

1. With the Links view open, click the plus sign to the left of the index.html (or whatever your home page is called) icon. The view expands to show all pages within your site that are linked to the home page (**Figure 15.41**).

2. Click the plus sign to the right of your home page. Pages within your site to which your home page is linked appear.

Notice that the pages that appear when you expand the view also have plus signs next to them. Click one on the left of a page to see other pages that link to it. That's what I did in **Figure 15.42**.

If you view links from the current page (with the plus sign to the right of the source page) you will see not only files to which the page contains links, but also images and URLs. **Figure 15.43** shows a page that includes links to several files, remote Web site URLs, and an e-mail address.

The toolbar and the Links view itself give you several options for altering the display of your site. You can also use the View Controller to change Links view options.

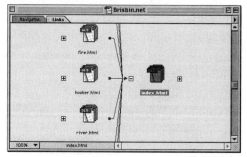

Figure 15.41 When you click a plus sign to the left of a page icon in the Links view, you see all of the pages within your site that link to that page.

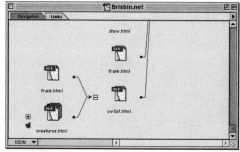

Figure 15.42 Here is my home page and pages containing links to it (on the left) and pages the home page links to (on the right).

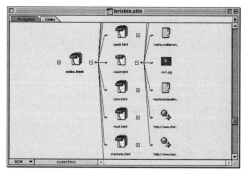

Figure 15.43 Clicking the right plus sign shows all items, including images, Web site URLs, and e-mail addresses that the source page links from.

THE LINKS VIEW

Figure 15.44 The Toggle Orientation button on the toolbar changes the Links view from vertical to horizontal and back again.

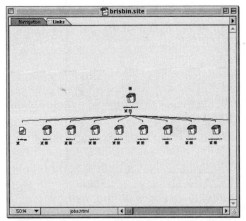

Figure 15.45 Here's my site in the Links view, viewed horizontally.

Figure 15.46 Use the Unfold All button to view all links in your site.

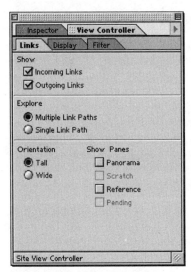

Figure 15.47 Change display options for the Links view in the View Controller.

To change the display of the Links view:

1. Use the popup menu in the lower-left corner of the Links view to enlarge or reduce the magnification of the pages in the Links view window.

2. Click the Toggle Orientation button on the toolbar (**Figure 15.44**) to see links horizontally (**Figure 15.45**).

3. To see all links within the site, click the Unfold All button (**Figure 15.46**) on the toolbar. All link relationships are expanded. You can collapse the entire site by clicking the Unfold All button again.

✔ Tip

■ When you work with a file in Links view, it behaves as it does in the Site view or Navigation view. You can use a context-sensitive menu or toolbar button to open the file in GoLive or in a browser or reveal it on the desktop. When you click once on the file, its Inspector appears.

To change the Links view with the View Controller:

1. With the Links view visible, click the View Controller tab in the Inspector.

   or

   Choose Window > View Controller. The View Controller appears, displaying the Links tab by default (**Figure 15.47**).

2. Under the Show label, uncheck Incoming Links or Outgoing Links if you want to hide either kind of link.

3. Under the Explore label, choose Single Link Path if you want to see only links that are part of the path you have expanded.

continues on next page

THE LINKS VIEW

4. Under the Orientation label, choose Wide if you want to view the Links view horizontally.

✔ Tips

■ You can change display and filter options for the Navigation view or the Links view, using the View Controller. The options under these two tabs are the same for both views.

■ You'll learn about the options under the Show Panes label in the "Peripheral Panes" section of this chapter.

To set display and filter options for the Navigation view or Links view:

1. Open the Navigation or Links view and then the View Controller.

2. Click the Display tab (**Figure 15.48**).

3. Choose Outline to see the Navigation or Links view as a hierarchical list of objects. Note that if you choose Outline, the other options in the Display tab disappear from the View Controller, except for the Show Columns popup menu that gives you control over the columns that appear in the outline.

4. With the Graphical view option selected (default), choose an option from among the Show Items as radio buttons. Your choices are Icons (the default), Thumbnails, Frames, or Ovals (**Figure 15.49**).

5. Under Item Label, choose Page Title to show the title of the page, rather than the file name.

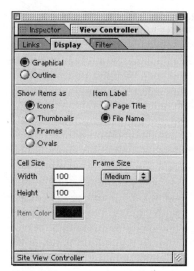

Figure 15.48 The Display tab of the View Controller allows you to change the look of the Navigation or Links view.

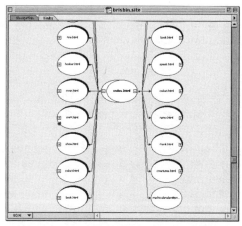

Figure 15.49 Here's the Links view when you choose to view items as ovals, rather than icons.

THE LINKS VIEW

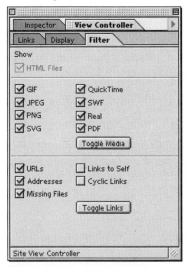

Figure 15.50 The Filter tab of the View Controller allows you to hide some items from the Navigation view or Links view.

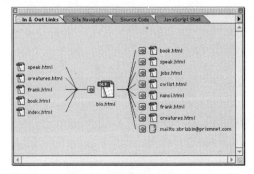

Figure 15.51 This page is linked to other pages, and has links coming from it, as well. Notice that some of the links on the right are Web site URLs and e-mail addresses.

6. Choose options for the size and color of objects in Navigation or Links view, under the Cell Size and Frame Size labels. Cell Size (measured in pixels) controls the size of icons in the Navigation or Links view, while Frame Size ranges from Small to Large and controls the distance between icons.

7. Click the Filter tab in the View Controller (**Figure 15.50**).

8. Uncheck file types that you do not want to see in the Navigation or Links view. Items that are checked will appear when you expand the views to see individual pages that contain the file types listed.

9. Click the Toggle Media button if you would rather see no media objects. Click again to view them all.

10. Click checkboxes next to the types of links that you do not want to see in the Navigation or Links view. The Toggle Links button turns them all on or off.

✔ Tips

■ Another way to view links—a way that works in all site views—is to use the In & Out Links palette. Choose Window > In & Out Links, and select an object in the Site, Navigation, or Links view. The In & Out Links palette will appear (**Figure 15.51**). You'll probably want to enlarge it with the grow box. When you click a file within your site, the In & Out Links palette displays items that link to the selected page (left) and items that are linked from the page (right).

■ Though the options for changing the display and filtering for the Navigation and Links views are the same, changing options for one view does not affect what you see in the other view.

THE LINKS VIEW

Peripheral Panes

In addition to the main graphical site views, GoLive includes four *peripheral panes*— alternative site views you can use while you also work in Navigation or Links view, or in the Design view (introduced in Chapter 14, "Building Sites").

Peripheral panes have several uses: you can use them to get a wide angle view of your site, looking at it as a whole while you work on smaller groups of pages and links in the Navigation, Links, or Design view. Peripheral panes also allow you to focus on a particular portion or perspective of a large site, without forcing you to scroll endlessly through its contents in the main site views.

There are four peripheral panes available.

- ◆ **Panorama pane** shows the site "from 30,000 feet." You see the entire site, reduced in size and with simple boxes representing pages or links, rather than icons. A movable box within the view lets you choose which portion of the site you want to focus on in the main (Navigation or Links) view.

- ◆ **Scratch pane** displays HTML and media files that are stored within the root folder of the site, but which are not linked to any other file that's part of the site. You can only use the Scratch pane in Navigation view.

- ◆ **Reference pane** shows images or other media files that are included within a selected HTML page. When you click the HTML file in the Navigation or Links view, all media files that are part of that page appear in the Reference pane.

- ◆ **Pending pane** shows pages that have a logical parent-child relationship (children are in a folder that's located in the same folder as the parent) or sibling relationship, but are not hyperlinked.

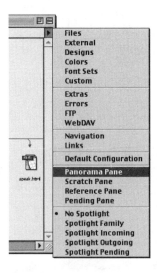

Files
External
Designs
Colors
Font Sets
Custom

Extras
Errors
FTP
WebDAV

Navigation
Links

Default Configuration

Panorama Pane
Scratch Pane
Reference Pane
Pending Pane

• No Spotlight
Spotlight Family
Spotlight Incoming
Spotlight Outgoing
Spotlight Pending

Figure 15.52
Choose a peripheral pane from the menu in the Navigation or Links view.

Show Panes

☐ Panorama
☐ Scratch
☐ Reference
☐ Pending

Figure 15.53 Choose a peripheral pane (or more than one) by clicking a checkbox in the View Controller.

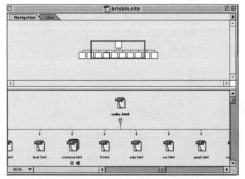

Figure 15.54 This Navigation view window includes a Panorama pane at the top. You can drag the box in the pane to focus on a portion of the site in the Navigation view.

To view a peripheral pane:

1. Open a site to the Navigation or Links view.

2. Choose a peripheral pane (Panorama, Scratch, Reference, and/or Pending) from the Pane menu under the right-facing arrow in the upper-right corner of the Navigation or Links view window (**Figure 15.52**).

3. Choose Window > View Controller and under the Show Panes label, click the checkbox for the peripheral pane(s) you want (**Figure 15.53**). The pane opens in the Navigation or Links view window (**Figure 15.54**).

✔ Tips

■ You can view more than one peripheral pane at a time. Just choose the second one from the menu, or click the checkbox.

■ To adjust the size of the panes you're viewing, drag the border between the panes.

■ When you view a peripheral pane in the Navigation or Links view, the pane is attached to that view. If you switch views and then switch back, the peripheral pane settings are those that were in effect the last time you worked in that view.

■ To remove a peripheral pane, click the menu item or checkbox you used to add it in the View Controller. The pane disappears.

PERIPHERAL PANES

To view a peripheral pane in the Design view:

1. Open a site and a site design.

2. If the Inspector is visible, click the View Controller tab.

   or

   Choose Window > View Controller.

3. In the View Controller (**Figure 15.55**), click the checkbox for the peripheral pane you want to view. The pane appears in the Design view window. Note that you can't use the Scratch pane in Design view.

Working with peripheral panes

Each peripheral pane gives you a different way to view and change your site.

To use the Panorama pane:

1. Open a site view (Navigation, Links, or Design) and display the Panorama pane.

2. Move the box within the Panorama pane by clicking and dragging the border. The portion of the site you see in the main site view changes as you drag (**Figure 15.56**).

3. Click a page in the Panorama pane. Notice that it is selected both in the peripheral pane and in the main site view (**Figure 15.57**).

   When you select an object in the Panorama pane, it's just as if you had selected it in the main site view. You can view its Inspector, expand or collapse its relationship to other pages in the site, or even move the page around.

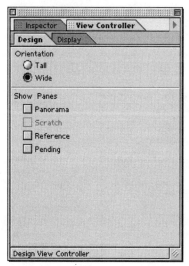

Figure 15.55 Choose a peripheral pane in the Design view's View Controller.

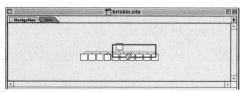

Figure 15.56 Drag the box around the Panorama pane to change the focus from one portion of your site to another.

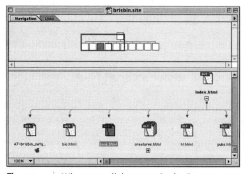

Figure 15.57 When you click a page in the Panorama pane, it is selected there and in the Navigation or Links view. You can work with the object in either pane.

PERIPHERAL PANES

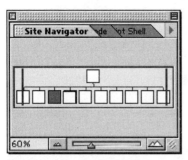

Figure 15.58 The Site Navigator.

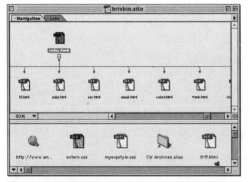

Figure 15.59 Here's the Scratch pane, showing files and other items that are not linked to the selected page, but are stored in the same folder with it.

Figure 15.60 When you drag a page from the Scratch pane to the site hierarchy in the Navigation view, the page appears there, but with a bug below it, indicating that you need to compete the hyperlink.

✔ Tip

■ The Site Navigator works just like the Panorama pane. You may choose to use it if you just need to move the view of your site around. Unlike the Panorama pane, the Site Navigator view is simply a representation of the site: you can select objects within it. To use the Site Navigator, choose Window > Site Navigator. It appears in **Figure 15.58**.

To use the Scratch pane:

1. Open a site to the Navigation view and display the Scratch pane. Note that you can't use the Scratch pane in Links view.

2. Click a page in the main part of the Navigation view. Items in the folder containing that page that are not linked to it appear in the Scratch pane (**Figure 15.59**).

3. To move a page from the Scratch pane into the hierarchy of the site, drag it into the main Navigation view pane. The page is moved, but appears with a bug icon below it, indicating that you need to complete the hyperlink between it and the parent page (**Figure 15.60**).

4. To complete the link, open the selected page (double-click its icon in the Navigation view) and make a link to the parent page in the hierarchy. When you save and close the page, the bug disappears from the selected page.

PERIPHERAL PANES

To use the Reference pane:

1. Open a site to the Navigation or Links view and display the Reference pane.

2. Click a page icon in the main Navigation or Links pane. Icons for media files on that page appear in the Reference pane (**Figure 15.61**).

3. Click another page in the Navigation or Links view to see the media files linked to it.

✔ Tip

■ Just as the Site Navigator and Panorama pane have a lot in common, the Reference pane shares some capabilities with the In & Out Links palette (see "The Links View" section of this chapter). In fact, the In & Out Links palette is a bit more versatile because you can use it in any site view, and because you can Point & Shoot from the palette to an object within your site, should you need to change a link. You can get to the In & Out Links palette by choosing Window > In & Out Links.

To use the Pending pane:

1. Open a site to the Navigation view and display the Pending pane. Note that you cannot display the Pending pane in the Links view.

2. Click a page icon in the Navigation view to select it. Sibling or child pages that are not linked appear in the Pending pane (**Figure 15.62**).

3. Double-click the selected file to open it.

4. Add a hyperlink to one of the pages that appears in the Pending pane. When you save and close the file, the file you linked to no longer appears in the Pending pane.

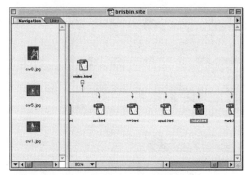

Figure 15.61 The Reference pane (left) shows all of the media files (JPEG images, in this case) that are embedded in the selected HTML page.

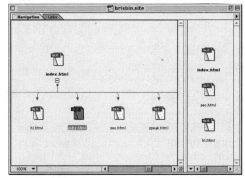

Figure 15.62 When you select a file in the Navigation view while the Pending pane is visible, sibling and child files of the selected file appear in the Pending page.

Figure 15.63 Name and color a new collection in the Edit Collections dialog box.

Collections

Large and even medium-sized sites tend to be organized into groups of pages, rather than simply as a bunch of individual pages that all link to the home page. When you work with these pages, it may be easier for you to work with them as a group than as individuals. GoLive's Collections feature makes this easier.

A collection is a group of pages that can be viewed, edited, and moved as one, within one of GoLive's graphical site views—Navigation, Links, or Design view.

To create a new collection:

1. Open a site and display the Navigation, Links, or Design view.

2. Choose Design > Edit Collection. The Edit Collections dialog box appears.

3. Click New.

4. Name the collection (**Figure 15.63**).

5. If you want to assign a different color to the collection, click the color box next to the Name field and choose a color from the dialog box that appears.

6. Click OK to create the collection.

COLLECTIONS

To build a collection from existing pages:

1. Select pages in the Navigation, Links, or Design view that you want to include in a collection.

2. Choose Design > Remember Selection. GoLive creates a collection and gives it a generic name.

   or

   Control-click (Mac) or right-click (Windows) and choose Remember Selection from the contextual menu (**Figure 15.64**).

3. To give the collection a custom name, choose Design > Edit Collection and click the collection you just created. Change its name in the Name field.

To add items to an existing collection:

1. In the Navigation, Links, or Design view, click the icon for a page you want to add to the collection.

2. Control-click (Mac) or right-click (Windows) on the page's icon and choose Toggle Collection > <collection name>. The page is added to the collection you selected.

To work with a collection:

1. Choose Design > Reselect Collection > <collection name> where *collection name* is the collection you want to work with.

2. Open, move, delete, or choose another file management option that you want to perform on the collection as a whole.

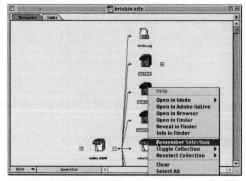

Figure 15.64 Select a group of pages you want to include in a collection and then control-click (Mac) or right-click (Windows) and choose Remember Selection from the contextual menu.

COLLECTIONS

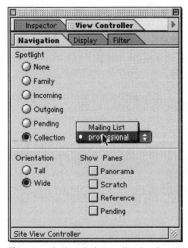

Figure 15.65 Spotlight a collection in the Inspector.

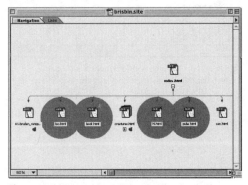

Figure 15.66 Here's a spotlighted collection in the Navigation view.

Spotlight collections

In the Navigation view section of this chapter, I introduced the concept of spotlighting portions of your site. When you spotlight a page, family, or group of links, they are highlighted in the Navigation view. You can also spotlight collections, making them easier to identify and work with.

To spotlight a collection:

1. Open a site in the Navigation view.

2. If it's not visible, open the View Controller (choose Window > View Controller, or click the View Controller tab in the Inspector).

3. Under the Spotlight label, click the Collection button (**Figure 15.65**).

4. Choose a collection to spotlight from the adjacent popup menu. The collection is spotlighted (**Figure 15.66**). You may need to expand the site view (with the plus sign below the spotlighted page), to see all items in the collection.

COLLECTIONS

Troubleshooting Sites

Earlier in this chapter, I explained how to update your site by changing file names and how to keep it organized by examining your site with the Navigation and Links views. Changing things, though, can introduce errors. GoLive includes several tools for finding and fixing errors.

To identify errors in the Site window:

1. Open a site to the Site window. If you don't see the Site window, choose Site > View > Files.

2. In the Site window, click the Status header (**Figure 15.67**) to sort files and folders by their status within the site. GoLive sorts files with no errors at the top of the list.

3. To bring broken files to the top of the window, click the Ascending/Descending arrow, located at the upper-right corner of the Site window.

The Site window in **Figure 15.68** shows five of the possible Status indicators.

◆ A **checkmark** indicates that the file contains no errors and that all the files or URLs it points to are where they should be.

◆ A **bug** indicates that the file contains broken links.

◆ An **error indicator** in the Status column of a folder warns that files within the folder contain errors.

◆ A **stop sign** indicates that a file is missing.

◆ A **warning marker** indicates an empty file.

✔ Tip

■ E-mail addresses do not display Status indicators because there isn't a way to verify them.

Figure 15.67 Click the Status header to sort the objects in the Site window by their status within the site. By default, files without errors are sorted to the top. Reverse the sort order with the Ascending/Descending button in the upper-right corner of the Site window.

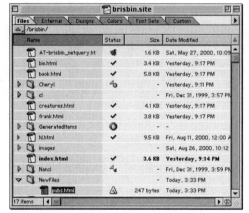

Figure 15.68 This Site window includes files and folders that are in good shape and some with errors.

Figure 15.69 A bug icon in the Status column indicates a problem with a link on this page.

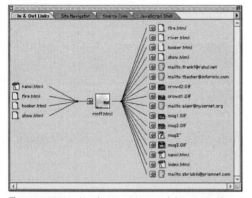

Figure 15.70 Notice the question mark icon near the bottom right of the In & Out Links palette? That's the source of the problem, noted by the bug icon, that appears next to the rmff.html page in the Site window.

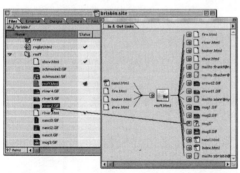

Figure 15.71 To fix a broken link in the In & Out Links palette, drag from the Point & Shoot icon next to the problem link to the correct file in the Site window.

To check pages for errors:

1. Locate items in the Site window with a "bug" icon in the Status column (**Figure 15.69**).

2. Double-click the file to open it.

3. Choose Edit > Show Link Warnings.

4. Look for any obvious problems: missing images, for example. If you find a broken image link, click it to display the Inspector and try to fix the problem by locating the file that should be linked.

5. Links that are broken are highlighted on the page. Click a broken link and use the Inspector to fix it.

6. When you've fixed all the links on the page, save and close the file. The Site window should now display a checkmark in the Status column for the file you've worked on.

✔ Tip

■ Another way to check for and fix links is to use the In & Out Links palette. In the Site window, click a file with a bug icon, then choose Window > In & Out Links (**Figure 15.70**). In the In & Out Links palette, look for objects with error indicators. You can fix these links by clicking on the Point & Shoot icon in the In & Out Links palette, and dragging to the correct file in the Site window (**Figure 15.71**).

To check a site for missing files:

1. Open the secondary pane of the Site window by clicking the double arrow icon in the lower-right corner of the Site window (**Figure 15.72**).

Figure 15.72 Click the double arrow icon to open the secondary pane of the Site window.

2. Click the Errors tab in the secondary pane to display folders containing broken site items.

3. Click the triangle next to the Missing Files folder to open it. A list of files to which others link, but which can't be found in the site hierarchy, appears (**Figure 15.73**). These files may have been deleted entirely, or may have had their names changed, possibly because the site has been edited by multiple people.

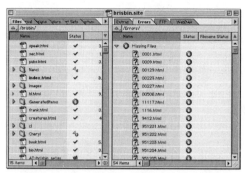
Figure 15.73 Files that can't be found in the site appear in the Missing Files folder, within the Errors tab of the Site window.

4. Click a missing file. The Error Inspector displays the URL for the missing file (**Figure 15.74**). This information may give you a clue to the file's actual whereabouts.

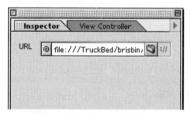
Figure 15.74 The Error Inspector shows the URL for the missing file—the broken link that appears in the source file.

5. If you can't resolve the broken link with its URL, choose Open In & Out Links from the toolbar (or choose Window > In & Out Links). The missing link appears on the right, and the file or files that use it appear on the left (**Figure 15.75**). Now you determine which pages in your site use the missing file, and you can decide whether to solve the problem by eliminating the link, by recreating the file, or by finding the original.

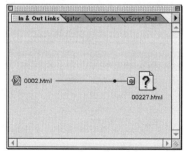
Figure 15.75 When you click on a file in the Missing Files folder, it appears in the In & Out Links palette, along with the file or files which link to it.

Figure 15.76 Click the Find Files in Site button to look for files you've lost.

Figure 15.77 The Find dialog box, with the In Site tab selected, appears when you click Find Files in Site.

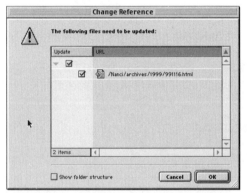

Figure 15.78 When you recreate a link to a formerly missing file, the Change References dialog box appears, allowing you to verify that you want to change the link to the file, wherever it appears within your site.

To find the file if you think it has been misplaced within the site:

1. Click Find Files in Site (**Figure 15.76**) from the toolbar. The Find dialog box appears, displaying the In Site tab (**Figure 15.77**).

2. Type all or part of the name of the file you want to look for.

3. Click Find.

4. If GoLive finds the file, it will be highlighted in the Site window. If the file has been moved to the wrong folder, you can drag it back into its original location within the site. In that case, a Change Reference dialog box will appear.

5. In the Change Reference dialog box, click OK to update the site.

To update the link if you find a file:

1. With the folder containing the newly found file visible in the Site window, open the In & Out Links palette if it isn't already open.

2. Click the missing file icon in the Missing Files folder. The missing file and the item(s) to which it is linked appear in the In & Out Links palette.

3. Point & Shoot from the missing file in the In & Out Links palette to the file in the primary Site window pane. When you release the mouse button, the Change Reference dialog box appears (**Figure 15.78**).

4. Click OK to fix the link. The formerly missing file disappears from the Missing Files folder.

TROUBLESHOOTING SITES

To find a file if you think it has been renamed:

1. In the In & Out Links palette, note the files to which the missing file should be connected. Write the file names down or print the In & Out Links window. You can print the contents of the window by choosing Print from the Pane menu of the In & Out Links palette.

2. Search the site manually, or with the Find command, for files that may be the one you're looking for.

3. When you locate the file you want, you can restore its original name (by typing it in the Name field of the File Inspector), in which case all of the links will be repaired. Or open the file and add links according to the list you made from the In & Out Links palette.

✔ Tips

- You can print a list of the items in the Missing Files window. Just click within the window and choose File > Print. The list may help you determine any systemic problems with file naming that affect your site.

- When you view a missing file in the Error Inspector, you may not be able to see the full URL. One way around this is to move your cursor over the missing file object in the In & Out Links palette. The relative URL for the item appears in the lower-left corner of the palette (**Figure 15.79**).

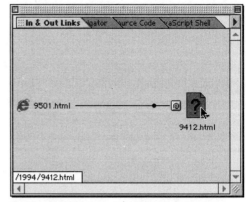

Figure 15.79 When you move the cursor over a missing file in the In & Out Links palette, the URL for the file appears in the lower-left corner of the palette.

TROUBLESHOOTING SITES

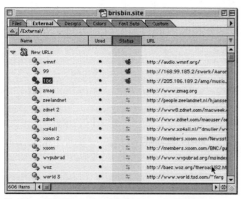

Figure 15.80 When you check external references, GoLive lets you know which URLs are valid, and which ones it could not verify by connecting to them. If you see a bug icon, GoLive was unable to connect to it.

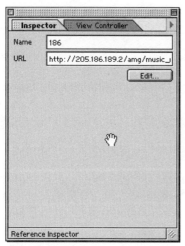

Figure 15.81 The Reference Inspector appears when you click a URL in the Site window. With the Inspector, you can view and edit the URL.

To locate and repair external URLs:

1. If you don't have a continuous connection to the Internet, connect to the Internet.

2. Click the External tab in the Site window.

3. Choose Site > Check External Links. GoLive checks URLs to see whether they are valid. When the process is complete, the results appear in the Status column of the External tab (**Figure 15.80**).

4. Click the Status label to sort URLs by their Status. If GoLive could not connect to a particular URL in your site, the bug icon appears in the Status column for the URL.

5. If you have found a "buggy" URL, click it to open the Reference Inspector (**Figure 15.81**), or view the URL in the Site window's URL column.

6. With the URL selected in the Site window, choose Window > In & Out Links to see which files within your site link to the URL. This step may help you remember what the URL is, and whether it's likely to be in working order. Open the file containing the URL if you need more information.

continues on next page

TROUBLESHOOTING SITES

7. Make sure the URL is selected in the Site window and examine the URL for any obvious problems. If the full URL isn't visible, click the Edit button. The full URL appears in a new dialog box.

8. If all the information you've gathered leads you to believe that the URL should be valid, copy the URL from the Reference Inspector and paste it into your Web browser.

9. Connect to the Web and check the URL.

10. If the URL does not work, delete it from your site and remove or replace any links to it. If it does work, try using the Check External Links command again to see if GoLive can connect to the URL.

To find and fix orphan files:

1. In the Errors tab of the Site window, open the Orphan Files folder. The folder will not be present if there are no orphan files. An orphan file is one that is linked to a file within your site and is stored on your hard disk, but can't be found within your site's folder hierarchy.

2. Drag the orphan file into the Files tab of the Site window. The Copy Files dialog box appears, asking if you want to update references to the relocated file. If you click OK, files within your site that link to the file will be updated and the formerly orphaned file will be added to your site.

Site Reporting

As useful as the graphical site views and troubleshooting tools in GoLive are, there are times when nothing will do the job like a text-based report: a list of files, objects, links, and other site elements that you can use to share information about your site, or just to track your work for your own use. GoLive's site reporting tools are located in the Find dialog box. With site reporting tools you can create and save queries that gather a wide variety of information about the contents and current condition of the site.

✔ Tip

■ Though you'll find site reports in the Find dialog box, this is not the place to go when you're searching for a wayward file within your site. To search by file name, click the In Site tab of the Find dialog box (conveniently located right next to the Site Reports tab) and enter part or all of a file name you want to locate.

Site Reports options

You can search for five kinds of site information, using the Site Reports tab.

◆ **File Info** includes options for file size, download time (based on file size and type), and date information.

◆ **Errors** lets you look for the kind of problems you would find under the Errors tab of the Site window, as well as image tags missing some attributes, or HTML that is incompatible with one or more versions of Microsoft or Netscape browsers.

◆ **Site Objects** allows you to search for components, fonts, and colors (all stored as objects within a GoLive site) or pages that include a URL (Web site address or e-mail) that is stored in the site's External tab.

continues on next page

◆ **Links** gives you the option of searching for files with one of several prefixes, or with a particular extension. You can also look for pages with external links.

◆ **Misc** lets you look for files that have a relationship with other files by virtue of their position in the site hierarchy. Specify a particular file and search for others that are within a set number of clicks of that item.

To create a site report:

1. Choose Site > Site Report. The Find dialog box appears with the Site Reports tab selected (**Figure 15.82**).

2. Choose one of the criteria in the File Info tab (shown by default) and click the checkbox to activate fields for that criterion.

3. Choose an option from a popup menu and enter a value in the adjacent field. **Figure 15.83** shows a search for site files larger than 100000 bytes.

4. Choose additional search criteria from the current tab or from one of the others. Site reports can be based on several search criteria.

5. Once you've selected all the criteria you want, click the Search button. When GoLive has finished searching your site, a Report Results window appears showing the files that match your criteria (**Figure 15.84**).

✔ Tip

■ If you choose and change multiple search criteria, be sure before you search that you only have the criteria you want to use selected. Since you can only see one of the five query tabs, it's possible, if you change queries, that an old one is still selected, which may give you incorrect or irrelevant results.

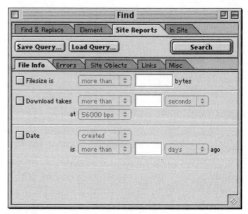

Figure 15.82 You create site report queries in the Site Reports tab of the Find dialog box.

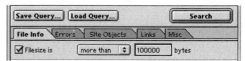

Figure 15.83 This search will locate all files that are larger than 100000 bytes (100 K).

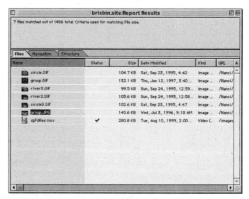

Figure 15.84 Site Report search results look like this. You see the name, modification date, and URL (among other things) that are associated with each file.

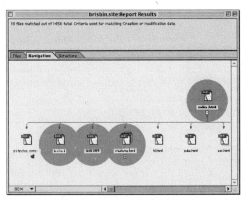

Figure 15.85 The Navigation tab of the Report Results window spotlights found files within the navigation hierarchy of the site.

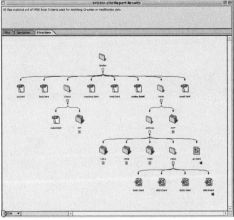

Figure 15.86 In the Structure view, you see all the files that turned up in a Site Report search. They are displayed in their locations within the site's file hierarchy.

The Report Results window contains three tabs that display your search results differently:

◆ **Files** lists files that match your search criteria.

◆ **Navigation** shows the Navigation view, just as if you had chosen the Navigation view for your site. In a site report, the files that matched your search criteria are spotlighted (**Figure 15.85**). You cannot change or move items in this version of the Navigation view.

◆ **Structure** displays search results from the point of view of their position in the site hierarchy. The root folder and any folders that are part of the results file(s) family appear in the Structure tab (**Figure 15.86**).

✔ Tip

■ To work with items that come up as search results, Control-click (Mac) or right-click (Windows) on the object in the Files tab of the Report Results window. You'll see the usual file opening options. You can also see where the file appears within the site by looking at the File Inspector or the URL column of the Files tab.

Reusing site queries

The kind of information you can gain from a site report is often information that you want to have access to again and again. You might, for example, generate a new site report before each site update, or at some other regular interval. You may design a report that helps you spot site trouble spots and maintain the integrity of your links and navigation hierarchy. GoLive allows you to create and then save site report queries so that when you are ready to repeat one, it's quickly available from the Site Reports tab of the Find dialog box.

continues on next page

SITE REPORTING

To save a site report query:

1. Create a query that you would like to save for future use. Include as many search criteria as you like.

2. Do a search using the query to see how much information you are able to gather.

3. When you are satisfied with the query, click Save Query in the Site Reports tab.

To use a saved query:

1. With a site open, choose Site > Site Reports.

2. Click Load Query.

3. Locate the query you saved in the Open dialog box that appears and click Open.

4. In the Site Reports tab, click Search. Results appear in the Report Results window.

✔ Tips

■ Site report query files contain the extension .glqs. Preserve this extension when you name saved queries.

■ You can store queries anywhere you like. The Site data folder is a good place. If you use a lot of queries, you could create a folder for them within the Site data folder.

■ If you decide to change a query you've already created and save, there's no automatic way to update it. You'll have to resave it with the same name as the older version of the query, and in the same folder, overwriting the older version.

Publishing Your Site

After the text is typed, images placed, links connected, and errors checked it's time to put your site on the Web. If your Web server is located in your own office, this may simply be a matter of copying folders to the server machine. If you use an Internet service provider (ISP), you'll need to use FTP to transfer your files to a remote server.

Wherever your Web site lives, Adobe GoLive can help you get everything in order for the big upload.

In this chapter, I cover:

◆ Choices for publishing your site

◆ Two kinds of FTP

◆ Exporting a site

◆ Using WebDAV

Four Ways to Publish Your Site

GoLive provides four ways to move a site, or pages of a site, from your computer to your Web server. You can use the following:

- FTP browser
- FTP tab of the Site window
- Site export
- WebDAV

The FTP browser and the FTP tab of the Site window are each FTP (File Transfer Protocol) clients. An FTP client allows you to add or remove items from a Web server using Internet-standard commands, and based on password-protected access to the server's files. If you don't use GoLive's FTP features, you'll have to use a stand-alone FTP client program, such as Anarchie (Mac) or WS-FTP (Windows).

The Site export feature doesn't actually upload files to a Web server, but it does allow you to prepare your files for uploading. Finally, GoLive's WebDAV client tool gives you access to WebDAV servers. A WebDAV server not only stores and delivers Web pages, but also allows several members of a workgroup to add and edit files to a Web site while managing file versions and tracking who is currently working with a given file.

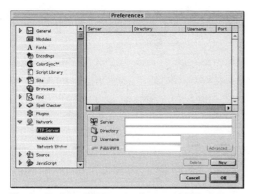

Figure 16.1 Set up FTP servers for use with the FTP Browser in the FTP Server portion of the Preferences window.

Figure 16.2 When you click New in the FTP Server Preferences window, you can begin setting up an FTP server.

The FTP Browser

Just like any FTP client (you may have used Fetch, Anarchie, Transmit, WS-FTP, CuteFTP, or a Web browser to exchange files with an FTP server), GoLive can upload and download files—from one file at a time to a whole site's worth. The GoLive FTP browser is designed to let you pick and choose files to copy, and to give you a clear picture of the directory structure available on your FTP server. Like other FTP tools, it can also be used to grab any file stored on a remote server, whether or not it's a component of your Web site.

To configure the FTP browser:

1. Choose Edit > Preferences.

2. Click the triangle (Mac) or plus sign (Windows) next to the Network label and click FTP Server (**Figure 16.1**).

3. Click the New button to activate the fields at the bottom of the window (**Figure 16.2**).

4. Enter the URL of your server, the directory path to your files, and your username and password. If you don't have this information, contact your Webmaster or ISP.

5. To add another server, repeat steps 3 and 4.

6. When you've finished adding servers, click OK to close the Preferences window.

✔ Tip

- Not sure of the name of the directory your files are stored in? Many ISPs set up server access so you don't need to know the directory name before connecting for the first time. To find out if your directory is set up like this, enter the server name and your username and password, leaving the Directory field blank. When you connect to the server, you'll be able to determine whether you're in the right directory or you can navigate to it when connected.

To use the FTP browser:

1. If you are not already connected to the Internet, be sure that you can make a connection from your computer before proceeding with these steps. If you can connect, but aren't already online, GoLive will connect you automatically.

2. With GoLive open (you can be working within a site or not), choose File > FTP Browser. The FTP Browser window appears (**Figure 16.3**).

3. Choose a server from the popup menu to the right of the Server field (**Figure 16.4**).

4. Click the Connect button. GoLive will attempt to open an Internet connection via PPP, TCP/IP, or over your LAN connection, and will open the FTP server when it succeeds. The server's directories and files appear (**Figure 16.5**).

5. Navigate through the window just as you would in the Finder or Windows Explorer, or in the Site window of a GoLive site, to locate a folder into which you want to upload files.

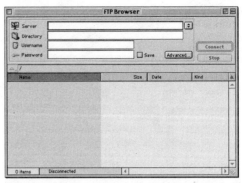

Figure 16.3 The FTP Browser window shows the configuration information for the server.

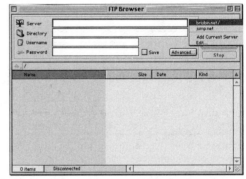

Figure 16.4 In this window you can choose a server to work with, add the currently displayed server to the list of available servers, or edit the current server's information.

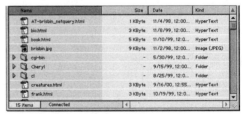

Figure 16.5 When you connect to an FTP server, files and directories appear. They look pretty much like Mac or Windows files and folders.

THE FTP BROWSER

6. To upload a file or folder, drag it from the Finder, Windows Explorer, or from the left pane of the GoLive Site window into the FTP server window (in the right pane of the Site window), onto the appropriate directory label. The file or folder is copied.

7. When you've finished working with this server, click the Disconnect button on the toolbar. If you're connected to the Internet via a dial-up connection, you will need to disconnect from your dial-up connection separately.

✔ Tips

■ You can download items from a Web server by double-clicking them in the FTP server window—the right pane of the Site window. When you do, you'll be presented with a standard Save dialog box. Navigate to the folder you'd like to use, and GoLive will copy the file.

■ You can also download files to your hard drive by dragging them into the Files tab in the left pane of the Site window or into the Finder or Windows Explorer.

■ You can use the labels at the top of the FTP Server window to sort server directories and files, just as you would in the Finder or GoLive Site window.

The FTP Tab

You can use the FTP Browser to work with a GoLive site or with any file you want to upload to or download from a Web server. The FTP client included in the GoLive site management interface is specifically geared to the needs of those who manage their Web resources with GoLive's site management features. When you use the FTP tool within the Site window, GoLive helps you determine which files to upload and does the work of copying files and folders for you. It's much easier to work with the FTP tool of the Site window than with the FTP Browser when you're uploading a site for the first time, or when you need to perform a major, complicated update later on.

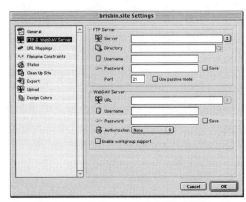

Figure 16.6 Set up FTP server access in the FTP and WebDAV portion of the Site Settings window.

✔ Tip

■ To completely configure the FTP client for uploading, you must be connected to the Internet. If your connection is not constant (usually a dial-up connection), connect to the Internet before you begin setting FTP options in this section.

To set up server access within the FTP tab:

1. Open a site that is ready to be uploaded to a Web server.

2. Click the Site Settings button on the toolbar.

   or

   Choose Site > Settings.

3. In the Site Settings window, click the FTP & WebDAV Server item. The result appears in **Figure 16.6**.

4. Enter the name, directory, username, and password for your FTP server in the FTP Server section of the window. If you don't have this information, consult your Webmaster or ISP.

Figure 16.7 Click the folder icon to open a list of available directories on the FTP server.

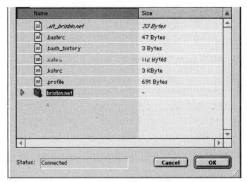

Figure 16.8 Choose the directory containing the root (top-level directory) of your site, then click OK.

To locate the directory for your site:

1. If you know your server and account information, but not the directory where your files are to be stored, fill out the server name and account access fields as describe above, then click the folder icon next to the Directory field (**Figure 16.7**). GoLive connects to the server and displays a file and directory listing (**Figure 16.8**).

2. Click a directory to select it, or open the directory to locate a subdirectory. When you find the directory that will (or already does) contain the *root*—the highest level directory—of your Web site, click to select it, then click OK. The full directory path appears in the Directory field of the Site Settings window.

✔ Tip

■ (Mac) GoLive supports the Mac OS keychain, a password management tool built into the OS that allows you to enter a single password for all keychain-supporting applications. If you have set up a keychain on your Mac, GoLive will ask whether you would like to manage FTP server access within the keychain. If you do, the password for servers you add in GoLive are added, and you no longer need to enter the password each time you log on. If you don't want to use the keychain to manage FTP access, or haven't set up the keychain elsewhere in Mac OS, just choose not to add FTP passwords to the keychain when prompted.

THE FTP TAB

To configure site settings for FTP uploading:

1. In the Site Settings window, click the Upload label on the left side of the window. Once you have finished setting up FTP server access, you can customize the way GoLive manages FTP uploads here.

2. Click the Site specific settings checkbox. The fields in the window are activated (**Figure 16.9**).

3. Choose whether to use the Publish status of folders and/or files to determine which files will be uploaded to the Web server. If you leave the boxes checked, only files that are labeled Publish (which is what they are labeled by default) will be uploaded.

4. Leave the "Upload referenced files only" option checked to instruct GoLive to ignore files that are not linked to anything within your site.

5. Use the "Show list of files to upload" and "Show options dialog" checkboxes to override publishing settings before files are transferred to the server.

6. Check some or all of the three "Strip HTML code for" checkboxes to have GoLive remove GoLive-specific code, comments, or extra spaces.

7. Click OK to close the Site Settings window.

To upload your site:

1. With a GoLive site open, choose FTP Server Connect/Disconnect from the toolbar.

   or

   Control-click (Mac) or right-click (Windows) in the Site window, and choose FTP Server > Connect.

   or

   Choose Site > FTP Server > Connect.

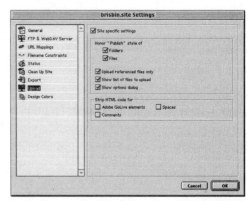

Figure 16.9 Set publishing options in the Upload pane of the Site Settings window.

Figure 16.10 When you connect to an FTP server, the contents of the server appear in the FTP tab of the Site window.

2. If you have set up GoLive to request a password each time you connect to the server, you will be asked for it now. Type your password. When GoLive has connected to the FTP server, the right pane of the Site window opens (if it's not already visible) and displays the directory for your site (**Figure 16.10**).

3. Choose an upload option: you can upload an entire site, update all files in a site that have changed, or select specific items to upload. There are four upload options:

▲ **Upload all** copies all files within the site to the Web server.

▲ **Incremental upload** moves files that have been created or changed since the last site upload (items whose modification dates are later on the local site than on the server).

▲ **Upload modified items** uploads only files that have been edited in GoLive since the last upload.

▲ **Upload selected** copies items that are selected in the Site window at the time of the upload, regardless of their modification status.

The process is basically the same for each kind of upload—GoLive locates files to be uploaded, then gives you the final choice about whether to upload them or not. The initial choice of files varies, depending on which upload option you choose. You're given this choice by default. If you don't want to be prompted to choose files for uploading, you can disable this option in the Upload portion of the Site Settings window.

To upload an entire site:

1. Choose Site > FTP Server > Upload All.

   or

   Control-click (Mac) or right-click (Windows) in the left pane of the Site window and choose FTP Server > Upload All from the menu. The Upload Options window appears (**Figure 16.11**). Its options duplicate those in the Upload pane of the Site Settings window, described earlier in this chapter.

2. Choose upload options that instruct GoLive what files to upload and how to deal with the files before they are uploaded.

3. To strip GoLive specific code, comments, or extra spaces from HTML code, click the Strip HTML Code button and choose the options you want to use from the HTML Options window.

4. Click OK to return to the Upload Options window.

5. If you want to apply the same options each time you upload, click the Don't show again checkbox and then the Set as default button. The next time you upload your site, GoLive will use the options you have set here.

6. When you're satisfied with the settings you've chosen, click OK. If you have chosen to see a list of files before they are uploaded, GoLive builds and displays the list (**Figure 16.12**). If your site is large, this may take some time.

7. If you want to prevent a file or folder from being uploaded, uncheck it in the list.

8. To display files within a folder, click next to the folder to open it.

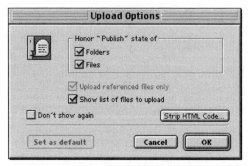

Figure 16.11 The Upload Options window is your chance to choose the kinds of files you want to upload.

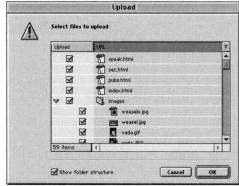

Figure 16.12 One last chance to change your mind: if you have instructed GoLive to display a file list before the upload begins, this window will appear before the upload begins. Uncheck files you don't want uploaded, and then click OK.

9. When you're satisfied with your selections, click OK to begin moving files to the Web server. While the upload is in progress, GoLive displays a status box. When the upload is complete, the box disappears and the directory of files on the server is updated.

✔ **Tip**

■ (Mac) If you experience excessive slowness when uploading a large site, quit GoLive and allocate more RAM to the application before uploading.

To upload changed items only:

1. Open a GoLive site and connect to an FTP server on which your site is already present.

2. Choose Incremental Upload or Upload Modified Items from the toolbar, contextual menu, or Site menu.

3. Perform steps 2–6 from the previous section. GoLive locates and then displays the files to be uploaded if you have chosen to see a file list before the upload.

4. Uncheck files or folders (if any) that you want to exclude from the upload and then click OK. When the upload is complete, GoLive updates the contents of the FTP tab of the Site window.

5. Disconnect from the server by choosing FTP Server Connect/Disconnect from the toolbar or FTP Server > Disconnect from the contextual menu.

✔ **Tip**

■ When you disconnect from the server, the list of uploaded files on the right pane of the Site window disappears, leaving an empty pane. If you want to work with the list of uploaded files (to compare it to the original list, sort it, etc.) do so before breaking your connection to the server.

THE FTP TAB

To upload selected items:

1. Open a site in the Site window, then connect to an FTP server.

2. Click to select files or folders you want to upload.

3. Control-click (Mac) or right-click (Windows) and choose FTP Server > Upload Selection from the contextual menu.

4. Make any changes you wish in the Upload Options window and click OK. If you have chosen to see a file list, uncheck files to exclude in the Upload window, then click OK to begin the upload.

✔ Tip

■ If you're thinking that it would be easier to drag selected files and folders from the Site window to the FTP tab, you're right, except that you don't have access to GoLive's upload filtering options. Your files are simply copied, replacing old versions or added to the site without regard to their status. Dragging files is a simple way to quickly add or update a file or two to your site.

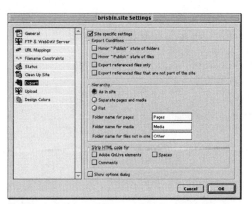

Figure 16.13 Choose Export options in the Site Settings window before you begin the export.

Exporting a Site

If you're not quite ready to upload your site, or if you need to prepare it according to a structure established by your Webmaster or ISP, you can use the Export Site command as the first step to publishing the site to a Web server.

Although most people won't find the Export option a better choice than using FTP, there are a few circumstances in which it could be useful. If, for example, your Web server is a Mac or PC on your network, you can export a site and drag it into the proper directory on the server using the familiar Finder or Windows Explorer interface and using your existing file access privileges. You can also specify publishing options, like requiring that an exported site include only files that are being used within the site, or that include a Publish state ("flag").

✔ Tip

■ Like FTP, GoLive's site export includes the option to modify settings that govern which items in a site are uploaded. You can activate these settings in the Export pane of the Site Settings window (**Figure 16.13**) or at the time you export the site. To do the latter, you'll need to click the Show options dialog checkbox at the bottom of the Export pane.

To export a site:

1. With a site open and the Site window visible, choose Site > Site Export.

   or

   Control-click (Mac) or right-click (Windows) and choose Site Export from the contextual menu. If you chose to display options when you export your site, the Export Site Options window appears (**Figure 16.14**). If you didn't make that choice, skip to step 4.

2. If you want to export the site using a different folder hierarchy than it has now, choose Separate pages and media or Flat. The Separate pages option will create one folder for HTML pages and one folder for media files. A Flat structure will place all files in the same folder. This usually isn't the best way to structure a site, but you do have the option if you don't want to use folders.

3. Select an option under the Honor "Publish" state of label to exclude files or folders whose status is something other than Publish in the Reference Inspector. Unless you've changed these status options, all of the files in the site are set to be published.

4. Click one or both of the Export referenced files options to limit the site export to those files that are linked to others within the site. Note that Export referenced files only cannot be selected unless Files under Honor "Publish" state of label is unchecked.

5. Click the Strip HTML Code button to see options (in the HTML Options window) that remove GoLive-specific code, extra space, and/or comments before site files are exported. When you've selected the options, click OK to return to the Export Site Options.

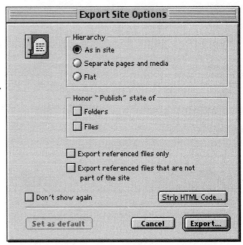

Figure 16.14 Most of the options that appear in the Site Settings window are in the Export Site Options window. You will only see this window if you have chosen the Show options dialog checkbox in the Export pane of the Site Settings window.

EXPORTING A SITE

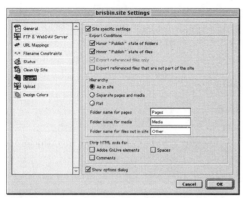

Figure 16.15 To export the site into folders for HTML, media, and other items, click the Separate pages and media button and rename the folders for each type of file, if you like.

6. Click Export to begin the export process. (The Export Site Options window will close automatically.) GoLive presents a Save dialog box so that you can choose a location for the exported site.

7. Navigate to a location on your hard drive where you would like to store the exported site and click Save. GoLive exports the site.

✔ Tips

■ GoLive will publish files whose status you have set to Always, but not those files within a folder whose status is Never.

■ When you export a site with separate folders for media and HTML files, GoLive creates folders called Pages, Media, and Other by default. You can use different names by setting them in the Site Settings window before you export your site (**Figure 16.15**). Open the Site Settings window, click the Export label and then the Site specific settings checkbox. The folder names (and all of the other options in the window) are activated, allowing you to change them.

WebDAV

WebDAV (Web Distributed Authoring and Versioning) is a server-side technology that makes it possible for a group of designers to work collaboratively on a single Web site, all from different, even remote, locations.

To use WebDAV with GoLive, your Web server must not only support it, but the Webmaster who runs the server must have implemented it. It's not simply a matter of uploading files to the server and working collaboratively. The information in this section will only apply to those who have access to a WebDAV server.

GoLive supports uploading of files to WebDAV-enabled servers. The server manages group access and transmits information about who is working on which file.

To use WebDAV, the server you're using must support it. At this writing, the Apache Web server (using the mod_dav module) and Microsoft's IIS 5 and Novell NetWare 5.1 all support WebDAV. Check with your Webmaster or ISP to see if your Web server supports WebDAV, and if you can use it.

✔ Tips

- If you are currently unable to use it, but are interested in learning more about WebDAV, check out WebDAV Resources at http://www.webdav.org.
  If you're a Mac user, also see http://www.webdav.org/goliath/

- If you would like to try WebDAV, you can sign up for a free account at http://www.driveway.com. Driveway allows you to store files (not an infinite amount, mind you) on their Web server for free. The site is also WebDAV-enabled, meaning that you can establish a WebDAV session from GoLive or any other client software that supports WebDAV.

Figure 16.16 Set up WebDAV servers in the WebDAV pane of the Preferences window.

GoLive and WebDAV

GoLive's WebDAV interface looks and acts a lot like the FTP tab of the Site window. You configure and upload files to a WebDAV server the same way you do using GoLive's FTP tools.

You can work with WebDAV servers using one of GoLive's two WebDAV client interfaces—the WebDAV tab of the Site window or the WebDAV Browser.

First, set up global WebDAV access from GoLive, then connect to a specific server to transfer files.

To set up global WebDAV server access:

1. Choose Edit > Preferences.

2. Click next to the Network label to view Network preferences.

3. Click the WebDAV label. The WebDAV pane appears.

4. Click New to activate the fields (**Figure 16.16**).

5. Type the WebDAV server's address in the Address field, and your username and password in the corresponding fields.

6. If your WebDAV server requires authorization—a password—choose Basic from the popup menu. Otherwise, choose None to indicate that you don't need authorization to access the server.

   If you're not sure how to fill out these fields, consult your Webmaster or ISP for information.

7. Click OK to close the Preferences window, or click New to add another WebDAV server.

✔ **Tip**

■ Setting up WebDAV servers in the Preferences window makes them immediately available in the WebDAV tab of the Site window and in the WebDAV Browser. You can also configure individual servers from within these WebDAV clients.

WEBDAV

To enable WebDAV server access in the Site window:

1. Open a GoLive site.

2. Choose Site > Settings.

   or

   Choose Site Settings from the toolbar.

3. Click the FTP & WebDAV Server label.

4. In the WebDAV Server area (**Figure 16.17**), type the URL of the server, along with your username and password.

5. Choose an authorization type (None or Basic) from the Authorization popup menu. Your Webmaster or ISP should be able to supply this information along with your username and password.

6. Click Enable workgroup support if several people will be uploading files to your site via the WebDAV server.

7. Click OK to finish configuring the WebDAV server.

To connect to a WebDAV server from the Site window:

1. Open a GoLive site and set up access to a WebDAV server.

2. Choose Site > WebDAV Server > Connect.

   or

   Choose WebDAV Server Connect/ Disconnect from the toolbar.

   or

   Control-click (Mac) or right-click (Windows) in the left pane of the Site window and choose WebDAV Server > Connect from the menu. GoLive makes a connection to the server and its contents appear in the WebDAV tab of the Site window (**Figure 16.18**).

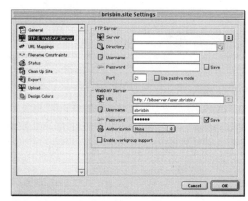

Figure 16.17 In the Site Settings window, enter the server name, along with your username and password to connect to a WebDAV server.

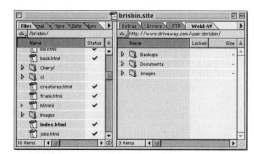

Figure 16.18 You won't see files in the WebDAV tab unless you're connected to the server, as indicated here.

WEBDAV

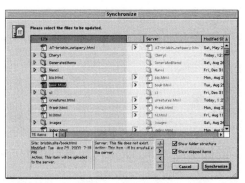

Figure 16.19 The Synchronize window shows files and folders on the local and server sides.

Uploading and downloading files

When you move files to and from a WebDAV server, you synchronize them. GoLive uses information about your site and about the files stored on the server to build a record of when and by whom files are modified. When you upload or download files, GoLive reports on the files on both sides, letting you know which versions are newer and whether the files in question are out of sync with one another—if the local and server versions have both been modified since the last synchronization, for example.

To upload files to a WebDAV server for the first time:

1. Open a GoLive site.

2. Connect to a WebDAV server.

3. When GoLive presents a dialog box letting you know that the two sites (your local files, and the remote site's file) need to be synchronized, click Yes to upload all files (the entire site, in this case) to the remote server. If you click No, you can add files by dragging them from the left to the right pane of the Site window.

To upload files after working on a site locally:

1. Open a site and connect to a WebDAV server containing a version of the site.

2. From the site menu or contextual menu, choose WebDAV Server > Upload Modified Items. GoLive communicates with the server. When the process is complete, the Synchronize window appears (**Figure 16.19**).

continues on next page

WEBDAV

3. Examine the file list in the Synchronize window. If you want to change what happens to a file, click the button in the column between the local site and server columns of the window to change the file's status (**Figure 16.20**). Possible file status indicators are:

- ▲ **Right-pointing arrow**: the file will be copied to the server.

- ▲ **Left-pointing arrow**: the file will be copied to the local hard drive containing your site if the remote file is older than the local one. If the dates are the same, or if the remote file is newer, the local file is not copied

- ▲ **An X**: the file will be deleted.

- ▲ **A warning icon**: the file has been modified on both the local hard drive and the WebDAV server.

- ▲ **A slash**: the file is set to be skipped, even if it has been modified since the last upload.

- ▲ **No icon**: no action will be taken.

4. To see an explanation of the condition of a file, click the file name or icon, on either side of the window. Information about the file and its status appears below the list of files to be synchronized (**Figure 16.21**).

5. When you are satisfied with the synchronization options you've chosen, click Synchronize.

To use the WebDAV Browser:

1. Choose File > WebDAV browser. You need not have a GoLive site open. The WebDAV Browser appears (**Figure 16.22**). If you have set up a WebDAV server in the Preferences window, access information for the server appears in the WebDAV Browser.

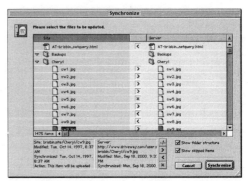

Figure 16.20 You can choose to add or skip files from synchronization by clicking on the status indicators in the middle column.

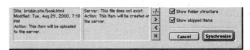

Figure 16.21 Click a file's name or icon in the Synchronize window to see information about the file at the bottom of the window.

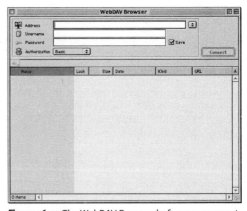

Figure 16.22 The WebDAV Browser before you connect.

WEBDAV

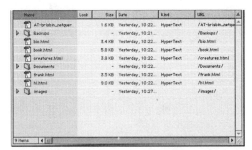

Figure 16.23 When you connect to a server using the WebDAV Browser, your files appear in the lower portion of the window. You can then drag and drop files into the window to upload them to your server.

2. If you don't have WebDAV access set up, enter your server name, username, and password in the fields provided.

3. With all information entered, click Connect. The contents of your Web directory appear in the WebDAV Browser (**Figure 16.23**).

✔ **Tip**

■ Frankly, the WebDAV Browser isn't particularly useful. Since the whole point of WebDAV is to take a look at your local site versus the server, it makes more sense to use the WebDAV tab of the Site window to upload and download files. You also won't have access to WebDAV synchronization features when you use the browser. If you're not managing your site with GoLive, however, using the browser is your only choice for adding files to a server using WebDAV.

Workgroups and WebDAV

The whole point of WebDAV is collaboration. A group of Web page designers can work on a single site stored on a WebDAV server without fear of overwriting the latest version. GoLive supports collaboration by providing tools to synchronize local and remote files (described in the previous section) and to check files in and out to users who work on them locally and then return them to the server.

✔ **Tip**

■ If you intend to use WebDAV to collaborate, be sure to choose the Enable workgroup support option in the FTP & WebDAV Server pane of the Site Settings window.

WEBDAV

To check out a file from the WebDAV server:

1. Open a GoLive site and connect to a WebDAV server.

2. Select a file or files in the WebDAV tab of the Site window, which appears when you connect to the server.

3. Control-click (Mac) or right-click (Windows) on the file you want to check out, and choose Check Out from the contextual menu. When GoLive has finished updating the server, a pencil icon appears next to the icon of the file you've checked out in both the Site window and in the WebDAV tab, indicating that you now "own" this file and nobody else in the workgroup can modify it.

4. Double-click the local (Site window) copy of the file to edit it in GoLive. Check the file back in to the WebDAV server when you have finished editing it.

To check in files from the WebDAV server:

1. Open a GoLive site and connect to a WebDAV server.

2. In the Site window, control-click (Mac) or right-click (Windows) on a file you want to check in to the WebDAV server and choose Check In from the contextual menu. The pencil icon disappears and the file is now available for others to check out and edit.

3. Enter a comment in the Check In box when it opens, or just click OK.

WEBDAV

USING ACTIONS

In addition to building Web pages with Adobe GoLive, you can use the software to add interactivity to pages, using actions.

Actions are prepackaged collections of JavaScript and Cascading Style Sheets that allow you to add interactivity and automation to your pages by simply entering values in the Inspector palette. GoLive does all the coding for you, so you don't have to know JavaScript to use actions. But if you do, you can create your own actions, as I will discuss later in the chapter.

In this chapter, I cover:

◆ Tools for adding actions

◆ Adding action icons

◆ Configuring actions

◆ Creating your own actions

◆ The GoLive Software Developer's Kit (SDK)

Action Tools

You will work with three sets of tools when using actions in GoLive: some of the icons on the Smart tab of the Objects palette, the Action Inspector, and the Actions palette.

Action icons

GoLive includes several actions that you can use by dragging an icon from the Smart tab of the Objects palette (**Figure 17.1**) onto a Web page. The Smart tab also includes icons you will use to configure actions; namely, Rollover, URL Popup, Body Action, Head Action, and Browser Switch icons.

The Smart tab also contains objects you need to add smart images created in Adobe applications like Photoshop and Illustrator. These smart objects are covered in Chapter 5, "Working with Images."

Action Inspector

When you have applied an action, you configure it in the Action Inspector (**Figure 17.2**). Once you choose a particular action, the Inspector displays a set of options that are specific to that action.

The Actions palette

When you have selected an image or other HTML element that can take an action, you can use the Actions palette to add and configure the action. To activate the Actions palette (**Figure 17.3**), choose Window > Actions. To activate the palette, you must first select an item in the Document window that can accept an action.

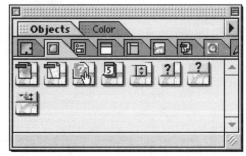

Figure 17.1 Open the Smart tab of the Objects palette to work with actions.

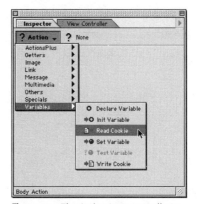

Figure 17.2 The Action Inspector allows you to select an action, and has settings specific to each.

Figure 17.3 Set up actions in the Actions palette, available from the Window menu.

Figure 17.4 The Modified Date stamp icon.

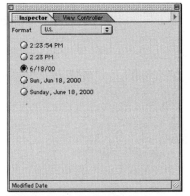

Figure 17.5 Use the Modified Date Inspector to select a date format by clicking the radio buttons next to sample formats.

Figure 17.7 This date is displayed in French Canadian fashion.

Figure 17.6 The Modified Date Inspector's Format popup selects local variations in how date or time is displayed.

Adding Action Icons

Let's start simply by adding action icons to a document. In the next section, we move on to full-fledged actions.

Modified Date stamp

The Modified Date stamp adds a static date and time, visible in one of several different formats, to your page. The date and time are derived from your computer's clock. Each time you save the page, the date or time information is saved in the specified format. The date that appears when a visitor opens your page in a browser is the date on which you last modified the page.

To add a Modified Date stamp:

1. Open a document in the Layout Editor and choose a location for the modification date or time.

2. Double-click or drag the Modified Date icon (**Figure 17.4**) from the Smart tab of the Objects palette onto the page. A date and time stamp appears.

3. Using the Modified Date Inspector (**Figure 17.5**), choose a display format by clicking one of the radio buttons. The first two formats will display time, the last three will display the date.

4. To change the language of your stamp, choose one from the Format popup menu in the Inspector (**Figure 17.6**). Selecting the language or format of the stamp changes the sample in the Document window (**Figure 17.7**).

continues on next page

ADDING ACTION ICONS

5. In the Document window, select the stamp. You can edit the stamp's appearance, just as you would any text item, with the toolbar or the Text Inspector, which appears when you select the stamp.

6. To add a second stamp, repeat steps 1–5 and choose a format.

✔ Tips

■ You can use a Modified Date stamp just as though it were an HTML element: for example, drag it onto a layout grid, into a text box within a layout grid, or add it to a floating box.

■ Many Web authors create date and time stamps displaying the current date and time to a user visiting the page. The Web server must be running a CGI application or other program that supports that function for this to work, and the Web page must contain code linking the page to the CGI. Your Internet service provider must support them, and you must create or acquire the code to add such a feature to your own page and then connect it to the CGI.

Rollovers

You can set a button image to effectively change its appearance when a visitor moves the mouse over the button, and/or clicks on it. This interactive effect is commonly referred to as a *rollover*.

Before you can add a rollover to your page, you'll want to decide how the image should change when your visitors mouse over it, and/or when they click it. You will probably choose to create different iterations of a single image, though you might decide to display a completely different one when the user moves across it. If you decide to use an iteration of one image, you will need to create the variants using an image-editing tool,

Figure 17.8 Choose the Rollover icon from the Smart tab of the Objects palette.

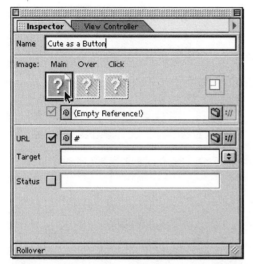

Figure 17.9 Click Main in the Rollover Inspector to attach an image reference for the rollover's main image.

like Adobe Photoshop. Start with the original image, and edit it, saving each version at the same size as the first image. When you have three images (the original, the version that appears when a user mouses over it, and a final one that appears when the user clicks on the image), you're ready to create it using the GoLive Rollover icon.

In this exercise, you need to create the following images:

◆ **The Main image** appears when no activity is taking place on it.

◆ **The Over image** displays when the mouse pointer moves over the image area.

◆ **The Click image** is displayed fleetingly when the image is clicked.

You'll also need to choose the URL your button will link to when clicked. The following steps assume you have created the images and chosen the URL.

To create a rollover:

1. With a document open in the Layout Editor, double-click or drag the Rollover icon (**Figure 17.8**) from the Smart tab of the Objects palette. The icon that appears in the Layout Editor looks like a standard image placeholder. The Rollover Inspector is activated.

2. In the Rollover Inspector, name the button rollover.

3. Click the box marked Main (**Figure 17.9**).

continues on next page

ADDING ACTION ICONS

4. Browse or Point & Shoot to locate the image that appears when the page loads. The image appears, both in the Document window and in the Main area of the Inspector (**Figure 17.10**).

5. Click the box labeled Over to select it. The URL checkbox is now checked and the URL field is activated.

6. Browse or Point & Shoot to the image you want users to see when the mouse moves over the first image you linked. This new image will appear in the Over area.

7. Select the Click box and repeat step 6, placing an image that will replace the original when a visitor clicks on the button (**Figure 17.11**).

8. To use the image as a hyperlink, be sure the check box adjacent to the assigned URL is checked. Browse or Point & Shoot to a page you want to link to, or type a complete URL.

9. You can target the link to a new location (such as a window, frame, or an anchor) with the Target popup menu.

10. If you wish to display a message in the browser's Status area when a user mouses over the link, click the Status checkbox and enter a short message in the text box.

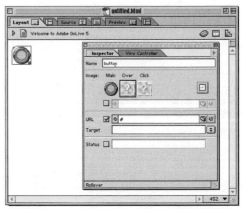

Figure 17.10 Assigning a Main rollover image displays it both in the Inspector and the Document window.

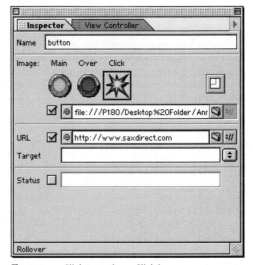

Figure 17.11 Click to assign a Click image.

Figure 17.12 The Rollover Inspector's Size box can be used to equalize sizing variations among a button set.

✔ Tips

- To add rollover properties to an image already on your Web page, drag the Rollover icon over the existing image. Then configure the button image as described in steps 5–9, above.

- You don't have to create both an Over image and a Click image. You can use one or both options with your button.

- If you decide to use completely different images for the three elements of button animation, you must make sure the images are the same size. If they aren't the same size when you create them, they may be stretched or shrunken to fit into the image placeholder you've created for them in your document. If you want to try to reach a happy medium when working with images that are different sizes, you can experiment using the Size box in the Rollover Inspector (**Figure 17.12**). With your two or three images placed and configured, click the one whose size most closely matches the image size you have in mind. Then click the Size box. The placeholder box changes to fit the image you've selected.

- To see how your rollover works, click the Preview tab in the Document window. Mouse over your image and then click it.

- Adobe's ImageReady software is helpful in preparing rollovers for final insertion into GoLive pages. It's bundled with Adobe Photoshop.

ADDING ACTION ICONS

URL popup menus

URL popup menus are used to add navigation elements to a page. Use one to provide visitors a compact menu of destinations within your site, or to other sites.

To create a URL popup:

1. With a document open, drag or double-click the URL Popup icon (**Figure 17.13**) in the Smart tab of the Objects palette to the Document window, A small popup box appears in the Document window. Click to activate the URL Popup Inspector (**Figure 17.14**).

2. In the Inspector, click the line that says Adobe Systems, Inc., assuming you do not plan to offer visitors a direct link to the makers of GoLive. Make text changes in the Label and URL fields to reflect the names of the pages to be linked and their URLs.

3. Click New to add another item to the popup and add a Label and URL for the new item on the menu (**Figure 17.15**).

4. Repeat step 3 to build a complete popup URL navigation system.

5. Take a look at your new popup by clicking the Preview tab in the Document window and clicking on the menu to view its items.

✔ Tips

- You can also use Point & Shoot to connect the popup to URLs.

- The Inspector allows you to specify locations within the page or frameset in the Target popup.

- Click Delete to delete a URL from the list.

- Click Duplicate to create a duplicate item. It can save a lot of typing when you're entering long URLs!

Figure 17.13 Choose the URL Popup icon from the Smart tab of the Objects palette.

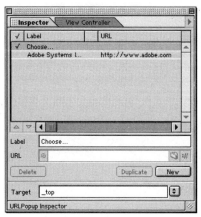

Figure 17.14 The URL Popup Inspector is where you add URLs that will appear within the menu.

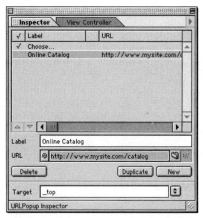

Figure 17.15 Click New to add a new item to the menu. Add a label and URL to complete it.

- The first item in the URL Popup Inspector is labeled Choose. That's what a visitor will see before selecting the menu in a browser. You can change the label to anything you like by clicking the item and editing the Label field.

Figure 17.16 Choose the Browser Switch icon from the Smart tab of the Objects palette.

Browser switching

Not all browsers are created equal. To begin with, they are designed by the software equivalents of the Hatfields and McCoys. Certain capabilities are possible only with certain browsers, at certain revision levels.

A browser switch is a useful way to take visitors whose browsers are incapable of interpreting some of the more advanced features of your page to pages that don't use those features. To build such a page, you'll either have to make a "parallel" site without advanced features like style sheets and JavaScript, or you'll have to add text that informs the user that the site may not display properly in an older browser. You can use a browser switch to either direct the user to a different page, or to display one that indicates they should get a newer browser before viewing your site.

Browser switch is a Head Action. All Head Actions take place before the page loads, which minimizes wasted time loading pages to browsers that don't fully support them.

To create a browser switch:

1. Open the current document's Head section by clicking on the triangle next to the page title, near the top of the Document window.

2. Double-click or drag the Browser Switch icon (**Figure 17.16**) from the Smart tab of the Objects palette to the Head section of the Document window. A browser switch icon appears.

continues on next page

ADDING ACTION ICONS

3. Click the icon once to activate the Browser Switch Inspector (**Figure 17.17**).

4. If you want GoLive to determine which browsers your page is compatible with, leave Auto—the default setting—checked in the Inspector.

5. To determine manually which browsers or platform to support, uncheck Auto.

6. To choose specific browsers, click the browser versions that you *think are compatible* with your page's JavaScript and/or Cascading Style Sheet features. (The infinity sign means all versions.) If a visitor uses a browser version you did not check, he or she will be redirected to a different page, to be specified.

7. Specify a preferred platform (Mac or Windows). The unchecked platform will be redirected.

8. Browse or Point & Shoot to the alternative page, using the Alternate Link field.

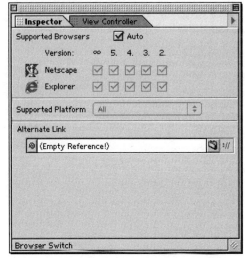

Figure 17.17 The Browser Switch Inspector.

Configuring Actions

Actions are scripted events executed when a *trigger* is activated. Actions can be used to change the appearance of a page or its elements, open alert windows, play media files, and much more. GoLive's assortment of actions can be added to pages, adding interactivity to animations, text, and images, by using mouse- and keyboard-based triggers.

Triggers

Just as a sentence consists of a subject and a verb, an action consists of a *trigger* and an *event*. When the trigger is applied, the specified event occurs. GoLive provides nine event triggers that invoke actions:

- Mouse click
- Mouse enter
- Mouse exit
- Double-click
- Mouse down
- Mouse up
- Key down
- Key press
- Key up

You have access to additional action triggers when you add an action to the Head section of a document. The following triggers are available from the Exec.popup menu in the Action Inspector. These triggers are associated with the page to which they belong. An OnLoad trigger, for example, causes an action to occur when the page is loaded. They are:

- OnLoad
- OnUnload
- OnParse
- OnCall

Action placement

There are three locations within a GoLive document where you can add actions. They are:

◆ **Head Actions** are added in the Head section, and applied to the page as a whole.

◆ **Body Actions** can be applied to hyperlinked text, images, or any other item within the body of the page.

◆ **TimeLine Editor Actions** control animations based on floating boxes moving over time. These Actions are configured with the TimeLine Editor. I will cover animation in Chapter 18, "Animation and QuickTime."

To add an action to the Head or Body section of a document, use the Head Action or Body Action tools in the Smart tab of the Objects palette, respectively.

The process of adding actions is similar, regardless of what the action does, or what trigger you plan to use. I'll describe the general procedure, and then move to explanations of what the Actions are and how to use them.

To set up an action triggered by a mouse or keyboard event:

1. In the Layout Editor, select text or an image on the page. In **Figure 17.18**, I have placed an image of a left-pointing arrow that will return the visitor to the page from which he or she came.

2. Create a link by clicking the New Link button on the toolbar.

   or

   Click the Link button in the Text or Image Inspector. The URL field (in the Link tab of the Text or Image Inspector) lights up, allowing you to type within it.

Figure 17.18 Select an image, then add an action to it.

Figure 17.19 The Actions palette displays the options for the hyperlinked image.

Figure 17.20 The plus button adds an action event to be associated with a trigger.

Figure 17.21 Go Last Page is the event that will be associated with the image.

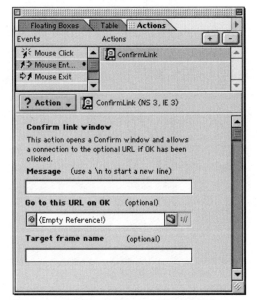

Figure 17.22 Like most actions, the ConfirmLink Window's Inspector includes an explanation of what it does, on which browsers, and what information it needs from you to do its job.

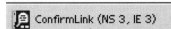

Figure 17.23 The ConfirmLink action confirms that it can be used by version 3 and later of Netscape Navigator or Internet Explorer.

3. To associate an action with selected text or an image, type a number sign (#) in the URL field of the Inspector after deleting the text "(Empty Reference)" from the field.

4. With the image still selected, choose Window > Actions to view the Actions palette (**Figure 17.19**).

5. Choose Mouse Click (one of the three triggers from the Events list on the left).

6. Click the + button, located above the Actions list (**Figure 17.20**). The Action popup menu is enabled.

7. Choose an action event from the Action popup menu. I have chosen Link > Go Last Page (**Figure 17.21**). The action is complete. JavaScript has been added to the document and will execute the event when the button is clicked.

✔ Tips

■ Multiple actions can be added to a selected item. Repeat steps 5 through 7.

■ Delete an action by selecting it in the Actions palette and clicking the Minus (-) button.

■ Not sure what an action does? Choose it from the Actions palette and read the explanation that appears at the bottom of the window (**Figure 17.22**). Not all actions have explanations, but some do.

■ The Actions palette will also indicate which browsers an action is likely to work with. Note in **Figure 17.23**, the ConfirmLink action works with Netscape 3 and above, and Internet Explorer 3 and above.

Types of actions

The following actions included with GoLive support a variety of events.

Many of the actions I am about to describe are complex, and several use one action to trigger another.

GoLive includes 44 actions—events invoked by some of the above triggers. In addition, 14 actions are part of ActionsPlus, a collection of actions that Adobe began bundling with GoLive 4.

Actions are arranged in these categories (each category has its own menu item and a submenu containing the actions in that category) in the Action Inspector and the Actions palette.

◆ ActionsPlus   ◆ Multimedia

◆ Getters   ◆ Others

◆ Image   ◆ Specials

◆ Link   ◆ Variables

◆ Message

✔ Tips

■ The actions in the ActionsPlus folder were created by independent developers and bundled with GoLive by Adobe. For a full description of these actions and their use, see "Using ActionsPlus Actions," on page 269 of the User Guide.pdf file that is installed along with the GoLive application.

■ Some Actions described in the following section are designed to work with GoLive's animation features. Before proceeding with animation actions, read Chapter 18, "Animation and QuickTime."

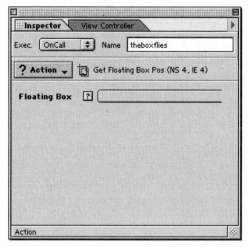

Figure 17.24 The Get Floating Box Position Inspector.

Getter actions

◆ **Get Floating Box Position** is a Head Action that grabs the top-left coordinates of a floating box. You can use this data to invoke another action that acts upon this information.

◆ **Get Form Value** reads the data that a user inputs into a specified form field. The information can either be passed to another Action or displayed.

To create a Get Floating Box Position action:

1. Create an animation consisting of two floating boxes: one with an animation path and the second with no movement assigned to it.

2. Drag the Head Action icon from the Smart tab of the Objects palette into the document's Head section.

3. In the Action Inspector, choose OnCall from the Exec. Popup menu.

4. Give the new action a name in the Name field.

5. Choose Getters > Get Floating Box Position from the popup menu in the Action Inspector (**Figure 17.24**).

6. Choose a floating box from the popup menu. This is the box whose position will be passed by the action.

7. Add a second Head Action to the document's Head section.

8. Configure that action by choosing Specials > Idle in the Action Inspector.

continues on next page

9. Uncheck the Exit Idle If Condition returns True checkbox (**Figure 17.25**).

10. Under the Condition tab, choose a Specials > Timeout action and edit the timeout value.

11. Click the True tab, and choose Multimedia > Move To from the Action popup menu. This Action allows you to specify the location to which your floating box will move.

12. Choose the floating box from the popup menu.

13. Click the buttons next to the Pos. field twice, so that the green question mark appears.

14. From the popup menu, choose the Get Floating Box Position action you created earlier.

15. Click the False tab.

16. Repeat steps 11–14.

To create a Get Form Value action:

1. Before creating this action, you must first add a form to your GoLive document. For more information about creating and using forms, see Chapter 8, "Working with Forms."

2. In the Action Inspector, choose OnUnload from the Exec. popup menu.

3. Add an action to the Head section of a document.

4. Choose Getters > Get Form Value from the popup menu in the Action Inspector (**Figure 17.26**).

5. In the Form field, enter the name of the form from which you want to extract information.

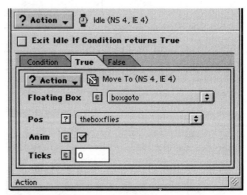

Figure 17.25 Assigning the names of the floating boxes and their positions.

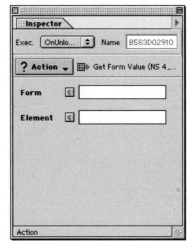

Figure 17.26 Add a connection to a form in the Action Inspector.

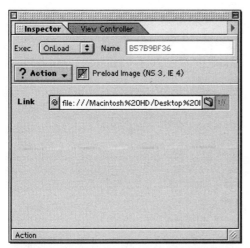

Figure 17.27 Select an image to preload in the Action Inspector.

6. Enter the name of the form element (the name you've assigned to the element itself, not the element type) in the Element field.

7. Add additional Get Form Value actions for each form field whose data you want to extract.

8. Create a repository of some kind (such as a cookie, probably in another action) for the form data retrieved by the Get Form Value action.

Image actions

◆ **Preload Image** is a Head Action that caches images before the body of an HTML page loads. Caching a large graphic makes it possible for all of a page's images to appear simultaneously. Preloading an image is commonly used with rollovers. They run more quickly, since their component images are present when the page is loaded.

◆ **Random Image** replaces the image to which you attach an action with a random image, one among several you specify.

◆ **Set Image URL** exchanges the current image for another, based on a trigger you specify.

To preload an image:

1. Add an action to the Head section of a document.

2. In the Action Inspector (**Figure 17.27**), choose Image > Preload Image from the Action popup menu.

3. Browse or Point & Shoot to locate an image to preload. A link to the image appears in the Action Inspector.

To add a random image action:

1. Create a mouse or key event action, as described in the "To set up an action triggered by a mouse or key event" section of this chapter.

2. Choose Image > Random Image from the Action popup menu. Several image selection fields appear.

3. Browse or Point & Shoot to locate an image you want to appear randomly when your trigger is activated.

4. Repeat the previous step for up to two more images. Enlarge the Inspector window if needed, to show all three URL fields (**Figure 17.28**).

To set an image URL:

1. Choose an image you want to exchange. If it doesn't already have a name, click the More tab of the Image Inspector and type a name in the Name field near the Is Form area. Be sure not to check the Is Form checkbox.

2. Create a mouse or key event action, as described in the "To set up an action triggered by a mouse or key event" section of this chapter.

3. Choose Image > Set Image URL from the Action popup menu in the Actions palette.

4. Choose the named image from the Image popup menu in the Actions palette.

5. In the Link area of the Actions palette, browse or Point & Shoot to an image to add its URL. The completed Actions palette looks like **Figure 17.29**.

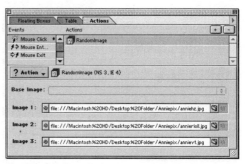

Figure 17.28 Three images are assigned in the Random Image Inspector.

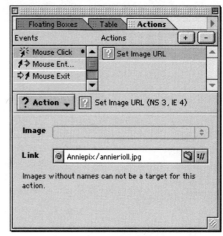

Figure 17.29 The Set Image URL Action will exchange the currently displayed image for one you specify in this Inspector.

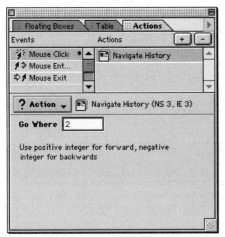

Figure 17.30 The Navigate History Action Inspector lets you direct the user forward or backward to the links they have visited.

Link actions

◆ **Get Last Page** returns the visitor to the previously viewed page when he or she clicks on the link.

◆ **Goto Link** sends a visitor to a URL you select.

◆ **Navigate History** uses browser history information—what pages a visitor has visited in what order—to take him or her forward or backward by a specific number of pages.

◆ **Open Window**, as the name implies, opens a new window when triggered, causing a linked page to be displayed in the window.

To add a Get Last Page or Navigate History action:

1. Create a mouse or key event action, as described in the "To set up an action triggered by a mouse or key event" section of this chapter.

2. Choose Link > Get Last Page, or Link > Navigate History from the Action popup menu in the Actions palette. The Navigate History Action appears in **Figure 17.30**. If you're creating a Get Last Page action, you're done.

3. To complete a Navigate History action, in the Go Where field type in a number of history items (negative numbers go backward, positive go forward) to move when the action is triggered.

To create a Goto Link action:

1. Create a mouse or key event action, as described in the "To set up an action triggered by a mouse or key event" section of this chapter.

2. Choose Link > Goto Link from the Action popup menu. Goto Link options appear.

3. Type a remote URL or locate a URL within your site that you want to link to (**Figure 17.31**).

4. If you want to choose a location for the new page to appear, use the Target field to specify the location.

✔ Tip

■ If it sounds like a Goto Link action does just what a normal hyperlink does, you're right, assuming that you've chosen a mouse click trigger. Using other triggers—like Mouse Enter, for example—makes things considerably more interesting. This isn't standard operating procedure on the Web, though, so be sure to give your visitors some kind of warning that invoking the trigger you set will send them to another page or another site.

To create an Open Window action:

1. Create a mouse or key event action, as described in the "To set up an action triggered by a mouse or key event" section of this chapter.

2. Choose Link > Open Window from the Action popup menu in the Actions palette.

3. Type a URL, browse, or Point & Shoot to the linked page that will appear in the new window (**Figure 17.32**).

4. If necessary, use the Target field to specify in what window the new page should open.

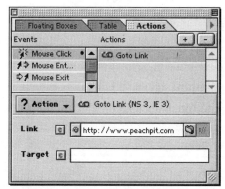

Figure 17.31 In this example, the Goto Link action functions like a conventional hyperlink.

Figure 17.32 The Inspector for the Open Window action lets you specify a window to be opened and how that window is displayed.

5. To control the appearance of the window itself, use the other controls in the Inspector. Start by specifying a size (in pixels) for the new window when it appears onscreen.

6. Click the Resize checkbox to allow the user to resize the new window.

7. Leave any of the six browser display buttons checked to show scroll bars, menus, directory buttons, status indicators, toolbars, and location bars.

Message actions

- **Document Write** fills an inline place-holder with text or with HTML.When used with a Body action, it can replace the Body action with text or HTML when the Document Write action is invoked.

- **Open Alert Window** displays a browser alert window onscreen when triggered.

- **Set Status** displays a custom message in the status field at the bottom of the browser window.

To create a Document Write action:

1. Add any mouse or key event action to the Body section of a document.

2. Drag the Body Action icon from the Smart tab of the Objects palette to the Document window.

3. Choose Message > Document Write from the Action popup menu in the Body Action Inspector.

4. Type some HTML code or text into the HTML field to display text when the action you created in step 1 is triggered.

   or

   Click the button next to the HTML field twice. The button changes from a "c" to a question mark and you can choose the action you created in step 1 from the popup menu that now appears in the HTML field.

To create an Open Alert Window action:

1. Create a mouse or key event action, as described in the "To set up an action triggered by a mouse or key event" section of this chapter.

2. Choose Message > Open Alert Window from the Action popup menu. The Message field appears.

3. Type the text you want to appear in the alert window (**Figure 17.33**).

To create a Set Status action:

1. Create a mouse or key event action, as described in the "To set up an action triggered by a mouse or key event" section of this chapter.

2. Choose Message > Set Status from the Action popup menu.

3. Enter the status message in the text field that appears.

Multimedia actions

♦ **Drag Floating Box** allows a visitor to drag content (contained in a floating box) around in the browser window.

♦ **Flip Move** allows you to move a floating box from a starting point to another position on the page, and back again when triggered a second time.

♦ **Move By** specifies the vertical and/or horizontal movement of a floating box. When triggered, the box moves according to the measurement in the Move By Action and no further.

♦ **Move To** behaves just like Flip Move, except that it doesn't return the floating box to the original position when triggered again.

♦ **Play Scene and Stop Scene** actions control the start and stop points of animations created in the TimeLine Editor.

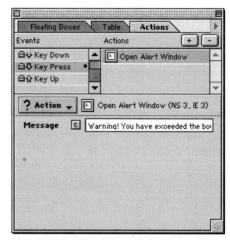

Figure 17.33 An Open Alert Window action will display a small window containing a message under the specified condition.

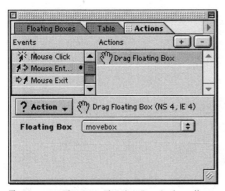

Figure 17.34 The Drag Floating Box Action allows the visitor to drag a floating box and its contents around the browser window.

◆ **Play Sound and Stop Sound** actions control the stopping and starting of sounds.

◆ **ShowHide** controls the visibility of a floating box on the page.

◆ **Stop Complete** stops all animation, including visual and audio playback. It is useful to give visitors a trigger that allows them to stop animation if their Internet connection is slow, or if they simply don't want to bother with it.

◆ **Wipe Transitions** create a fading effect that applies to floating boxes as they enter and leave the visitor's view.

To add a Drag Floating Box action:

1. Choose or create a floating box. If the box is empty, add content to it.

2. If you like, rename the box in the Floating Box Inspector from the generic name assigned to it by GoLive. If you don't rename the box, note its default name. You'll be referring to it by name when you create the action.

3. Add a Head Action to the floating box.

4. Choose Multimedia > Drag Floating Box from the Action popup menu in the Action Inspector. The Inspector displays the Floating Box popup menu containing all floating boxes within the current document.

5. From the menu, choose the box that you want visitors to be able to drag (**Figure 17.34**).

To add a Flip Move action:

1. Within a document that contains at least one floating box, create a mouse or key event action, as described in the "To set up an action triggered by a mouse or key event" section of this chapter.

or

With the TimeLine Editor open, Command-click (Mac) or Control-click (Windows) the Action track to add an action marker.

2. Choose Multimedia > Flip Move from the Action popup menu in the Action Inspector. The Inspector displays positioning fields for the action (**Figure 17.35**).

3. Choose a floating box from the popup menu.

4. Click the Get button on the Pos1 line to establish the initial coordinates (in pixels) of the floating box. GoLive fills in the coordinates.

5. In the Document window, drag the floating box to the position you want to move it to, and click Get on the Pos2 line in the Inspector, to fill in the second set of coordinates.

6. Leave the Anim box checked to cause the flip move to work.

7. To make an object move faster or more slowly, raise or lower (respectively) the number of ticks in the Ticks field. A tick is $\frac{1}{60}$ of a second.

✔ Tip

■ When you drag the floating box to set its coordinates, you'll lose contact with the Inspector associated with the image or text you're using to trigger the Action. Don't worry about that. When you have finished dragging the floating box, click immediately on the text or image, activating the Action Inspector. Click Get to set up the Flip Move, and you're ready to test it.

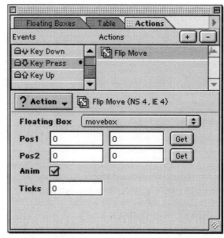

Figure 17.35 The Flip Move action moves a floating box and its content to a specified location on the page, and then back again.

CONFIGURING ACTIONS

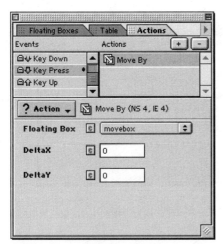

Figure 17.36 Move By actions move a floating box and its content vertically or horizontally by a specified amount when triggered.

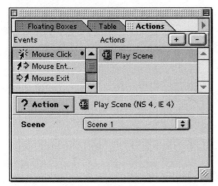

Figure 17.37 Under a specified trigger, the Play Scene action starts an animation controlled by the TimeLine Editor.

To create a Move To action:

◆ Follow steps 1–7 in "To add a Flip Move action," but, in step 2, choose a Move To action instead.

To create a Move By action:

1. Within a document that contains at least one floating box, create a mouse or key event action, as described in the "To set up an action triggered by a mouse or key event" section of this chapter.

   or

   With the TimeLine Editor open, Command-click (Mac) or Control-click (Windows) the Action track to add an action marker.

2. Choose Multimedia > Move By from the Action popup menu in the Actions palette (**Figure 17.36**).

3. Choose the floating box to be moved from the popup menu.

4. Enter DeltaX and DeltaY coordinates— the horizontal (X) and vertical (Y) movement, measured in pixels.

To play and stop scenes:

1. Create an animated scene (see Chapter 18), using the TimeLine Editor.

2. Create a mouse or key event action, as described in the "To set up an action triggered by a mouse or key event" section of this chapter.

3. Choose Multimedia > Play Scene from the Action popup menu in the Actions palette (**Figure 17.37**).

4. Choose the scene you created from the Scene popup menu.

continues on next page

CONFIGURING ACTIONS

5. To stop the scene, create a second action by clicking the + button. This adds a second event to the current trigger.

6. Choose Multimedia > Stop Scene from the Action popup menu in the Actions palette.

✔ Tip

■ Triggers for Play Scene and Stop Scene actions must be mouse events (mouse up, mouse click, mouse enter, etc.). If you choose a non-mouse event, the icon that appears next to the name of the Action you select will have an "x" through it. **Figure 17.38** shows an incompatible trigger and action. The x, your visual cue that you need to choose a different trigger, appears whenever triggers and actions are incompatible.

To play and stop sounds:

1. Add a sound to your page using a plug-in icon from the Basic tab of the Objects palette.

2. Name the plug-in in the More tab of the Plugin Inspector.

3. Create a mouse or key event action, as described in the "To set up an action triggered by a mouse or key event" section of this chapter.

or

With the TimeLine Editor open, Command-click (Mac) or Control-click (Windows) the Action track to add an action marker.

4. In the Actions palette, choose Multimedia > Play Sound from the Action popup menu.

5. Click the + button to add a Stop Sound action.

6. Choose the plug-in name you used before to complete the action.

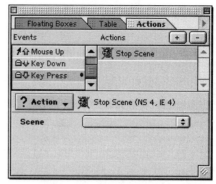

Figure 17.38 An incompatible trigger and action are indicated by the two bright X's.

CONFIGURING ACTIONS

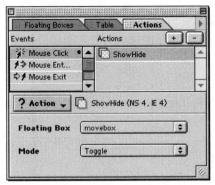

Figure 17.39 The ShowHide action controls whether or not a specified floating box is visible.

To add a ShowHide action:

1. Create an animation including a floating box.

2. With the TimeLine Editor open, Command-click (Mac) or Control-click (Windows) the Action track to add an action marker.

3. Choose Multimedia > ShowHide from the Action popup menu in the Actions palette.

4. Choose a floating box from the Floating Box popup menu.

5. Choose Show, Hide, or Toggle (switch between Show and Hide) from the Mode popup menu (**Figure 17.39**).

✔ Tip

■ You can use ShowHide actions in pairs, creating separate triggers for each position.

To add a Stop Complete action:

1. Create a mouse or key event action, as described in the "To set up an action triggered by a mouse or key event" section of this chapter.

2. Choose Multimedia > Stop Complete from the Action popup menu in the Actions palette.

To create a Wipe Transition action:

1. Within a document that contains at least one floating box, create a mouse or key event action, as described in the "To set up an action triggered by a mouse or key event" section of this chapter.

   or

   With the TimeLine Editor open, Command-click (Mac) or Control-click (Windows) the Action track to add an action marker.

continues on next page

CONFIGURING ACTIONS

2. In the Actions palette, choose Multimedia > Wipe Transition from the Action popup menu.

3. Choose the floating box you want to wipe from the Floating Box popup menu (**Figure 17.40**).

4. Choose a wipe direction from the Transition menu (**Figure 17.41**).

5. Enter a number of transition steps in the Steps field. The larger the number, the smoother and less jumpy the transition will be.

Other actions

◆ **Netscape CSS Fix** works around a bug that causes some versions of Netscape 4.0 browsers to lose Cascading Style Sheet information when the page is resized.

◆ **ResizeWindow** changes the size of the browser window when triggered.

◆ **Scroll Down, Left, Right, or Up** moves the browser display by the number of pixels, and in the direction you set, when it is triggered.

◆ **Set BackColor** changes the background color of the current window.

To add a Netscape CSS fix action:

1. Drag the Head Action icon into the Head section of a document containing Cascading Style Sheet information.

2. In the Action Inspector, choose Others > Netscape CSS Fix from the Action popup menu.

3. Leave the OnLoad option (the default) selected in the Exec. Popup menu.

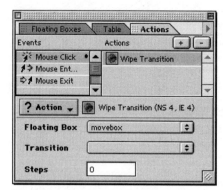

Figure 17.40 Specify Wipe Transitions in the Actions palette.

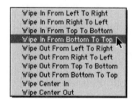

Figure 17.41 The available wipe directions for a Wipe Transition are listed in a popup menu in the Actions palette.

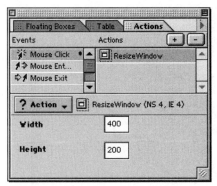

Figure 17.42 The Actions palette for the ResizeWindow action specifies the size of the window (in pixels) to be achieved under the specified trigger.

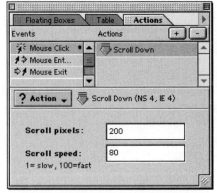

Figure 17.43 All of the Scroll actions—down, left, right, and up—are configured in the same way, allowing you to specify scroll movement and speed.

To add a ResizeWindow action:

1. Create a mouse or key event action, as described in the "To set up an action triggered by a mouse or key event" section of this chapter.

   or

   With the TimeLine Editor open, Command-click (Mac) or Control-click (Windows) the Action track to add an action marker.

2. In the Actions palette, choose Others > ResizeWindow from the Action popup menu.

3. Enter the Width and Height (in pixels) that you want to apply to the page when this action is triggered (**Figure 17.42**).

To add a Scroll action:

1. Create a mouse or key event action, as described in the "To set up an action triggered by a mouse or key event" section of this chapter.

   or

   With the TimeLine Editor open, Command-click (Mac) or Control-click (Windows) the Action track to add an action marker.

2. In the Actions palette, choose Others > Scroll Down, Scroll Left, Scroll Right, or Scroll Up from the Action popup menu.

3. Choose the number of pixels to scroll when the action is triggered.

4. Enter the speed from 1–100 (100 is fastest) at which the action will scroll (**Figure 17.43**).

CONFIGURING ACTIONS

423

To set a BackColor action:

1. Create a mouse or key event action, as described in the "To set up an action triggered by a mouse or key event" section of this chapter.

   or

   With the TimeLine Editor open, Command-click (Mac) or Control-click (Windows) the Action track to add an action marker.

2. In the Actions palette, choose Others > Set BackColor from the Action popup menu.

3. Click the box next to Background Color (**Figure 17.44**), activating the Color palette.

4. Choose a color from the Color palette by clicking and holding the mouse button.

5. Drag the color swatch into the Background Color box in the Actions palette.

Special actions

◆ **ActionGroup** gathers several actions together to be triggered at the same time.

◆ **Call Action** calls another action anywhere on the page. Use this action to call an action stored in the Head section of the page.

◆ **Call Function** calls any custom JavaScript function that you have added to the page. This action gives JavaScript programmers a special action to trigger their scripts.

◆ **Condition** actions are triggered based on whether defined conditions (such as other actions) occur. They use the Text Variable, Intersection, and Timeout actions.

◆ **Idle** actions periodically determine whether a condition has been met. They work with floating box intersection actions and timeout actions, and yield a true/false result.

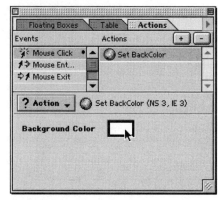

Figure 17.44 In the Actions palette, click the Background Color box to open the Color palette.

Figure 17.45 Add actions in the Actions palette to chain actions together.

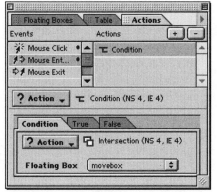

Figure 17.46 Specify whether floating boxes should overlap in the Condition section of the Action Inspector.

To create an Action Group:

1. Create a mouse or key event action, as described in the "To set up an action triggered by a mouse or key event" section of this chapter.

   or

   With the TimeLine Editor open, Command-click (Mac) or Control-click (Windows) the Action track to add an action marker.

2. In the Actions palette, choose Specials > Action Group from the Action popup menu.

3. Click the + button to add the first action to your group (**Figure 17.45**) and configure the action.

4. Click the + button to add more actions.

5. Configure these actions.

To add a Condition action:

1. In a document containing at least two floating boxes, drag the Head Action icon to the Head section of a document.

2. In the Action Inspector, choose Specials > Condition from the Action popup menu. New tabs and a new Action popup menu appear in the Action Inspector.

3. Choose Specials > Intersection from the Action menu below the Condition tab (**Figure 17.46**), to specify the intersection of two floating boxes—whether or not they overlap.

4. From the popup menu labeled Floating Box, below the Actions menu, choose the floating boxes whose intersection (or lack thereof) should trigger a conditional action.

continues on next page

CONFIGURING ACTIONS

5. To choose what will happen if the condition is met, click the True tab in the Action Inspector, then choose and configure an action.

6. To choose what will happen if the condition is not met, click the False tab in the Action Inspector, then choose and configure an action.

To set a conditional timeout action:

1. Create a Condition action, as described in the previous set of steps.

2. From the Actions popup menu below the Condition tab in the Action Inspector, choose Specials > Timeout to set a conditional action that will occur when a set amount of time has passed.

3. In the TimeOut field, set the number of seconds to wait.

To add an Idle action:

1. Add an action to the Head section of a document.

2. In the Action Inspector, choose Specials > Idle from the Action popup menu.

3. Check the Exit Idle if Condition returns True checkbox.

4. Under the Condition tab of the Action Inspector, choose Specials > Intersection, or Specials > Timeout from the Action popup menu to specify a condition.

5. Add actions that should be triggered if the condition is true or false, under the respective tabs in the Action Inspector.

Creating Your Own Actions

If you know how to write JavaScript, and are willing to learn a few conventions of action-building in GoLive, you can build your own actions, or modify those that already exist.

Actions are GoLive files, written within an HTML document. They must contain a title, action tags, JavaScript, and a layout grid, which is used to create the fields that appear in the Actions palette and Action Inspector when you select the action. All actions must contain these basic elements in order to function properly.

Action files must have the file extension .action. Script files, which use the .scpt file extension, are made up of JavaScript code only.

Actions are stored in their own folder within the GoLive application folder. The Actions folder is located inside the JScripts folder, which in turn is located in the Modules folder. Any action appearing in a folder within the Actions folder appears as an action in GoLive's Actions palette and Action Inspector.

To open an action for editing in GoLive:

1. Choose File > Open, and navigate to the Message subfolder of the Actions folder (the path is \Modules\Jscripts\Actions\Message).

2. Select and open an action. The action opens.

✔ Tip

- Starting with an existing action is a great way to get a start on building your own, but it's a good idea to either duplicate an action you want to base your action on, or save the action you open immediately with a new name, so that you don't over-write an existing action.

Anatomy of an action file

An action file is made up of four parts. In **Figure 17.47**, from top to bottom, the components are: title, tags (enclosed in blue rectangles), the JavaScript (indicated by the coffee bean icon) executed when the action runs, and the layout grid that builds the Inspector fields.

Special tags are required to identify an action, to create the parameter controls, and to generate the JavaScript code. These special tags appear as blue rectangles in the Document window. Click the triangles to view the attributes and values of these tags. The values can be edited, but their names cannot.

Learning the programming required to make an action is beyond the scope of this book. If you have the JavaScript chops and an understanding of how CSS works, start by examining the actions included with GoLive before experimenting with your own. You will find a comprehensive tutorial on making your own actions in Appendix B of the User Guide.pdf file on the GoLive 5 CD. The tutorial covers syntax and other technical details you need to know to make a useful, stable action.

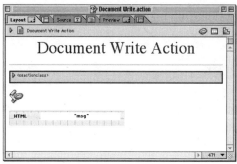

Figure 17.47 The four parts of an action file: title, tags, JavaScript code, and a layout grid.

To add a new action to GoLive:

1. Quit GoLive.

2. In the Finder (Mac) or Windows Explorer (Windows), navigate to Adobe GoLive\ Modules\Jscripts\Actions.

3. Create a new directory within the Actions directory for your actions, or open one of the subfolders corresponding with an existing category your action fits in.

4. Drag the actions you've written, downloaded, or purchased into the directory you created, or into an existing action directory.

5. Launch GoLive and verify that your new actions appear in the Actions palette.

✔ Tips

■ GoLive verifies that a file is an authentic action by affirming the presence of the <csactionclass> in the file. It does no other error checking. If GoLive crashes when a new action is added, that action most likely contains errors that GoLive does not check for. If removing that file from the Actions folder corrects the problem, your suspicions would be confirmed. Any new action you are developing should be stored outside of the Actions folder until you are certain it is correct.

■ If any new actions have problems that prevent GoLive from using them, GoLive warns you as soon as it has completely launched. It also creates a text file in the main GoLive folder, detailing the problem.

CREATING YOUR OWN ACTIONS

The GoLive SDK

If you know JavaScript and understand the ins and outs of Cascading Style Sheets, then the GoLive Extend Script SDK (Software Developer's Kit) is for you.

The GoLive Extend Script SDK can be used to add customized features to the user interface and behavior of GoLive itself and the sites it is used to produce by combining JavaScript and CSS tags.

The SDK supports (as does GoLive itself) JavaScript version 1.4 and defaults to Netscape. However, you can change this default preference to either Microsoft Jscript or ECMA-262. Custom Extend Script extensions can call external custom C, C++, or JavaScript libraries. To use the C or C++ programming languages requires detailed knowledge of these languages. Programs you write in these languages must be compiled before they can be used.

Figure 17.48 Enable the Extend Script module in the Preferences window, if it isn't enabled already.

✔ Tips

- Developing with the GoLive SDK requires that you restart GoLive whenever you need to test a new version of the extension you're working on. Even on the fastest systems, GoLive can take a lot of time to load. To reduce loading time, choose Edit > Preferences and click the Modules label. Disable modules that aren't directly related to the extension you are writing. Quit and restart GoLive to confirm your action. You may have to experiment with a list of modules which must be loaded for your extension or other features of your site to be functional.

- To use the GoLive SDK, the Extend Script module must be installed and active. To find out whether or not it is, open the Preferences dialog box by choosing Edit > Preferences. Click Modules and select Extend Script (**Figure 17.48**). You will need to restart GoLive to apply your changes.

THE GoLIVE SDK

Figure 17.49 The Menus and Dialogs sample directory in the Extend Scripts folder.

The SDK Samples Folder

To work with the SDK, you must copy its components from the GoLive 5.0 CD to your hard disk. You will find it at the root level of the CD, in a folder called Adobe GoLive SDK 5.0r1.

To use an SDK sample:

1. Install the SDK.

   (Mac) Copy the Adobe GoLive SDK 5.0r1 folder to your hard drive.

   (Windows) Run the Adobe GoLive installer program and click the Custom button when the installer opens. Check the Adobe GoLive SDK checkbox and run the installer.

2. Open GoLive and choose Edit > Preferences and click the Modules label.

3. If it isn't checked, click the Extend Script checkbox to enable the module.

4. Quit GoLive.

5. Locate the Adobe GoLive SDK 5.0r1 directory on your hard drive and open it, and then open the Samples directory within it.

6. Open the Adobe GoLive directory and then the Modules\Extend Scripts directory.

7. With both these directories open, drag one of the directories from the Samples folder into the Extend Scripts folder. In **Figure 17.49**, the Menus and Dialogs sample directory has been added to the Extend Scripts directory.

continues on next page

THE GOLIVE SDK

8. Reopen GoLive.

9. Note that a new menu has been added to GoLive called SDK Test (**Figure 17.50**). Experiment with the menu items to see what the new menu items do.

Learning the SDK

It is beyond the scope of this book to teach you the JavaScript and CSS skills required to make use of the extensive potential of the GoLive SDK.

Luckily, GoLive includes a detailed manual for using the SDK, in Adobe Acrobat format. This manual, though it presumes a knowledge of both JavaScript and CSS, will show you how to use the SDK to customize your work environment and, by extension, your site. You will find it in the Documentation folder within the Adobe GoLive SDK 5.0r1 directory.

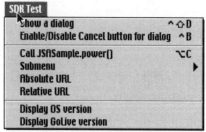

Figure 17.50 The SDK Test menu appears when you enable the Extend Script module and add SDK samples to GoLive's Extend Scripts folder.

ANIMATION AND QUICKTIME

I've described how you can use Adobe GoLive's dynamic HTML tools to position text and objects, (Chapter 12, "Layers and Positioning") and how actions can add interactivity to a page (Chapter 17, "Using Actions"). Now, for the final piece of the DHTML puzzle: animation, the ability to cause objects to look as if they're moving within a Web page.

DHTML animation allows you to move layers (floating boxes, in GoLive-speak), change their dimensions and visibility, and rearrange them relative to one another by altering their stacking order. GoLive's TimeLine Editor allows you to build animations and configure their elements in ways similar to those used by video producers to combine images, sound, and effects.

This chapter also describes how you can use GoLive's built-in QuickTime Editor to create and edit video that you can use on your Web pages.

In this chapter, I cover:

◆ Animation prerequisites

◆ Using the TimeLine Editor

◆ Setting up floating boxes for animation

◆ Using the QuickTime Editor

◆ QuickTime tracks

Animation Prerequisites

You create DHTML animation by filling floating boxes with content and then specifying a path along which the floating box moves on the page—by creating a *timeline*. Timelines use a combination of JavaScript and Cascading Style Sheet positioning features to control the movement and appearance of layers (floating boxes) on the page. You can add bells and whistles to animated content with actions that control the way animated objects move or how they interact with other items on the page.

Some of the tools you use to build animation should be familiar to you, if you've read Chapters 12 and 17. Chapter 12, "Layers and Positioning," introduced the floating box, the HTML element within which all animated objects reside, and described how to configure and stack multiple boxes. Chapter 17, "Using Actions," describes how to use JavaScript actions to incorporate interactivity, and includes details about all of the actions included with GoLive.

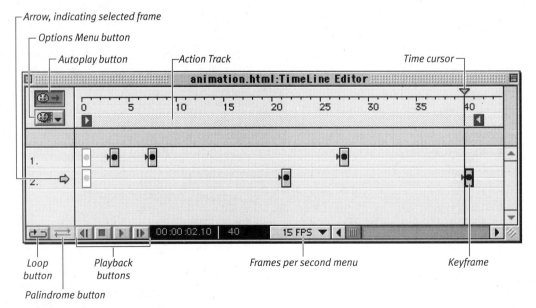

Figure 18.1 The TimeLine Editor's interface controls.

I need to introduce you to one more tool that is essential to building DHTML-based animations. It's called the TimeLine Editor (**Figure 18.1**). The TimeLine Editor is a tool that allows you to dynamically control a layer's visibility and position within the browser window.

✔ Tip

■ Visitors to a Web site need at least a 4.0 browser to view animated content.

Animation 101

Before getting started, familiarize yourself with the following terminology:

◆ **Actions** were described in Chapter 17. An action is a packaged combination (or set) of JavaScripts and Cascading Style Sheet settings that control the behavior of the page, or . of objects on the page. Actions specific to animation trigger playback, add sound, dynamically change content, and control other functions.

◆ **Animation frames** (not to be confused with HTML frames) are the base time unit of animation. Because of the human eye's persistence of vision, a sequence of still images that are presented quickly enough can simulate movement. Each image is a frame. The greater the number of frames per second (FPS) the smoother the animation will appear.

◆ **Frames** are individual "states" that occur within an animation. Like video, frames do not actually move, but are made up of still images that, when played quickly, give the appearance of movement.

◆ **Keyframes** are points that you define during animation where things happen. You can change an object's direction, show or hide it, change its position relative to other parts of the animation, and so on.

◆ **Time tracks** are the representative time scales. They show time, *not direction*, of the actual animation, and always read from left to right. Individual or multiple keyframes are inserted into time tracks, where their action or interactions occur at certain time points.

◆ **Scenes** are multiple animations appearing on the same page. Multiple scenes can be played back automatically or controlled by scripted actions, such as buttons which can be clicked to start an animation sequence.

Animating Floating Boxes

Any text or object that can be put into a floating box can theoretically be animated. Practically, however, you should not attempt to animate tables and layout grids. In most cases, you will be animating images. The optimal objects for animation are GIF images with transparent backgrounds because they show just about all of the underlying page beneath them as they chart their course across your page.

Before you can animate, you must first add and configure the objects that are to be animated, along with the floating box that will contain the animated content.

To prepare objects for animation:

1. Choose an object you want to animate. If you will be animating an image, prepare it by saving it as a transparent GIF. This format removes the image's background, so that it appears transparent when placed on your page. You can use tools such as GIFConverter or GraphicConverter (Mac) or Paint Shop Pro (Windows) to do this. If Adobe Photoshop is installed on your computer, you can use GoLive to make the image transparent. See Chapter 5, "Working with Images," for details on GoLive's Save for Web feature.

2. If your animation will include multiple versions of the same image that change as you animate them, duplicate the original image and make the changes to the image that will appear as the image comes into view within the animation.

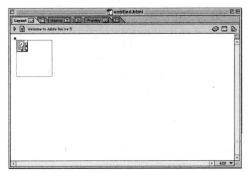

Figure 18.2 Drag an image placeholder into a floating box to begin building an element that will be animated.

To create a floating box for animation:

1. Add a floating box to a document by dragging or double-clicking the Floating Box icon from the Basic tab of the Objects palette.

2. Drag the Image icon from the Basic tab of the Objects palette into the floating box (**Figure 18.2**). If you double-click to add the image, it may appear as though the placeholder overlaps, or is actually inside the floating box, but it won't be within the box unless you drag it there, either from the Objects palette or from within the Document window.

3. Select the floating box and change its name in the Floating Box Inspector from *layer1* to something more descriptive. The name cannot include spaces or numerical characters.

4. Select the image placeholder and locate an image using the Image Inspector. Choose an image that you have already made transparent, as described in the previous section.

✔ Tips

- Text may also be animated, as long as it sits inside a floating box.

- Do not drag an image file from the Finder or Windows Explorer directly into the floating box. If you do, the image will become the background image for the floating box. Always link the graphic through its Inspector.

ANIMATING FLOATING BOXES

To begin creating an animation:

1. Select the floating box you wish to animate. It should already contain an image or other element. To select the floating box, click the border of the floating box, the yellow SB marker, or the name of the floating box in the Floating Boxes palette.

Figure 18.3 Clicking the TimeLine Editor button in the toolbar opens the editor.

2. Click the TimeLine Editor button (**Figure 18.3**), which is located above and to the right of the Document window, between the Scripts Editor button and the CSS buttons. The TimeLine Editor (**Figure 18.4**) opens. When you open it for the first time, the TimeLine Editor's window shows one time track and one keyframe. This keyframe represents the position in time of the selected floating box. The keyframe for the first position of the animation frame also maintains the distance of the floating box from the upper-left corner of the Document window.

   When you choose coordinates for a floating box within the Document window, those coordinates are always relative to the upper-left corner—the origin—and are expressed in pixels.

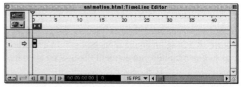

Figure 18.4 The TimeLine Editor, when opened the first time, shows one time track and a starting keyframe.

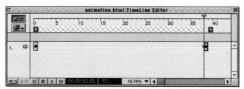

Figure 18.5 Adding the endpoint to the animation places a keyframe at the end of the TimeLine Editor's time track.

3. With the keyframe in place and the floating box still selected, Command-click (Mac) or Control-click (Windows) on a position in the time track of the TimeLine Editor to insert a new keyframe (**Figure 18.5**).The time track displays the passage of time in frames.

4. Make sure that, if you want to have a 5-second animation at 15 frames per second, you click or drag the second keyframe to 75 on the time track's scale (15 x 5 = 75).

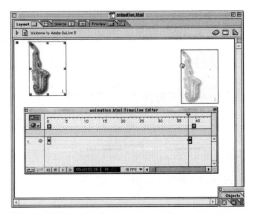

Figure 18.6 Drag the floating box to the position it should occupy when the animation is over.

Figure 18.7 The grayed-out line indicates the trajectory of the floating box between the starting point and the ending point.

Figure 18.8 Click the right-pointing triangle (the Play button) to watch the animation play.

Figure 18.9 Click the Loop button to cause the animation to play over and over again.

Figure 18.10 The Palindrome button only works when the Loop button is active. Selecting Palindrome plays the animation forward and backward, in a loop.

5. With the second keyframe selected in the TimeLine Editor, drag the floating box to the position in the Document window where you want it to be located at the time represented by the second keyframe (**Figure 18.6**). Note the grayed-out line in the Document window, indicating the path you have defined. (**Figure 18.7**).

To fine-tune the animation:

1. Return to the TimeLine Editor, and click the first (leftmost) keyframe. Your selected floating box should return to its starting position.

2. At the bottom of the TimeLine Editor is a set of playback controls (**Figure 18.8**). Click the Play button (the right-pointing triangle). You now can see your animation move from its original position to its new position, stopping at the position and time specified in the last keyframe. The two buttons to the left of the playback controls determine whether or not the animation will be looped.

3. To play an animation in an endless loop, click the Loop button (**Figure 18.9**). To cause the animation to play forward, then backward, click the Loop button, then click the Palindrome button (**Figure 18.10**).

continues on next page

ANIMATING FLOATING BOXES

4. To change the speed of the animation, choose a different number of frames-per-second from the frames-per-second menu at the bottom of the TimeLine Editor (**Figure 18.11**). If you choose a setting higher than 15 FPS, be sure to test the animation's smoothness on several computers, including some that are more than a year or two old. High-speed animation can be very processor-intensive, making it difficult to play on slower computers.

5. Drag the first keyframe to the right. A "ghosted" keyframe remains (**Figure 18.12**). When the animation is played, the contents of the floating box are not visible until the position of the "solid" keyframe is reached.

✔ Tip

- While you set the timing of animation actions in the TimeLine Editor, you change the actual movement or position of a floating box by dragging the box itself. When selecting the box, make sure that the cursor changes into a horizontal hand (**Figure 18.13**) *before* dragging the floating box. If you accidentally select the contents of the box rather than the box itself, you may end up animating an empty floating box!

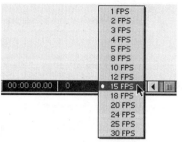

Figure 18.11 Choose the number of frames-per-second from the FPS menu at the bottom of the TimeLine Editor window.

Figure 18.12 Moving the starting point of the animation causes the floating box to remain invisible until the animation reaches its first "live" keyframe.

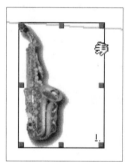

Figure 18.13 To move a floating box *and* its contents, grab the border of the box, making sure that the cursor is a horizontal hand.

ANIMATING FLOATING BOXES

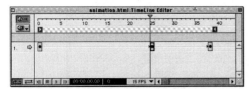

Figure 18.14 Adding a new keyframe between the start and finish keyframes creates a point at which the animation can change trajectory.

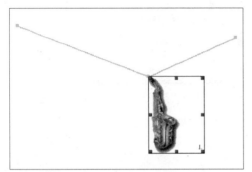

Figure 18.15 Dragging the floating box away from the line between start and finish points in the animation changes the path.

To add an intermediate point in the animation:

1. In the Document window, select the floating box.

2. In the TimeLine Editor, Command-click (Mac) or Control-click (Windows) on the timeline to insert the new keyframe (**Figure 18.14**).

3. With the new keyframe selected, drag the floating box to a new position in the Document window. This will be the position of the floating box when it reaches that point in the TimeLine Editor.

✔ Tip

■ The path of your floating box need not be straight. The box's path can dip below (**Figure 18.15**) or ascend above the starting and ending points of the animation path.

ANIMATING FLOATING BOXES

Complex animation paths

You can specify the shape of the path an animated floating box takes as it moves across the page. GoLive gives you several path shapes to choose from, or you can record your own by dragging a floating box across the Document window. GoLive records the path you take, and you can modify the path using the TimeLine Editor, if you like.

To specify a complex animation path:

1. In an animation with three keyframes, select the middle keyframe in the TimeLine Editor.

2. In the Document window, drag the floating box to a position you want it to occupy at the middle keyframe.

3. From the Animation menu in the Floating Box Inspector (**Figure 18.16**), select a path type.

   ▲ **Linear**, the default, moves the animation in a straight line during the selected segment.

   ▲ **Curve** creates a curved path (**Figure 18.17**).

   ▲ **Random** sends the floating box hurtling on a zany, nonlinear path (**Figure 18.18**).

   ▲ **None** causes the floating box to fly between the keyframe positions without appearing to travel along a path.

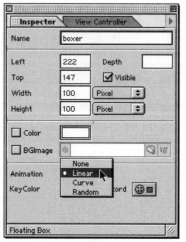

Figure 18.16 Choose an animation path type from the Animation menu in the Floating Box Inspector.

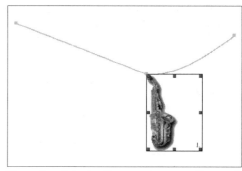

Figure 18.17 Selecting Curve creates a smooth curved path between the keyframes.

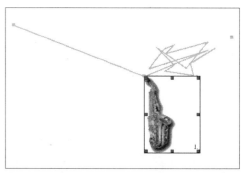

Figure 18.18 Selecting Random makes the path wild and nonlinear.

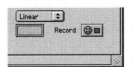

Figure 18.19 Click the Record button in the Floating Box Inspector to record a complex animation path.

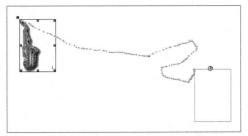

Figure 18.20 Releasing the mouse button stops the recording and displays the path from the original position of the floating box to the location where you stopped recording.

If you want to specify a path for the floating box to travel, you can do so by telling GoLive to *record* the path for you as you drag the floating box across the Document window. When you've finished dragging, you can fine-tune the path you've recorded.

To record a complex animation path:

1. Insert a floating box with content in the Document window, establishing a start point in the TimeLine Editor.

2. In the Floating Box Inspector, click the Record button (**Figure 18.19**). From this point on, movements of the floating box will be captured by GoLive as you drag the box.

3. In the Document window, drag the floating box along the path you want your animation to take.

4. Release the mouse button when you have finished the path. This stops the recording. When you do, the path appears in the Document window (**Figure 18.20**). In the TimeLine Editor, new keyframes appear.

5. Select a keyframe and drag it to a new position on the timeline to edit the length of animation segments. With a keyframe selected, you can edit the path you've created by moving the floating box in the Document window.

✔ Tip

- When you create a complex path by recording as you drag, GoLive creates lots of keyframes in the TimeLine Editor. You can often delete keyframes without affecting the animation. To do so, click the keyframe, then press Delete.

ANIMATING FLOATING BOXES

Animating multiple floating boxes

You can include multiple floating boxes in an animation. The TimeLine Editor allows you to manage and set up each box on its own timeline.

To animate several objects:

1. Add three floating boxes to a new document. In this example, I have added the images of different playing cards to each of the floating boxes. The ace occupies box #1; the deuce is in box #2, and the king, box #3.

2. Give each box a descriptive name in the Floating Box Inspector. These optional descriptive names must not contain spaces or numerical characters.

3. Open the TimeLine Editor. Note that each floating box has its own timeline.

4. Select box #2 in the TimeLine Editor and position it in the middle of the Document window. Note the arrow pointing to the time track for the selected box (**Figure 18.21**).

5. Add keyframes at the 10, 20, 30, and 40 frame positions for box #2. Do not move this floating box from its position in the Document window.

6. Click the Loop button, then the Play button. The timeline will move, but the floating box will not.

7. Select box #1 in the Document window. Note that the arrow in the TimeLine Editor now points to box #1. In the Document window, move this box to a position to the left of and slightly above box #2 (**Figure 18.22**).

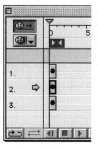

Figure 18.21 The keyframe for the second floating box is selected in the TimeLine Editor.

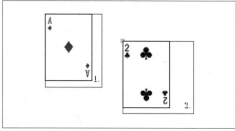

Figure 18.22 The first floating box—containing the ace—is positioned above and to the left of the second floating box (deuce).

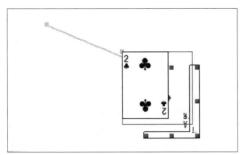

Figure 18.23 Drag the box containing the ace to a position "under" the deuce. Stacking order controls which card appears to be on top.

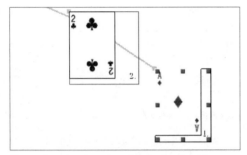

Figure 18.24 Continue dragging the first (ace) box to a position below and to the right of the deuce.

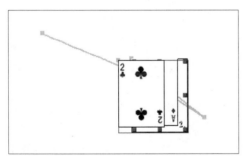

Figure 18.25 Change direction for the next keyframe, dragging the ace once again "under" the deuce.

8. With box #1 still selected, add a keyframe at the frame 10 position in the TimeLine Editor.

9. In the Document window, drag box #1 onto box #2 (**Figure 18.23**). Box #1 will appear to go *beneath* box #2 because of its position in the stacking order. The initial stacking order of floating boxes is based on the order in which they were created. The later the floating box was added to the Document window, the higher it will be in stacking order.

10. In the time track for box #1, insert a keyframe at 20 frames, then move the floating box to a position to the right of box #2 (**Figure 18.24**).

11. Insert another keyframe at frame 30.

12. Move box #1 back onto box #2 in the Document window (**Figure 18.25**).

13. In the TimeLine Editor, insert a keyframe for box #1 at frame 40.

continues on next page

ANIMATING FLOATING BOXES

14. Move box #1 to the left of box #2, to box #1's approximate starting point (**Figure 18.26**).

15. Test the animation by clicking the Play button in the TimeLine Editor. Box #1 should move down and to the right, onto box #2, sliding "underneath" it in both directions.

16. Select box #3. In the example, this is the floating box containing the king of hearts. Now, you want to cover the deuce (box #2) at the point where the ace (box #1) is tracking back to its starting point and crosses the deuce.

17. Click and hold the first keyframe of box #3, and drag it to frame 30 (**Figure 18.27**). Note that the starting keyframe for box #3 is now grayed out, indicating that this animation element will not be visible until frame 30.

18. Drag box #3 over box #2 at this position. In this example, the king completely covers the deuce.

19. Add another keyframe at frame 40 without moving box #3. The king continues to cover the deuce at frame 40. Stacking order can be set at each individual animation position.

20. Click the first keyframe of box #1 (ace in the example) and type 1 in the Depth box in the Floating Box Inspector.

21. Move to the right, selecting the other keyframes in turn, and set the depth (stacking order) to 1, 2, 3, and finally, 2 at frame 40.

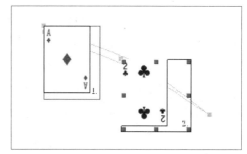

Figure 18.26 Returning to the approximate starting point completes a yo-yo–like animated relationship with the deuce.

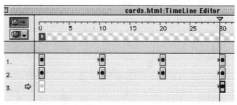

Figure 18.27 Drag the initial keyframe for box #3, so it lines up with the third keyframes of the other boxes. This will keep the king of hearts out of the action until that point in the timeline.

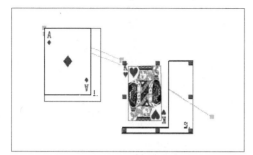

Figure 18.28 In the Document window, set the first visible keyframe so that the king of hearts "lays over" the deuce. Change the stacking order in the Depth box of the Floating Box Inspector to make the king appear as the ace passes over the deuce.

22. Select the keyframes for box #2, one by one, and set the depth of the box to 2, 2, 1, 1, and 1 at frame 40 (**Figure 18.28**).

23. Select the keyframe at frame 30 for box #3 (king of hearts) and set its depth to 2. Select the keyframe at frame 40 and set it to 2 as well.

24. Click Play. In the example animation, the ace crosses *under* the deuce and to the right. Returning, it crosses *over* the deuce, which is seemingly replaced by the king of hearts.

Note that, when played, the relationship between the floating boxes remains the same.

About stacking order

To understand how multiple floating boxes interact, you need to understand the concept of *stacking order.* You learned a bit about using stacked floating boxes in Chapter 12, "Layers and Positioning." Let's take a look at how stacked layers affect animation.

Stacking order, also called the *z-index,* assigns a number to each floating box, corresponding to its position in the stack of floating boxes on the page.

Stacking order applies to floating boxes and their content whether they are static or animated. Stacking order can be used to establish relative motion when more than one floating box is animated. Objects can appear to orbit each other, for example.

ANIMATING FLOATING BOXES

Working with Multiple Animations

There is no practical limit to the number of animated floating boxes you can include in a single page, but Web designers—and the boundaries of good taste—caution that too much animation on a page leads to instability and visual clutter.

GoLive lets you create and group multiple animations into *scenes*. With the TimeLine Editor, you can build multiple animated scenes. You may then run the scenes concurrently, sequentially, or control them with actions. To learn about GoLive actions, see Chapter 17, "Using Actions."

Floating boxes and their contents are the cast for your animations. You are the director. You can move your cast members in and out of the scenes, and control their motion and visibility. The floating box cast can be a part of one or all of the scenes. It's all up to you.

✔ Tip

■ Do not attempt to control one floating box from two different scenes at the same time.

To make a two-scene animation:

1. Create a complete animation.

2. Select Rename Scene from the Options menu (**Figure 18.29**), in the upper-left corner of the TimeLine Editor.

3. Name the new scene in the resulting dialog box and click OK.

4. Choose New Scene from the Options menu and name the second scene. Two new time tracks appear in the TimeLine Editor (**Figure 18.30**) and the new scene is displayed. Note that the set of floating boxes used in your first animation also

Figure 18.29 Click the Options menu in the TimeLine Editor to rename a scene or add a new one.

Figure 18.30 A new set of tracks indicates the presence of a new scene in the TimeLine Editor.

WORKING WITH MULTIPLE ANIMATIONS

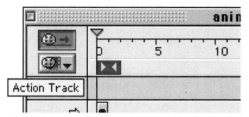

Figure 18.31 The Action Track of the TimeLine Editor is just above the area containing keyframes.

appears in this new set of time tracks. The entire cast of floating boxes is at your disposal.

5. Select the floating boxes to be used in the second scene and, by adding keyframes, build paths for the boxes' passage through the page. You may also choose to record the path of the floating box.

6. Preview the animation and edit the keyframes in the time track to be sure that the animation is as smooth as possible.

✔ Tip

- The default method for playing back multiple scenes is to play them back simultaneously after the page loads. Read the next section to learn how to use the Action Track to control the timing of playback.

Controlling animation with the Action Track

Just above the numbered timelines in the TimeLine Editor is the Action Track (**Figure 18.31**). Actions inserted into this track are the same kinds of actions I showed you in Chapter 17, several of which are designed specifically to be used with and control animation. Among the animation tasks you can control with an action is playback of the animation. Actions occur when triggered—when an event such as a mouse click or key press occurs, the action takes place.

To control sequential playback with an action:

1. Click the Autoplay button in the TimeLine Editor to deselect it on your second scene. Turn off looping and palindrome.

continues on next page

2. Select the first scene.

3. Command-click (Mac) or Control-click (Windows) at a point near the end of the last keyframe in the Action Track (**Figure 18.32**). The question mark icon in the Action Track indicates that GoLive wants you to select an action. The Action Inspector becomes visible.

4. In the Action Inspector, choose Multimedia > Play Scene from the Action menu (**Figure 18.33**). Select the name of the second scene from the popup list. The action icon (**Figure 18.34**) replaces the question mark in the Action Track.

5. Use the playback controls to preview the animation.

✔ Tip

■ You can use other actions to further refine playback. For example, if you assign the Play Scene Action to a button, visitors to your page will be able to start an animation with a click of their mouse. For more on actions, see Chapter 17, "Using Actions."

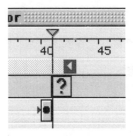

Figure 18.32 To add an action to an animation, Command-click (Mac) or Control-click (Windows) in the Action Track of the TimeLine Editor.

Figure 18.33 Select Play Scene as the controlling action from the Multimedia submenu in the Action Inspector.

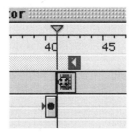

Figure 18.34 The action's icon replaces the question mark.

QuickTime Authoring and Editing

Apple's QuickTime video format—actually, you can include any combination of video, still images, and sound—is supported by any browser with the QuickTime plug-in installed. Chapter 13, "Working with Rich Media," showed you how to add a QuickTime movie to a Web page with GoLive. In this section, you'll learn how to build or edit QuickTime movies in GoLive. Although QuickTime movies are often created and built using video-editing software, GoLive's robust QuickTime Editor allows you to edit QuickTime without ever leaving GoLive. Centralized authoring seamlessly integrated into the page development process makes using QuickTime within GoLive a very attractive option.

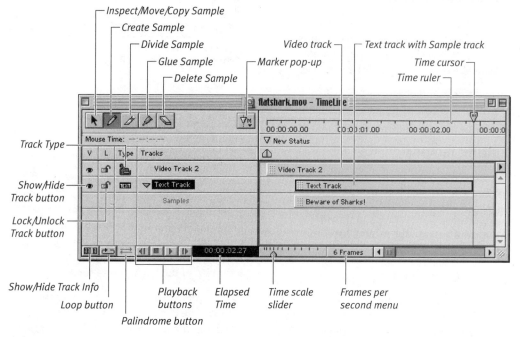

Figure 18.35 The TimeLine window in the QuickTime Editor looks something like the TimeLine Editor used to build animations.

QuickTime Authoring Tools

To edit movies in GoLive, you'll use the Movie Viewer and the Track Editor. The Viewer allows you to play and control movies, while the Track Editor controls the tracks and sequencing that comprise the movie. The Objects palette's QuickTime tab includes icons that allow you to add tracks and effects to the timeline. When the Movie Viewer is open, the toolbar contains QuickTime-specific buttons. Finally, like most other GoLive elements, you will use inspectors to configure movies and their elements.

If you've read the section of this chapter about animation and gotten to know the TimeLine Editor, you're well on your way to understanding the QuickTime TimeLine window (**Figure 18.35**). Both use a timeline metaphor, with keyframes indicating positions where action is to take place.

The QuickTime palette

QuickTime has its own tab in the Objects palette (**Figure 18.36**). This tab contains icons for each of the many types of media that can be added to a QuickTime movie.

To add tracks and other objects to a QuickTime movie, just drag a QuickTime tab icon into the TimeLine window.

Editing movies

You can either work with existing QuickTime movies or build new ones using GoLive's QuickTime Editor.

To open an existing movie for further editing:

1. Choose File > Open.

2. Locate a movie file, and open it. The movie opens in the Movie Viewer window, with the Preview tab selected (**Figure 18.37**).

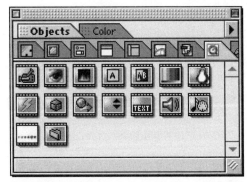

Figure 18.36 Add new tracks to a QuickTime movie with icons from the QuickTime tab of the Objects palette.

Figure 18.37 When you open a movie in the Movie Viewer, it appears with the Preview tab active.

The Background Track

When you open a new QuickTime movie document, the movie already has a single track, called the Background track.

The Background track's only purpose is to keep the Movie Viewer window open. The size and color specified in the New QuickTime Movie dialog box determine the size of the Background track.

Once you add an image or video to the movie, the Background track is eliminated, because the dimensions of the Video track will determine the size of the window.

Figure 18.38 Click this button on the toolbar to open the TimeLine window.

Figure 18.39 If an existing movie is imported with video and sound tracks, they show up as separate tracks.

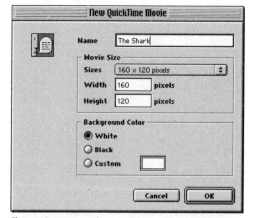

Figure 18.40 Name the movie in the New QuickTime Movie dialog box.

Figure 18.41 The TimeLine window opens, with the Background Track visible.

3. Click the Show TimeLine Window button on the toolbar (**Figure 18.38**) to display the TimeLine window.

   or

   Choose Movie > Show TimeLine. The tracks contained in the open movie will be displayed (**Figure 18.39**).

To create a new QuickTime movie:

1. Choose File > New Special > New QuickTime Movie.

2. Type a name for the movie in the Name field of the New QuickTime Movie dialog box (**Figure 18.40**). The filename must end with the .mov extension.

3. Choose a size in pixels from the popup menu, or type in your own dimensions, expressed in pixels, in the Width and Height fields.

4. Choose a color for the background track. The default is white. You can change it to black, or choose a custom color by clicking the Custom radio button and selecting a color.

5. Click OK. The Movie Viewer opens with the specified background color in place.

6. Open the TimeLine window. The background track is the only current track, and appears in the TimeLine window (**Figure 18.41**).

To annotate and view properties of a movie:

1. Click in the Movie Viewer to activate it and show the Movie Inspector. Make sure the whole movie is selected and not just one of its component parts. The Movie Inspector's Basic tab (**Figure 18.42**) contains information about the movie: You can choose a few options in the Basic tab, which I will cover in subsequent sections of this chapter.

2. Click the Annotation tab (**Figure 18.43**), and fill in the information you find useful. This is where information about the ownership and authorship of the movie is established and maintained.

Figure 18.42 Information about the movie appears in the Movie Inspector's Basic tab.

Figure 18.43 The Annotation tab, among other things, establishes ownership of the movie.

About Flattening

The first time you save a QuickTime movie, it will be *flattened*. Flattening is not compressing. Flattening takes all the file references in the QuickTime movie— that is, tracks which point to files elsewhere on your hard drive—and includes them in the core file, which then grows in size. Movies *must* be flattened to load onto a Web server and display on the Web.

QuickTime Tracks

Tracks are the basic unit of the QuickTime TimeLine window. When you add audio, video, or other supported formats into the QuickTime Editor, each occupies a *track*. There are different track types for different kinds of information. Besides video tracks, the other track types are:

♦ **Picture tracks** can make a slide show of your still images.

♦ **Sound and Music tracks** can contain AIFF/AIFC, standard MIDI, System 7 sound, WAV, MP3, or Sound Designer files.

♦ **Sprite tracks** select from a pool of still images, assigning them actions and behaviors.

♦ **SWF tracks** contain images made in Macromedia Flash and Adobe LiveMotion.

♦ **Streaming tracks** can be used to set up on-demand movies through either RTSP or HTTP protocols.

♦ **3-D tracks** contain QuickTime 3-D files.

♦ **HREF tracks** embed hyperlink information into a movie.

♦ **Folder tracks** are used to organize groups of other tracks.

♦ **Chapter tracks** divide a movie into segments so your visitors can view your movie a bit at a time.

♦ **Text tracks** contain text (titles, for example) displayed with your movie.

♦ **Filter tracks** allow you to select special effects such as transitions between scenes.

Most of the work involved in QuickTime authoring involves controlling the types of material brought into the TimeLine window and manipulating the order, visibility, and behavior of the individual tracks with respect to the movie as a whole.

Sample Tracks and Sample Tools

Sample tracks are used by some types of QuickTime tracks to control certain qualities of the track. Adding one of the track icons to the TimeLine Editor opens a Sample track and its associated Inspector.

The five Sample tools—inspect/move/copy, create, divide, glue, and delete (**Figure 18.35**)—are used to make the Sample track, which—in conjunction with the Sample Track Inspector—assigns certain characteristics to the Sample track and to the QuickTime track itself. The Sample track acts as the QuickTime track's controller. The Sample tools are used to position and edit them in the TimeLine window.

Adding Video tracks

Video tracks, or moving video images, are what most people think of when they think of QuickTime.

To insert tracks from another movie:

1. Open an existing movie or create a new one.

2. Open the TimeLine window (Movie > Show TimeLine).

3. Drag the Video Track icon (**Figure 18.44**) from the QuickTime tab of the Objects palette onto the track list in the left pane of the TimeLine window (**Figure 18.45**). An Open dialog box appears.

4. Choose the QuickTime movie containing the video track you want to add. The first visible track of the selected movie is imported, and the track appears on the track list. If the imported movie has a sound track, both a video and a sound track appear in the TimeLine window (**Figure 18.46**).

5. Rename the track if you wish by double-clicking its name in the track list. The track's name is selected. You can also change a track's name by clicking on it and editing the name in the track's Inspector (**Figure 18.47**).

Figure 18.44 The Video Track icon appears on the QuickTime tab of the Objects palette.

Figure 18.45 Drag the Video Track icon from the QuickTime tab of the Objects palette to the track list area of the TimeLine window.

Figure 18.46 Video and sound are imported on two separate tracks.

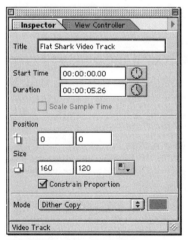

Figure 18.47 Like other track Inspectors, the Video Track Inspector is used to name the track, as well as set its dimensions and position on the page.

QUICKTIME TRACKS

To copy an individual track from another movie:

1. Open the source movie and the destination movie in GoLive.

2. Select the source movie.

3. Open the TimeLine window.

4. Select the track you wish to copy from the source movie.

5. Choose Edit > Copy.

6. Switch to the destination movie and make sure the TimeLine window is open.

7. Choose Edit > Paste. The track copied from the source file appears in the TimeLine window's track list.

8. Rename the imported track.

✔ Tip

- You can also import animated GIF images into a QuickTime movie. Drag the Video Track icon into the TimeLine window to set up an empty track, then choose the animated GIF file, which will be converted into a video track.

To control the properties of a video track:

1. Click a video track in the TimeLine window to view the Video Track Inspector.

2. Set the time during the movie at which you want the video track to start in the Start Time field.

3. Use the Duration box to set the length of the video track.

4. Click the Scale Sample Time checkbox to have other tracks containing samples (such as sprites, text, chapters, HREF, or filters) change their look proportionately with changes made to the video track.

continues on next page

QUICKTIME TRACKS

5. Set the x and y coordinates for the movie in the Position fields (**Figure 18.48**).

6. Set the size of the track in pixels.

7. To scale the size properties of the track with respect to other tracks, click the button to the right of the size field and choose Normalize Track/Set Track Dimensions.

8. Use the Mode menu to choose how the video track overlays other tracks.

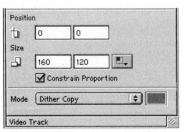

Figure 18.48 Choose size and positioning options for a video track in the Video Track Inspector.

▲ **Dither Copy** overlays the selected track, using dithering—a method of color substitution—to add colors by combining colors in the existing palette.

▲ **Copy** does the same thing as Dither Copy, but without dithering, making the track less color rich for systems capable of displaying 256 or more colors.

▲ **Blend** makes the selected track translucent, allowing the visual tracks below it to be seen. The degree of translucency is determined by selecting a color with the Color box next to the Mode menu. The lighter the color, the greater the degree of translucency.

▲ **Transparent** defines a color that will be transparent in a visual track.

▲ **An alpha channel** is a special color channel used for making a masked (or left out) section of a background image. To set qualities in a track's alpha channel, use the final five modes:

▲ **Straight alpha** and **Straight alpha blend** combine the color qualities of each pixel with the background pixel at the same location in the movie, based on the value set in the alpha channel.

▲ **Premul white alpha** supports images created on a white background with a premultiplied alpha channel.

QUICKTIME TRACKS

Figure 18.49 Use the Picture Track icon from the QuickTime tab of the Objects palette to add tracks for still images.

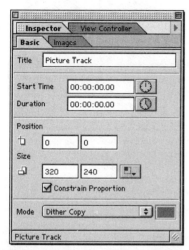

Figure 18.50 Configure a picture track in the Basic tab of the Picture Track Inspector.

Figure 18.51 Add images to the track in the Images tab of the Picture Track Inspector.

▲ **Premul black alpha** supports images created on a black background with a premultiplied alpha channel.

▲ **Composition (Dither Copy)** is a special mode that uses color dithering to benefit video tracks created from animated GIF files.

Adding Picture tracks

Picture tracks contain still images that can be arranged to make a version of an online slide show. The pictures are deployed like a video track, using the TimeLine window.

To add a picture track:

1. With the Movie Viewer window and TimeLine window open and active, drag the Picture Track icon (**Figure 18.49**) from the QuickTime tab of the Objects palette on to the track list of the TimeLine window. The Picture Track Inspector appears (**Figure 18.50**).

2. In the Picture Track Inspector, name the track and choose a start time, duration, position, and size, just as you did for the video track in the previous section.

3. Click the Inspector's Images tab (**Figure 18.51**).

4. Choose whether this image will be inserted at the current time marker position (Insert Images) or if the image will be part of a slideshow, replacing previous images (Replace Images).

5. Click Import and select an image to add in the Open dialog box. You can add multiple images if you like.

6. Click Done to finish adding images.

continues on next page

QUICKTIME TRACKS

7. In the Compression Settings dialog box that appears (**Figure 18.52**), change the compression, bit depth, and quality settings if you wish, then click OK to return to the Picture Track Inspector.

8. Set other properties for the image or images:

▲ **Images Constrain Proportion** scales down oversized images to the size of the movie.

▲ **Background Color** sets the picture track's background color, selected from a color palette.

▲ **Slideshow Time Interval** specifies the duration of visibility for the image.

▲ **Loop** determines how many times a sequence of pictures sharing the same track will be cycled.

9. In the Movie Viewer, click the Play button (**Figure 18.53**) to preview the movie, including the new picture track.

Figure 18.52 After you have chosen an image or images for the picture track, GoLive presents a Compression Settings dialog box where you can choose the type and quality of compression you want to apply to the image.

Figure 18.53 Click Play when you're ready to preview a movie and the new picture track.

Figure 18.54 Add a sprite track with the Sprite Track icon from the QuickTime tab of the Objects palette.

Figure 18.55 A sprite track in the TimeLine window. Notice that there's an expansion triangle next to the track, allowing you to control sprites within a track individually.

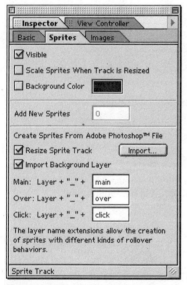

Figure 18.56 The Sprite Track Inspector sets the properties for the Sprite.

Sprite tracks

Like video tracks, sprite tracks contain images that form movies. But instead of continuous video, sprite tracks consist of images, sequenced and animated, to create the effect of movement. A sprite is typically a static image that moves through a movie in a certain way. Creating sprites requires several steps: first, you create the sprite track within a movie. Next, you import graphics into an image pool from which you will draw when you create and animate individual sprites.

To add a sprite track:

1. With a movie open and the TimeLine window visible, drag the Sprite Track icon (**Figure 18.54**) from the QuickTime tab of the Objects palette into the track list. A new sprite track appears in the track list (**Figure 18.55**) and the Sprite Inspector appears.

2. Name and set options in the Sprite Track Inspector's Basic tab as you have for other kinds of QuickTime tracks.

3. Click the Sprites tab of the Sprite Track Inspector and set preferences related to the appearance and activity of sprites (**Figure 18.56**).

   ▲ **Visible** toggles the visibility of the Sprite track in the Movie Viewer window.

   ▲ **Scale Sprites When Track Is Resized** is used to smooth vector graphics when the sprite track is resized.

   ▲ **Background Color** sets the background color of the sprite track. The default color is black. Select another color with the Color palette.

   ▲ **Add New Sprites** is a dialog box where you enter the number of sprites to be added to the sprite track. It can't be set until you add images to the pool available to the sprite track.

To add images to a sprite track's image pool:

1. Select the sprite track from the track list. Click the Images tab of the Sprite Track Inspector and select a still image to use as the first sprite (**Figure 18.57**).

2. In the Sprites tab of the Sprite Track Inspector, enter the number of sprites to be added in the Add New Sprites box (**Figure 18.58**).

3. Return to the Inspector's Images tab, then click Import.

4. In the resulting file dialog box, navigate to the folder containing your images. Select each one, then click Add. When all the images are added, click Done.

5. In the Compression Settings window (**Figure 18.59**), select a compression scheme for your images. I have selected the default JPEG settings.

6. Select the color depth from the Best Depth popup menu. Your choices, unless you have chosen one of the more esoteric compression schemes, will likely be Color and Grayscale.

7. Select a level with the Quality slider. The greater the compression, the more quality suffers. Conversely, the higher the quality, the greater the download time. Check the preview window to see that you select the best compromise between file size and image quality.

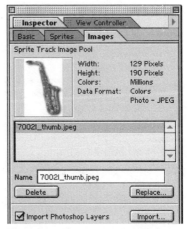

Figure 18.57 The Images tab of the Sprite Track Inspector is where you add to the pool of images for the sprite track.

Figure 18.58 Enter the number of sprites to be added in the Add New Sprites box, located in the Sprites tab.

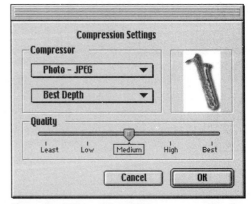

Figure 18.59 When adding JPEG images as sprites, the Compression Settings dialog box opens to give you a choice of settings.

Figure 18.60 Each sprite is assigned its own subtrack, beneath the Sprite track.

8. Click OK to close the Compression Settings dialog box. The sprite images appear in a subtrack below the Sprite track (**Figure 18.60**), each assigned a name (Sprite 1, Sprite 2, etc.) and each assigned a keyframe on each track.

9. Click one of the new sprites to open the Sprite Object Inspector.

10. Rename the sprite so that you can easily identify it.

11. Click the Sprite track, and open the Basic tab in the Sprite Track Inspector. Use the settings to experiment with the position of the selected Sprite in the Movie Viewer.

Adding behaviors to sprites

As anyone who has read Shakespeare's *The Tempest* knows, sprites are trainable. Adobe calls sprites that have had behaviors added *wired sprites*.

Using the Sprite Sample Inspector with the Sprite track selected, you can add interactivity up to and including full rollovers and navigational buttons, all from within QuickTime. Basically, wiring a sprite with action is exactly like adding action to any other element. You choose the sprite and select an event from the Sprite Sample Inspector which will trigger the action (usually a mouse movement of some sort). Then, from an Action popup menu, select an action—such as jumping to another URL. A description of the selected action appears, along with dialog boxes you must fill in for the action to work.

✔ Tip

■ Photoshop files with layers can also be imported as sprites, with the added advantage of having each layer treated as an independent, controllable image.

Adding SWF tracks

SWF is a file format used by Macromedia Flash and Adobe LiveMotion. This advanced technology makes stunning animations and, using GoLive's QuickTime authoring, can be presented as QuickTime movies.

Just drag the SWF icon from the QuickTime tab of the Objects palette into the TimeLine window and add an SWF file when prompted. A new track handles the SWF file, matching its duration and frame speed. Use the SWF Track Inspector to configure the track further.

Adding Streaming tracks

There are two schemes for streaming video, HTTP and RTSP (Runtime Streaming Protocol). If you have the dedicated server required for streaming and the know-how to develop streaming content, you can use GoLive to add a streaming track to your movie. To do this, drag the Streaming Track icon from the QuickTime tab of the Objects palette and configure the new track in the Streaming Track Inspector.

Adding QuickDraw 3D tracks

QuickDraw 3D is an Apple graphics format that allows you to include 3-D animation within QuickTime movies. Configure these files with the QuickDraw 3D icon (found on the QuickTime tab of the Objects palette) and the QuickDraw 3D Inspector.

Figure 18.61 The Sound Track (left) and MIDI (Music) Track icons appear in the QuickTime tab of the Objects palette.

Adding Music and Sound tracks

If you import a video file without sound into the QuickTime Editor, chances are you'll want to add some sort of sound track to increase its effectiveness on the Web. Whether it's a voice-over or a music track, sound adds impact to visual presentations. Adding a sound track is just a matter of dragging and dropping a new track into the QuickTime Editor.

✔ Tips

■ GoLive supports AIFF, AIFC, System 7 (Macintosh) sound, WAV, MP3, and Sound Designer II file formats. Music is specifically defined as standard MIDI format, which can be played back using QuickTime's musical instruments.

■ The QuickTime Editor cannot produce sound or music tracks. It can only add them as tracks within QuickTime movies. You will need a sound editing application to build or modify the sound track, or a music application to produce MIDI files.

To add a music or sound track to a QuickTime movie:

1. Open a movie containing at least one video track and the TimeLine window.

2. Drag the (MIDI) Music Track or Sound Track icon from the QuickTime tab (**Figure 18.61**) of the Objects palette onto the TimeLine window's track list.

3. Using the Inspector, open the audio file.

4. Click Play in the TimeLine Editor to see how well the sound file synchronizes with existing video tracks.

5. To change the duration of the sound or music track, enter a new duration value in the Sound Track Inspector, or change the start and end points of the track on the track list.

QUICKTIME TRACKS

Adding HREF tracks

HREF tracks contain URLs embedded in QuickTime movies. The HREF appears for a specified period of time during the run of the QuickTime movie, and viewers may elect to jump to the URL, or they may be sent there automatically.

If your site uses frames, HREF tracks can be used to cause a QuickTime movie occupying one frame to change the content of another frame. For example, the movie containing the HREF track can be used to change the content of another frame, while the movie in the first frame continues to play.

To add an HREF track:

1. Open a movie and the TimeLine Editor.

2. Drag the HREF Track icon from the QuickTime tab of the Objects palette, (**Figure 18.62**) into the TimeLine window. A new, empty HREF track opens. By default, the track is hidden so it will not overprint on the movie's visuals.

3. To make the URL track visible, click the eye icon in the track list (**Figure 18.63**).

4. Configure options for the HREF track in the HREF Track Inspector, if necessary.

5. In the TimeLine Editor, click the triangle next to the HREF track's name (**Figure 18.64**). The Samples track is displayed.

6. Click the Create Sample icon (**Figure 18.65**) to add a sample content bar to the Samples track (**Figure 18.66**).

7. With the Samples track selected, enter the URL in the Link field of the HREF Sample Track Inspector (**Figure 18.67**), or browse to find a page to link.

8. From the Target pop-up, choose where the link should open.

Figure 18.62 The HREF Track icon in the QuickTime tab of the Objects palette.

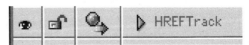

Figure 18.63 Click the eye icon to make the new HREF track visible.

Figure 18.64 Click the triangle next to the HREF track's name to display the Samples track.

Figure 18.65 The Create Sample icon.

Figure 18.66 The Create Sample icon is used to draw the sample content bar in the Samples track.

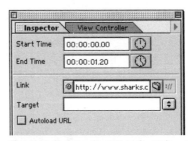

Figure 18.67 Enter the URL in the Link field of the HREF Sample Track Inspector.

QUICKTIME TRACKS

✔ Tip

■ If the Autoload URL box is checked in the HREF Track Inspector, the browser will automatically jump to the linked URL while the QuickTime movie is playing. If Autoload URL is not checked, the browser will only jump to the linked URL when the movie is clicked.

Using Folder tracks

Folder tracks are used to group the tracks in a QuickTime movie. Generally a folder will contain tracks of the same type, such as all the sound or video tracks used to make a movie.

To insert a Folder track, drag the Folder Track icon from the QuickTime tab of the Objects palette to the TimeLine Editor.

Once you have added a Folder track, you can add other tracks to the folder by dragging them over the folder.

Using Chapter tracks

Where Folder tracks store tracks of the same media type, Chapter tracks store tracks relating to a section of a QuickTime movie. Like chapters of a book, Chapter tracks and the tracks they contain can be arranged sequentially, dividing a large movie into segments whose titles appear in a pop-up menu when the QuickTime movie is played in the browser—something like a table of contents.

To create a chapter track:

1. Drag the Chapter Track icon from the QuickTime tab of the Objects palette to create a Chapter track.

2. Name the Chapter track in the Title field of the Chapter Track Inspector. The Chapter track needs to be at least 275 pixels wide.

continues on next page

QUICKTIME TRACKS

3. Click the triangle in the track to open the Samples track.

4. Click the Create Sample icon to set the duration of the track.

5. Open the Chapters Sample Inspector (**Figure 18.68**) and set the properties of the Sample. You can preview your chapter in the Movie Viewer window.

6. Resize the movie if necessary to accommodate the new popup menu, and choose chapters from the list to run.

Using Text tracks

By adding a Text track to your movie, you can add titles, subtitles, and even links to other Web pages.

To add a text track:

1. Drag the Text Track icon from the QuickTime tab of the Objects palette into the TimeLine Editor.

2. Set the track's properties in the Text Track Inspector (**Figure 18.69**).

3. In the TimeLine Editor, click the triangle to the left of the new Text track, opening the Samples track. Set the duration of the Samples track, using the Samples track icons.

4. With the Samples track selected, open the Text Sample Inspector (**Figure 18.70**). Select the Text tab and enter the text to be displayed in the Text box. Click Apply. The text appears on the Text Sample track.

5. Use the Align popup menu to align the text left, center, or right, within the Movie Viewer window.

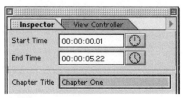

Figure 18.68 Name the chapter in the Chapters Sample Inspector.

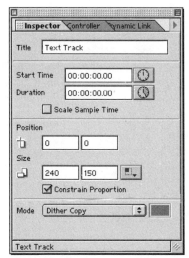

Figure 18.69 The Text Track Inspector.

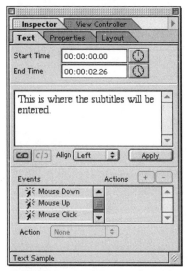

Figure 18.70 The Text Sample Inspector is where text is actually entered.

QUICKTIME TRACKS

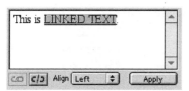

Figure 18.71 Text chosen for a link is highlighted and underlined in blue.

To add links to Text tracks:

1. In the Text tab of the Text Sample Inspector, select the text to be linked in the Text box.

2. Click the Link button. The selected text is highlighted and underlined in blue (**Figure 18.71**).

3. From the list in the lower-left corner of the Text Sample Inspector, select the event that will trigger the link action, typically a mouse click.

4. Select Go To URL from the Action popup menu.

5. Enter the URL to which the action will jump and click Apply.

✔ Tip

- Text properties also can be set in the Layout tab of the Text Sample Inspector. These include margin settings for the text box, background color for the text (set from the color palette), drop shadow for the type, and transparent—a setting used to hide the type in the background color.

Filter tracks

Transitions—the effects that connect one visual scene to another—have their own special track type. They are called Filter tracks, and there are three types:

- **Generic filters** are effects generated by the filters themselves. They are self-contained and need no video track.

- **One source filters** are applied to single video tracks.

- **Two source filters** are used as transition material between two video tracks.

QUICKTIME TRACKS

To add a Generic Filter track:

1. Create a movie containing two video tracks, open the TimeLine Editor, and be sure it is in a position *below* the Video track or Picture track you are going to alter.

2. Drag the Generic Filter icon from the QuickTime tab of the Objects palette to the TimeLine Editor. The Generic Filter Track Inspector appears (**Figure 18.72**).

3. With the new track in place and selected, set its properties in the Inspector.

4. Click the triangle to the left of the selected track to open a new Samples track. Use the Samples Track tools to set the duration of the track.

5. In the Generic Filter Sample Inspector (**Figure 18.73**), click Select.

6. Select one of the types of filters from the Select Effect window. I have chosen the Algorithmic Cloud Effect (**Figure 18.74**). Each effect appears in a preview window, and the parameters of each generic filter type can be changed in the Inspector.

7. Click OK when you are satisfied with the effect.

8. Preview the effect by playing the movie in the Movie Viewer.

To add a One Source Filter track:

1. Drag the One Source Filter Track tool from the QuickTime tab of the Objects palette into the TimeLine Editor, and be sure it is in a position *below* the Video track or Picture track you are going to alter.

2. With the new track selected, set its properties in the One Source Filter Inspector.

3. Choose the Video or Picture track you are going to alter with the Filter track.

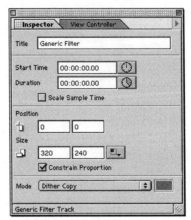

Figure 18.72 When you add a Generic Filter track, the Generic Filter Inspector appears.

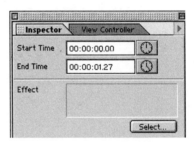

Figure 18.73 Click the Select button in the Generic Filter Sample Inspector.

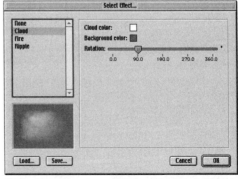

Figure 18.74 Choose an effect from the Select Effect window. The selected effect appears in the preview window, and numerical values can be changed there.

QUICKTIME TRACKS

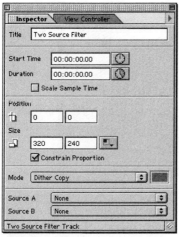

Figure 18.75 The Two Source Filter Track Inspector.

4. Click the triangle to the left of the Filter track to expand the track and add a Samples track.

5. Use the Create Sample tool to make a sample bar in the Samples track's content area. The One Source Filter Track Sample Inspector appears.

6. Click the Select button to open the Select Effect window.

7. Select one of the effects listed in the dialog box. Use the preview window and the parameters to determine which effect to use.

8. Click OK. The filter now occupies the content area of the Samples track. Play the movie in the Movie Viewer to see the effect in action. The filter's effects can be changed by moving the Samples track, or by accessing the Layout tab of the Movie Viewer.

✔ Tip

■ The One Source Filter Sample Inspector allows you to save filters for later use using the .qfx file extension. Open saved files by clicking Load in the same Inspector to be used by this or other movies.

To insert a Two Source Filter track:

1. Create a movie containing two video tracks.

2. Drag the Two Source Filter Track tool from the QuickTime tab of the Objects palette to the TimeLine Editor, making sure that the filter track appears below the video tracks on the track list.

3. Use the Two Source Filter Track Inspector (**Figure 18.75**) to set the properties of the track.

continues on next page

QUICKTIME TRACKS

4. Choose a video track from the Source A popup menu and one from the Source B menu.

5. In the TimeLine Editor, click the triangle to the left of the track to expand the track and open a Samples track.

6. Use the Create Sample icon to create a sample bar and Samples track content area. If you're specifically making a transition, make your Video tracks overlap slightly and create the Two Source Filter Sample track in the overlap. The Two Source Filter Sample Inspector appears (**Figure 18.76**).

7. Click the Select button to open the Select Effect dialog box.

8. Choose an effect from the list.

9. Click OK. The Sample content bar now contains the name of the selected effect (**Figure 18.77**).

10. Choose whether you want the effect to transition from Source A to B, or Source B to A.

11. Preview the movie in the Movie Viewer window to see the filter. You can adjust the filter in the TimeLine window or in the Layout tab of the Movie Viewer.

✔ **Tip**

■ The Two Source Filter Sample Inspector allows you to save filters for later use using the .qfx file extension. Open saved files by clicking Load in the same Inspector so they can be used in other movies.

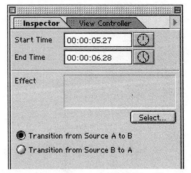

Figure 18.76 The Two Source Filter Sample Inspector.

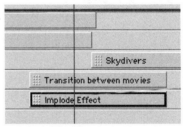

Figure 18.77 When you've added and configured a two source track, the TimeLine Editor looks like this.

BEYOND HTML

Adobe GoLive can help you weave your Web pages together with an ODBC-compliant (Open Database Connectivity) database, making a powerful Web presence. Whether you want to put your necktie collection online or build a complete e-commerce solution, GoLive's visual environment and tools can help you link the pages of your Web site to industry-standard databases with a tool called Dynamic Link.

GoLive can also write Extensible Markup Language (XML) code. XML offers a lot of advantages over the limitations of HTML for Web developers who need to build dynamic sites and who want to share Web content with other applications.

Dynamic Link

By now most of us have had the experience of requesting a piece of information from a database-driven Web site—airline schedules, a page describing an item up for auction, or a book review from the Sunday newspaper. When you interact with a Web site in this way, you are viewing dynamic content— Web pages whose contents are generated "on the fly," based on the specific information requested. This works on the Web because the HTML page where you enter your search request or click a link to dynamic content communicates with the Web server and with a database containing the information you're looking for. GoLive's Dynamic Link module allows you to build those links while you develop pages in GoLive. Once you make the links, GoLive generates the code needed to link to the database.

Dynamic Link is designed to support a variety of databases, but the version supplied with GoLive 5.0 supports only Microsoft's ASP (Active Server Pages) technology.

Dynamic Link and ASP

If you've ever noticed ".asp" at the end of a long URL, you've used ASP technology. When you click a link or a submit button, your browser sends a request to a Web server— usually a Microsoft Windows NT server. Your request is passed along to the database containing the information you've requested.

ASP is a Microsoft-specific technology. It can only be implemented on Microsoft Personal Web Server, Peer Web Server, and Microsoft Internet Information Server (version 3 or later). ASP-built pages can most reliably be viewed on 4.0 or later browser versions.

Lasso Studio Announced

Another string of letters you may have noticed when querying a database-driven Website is Lasso. Lasso is a database development tool from Blue World Communications, Inc. (www.blueworld.com). As this book went to press, Blue World was preparing to ship Lasso Studio for GoLive 5.

Like Dynamic Link for ASP, Lasso Studio will provide Web developers a visual development environment for building database-driven Web sites powered by the Lasso Web Data Engine. Lasso Studio will provide a set of wizards, editors, and translators to ease the development process.

You will still need to learn a few tags in Lasso's native language, LDML, and find a Lasso-friendly ISP to handle your Web and database serving requirements, but this alternative to Microsoft ASP server technology is an attractive solution for many developers.

Unfortunately, Lasso Studio was not available for evaluation when this book went to press.

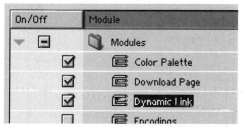

Figure A.1 To enable Dynamic Link, click the Dynamic Link Module checkbox in the Preferences window. You will have to restart GoLive to view and use Dynamic Link tools.

Microsoft Access, Microsoft SQL Server, Oracle, and any database that uses ODBC (including FileMaker Pro version 4.1 and later) are supported. Microsoft Data Access Components are required to use Access 2000 with ASP, and Microsoft Commerce Server is required to build an e-commerce site.

Dynamic Link is GoLive's method of connecting the Web pages you create to a database utilizing ASP. Because Dynamic Link uses GoLive's familiar graphical interface, there are advantages to using GoLive as your development tool.

Getting started with Dynamic Link

By now you've probably realized that you will need to coordinate several tools and technologies to make a database-driven Web site a reality. First, you'll need an ODBC-capable database application. Designing the database itself with the ultimate goal of using it to supply Web content is critical. Then, you'll need to find an Internet Service Provider capable of hosting your database and managing your Web server with the Microsoft products discussed earlier, or plan to host the database and an ASP-compatible Web server program on your own servers.

First, though, you'll need to enable the Dynamic Link module to GoLive's Modules folder.

To enable Dynamic Link:

1. Choose Edit > Preferences. The Preferences window appears.

2. Click the Modules label to display a list of available GoLive modules.

3. Click the Dynamic Link checkbox (**Figure A.1**) to activate the Dynamic Link module.

continues on next page

DYNAMIC LINK

4. Click OK to close the Preferences window, and quit GoLive.

5. Launch GoLive. Dynamic Link is now available. Notice that the palette containing the Inspector and View Controller now includes the Dynamic Link tab (**Figure A.2**).

With its convenient drag-and-drop and validation checking features, GoLive has some real advantages as an ASP development tool. GoLive's visual metaphor makes it possible for you to avoid lots of hand coding and scripting.

But GoLive's visual tools won't keep you sheltered from all of the hard work of database building. Developing an ASP-driven site requires knowledge of Windows NT server technology, know-how, and patience.

You will find an introduction to making an ASP site in the GoLive 5.0 User Guide. The Dynamic Link folder within the Adobe GoLive 5.0 folder is a basic demonstration site.

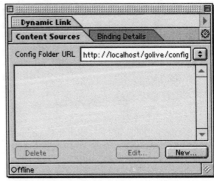

Figure A.2 Enabling the Dynamic Link module adds the Dynamic Link palette to the Window menu. It contains the two main tools of ASP: Content Sources to link to a database and Binding Details to link placeholding material to data.

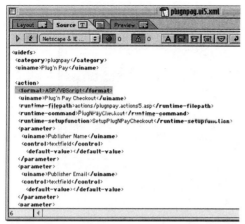

Figure A.3 A DTD displayed in the HTML Source Editor.

XML

Extensible Markup Language (XML) evolved from SGML—the granddaddy of all markup languages. XML allows developers to create their own tags, making it possible to integrate XML-based content with a variety of other data. Unlike the rather limited vocabulary of HTML, XML allows the developer to include a pointer to a Document Type Definition (DTD) at the top of a page. The DTD contains the developer's XML tags and their definitions. This string of code tells the receiving browser—up front—what the code making up the page's tags means. These tags are then interpreted for display by the receiving browser.

XML allows you to develop and maintain a vocabulary customized for the purposes of your particular data.

For example, <HR> will define a horizontal rule in HTML and display the rule in its proper position on a Web page. But, the XML tag <RULES> may be defined to show a set of rules and regulations. This information can be interpreted by a database compiling a list of rules and regulations, or a Web robot looking for a list of Web sites dealing with rules and regulations.

GoLive and XML

Much of the work of using XML is in the definition of elements. That's where GoLive comes in. Although you can't build an XML page visually in GoLive as you can an HTML page, you can open existing XML files in GoLive using the HTML Outline Editor.

The HTML Source Editor (**Figure A.3**) is even more revealing, with the definitions declared. This document is a DTD.

continues on next page

XML

XML definitions can be edited and written in GoLive using the XML Item Inspector (**Figure A.4**). Because of the nature of XML, the Layout Editor doesn't give you an indication of what your XML tags actually do. The XML Item Inspector allows you to define and modify the attributes of an XML tag when working in the HTML Outline Editor.

As it goes about its business, GoLive is itself using XML. **Figure A.5** shows four DTD files. These or any other DTD files can be viewed using GoLive's XML Item Inspector. (Don't change any of GoLive's internal XML code, though!)

XML is not for the beginning Web developer, and XML authoring is beyond the scope of this book. Fortunately, there are lots of XML resources on the Web that can help you learn and use it to structure your Web presence. Start at `http://www.w3.org/XML/`, the World Wide Web Consortium's XML reference site. Other sites include XML.com (`http://www.xml.com`), the XML Zone (`http://www.xml-zone.com`), and XMLephant.com (`http://www.xmlephant.com`).

Figure A.4 Each XML definition can be examined and edited in the XML Item Inspector.

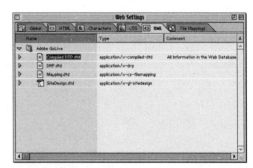

Figure A.5 GoLive itself uses XML, as you can see from these internal DTD files in the Web Settings window. Expert users of XML may want to tinker with these settings.

XML

INDEX

INDEX

nested frames 198-200
nesting tables 159-160
Netscape 244, 293
Netscape Communicator 98, 189, 201
Netscape CSS Fix actions 422
Netscape Navigator 85-87, 90
Never status 387
New Pages dialog box, Parent and Sibling
    menus 315
New Set button 25
noframes elements 201-202
non-breaking spaces 149, 155
non-file resources 321
None path 442

O

objects. *See also specific objects*
    animating 436, 444-447
    changing attributes 10
    coloring 13
    components sharing horizontal spaces
      with 344
    layout grids 77-81
Objects palette 8-9
    adding images to pages 101-102
    adding tags 209
    opening stationeries 342
    Site tab 302
One source filters 469-471
online help 26-27
Open Alert Window action 415-416
Open dialog box 30-31
open documents, linking 133
Open Window actions 413-415
opening
    actions for editing 427
    Align palette 78
    auxiliary palettes 14
    Color palettes 12
    documents in Web browsers 7
    files in Navigation view 21
    Inspector 10
    Objects palettes 8
    pages 30-31, 34
    smart objects 119
    stationeries 342
    toolbars 6-7
ordering
    keywords 225
    layers 271-272
orphan files, finding 368
Other folder 387
Outgoing spotlight option 347

outline toolbar, adding tags 210-211
Outline view 160
outlines, adding text 211
outlines of pages 206-209
Over image 399, 401

P

page, defined 126
Page font set 52-53
Page icon, creating links 133
Page Size popup menu 33
pages
    ActiveX controls 298-299
    adding images to 35-36, 40-41, 101-102, 104,
      106, 332
    anchoring site designs 311-312
    applying colors to 93-94
    backgrounds 35-36, 93-94
    building collections from 360
    checking for errors 363
    choosing sizes of 32-34
    coding
      head elements 221-230
      HTML Outline Editor 206-213
      HTML Source Editor 214-219
      Layout Editor 220
      Markup Tree palette 213
      Source Code window 220
      Web Settings database 231-240
    colors of 35-36
    comparing in different browsers 7
    creating 30-32
    entering text into 44-46
    home, replacing 39
    inserting tables 144-145
    JavaScripts 294
    links 130-131, 315-317
    named anchors 136-137
    opening 30-31, 34
    saving 37
    setting preferences for opening 34
    spotlighting 348
    in URLs 126
    viewing 18, 22, 349
    visually impaired users' ability to navigate 110
Pages folder 387
palettes 22-23. *See also specific palettes*
Palettes tab 91
Panorama pane 354, 356-357
paragraphs 56-57
parameters, Java 297
parent target attribute (add underscore at
    front) 139

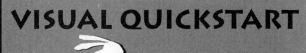